The Teacher as Learning Facilitator

Psychology and the Educational Process

Jay M. Smith

Adelphi University

Don-David Lusterman

Hofstra University

Wadsworth Publishing Company, Inc., Belmont, California

Education Editor: Roger Peterson

Production Editor: Anne Kelly

Designer: Kate Michels

Printed in the United States of America

1 2 3 4 5 6 7 8 9 10–83 82 81 80 79

Library of Congress Cataloging in Publication Data

Smith, Jay M
 The teacher as learning facilitator.

 Bibliography: p.
 Includes indexes.
  1. Educational psychology. I. Lusterman, Don-David, joint author. II. Title.
LB1051.S627   370.15   78-13599
ISBN 0-534-00587-X

Photo Credits:

Page 90: Yves De Braine/Black Star
Page 103: Robert W. ten Bensel
Page 111: (top photo) © Roger Lubin 1978/Jeroboam, Inc.
Page 112: Ray De Aragon
Page 114: James R. Holland/Stock, Boston
Page 126: Peter Menzel/Stock, Boston
Page 213: © Mitchell Payne 1978/Jeroboam, Inc.
Cover photo and all other interior photos: © Howard Harrison 1978.

To our parents, our wives, and our children

Brief Contents

Contents

Contents

Preface

We have written this book to introduce you to educational psychology. Whether you are an undergraduate planning to teach, a graduate student already teaching, or simply someone who would like to learn more about education, we feel this book has something for you. Educational psychology is concerned with applying psychological knowledge to help educators better understand and improve teaching and learning. In this book we focus on viewing the teacher as a learning facilitator—a helping person who makes the learning process easier. Although this book has been written especially for persons interested in classroom teaching, its concepts can also be useful to counselors, social workers, parents, coaches, health professionals, and any others involved with helping people learn.

Standard textbooks in education, and more specifically in educational psychology, are usually similar to textbooks in other social science fields—sociology, general psychology, economics, political science, etc. These texts introduce the reader to the field through a very comprehensive overview of current thinking and research. *The Teacher as Learning Facilitator* is different. In writing this text, we have tried to be selective, not comprehensive. Rather than overwhelm you with a great deal of information, we have included only those topics that we feel are particularly relevant to teaching. Some topics that are heavily emphasized in other educational psychology texts may either be absent or receive only brief treatment here. Our choice of topics has been heavily influenced by feedback from the more than 2,000 prospective and practicing teachers that we have taught in the years prior to and during the writing of this book. This choice also reflects our own values as teachers and psychologists.

Our point of view in this text is probably best described as humanistic-eclectic. A humanistic approach to educational psychology is one that sees both teachers and learners as "total persons" with abilities, attitudes, values, feelings, strengths, and weaknesses. The goal of this approach is to help teachers promote the growth of each student toward self-actualization—the full realization of his or her potential. We believe that the educational process must free rather than control students and prepare them to direct their own learning. This requires teachers to serve as guides or facilitators, rather than as directors or simply dispensers of knowledge. However, while we describe our goals as humanistic, our point of view is also eclectic. We see all the major schools of psychology—behaviorism, psychoanalysis, cognitive psychology, humanism, and social systems psychology—as contributing to the improvement of teaching.

Not only does the content of this book reflect a change from other texts, but its format and organization are also different. The idea for writing this book grew out of our team teaching experiences at Hofstra University. In our constant efforts to make our teaching personally meaningful to students and relevant to current problems, we could not find appropriate books. When we realized that we were not alone in our disappointment with current texts and that many other instructors were looking for a more innovative approach, the idea for this book was born. We feel that the following features make this book unique:

1. *Personal and informal writing style.* We have tried to establish a dialogue with you rather than simply throw information at you, and we have tried to write in clear, readable language.
2. *Action-orientation.* We have incorporated into the narrative of each chapter many teaching devices to stimulate your thinking about what you are reading and help you relate it to your own experiences. These devices include case studies, real classroom anecdotes, problems to solve, thought questions, a photo essay, values clarification activities, and various "explorations"—all designed to actively engage you as you read.
3. *Integration of theory and application.* This book is neither a collection of abstract psychological research and theory nor a how-to-do-it book for teachers. Rather, we introduce you to the real problems teachers face and help you see how theories suggest solutions for these problems.
4. *Inductive approach.* Throughout this book we urge you to reflect on your own relevant experiences and ideas before we introduce a topic more formally. In this way we try to make your learning more meaningful, linking new concepts to your prior knowledge.
5. *Wide margins and margin notes.* The wide margins are designed for your notes and written responses to the various thought questions and activities. Our own margin notes provide additional information, references, and questions. (References that are especially relevant to a particular section appear in the margin notes. More general references are listed at the end of each chapter and at the end of the book.)
6. *Annotated references and suggestions for action-oriented learning.* The references at the end of each chapter were carefully selected for readability. We hope you will seek out those that interest you. The "Suggestions for Action-Oriented Learning" following each chapter's references are ideas for projects to further your learning.

We have organized this book into four units. Unit 1, The Teacher, includes Chapters 1 to 4. In the first three chapters we encourage you to think systematically about what teaching is, how your own experiences have influenced your reasons for wanting to teach, your concept of yourself as a student, and your own emerging theory of teaching. In Chapter 4 we explore four theoretical perspectives—the behavioristic, humanistic, cognitive, and social systems views of teaching. Unit 2, The Learner, compiles a great deal of information on student characteristics that prospective teachers need to understand. In this unit (Chapters 5 to 9), we help you understand how people develop intellectually, socially, and emotionally; the nature of intelligence and individual differences; and motivation as it relates to learning.

In Unit 3, The Teaching–Learning Process, we explore the teaching–learning relationship through the complex interactions that take place between the teacher and the individual learner (Chapter 10), the teacher and the class (Chapter 11), and the teacher and the larger school and community (Chapter 12). Unit 4, The Teacher as Learning Facilitator, is the final unit of this book. In Chapter 13 we present a model of learning facilitation designed to help you eliminate barriers that interfere with learning and to help you find ways of promoting learning. Chapter 14 focuses on the evaluation of learning and teaching, and Chapter 15 is an epilogue, a closing statement that ties together many of the concepts presented throughout the book.

A final note on using this book: This book is designed for active use. You will learn much more if you do the activities and explorations and answer the thought questions as you come across them in each chapter. Write your responses in the spaces provided in the book; use the open spaces in the margins for notes and comments. If possible, participate in some type of field work for two or three hours a week—tutoring, assisting in a classroom, teaching music lessons, coaching, counseling, etc. Such a teaching-type experience will help you understand many of the problems teachers face. By keeping a weekly log of your thoughts and feelings about your field work, you will be able to reflect on your learning. Our students have told us that field work makes the content of this book come alive.

We hope this book helps you see yourself as a prospective teacher, aids you in understanding the relationship between psychology and the educational process, and provides you with some specific suggestions for helping people learn. Feel free to write to us with your comments, suggestions, questions, or criticisms. We value your feedback. You can reach us by writing to:

Jay M. Smith
Department of Education
Adelphi University
Garden City, New York 11530

Don-David Lusterman
Department of Counseling,
Psychology, and Research in
Education
Hofstra University
Hempstead, New York 11550

Good luck!

Acknowledgements

This book grew out of five years of team teaching. During that time, our ideas and our ways of communicating were shaped and reshaped by the constant input of our students. So we must begin here by acknowledging the more than 2,000 students without whose help this book could never have been written.

The dedication of the staff of Wadsworth Publishing Company was a source of continuing inspiration for us. If our book is about facilitating learning, Wadsworth seems to be about facilitating authors. Dick Greenberg gave us the original impetus we needed, enabling us to write our own book. And we must thank Roger Peterson for continuing the shepherding process where Dick left off. Jean-Francois Vilain's early efforts were greatly appreciated, and Anne Kelly's untiring work in bringing the book to completion was invaluable.

We must express our appreciation to several reviewers whose thoughtful criticisms forced us to clarify our thinking and writing through many successive drafts: Michal Clark, Bakersfield State College, California; Frank R. Cross, Oregon State University; Arthur Coladarci, Dean of Education at Stanford; Lita L. Schwartz, Pennsylvania State University at Ogontz; Meryl Englander, Indiana University; Donald Treffinger, University of Kansas; and Mary Jo Poole, St. Benedict's College in Minnesota.

We thank Arlene Gilligan and Aileen Hirsch for the insights they offered us as classroom teaching consultants. A number of typists provided patient minds and untiring fingers: Elsa Spector, Maryann Lombardi, Judy Lusterman, and especially, Brent Smith. Finally, we must thank our wives and children for the understanding and support they extended us through many weekends, evenings and holidays. We know how many hours we stole from them; we hope the results justify their sacrifices.

Unit 1
The Teacher

We have entitled the first unit of this book "The Teacher." As you begin to read the first chapter, you will notice that the focus of the unit is on helping you understand what it means to be a teacher. Throughout the unit (and for that matter throughout the whole book) we directly address you and your emerging questions and feelings about becoming a teacher. We have written this book to actively engage you both intellectually and emotionally. Therefore, it is very important for you to carry out the explorations and respond to the questions that are incorporated in the narrative. We have also provided in the margins additional questions that you may want to think about as you read. The more actively you involve yourself in the reading, the more you will get out of this book.

By now you have spent 13 or 14 years in school as a student. In that time you have encountered as many as 40 or 50 teachers and have developed all sorts of ideas about teaching as you have looked at school from a student's perspective. Now that you are seriously considering becoming a teacher yourself, you undoubtedly have many questions about teaching as well as some fairly definite ideas about how you would like to teach. Chapter 1, "The Teacher as Person," introduces you to thinking about the psychology of education in a very personal way. In this chapter we will ask you to begin to consider why you want to be a teacher, how the teaching of some of your teachers has affected you, and what types of people become teachers.

In Chapter 2 we will focus on "Your Personal Growth." This chapter will push you to look at the influences on your development—your family, school experiences, peer group, and the environment in which you have grown up. We will pay particular attention to the effect of these four influences on your self-concept as a student because we believe that your feelings about you as a student will have a real impact on your teaching and your relationships with students when you enter the classroom.

Chapter 3, we believe, is unique. Through a series of activities we will help you uncover some of the elements of your own emerging theory of teaching. We believe that you already have developed some serious notions about how people learn and which approaches to teaching are most effective. As you become aware of your own implicit theory, you will be better able to evaluate it in the light of other views about teaching.

Finally, in Chapter 4 we will explore four theoretical perspectives—the behavioristic, affective, cognitive, and social systems views of teaching. Our goal here is to have you contrast your own ideas with formal theories that have been carefully articulated and tested. In that way you will begin to become a "consumer of theories," with a variety of resources to draw from. As you leave Unit 1 you should have a clear understanding of your own emerging ideas about teaching and, at the same time, see the value of formal theories.

1
The Teacher as Person

Good teachers make learning exciting and actively involving. How often have you experienced classes like the one shown here?

As you read, try to recall the first teacher you encountered in school. What impact did that preschool or first-grade teacher have on your feelings about school and on your view of yourself?

A teacher is a very important person. The preschool or first-grade teacher often is the young child's first intensive contact with an adult who is not a parent or relative. Through teachers young children are exposed to the customs and values of their culture and its expectations for their growth and development. As children go through school in the elementary years, they spend as much as five or six hours per day, nearly 180 days a year, with a teacher. Junior high school and senior high school usually bring the student into contact with five or more teachers each year, and consequently the time spent with any one teacher is reduced. However, even more important than the amount of time spent with teachers is the quality of the relationship students have with them. As you can recall from your own experiences, the effects of good teachers (and, unfortunately, poor teachers as well) are powerful and long-lasting.

Since teachers have such a great influence on the development of children, and ultimately upon the future of our culture, we believe it essential that prospective teachers understand themselves as people and examine their own motivations and feelings about teaching. Such self-examination ought to be a starting point in the study of educational psychology. Therefore, the first few sections of this chapter will help you to:

1. Look into your own reasons for wanting to be a teacher.

2. Consider what types of teachers have affected you positively and negatively.

3. Understand, through autobiographical statements, how the family and school backgrounds of two people affected their experiences as teachers.

In beginning to think about your own motives for becoming a teacher, why not try this exploration?

Exploration 1–1: Examining Your Motives for Teaching

The 14 statements below represent primary reasons given by a number of college students for their decisions to become teachers. Read through the list and then determine which statement is the closest to your own primary reason for wanting to become a teacher, which is the next closest, etc., until you have ranked the whole list in order from 1 to 14. Try to rank all items even though some may be hard to differentiate in terms of rank order and others may not seem to apply to you. (Note: 14 (a) applies to females and 14 (b) applies to males.)

Explorations are activities intended to help you explore and clarify your own thoughts, feelings, and experiences as they relate to issues being discussed in the text. By actually writing down your responses to these activities, you will make your learning more active and your reading more enjoyable. This book is designed for you to write directly in it.

Your
Rank   Statement

____ 1. I am becoming a teacher because I want to share my love for my subject with others and help my students learn from me.

____ 2. I want to be a professional _____ (artist, musician, actor, or whatever), but will probably not be able to support myself on my income from that field. Chances are I'll teach so that I'll have enough money to support myself yet enough free time to do what I really want to do.

____ 3. Ever since I can remember, my parents and others have encouraged me to be a teacher, emphasizing that teaching is a good, respectable profession.

____ 4. I have always enjoyed and been good at things like helping other kids with homework, tutoring, camp counseling, and coaching. I decided to become a teacher because I wanted to work with children.

____ 5. One of my teachers really influenced my decision to become a teacher because of the model he (she) provided. I really looked up to that teacher and wanted to be like him (her).

____ 6. School was always such a rewarding and satisfying experience for me that I feel I would like to continue it as a teacher.

____ 7. As a child I always liked situations in which I could be in charge or be the leader. Because I felt important when other people listened to me and did what I said, I think I would enjoy being a teacher.

____ 8. Teaching is a good profession to fall back on as a second choice if I don't realize my first choice (e.g., becoming a physician, lawyer, psychologist, etc.).

____ 9. One of my parents is a teacher and I grew up learning about teaching, playing school, and wanting to become a teacher myself.

If you are planning to become something other than a teacher—e.g., a counselor, a speech therapist, a social worker, or even a lawyer—you might think about your reasons for your career goals as you read these statements. Then, try to summarize those reasons in a paragraph.

____ 10. I have decided to become a teacher so that I can work to change many of the bad things that I experienced as a student at the hands of some of my teachers. I want to make school an enjoyable place where real learning can occur.

____ 11. I had never really considered teaching as a career until I participated in a "teaching-type experience" (e.g., being a scout leader, camp counselor, Sunday school teacher, etc.) that led me to think that I might like to be a teacher.

____ 12. I want to be a teacher because I believe that schooling can be a positive force in a child's development, and I would like to contribute to that development.

____ 13. I see myself as a person committed to social change. By being a teacher I will be able to do my part toward creating a better world.

____ 14. (a) As a *girl* growing up I was encouraged to go to college and take education courses. Then after graduation I would have a career if I wanted one. And after marrying and having children, I would be able to go back to teaching when my children were older.
(b) As a *boy* growing up I had very few male teachers, especially in elementary school, and I feel I missed something by not having enough male models in school. I would like to help correct this situation by becoming a teacher.

You might use this exploration to interview a few teachers you know regarding their reasons for entering the teaching field. As you learn of their motives and the influences upon them, you should gain a clearer picture of your own reasons for becoming a teacher.

Having rank ordered the statements above, consider the following questions:

1. Are there any statements you feel should be added to the list to better reflect your own motives for entering teaching? If so, why not make up such a statement or two?

2. What have you learned from considering the statements about your own motives to teach? Try now to summarize in a paragraph why you want to be a teacher.

3. How do your own motives differ from those of other students in your class?

The purpose of having you compare your own motivations with those of other college students has been to get you thinking about teaching and looking at yourself. However, it should be emphasized that a person's motives toward a future career are influenced by a complex set of factors. The exploration you have just completed gives you only a surface picture of some of those factors. One's self-concept, early family experiences, needs and interests, socio-economic and ethnic group, schooling, and even physical qualities like sex or height are all important (Holland, 1966; Roe, 1957; Super, 1957).

At this point we will not attempt to provide answers to the questions that may be emerging in your mind since there is very little known about the relationship between motives for teaching and ultimate success as a teacher. Research evidence does suggest that for teachers and other helping professionals, self-awareness is an important factor in operating consistently and effectively. Consequently, we have included within this chapter other activities designed to help you take a step or two toward greater self-understanding.

Teacher Behavior in the Classroom

Imagine what your life would be like if you had never set foot in any of your classrooms or come in contact with any of the persons you have had as teachers from your preschool days to the current semester. Do any of your teachers stand out as especially good? Or especially bad? What do you think are some of the qualities that distinguish good teaching from poor teaching? While your teachers have probably strongly affected you for better or for worse, other aspects of schooling have also touched you deeply—the friendships you found in school, your family's values about education, the size of your classes, the structure of the classrooms and school buildings, the ways you have been taught, the kinds of texts and materials used, and the ways you have been tested. Later in this book we will consider the impact of each of these factors, but for now let us concentrate on that particularly important person, the teacher.

The actual behavior of a teacher in the classroom as she* interacts with students reflects both her motives for being a teacher and her implicit theory of what teaching is. We will examine the development of that implicit theory and its importance in depth in Chapters 2 and 3. Here we focus upon actual teaching behaviors and their positive or negative effects upon the learning experiences of students—especially your own experiences.

Exploration 1–2: Teacher Classroom Behaviors and Their Effects

Below are listed a series of 11 anecdotes describing interactions between a teacher and student(s) in a classroom. Read through the anecdotes, imagining yourself as a student in each of the classroom environments presented. Try to imagine the teacher's behavior and your own feelings as a student as vividly as possible. Then refer to the activity following the anecdotes.

1. Mr. Trevino becomes aware that Marty is hesitant about going to the blackboard to demonstrate a math problem, as

A good theoretical rationale for the importance of self-understanding in all helping relationships is found in Combs, Avila, and Purkey, Helping Relationships: Basic Concepts for the Helping Professions *(1971).*

Curwin and Fuhrmann, Discovering Your Teaching Self *(1975) is designed to help prospective teachers discover their own views, feelings, and motives regarding teaching.*

It might be useful to make notes on your own feelings in the space beside each anecdote.

---

* Since teaching is a profession with large numbers of both men and women, we will at times refer to a teacher with the pronoun *she* and at other times with the pronoun *he.* Rather than saying *his/her* we will alternate between *his* and *her.* Similarly, we will refer to a child or student sometimes as *he* and sometimes as *she* when we are speaking of children or students in general.

the other eighth graders are doing. Speaking to Marty individually, he says, "Marty, you seem to be a little unsure of this material, perhaps you would like to see me for a moment after class so that I can help you."

2. Mr. Lorenz is introducing a new song to his seventh-grade general music class by singing the song himself as he plays it on the piano. Noticing three boys talking, he stops and orders the boys to go to the back of the room. Then he continues singing.

3. Bob complains, "I don't know why we need to study this material on photosynthesis." Ms. Warren, his biology teacher, responds, "That's a very good question. Can anyone suggest a reason for studying photosynthesis?"

4. Mrs. Berger says to her ninth-grade French class, "I can't tell you how disappointed I am in you today. None of you is really thinking."

5. Mr. Barker's tenth-grade social studies class is beginning a unit on the civil rights movement of the 1960s, when Jack remarks under his breath, "I don't want to talk about any of those blacks. Now they have all the rights and we have none." Recognizing that Jack and probably many other students have very strong feelings about the issue, Mr. Barker says, "Let's see a show of hands regarding whether you are for, against, or neutral about studying this unit." He then initiates a discussion of why the students feel as they do.

6. "Why do states have capitals?" Miss Johnson asks her fourth graders. "So there's a place where the government of the state can be located," responds Martha. "Good thinking," replies Miss Johnson. "Does anyone have another reason?"

7. Barbara, a ninth grader, mutters barely audibly, "Why do we have to read *Julius Caesar* and this other stuff that no one cares about?" Hearing Barbara's comment, Mrs. Grover explains with great concern, "*Julius Caesar* is one of the most thrilling plays ever written about the process of governance."

8. After introducing himself to his fifth graders on the first day of class, Mr. Sawyer says, "I want you to know that I am a very strict teacher; we will work hard with no fooling around, and you'll learn a lot in this class."

9. Mrs. Phillips asks her senior civics class, "What are some of the things you might have felt and done had you been Vice-President Gerald Ford preparing to assume the U.S. presidency following the resignation speech of Richard Nixon in August 1974?"

10. Mr. Jones notices Bill beginning to doze in the last row in English class and calls in a sharp voice, "Bill, repeat the last thing I said."

11. Jane asks her sixth-grade teacher, "Is it alright if I choose a book for my book report that's not on the list you gave us?" Ms. Carlson replies, "Apparently the books on this list don't interest you. Do you already have a book in mind that you would like to read or must I spend my time helping you to find a book?"

Activity

Think back through all your elementary and secondary school experience and try to identify your best teacher and your worst teacher. It is up to you to decide what the criteria are for *best* and *worst*. Then read through the preceding anecdotes, placing a *B* beside each behavior that you feel is similar to something your best teacher might have done and a *W* beside each behavior that is similar to something your worst teacher might have done. (Note: Don't concern yourself with the fact that any subject and grade level may be different from your experience. Just focus upon the similarity of the teacher's behavior.) If a behavior doesn't seem similar to the teaching of either your best or your worst teacher, just skip it and go on to the next item.

Questions

1. Which behaviors describe your best teacher? Write the item numbers here: _____

2. Which behaviors describe your worst teacher? Write the item numbers here: _____

3. What overall pattern emerges? Try to summarize in a couple of sentences the behaviors of your best teacher and those of your worst teacher.

4. What seem to be the important overall differences between your best teacher and your worst teacher?

Interaction Analysis: A System for Analyzing Teaching Behavior

Professor Ned Flanders, an educational psychologist who has been concerned with teaching effectiveness for many years, has developed a system for examining teacher behavior in the classroom. His research led him to conclude that there are essentially two types of teaching behaviors—those involving direct influence and those involving indirect influence. Teachers who utilize primarily direct influence tend to do most of the talking—lecturing, giving directions, criticizing students for unacceptable behavior, and justifying their own authority. On the other hand, teachers who practice indirect influence encourage students to talk, ask more open-ended questions, praise and encourage student responses, and accept and clarify the feelings and ideas of students (Flanders, 1970).

Out of his research Flanders has developed a system for rating interaction in the classroom. The system, which provides 10 categories for recording verbal classroom interaction, is outlined in

Flanders' system focuses on verbal communication in the classroom. Some critics argue that it ignores too many other important aspects of classroom behavior, such as nonverbal behavior and body language (i.e., gestures, facial expressions, eye contact, etc.), student–student communication, or the quality of verbal communication that comes through in tone of voice, emphasis, etc.

Other psychologists concerned with teaching effectiveness (e.g., Combs et al., 1974) argue that the teacher's actual behavior is less important than

his perceptions of himself, his role as a teacher, and his students. In other words, the type of person a teacher is will have a greater impact on students than the observable behavior Flanders talks about. In Chapter 4 we will explore more deeply the differences between such a perceptual view of teaching and the behavioristic views held by Flanders and others.

Table 1–1. Observers trained in Flanders' interaction analysis use a chart for categorizing at three-second intervals any verbal behavior that may take place in a class. The purpose in acquainting you with Flanders' system here is to help you think about different types of teaching behaviors rather than to train you to systematically record classroom verbal interaction. The following exploration is designed to help you understand Flanders' model of teaching behavior and relate it to your previous thinking regarding best and worst teachers.

Exploration 1–3: Using Flanders' Interaction Analysis to Classify Teacher Behaviors

Go back to Exploration 1–2 and the 11 anecdotes of classroom interactions. Referring to Table 1–1, try to place into one of Flanders' first seven categories of teacher talk the teacher's verbal behavior in each anecdote. (Note: In some anecdotes the teachers engage in more than one type of verbal behavior.) Record below your responses and a *B* or *W*, indicating whether the behavior was characteristic of your best or worst teacher.

Anecdote Number	Flanders' Category Number and Title (for example, 1—Accepts Feelings)	Best or Worst (Use *B* or *W*)
1.	_____	_____
2.	_____	_____
3.	_____	_____
4.	_____	_____
5.	_____	_____
6.	_____	_____
7.	_____	_____
8.	_____	_____
9.	_____	_____
10.	_____	_____
11.	_____	_____

Questions

Flanders' is only one of many systems for analyzing teaching behavior. If you would like to learn more about some of the others, a good reference is: Rosenshine and Furst, "The Use of Direct Observation to Study Teaching," in R.M.W. Travers (ed.), Second Handbook of Research on Teaching (1973).

1. How do your choices of categories for each of the teacher behaviors above compare with those of others in your class? If there are differences, discuss them.

2. Look at the anecdotes you feel represent behaviors similar to those your best and worst teachers would engage in. Do you see any patterns? Do your best teachers tend to use primarily indirect influence (categories 1–4) or direct influence (categories 5–7)? What about your worst teachers?

Table 1-1. Categories for Flanders' Interaction Analysis

Teacher Talk				Student Talk	No Talk
Indirect Influence		**Direct Influence**			

Teacher Talk — Indirect Influence

1. *Accepts Feelings.* Accepts and clarifies the tone of feeling of the students in an unthreatening manner. Feelings may be positive or negative. Predicting or recalling feelings are included.

2. *Praises or Encourages.* Praises or encourages student action or behavior. Jokes that release tension, but not at the expense of another individual; nodding head and saying "um hm?" or "go on" are included.

3. *Accepts or Uses Ideas of Students.* Clarifies, builds, or develops ideas suggested by a student. As teacher brings more of his own ideas into play, shift to #5.

4. *Asks Questions.* Asks a question about content or procedure with the intent that the student answer.

Teacher Talk — Direct Influence

5. *Lecturing.* Gives facts or opinion about content or procedure; expresses his own ideas, asking rhetorical questions.

6. *Giving Directions.* Directions, commands, or orders that the students are expected to comply with.

7. *Criticizing or Justifying Authority.* Statements intended to change student behavior from unacceptable to acceptable pattern; bawling someone out; stating why the teacher is doing what he is doing; extreme self-reference.

Student Talk

8. *Student Talk — Response.* Talk by students in response to teacher. Teacher initiates the contact or solicits student statement.

9. *Student Talk — Initiation.* Talk initiated by students. If "calling on" student is only to indicate who may talk next, observer must decide whether student wanted to talk.

No Talk

10. *Silence or Confusion.* Pauses, short periods of silence, and periods of confusion in which communication cannot be understood by the observer.

Adapted from N. A. Flanders, Analyzing Teacher Behavior (Reading, Mass.: Addison-Wesley, 1970), p. 34. Reprinted by permission.

* Adapted from N. A. Flanders, *Analyzing Teacher Behavior* (Reading, Mass.: Addison-Wesley, 1970), p. 34. Reprinted by permission.

Does this picture remind you of any confrontations you have had with a teacher? Are there alternatives to criticizing students who misbehave?

It might be interesting to read Flanders' book Analyzing Teaching Behavior *(1970) (or some other reference on interaction analysis) and then use his categories to analyze the teaching behavior of some of your college teachers.*

3. Flanders believes, and cites research to support his belief, that indirect influence brings about more student learning and promotes more favorable attitudes toward the teacher and the learning activities than does direct influence. On the basis of your own school experiences, do you agree or disagree? Why?

The Lives of Teachers

Our primary focus here is on the influence of family and school experiences on both motives for teaching and actual classroom behavior. However, it should be pointed out that other influences, such as the teaching environment, one's faculty colleagues and administration, and one's length of experiences, are also important. Fuller (1969) has even found that one's stage of development as a teacher—preservice, student teacher, first-year teacher, etc.—has an important impact on one's concerns and problems in the classroom.

In the previous sections of this chapter, we have considered people's motives for entering teaching as well as the ways they interact with students in the classroom once they become teachers. Now in order to better understand some of these motives and behaviors, we will look at two autobiographical statements written by teachers.* Each of the statements acquaints you with "the life of a teacher" through her own analysis of the major influences affecting her growing up and experiences as a teacher. Read each of the statements carefully and try to imagine the type of person each teacher is and how she became that way.

Janice Schwartz: An Autobiographical Statement

Janice Schwartz has been teaching French for the past 15 years, first as an elementary school teacher and then in junior high school. She now teaches in a rather traditional junior high school in a white middle-class suburban community.

* In order to protect the anonymity of the teachers who provided us with these very personal statements, we have given them fictitious names.

I was an only child. I spent my earliest years in a very small town in Michigan and an even smaller one in California. At the age of 12 or 13, I moved to a large city in the West where I completed high school. I was expected to do well in school. I remember the first time I brought home a B-plus, rather than my usual As—it caused my mother to call the teacher to complain.

I found it somewhat easier to relate to adults than to other kids. In school I was a memorizer and a "brownnoser." I felt safest with things I could memorize and give back. School was largely a succession of tests and examinations. A "hundred" was what I aimed for. Often I would avoid a course because I feared it was one where I would have to think. I think I learned to be very cautious, and to avoid taking risks as much as possible. In fact, I was shocked to discover that I was doing very poorly in college, after my glowing high school record. I attended a college where you were really expected to think—and this terrified me. I was extremely upset . . . very nervous. My whole self-image was pretty shattered.

How does Janice's description of her school experience compare with your own experience? What type of student were you?

I met and married a fellow student, and left school soon after. The idea of teaching—or any profession, for that matter—had never entered my mind. Perhaps because I was a girl—now that I look back at it—I was never career oriented. The point was to find a husband—remember, this was in the late 1940s. And I did, in fact, get married at nineteen—I guess it was the fulfillment of many expectations, parental and other.

Do you think a young woman aged 19 would be subject to the same expectations today? Why or why not?

I kind of fell into teaching. When we had settled down in a suburb of New York, a neighbor asked me if I would help her learn French—this had been my major at college. Someone then suggested I might use my talents teaching French in the elementary school. This was around the time of Sputnik, and the idea of introducing languages in the elementary grades was just coming in. But no one had been trained for that work, so I started—without a degree and without any formal training in education.

At this point, I've had a great deal of coursework. And I think I've picked up some things from my coursework—some in the area of methods, interesting things to do in the classroom; some about relating better with kids, being a little more open. But probably the most noticeable change has come with my therapy in the last two years or so. I'm much more understanding with the students—a new awareness of what's going on. I don't find myself blowing up as much.

From time to time, new groups of teachers enter the system in unusual ways. An example from the 1960s was the influx of many young men who wanted to avoid being drafted during the Viet Nam War and for whom teaching provided an occupational deferment.

What do you think might be the effects of such influxes of teachers?

Still—I don't like the defiance and lack of respect that so many of the students show. I can't imagine my having said to one of my teachers, "Do I have to?" But when my students say "I won't!"—How dare they? It's very hard for me to realize that they have the right to say they don't want to do something.

List two or three ways Janice's experiences as a student may have influenced her views of her own students.

I think what I enjoy most about my career is that I continue to grow in my knowledge of the French language and literature and that I can justify going to France from time to time. But to tell you the truth, if you ask me if I had it to do over, would I consciously choose to become a teacher—no. The answer is no. I would not. If it were really possible to choose, I would not.

Roseanne Murphy: An Autobiographical Statement

Roseanne Murphy began her career as a music teacher. When her exceptional ability to motivate her students was noticed, she was called to take on the administration of her district's music program. She became interested in administration and is now the principal of an innovative elementary school in a racially and religiously integrated community.

14

The Teacher

I was born in the Bronx—a real old-time urbanite. I came out here to Bayville when I was about nine. I went through the Bayville public schools, but then was lucky enough to get a scholarship to St. Anne's, our local Catholic parochial high school. I'm an only child. My mother was widowed very young, and I grew up with my grandparents. Mother was in the insurance business. Grandfather was a lawyer, and grandmother was a wonderful housekeeper.

My family never really pushed me toward any particular profession, but I was always interested in music. While I was in high school I was accepted into the preparatory program of a very fine conservatory, and when I graduated from high school, I went on to take my degree in music performance at this same conservatory. I did well there, as I always had in school. I always liked studying—for the sake of learning. Marks came easily, but weren't very important to me. I liked to think, to delve.

I was a very inquiring child, and teachers responded well to me. The teachers I really loved were not at all run-of-the-mill. They were the ones who could shake you up—lead you into unknown paths. They did the unexpected. I enjoyed that sort of challenge. But the idea that I might someday teach never entered my mind, because, with a few exceptions, I saw teachers as—let's say—not the most stimulating people in the world.

After I married and had my children, I did get very curious about their schooling. There were things that bothered me. I saw many insensitive and apparently uncaring teachers. I wondered why there weren't more good ones. I guess I began to think that maybe I could be a good one. So I started taking some courses at Columbia University, Teachers College. This was in the early 1960s, a time of great ferment. Jerome Bruner's ideas were just then gaining recognition, and many teachers at T. C. were being shook up by them. There was a lot of soul-searching going on—a very exciting time.

I finally completed a master's degree in education and found a job in Oaktown as a music teacher. Oaktown was just beginning to change when I started my teaching career there. It had been a predominantly middle-class community, upwardly mobile, and with high aspirations for its children. Then a black and Spanish-speaking influx began. Many problems developed. The teaching staff was not prepared to respond to these youngsters. A tracking system was in effect, and, when all was said and done, it separated kids into two groups—"smart" and "dumb"—and the "dumb" ones were usually the black and Spanish-speaking kids. Being a music teacher, I saw all the children, and it struck me that this system was not good for any child—bright, average, or slow.

And the kinds of discipline problems that naturally flowed from the kid's own understanding of his worth in the eyes of the school system were pretty terrible. Most of the teachers blamed the kids rather than the system or themselves. I began to feel rather alienated from many of my fellow teachers. I sensed that, as children reacted against the teachers, teachers' images of themselves were violated in some way. Thus not only were the kids hurt but teachers as well. You couldn't really blame the teachers either. They were not prepared for this by their lives or their education. They were in "culture shock."

In any event, I found that I could relate to the kids and have some real success in my teaching. Soon I found myself assigned to supervising music for the district, and then I became principal of an elementary school. There were some open classrooms in this school, and I saw what was going on in these classrooms as somewhat of an answer for a lot of children. I proposed that we gather all the teachers in the

Do you think this is a common view of the teaching profession? Why is it that even today teachers do not receive the social status accorded other professionals with advanced training—doctors, lawyers, businesspeople, etc.?

For a discussion of Bruner's ideas on how children develop intellectually and the need for teaching approaches that respond to children's curiosity and promote discovery, see Chapter 5.

Have you ever attended a school in which there was tracking, i.e., separation of children into classes by ability? What do you feel are the pros and cons of such a system for both "fast" and "slow" students?

Clearly, Roseanne sees herself as a "change agent." Do you think many school principals see their job as creating change? Why or why not?

district who taught in an open manner and make one open school for the district. This made me a target for much harassment in the community, and I finally left because I felt I had accomplished all I could—but at least the school was created, and the community was confronted with an important issue.

I am now the principal of an elementary school in Bayville, which is also an integrated community.

It has been very exciting to be involved in the creation of a new type of school environment here in Bayville. I've been thinking recently about what skills are helpful in turning a school around. Certainly there were some teachers on the staff whose philosophy was similar to mine, but there were many who differed greatly. I find that, for myself, the best way to help the staff to grow and pull together is to say, by my actions, "Look, you do it, you try it, don't be afraid, I'll be there if you need backup." I think most teachers appreciate that. It's not a matter of clobbering them over the head with your own beliefs. It is a matter of taking them from where they are and helping them move. I don't say it's the fastest process in the world—it isn't. But if good things are happening, a direction is being set, then I think the time is well spent.

Perhaps the quality that has helped me most in my work has been my willingness to take risks, and my stubbornness once I've decided on a course of action. I mentioned earlier that my grandfather was really my father figure. His voice is still in me, saying, "Try it—if it doesn't work out, that's okay too." You know, very honestly, I don't think I could stand the straight and narrow path too long. I'd get bored. I guess I love this field because it's both my work and my play.

Is serving as a change agent an important reason for your desire to become a teacher? Why or why not?

What differences do you see between Janice's and Roseanne's attitudes toward risk? How do these differences affect their views of education?

An excellent source for further reading on the relationship between one's life and work is Studs Terkel's Working *(1975). In this book men and women from a wide variety of occupations talk openly about how they feel about their work.*

What Types of People Become Teachers

There is a great deal of information that can help answer the question "What types of people become teachers?" in terms of such demographic characteristics as sex, marital status, social-class background, community origin, educational attainment, religion, race, and ethnic group. The majority of teachers continue to be women, although the percentage of men in teaching is increasing, primarily as the result of more males becoming secondary school teachers. Statistics gathered for the 1971–1972 school year showed that 15.5 percent of elementary school teachers in the United States were male, while 54.2 percent of high school teachers were male. At that time approximately one in three public school teachers were male (Van Til, 1974). While it is becoming more and more common to find males in the later elementary grades, it is still a rarity to find a male preschool or first-grade teacher.

The teaching profession draws heavily on the middle class (especially the lower middle class) for its new recruits, with only small percentages of teachers coming from lower class or upper class backgrounds. The teaching ranks tend to be filled not from the families of professionals or businesspeople but from those of blue-collar workers and non–college-educated white-collar workers. Teaching has long been one of the professions most open to people seeking upward mobility—an opportunity to move up a notch or two from lower-middle-class social status (Stephens and Evans, 1973). In the

What do you think are the consequences, for both boys and girls, of the small number of male elementary school teachers?

Since the oversupply of teachers that began in the early 1970s, only a small proportion of people certified to teach have found jobs soon after graduation. The fact that teaching jobs are not as available as they once were will probably mean that only the most highly qualified and most sincerely motivated education majors will get jobs.

What do you feel are the pros and cons of this situation for students? For you as a prospective teacher?

How often have you had teachers who came from a racial, ethnic, or religious group different from your own? What special problems might teachers encounter in working with students whose background is not the same as their own?

past teachers tended to come from agrarian or small-town communities more often than they did from urban areas. As our society is becoming more urban, this pattern appears to be changing.

While six out of every 10 beginning teachers in 1954 were college graduates, today nearly 100 percent are. In addition, the combination of new, more rigorous state certification requirements and the oversupply of teachers that emerged in the 1970s has led to large percentages of teachers acquiring master's degrees and post-master's training. In 1957 only one teacher out of four held a master's degree (Charters, 1963); by the early 1970s the master's degree was increasingly taken for granted as a necessity for teachers (Van Til, 1974).

Although the overwhelming majority of American teachers continue to be native-born middle-class whites, with the affirmative action programs more and more blacks and members of other minority groups are being hired as teachers in the 1970s. In short, racial, ethnic, and religious homogeneity is gradually breaking down in the teaching profession just as it is in other areas of American life. Unfortunately, the data on the characteristics of those who have entered teaching in the mid-1970s, since the teacher oversupply, are not yet available to help us determine how fast the types of people entering teaching are really changing.

Whatever the facts regarding the social background of today's teachers, it might be useful for you to read and think about the following 1956 description of the majority of teachers:

> The majority of teachers are coming from homes which are culturally unpromising if not impoverished. They are coming from homes in which light popular books and magazines or none at all are the rule. If the future teacher's family subscribes to any magazines, it is likely to be *Collier's, Saturday Evening Post,* or the *Reader's Digest.* It is not likely to be *Harper's, Atlantic Monthly, Freeman, Saturday Review of Literature, American Mercury, Reporter,* or any other periodicals devoted to serious writing on political, social or cultural topics. The families from which teachers come are generally inactive both politically and in community affairs. Their social activities are likely to be confined to fraternal orders and lodges such as the Masons, Shriners, Order of the Eastern Star, Elks, Moose, International Order of Odd Fellows, or Knights of Columbus. Families in the upper-lower or lower-middle class usually have rather limited experience in the fine arts such as music or painting. Attending movies, playing cards, listening to radio and watching television, and visiting the neighbors are the most popular recreational outlets for these classes.*

Questions

1. Do you feel Lieberman's statement accurately describes most of the teachers you know in the 1970s? Or was it only appropriate to the 1950s? Explain your answers.

* From M. Lieberman, *Education as a Profession* (Englewood Cliffs, N.J.: Prentice-Hall, 1956), p. 466. Reprinted by permission.

2. To what extent does it describe you and your background?

3. Howard Becker, a sociologist, has confirmed Lieberman's findings, saying that most teachers could be placed as lower middle class on a scale of socioeconomic status. Both Becker (1969) and Leacock (1969) have found that teachers tend to have more positive attitudes toward students from middle class backgrounds than toward lower class students. Have you observed such attitudes in your own school experiences? How did they affect both you and your classmates?

This section of Chapter 1 has described characteristics of the teaching population as a whole; obviously, there are many individuals whose backgrounds do not fit this picture. This is always the case when we look at individuals rather than at groups. We should also point out that while a great deal is known about the demographic characteristics of the teaching population, research has been inconclusive about the relation of these characteristics to effective teaching.

Conclusions

The purpose of this chapter has been to introduce you to the psychology of teaching by providing an intensive exploration of the teacher as person. We have sought to stimulate your thinking regarding the following questions about teaching:

1. What motives do people have for becoming teachers?

2. What are some types of behaviors teachers engage in as they interact with students in the classroom? What are some of the positive and negative effects of those behaviors upon students?

3. How do a person's early growing-up experiences affect both her decision to become a teacher and her actual experience as a teacher?

4. What types of people become teachers?

The explorations, activities, expository material, questions, and autobiographical statements have all been designed not only to acquaint you with information about teachers as people, but more importantly to encourage you to begin to look at yourself—your school experiences, your background, your motives to become a teacher. Our approach has been purposely *inductive* rather than *deductive,* since we want you to think critically and draw your own conclusions about the topics.

Chapter 2 will help you examine even more directly your own growth. Through a variety of activities and explanatory discussions, we will provide you with a picture of the effect of your own family, school, and peer-group experiences upon your development. We feel strongly that before people can effectively understand the ways others develop and learn, they must understand themselves.

Inductive—*An inductive approach to teaching presents students with specific ideas, questions, or experiences and then encourages them to draw their own inferences, conclusions, and generalizations.*

Deductive—*A deductive approach (which is more typical of traditional texts and classroom presentations) provides generalizations, theories, and principles, and then assumes students will be able to apply this knowledge to specific situations.*

Some Good Books

Ashton-Warner, Sylvia. *Teacher*. New York: Simon and Schuster, 1963. The warm, personal autobiography of a teacher who used the discovery approach in teaching disadvantaged Maori children in New Zealand.

Greenberg, Herbert. *Teaching with Feeling*. New York: Pegasus, 1969. Greenberg explores the inner worlds, feelings, and thoughts of teachers in real-life situations. Greenberg believes that by becoming aware of their own emotions, teachers can improve their relationships with students and colleagues.

Hamachek, Don E. *Encounters with the Self*. New York: Holt, Rinehart and Winston, 1971. An excellent book concerned with self-concept, its development, and its relation to effective childrearing and teaching. Hamachek is very concerned with the personal aspects of being a teacher.

Kaufman, Bel. *Up the Down Staircase*. New York: Avon, 1964. A fictional yet very personally written account of life in a New York City school.

Kohl, Herbert. *36 Children*. New York: New American Library, 1967. A now classic account of a first-year teacher's struggle to make his Harlem classroom a place of joy, excitement, and true learning.

Kozol, Jonathan. *Death at an Early Age*. Boston: Houghton Mifflin, 1967. An exposé of life in a ghetto school in Boston, written by a young teacher who was dismissed for not following the course of study prescribed for his class. This is an excellent personal account of one teacher's experience in attempting to challenge an urban educational system that was unresponsive to the needs and interests of its students.

Rogers, Carl. *Freedom to Learn*. Columbus, Ohio: Merrill, 1969. A collection of essays that discuss the importance of self-directed learning and approaches to developing it. Particular emphasis is placed upon the teacher as person.

Ryan K., ed. *Don't Smile until Christmas: Accounts of the First Year of Teaching*. Chicago: University of Chicago Press, 1970. A collection of autobiographical statements on the first year of teaching by six beginning high school teachers.

Ryan, K. and James M. Cooper. *Those Who Can Teach*. 2nd ed. Boston: Houghton Mifflin, 1975. This popular textbook provides a good introduction to many current teaching issues.

Articles, Studies, and Other References

Combs, Arthur W. *Florida Studies in the Helping Professions*. Gainesville, Fla.: University of Florida Press, 1969. This report on the research of Combs and his colleagues focuses on the way effective teachers, counselors, nurses, and Episcopal pastors perceive themselves and others.

Hamachek, Don E. "Self-Understanding: A Prerequisite for Good Teaching." In Hamachek, *Behavior Dynamics in Teaching, Learning, and Growth.* Boston: Allyn and Bacon, 1975. This chapter in Hamachek's humanistically oriented educational psychology text presents a nice overview of thinking on the subject of the teacher as person.

Hawkins, David. "What It Means to Teach." *Teacher's College Record,* September 1973: 7–16. Hawkins provides a very personal essay on teaching as both art and science. He helps us see the full complexity of teaching as a continuous process of diagnosing, designing, and responding to the needs of students.

Jackson, Philip W. "Life in the Classroom: The Need for New Perspectives." In Jackson, *Life in Classrooms.* New York: Holt, Rinehart and Winston, 1968. In this chapter from his widely read book Jackson argues that in order to understand teaching, we should use the perspective of a social psychologist, because interaction and group dynamics make classroom life unpredictable and everchanging.

Suggestions for Action-Oriented Learning

1. Get involved in a field project where you can observe the growth and learning of children or adolescents and at the same time engage in some sort of helping relationship. This could involve, for example, tutoring a child who needs help in a school subject, observing the same class for a period or two each week, working in a day-care center, or being a big brother or big sister to a child in an orphanage. Continue the project throughout the current semester for at least an hour or two each week, keeping a weekly log of your experiences, feelings, and the things you learn about yourself and the people you work with.

Our experience has been that field work can be a valuable means of making learning come alive in an educational psychology class. Virtually all the students in our undergraduate course carry out such projects and prepare a final paper evaluating that learning at the end of the course.

2. Prepare an autobiographical statement examining in depth the factors you feel have influenced your decision to become a teacher. If you need a guide for format, refer to the two statements presented in this chapter.

3. Carry out a survey of a group of high school or elementary school students, asking them to describe in depth their best teacher and their worst teacher. Summarize your results and share them with your class.

In any attempt to survey, interview, or observe in a school it is important to get permission from school officials (usually the principal) in advance.

4. Make arrangements to observe in an elementary or secondary school classroom and become aware of the teacher's different behaviors by using Flanders' system of interaction analysis (see Table 1–1).

5. Conduct an in-depth interview of a teacher to find out why that person became a teacher and how he or she feels about teaching today. Contrast your own motives and views about teaching with those of the teacher you interview.

2
Your Personal Growth

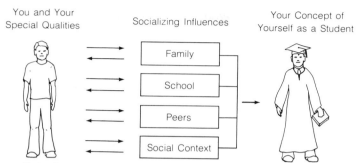

Figure 2–1. *Socializing Influences and Their Impact on the Development of Your Concept of Yourself as a Student*

This chapter is designed to help you examine some of the major factors that have influenced your personal growth. We will center upon one aspect of your *self-concept,* namely, your concept of yourself as a student. We will examine your personal growth in this way for two reasons: (1) The factors influencing the development of people's concepts of themselves as students are basically the same as those affecting other aspects of their development, such as social, emotional, or intellectual development. By considering your concept of yourself as a student you will get a better picture of your total development. (2) People's concepts of themselves as students, and their self-concepts in general (Combs, Avila, and Purkey, 1971; Hamachek, 1971), make a major contribution to their concept of themselves as teachers. Teachers bring to their teaching many of the attitudes, beliefs, feelings, and expectations they held as students. This chapter will serve as a link between Chapters 1 and 3 by furthering your thinking about your growth as a student in preparation for understanding your emerging views about teaching.

Figure 2–1 diagrams four key influences on your concept of yourself as a student. Take a few minutes to look carefully at the illustration since it provides the model from which we will operate throughout this chapter. The diagram shows how your concept of yourself as a student grows out of the interaction between you and your special qualities and the various influences of others. The influences of others we have chosen to call socializing influences because they are key influences in the *socialization process.* Figure 2–1, then, is an illustration of the way your concept of yourself as a student develops through your encounters with your social environment.

Your Concept of Yourself as a Student

Now that you have a picture of the model, try the activity below.

Exploration 2–1: Your Concept of Yourself as a College Student

Think about yourself as a college student at the present time. In three or four sentences describe your concept of yourself as a college student.

Self-concept—*"The way in which a person views or perceives himself—his attitudes, beliefs and feelings, and expectations about himself. The perceptions one has of oneself are not neutral or valueless: the self and its various aspects are viewed as good or bad, adequate or inadequate" (Patterson, 1973, pp. 155–156).*

By special qualities *we mean those characteristics, both positive and negative, that make you uniquely you; for example, your physical attributes, abilities, particular personality qualities, talents, and weaknesses.*

Socialization process—*The social learning process through which people learn the rules, customs, attitudes, values, and behavior expected of them by their culture.*

Some ideas that may be helpful in stimulating your thinking are:

1. To describe yourself you might want to select adjectives such as these—bright, average, weak, highly motivated, turned-off, hard-working, lazy, questioning, sincere, etc.

2. How do you feel about the picture you have of yourself as a student? Are you happy with the way you see yourself? Why or why not?

Compare your description with that of some other members of your class. You might discuss the extent to which your parents and teachers see you as you see yourself, or how your concept of yourself as a student affects your performance.

Now that you have described the way you are today as a student, look backward to your earlier experiences to see how this concept of yourself has evolved and changed over the years and what factors seem to have influenced the process of development. In the following exploration you will gather data to help you recall how you saw yourself as a student at various stages in your earlier years.

Exploration 2–2: Gathering Data on the Development of Your Concept of Yourself as a Student

If you can't find items for a category, take a few minutes to think about the category, using your memory to "reconstruct" the items. Take notes on the things you recall.

Try to gather as many of the items below as you can. They will help you to recreate the total range of your school experiences from preschool or first grade to the present.

1. Your old report cards from elementary school up.

2. Old photographs, especially those that relate to school.

3. Awards, prizes, honors, certificates, diplomas, etc., that you earned.

4. Old notebooks, term papers, reports, projects—especially those with grades and/or teacher comments.

5. Artwork, poetry, short stories.

6. Yearbooks, old school newspapers, class pictures, autograph books.

7. Diaries, old letters, especially if they relate to school.

8. Any other materials you and your family can uncover that communicate something about your school experience.

You might want to interview your parents or some former teachers to learn their views of you as a student. They can probably help you see changes in your view of yourself.

Look through the materials you have gathered and any notes you have made. Think about the memories this exploration has brought back to you. Then try to recall how you felt about yourself as a student as you went through the stages of school listed here and summarize those feelings in a few adjectives or a short sentence for each period.

Preschool

Primary grades (1–3)

Late elementary grades (4–6)

Junior high (7–8 or 7–9)

Senior high (9–12 or 10–12)

College (Summarize the statement you prepared in Exploration 2–1 and fill it in here.)

Questions

1. Did your concept of yourself as a student stay relatively the same or change over the years?
2. When were the times you felt most positive about yourself as a student?
3. When were the times you felt least positive about yourself as a student?

Can you identify any reasons for the positive or negative feelings you had about yourself as a student?

Interactionist—*An interactionist theory of development is the common view that psychological development is determined by an interaction between heredity (as fixed by genetic structure) and the environment in which a person matures.*

If you would like to read further on the topic of socialization you might look for D. A. Goslin (ed.), Handbook of Socialization Theory and Research *(1969).*

An especially good chapter within Goslin's book is Alex Inkeles' article "Social Structure and Socialization," pp. 615–632. Inkeles argues that in the United States the school is one of the chief agencies of socialization.

Socializing Influences and Their Impact on the Development of Your Concept of Yourself as a Student

The purpose of Explorations 2–1 and 2–2 is to help you see how your concept of yourself as a student has developed over the years you have been engaged in formal education. Let us now return to the model illustrated in Figure 2–1 to examine the socializing influences that, in part, have determined that picture. Figure 2–1 illustrates what psychologists call an *interactionist* theory of development. As you can see, the model shows that people's self-concepts as students emerge out of the interplay between "what they bring with them"—heredity—and "what they encounter in various social situations"—environment. This interactive process is quite complicated and is not easily represented graphically, since people are continually both influencing others, such as their parents, peers, or teachers, and at the same time being influenced by them. (The directions of the arrows in Figure 2–1 illustrate this two-way influence.)

The socializing influences represented in the model are organized into four major categories:

Family. Includes parents, siblings, and relatives—their attitudes toward school, expectations for school achievement, involvement with a child's education, and reactions to the child's school accomplishments.

School. The total environment of the school, including teachers, principals, counselors, their expectations for the child's abilities, performance, and personality, and the ways they react to him.

Peers. Includes the age-mates of both sexes who also are students. A child's friends and peers serve as models and communicate their feelings about appropriate attitudes and ways of behaving. They provide feedback about his abilities, school performance, and social relationships within the school.

Social Context. Includes the influence of the larger social environment within which the child lives; for instance, the child's socioeconomic status; his community and its location (rural, urban, or suburban); his racial, ethnic, and religious group; and the culture, times, and world conditions. The expectations of each of these social environments for the child's views and performance are passed on through word and example. Evaluation of the child's actual functioning as a student is continually communicated.

Exploration 2–3 will help you consider the influence of each of the above socializing influences upon your concept of yourself as a student.

Exploration 2–3: The Impact of Socializing Influences on the Development of Your Concept of Yourself as a Student

Look over the descriptive statements you prepared in Explorations 2–1 and 2–2. Then rank order in the following chart the impact of each of the four socializing influences on your self-concept during each of the major periods in your formal schooling. For each time period use a *1* for the most important influence, a *2* for the second most important influence, and so on. As you complete this activity, consider for each time period how and why each influence affected you.

Socializing Influence	Preschool (N–K)	Elem. (1–3)	Elem. (4–6)	Jr. High (7–8 or 7–9)	Sr. High (9–12 or 10–12)	College
Family						
School						
Peers						
Social Context						

Having filled in your rankings, examine the chart and reflect upon these questions:

1. Do the rankings you assigned to each of the four socializing influences change in each successive period or do they stay roughly the same?

2. Are there any points in your chart where there was a dramatic change in your rankings from one period to the next? (For example, in junior high school you may have ranked family 1, and in senior high school it may have dropped to 4.) Consider what might have taken place to bring about such dramatic changes.

You may now have begun to wonder, "Are my rankings similar to those of other people who have completed the chart?" In order to answer this question, why not compare your rankings with those of some of your classmates?

Psychologists, too, are interested in this question of similarities and differences among people. Similarities are important to psychologists as they seek to develop general psychological principles, theories, and laws that explain and predict the behavior of most people. Differences are important in helping psychologists understand and explain the uniqueness of each individual. Research designed to help psychologists formulate principles and laws that describe and explain the behavior of people in general is called *nomothetic research;* research that examines in depth individual uniqueness is called *idiographic research.* In understanding human behavior both types of research perspectives are essential since each

This distinction between the nomothetic and idiographic is often characteristic of the difference between the work of experimental psychologists and clinical psychologists. Experimental psychologists, through carefully controlled research, seek to develop

laws explaining the behavior of people in general. Clinical psychologists usually work with people on a one-to-one basis. Their goal of helping each client suggests an idiographic approach, which responds to the uniqueness of each individual.

In this chapter we have only briefly explored the formation of a person's self-concept by encouraging you to think about your own concept of yourself as a student. There is a large body of theory on the development of self-concept, and an excellent overview of a variety of these theories is provided by Hamachek in Chapter 2, "The Self and Perceptual Processes," of his book Encounters with the Self *(1971).*

Another author who has integrated a great deal of thinking about self-theory is Carl Rogers, whose On Becoming a Person *(1961) brings together much of his own idiographic research through his years of practice as a psychotherapist.*

An interesting new area of research that explores the ways dynamics within family systems affect the development of children is birth order. In Family Constellations *(1976), Toman presents data suggesting that personality attributes are related to birth order; e.g., firstborn children are different, as a group, from middle children or youngest children.*

More recently, Zajonc (1976) has published research results suggesting that intelligence declines with family size and birth order. In other words, the fewer children there are in a family, the smarter each is likely to be. And in general the older children in the family will have higher I.Q.s than the younger children. Zajonc and Marcus argue that with each new

of us shares some characteristics with others and at the same time possesses unique qualities.

In comparing your ratings of the factors influencing your view of yourself as a student with the ratings of others, you probably have found that there are both similarities and differences in your charts. Psychologists (e.g., Erikson, 1963; Havighurst, 1952) who have conducted nomothetic research on the socialization process have found that the family usually has the greatest impact on child development during the early years. As children get older, the influence of the school and their peers come more and more into play. The peer-group influence generally is not as great as that of the family and school during the early elementary grades, but by junior and senior high school its power over the individual is often profound and frequently at odds with the influence of family and school. As people mature, their social world gradually expands, including more and more outside influences and thus weakening the impact of any single one, especially the family.

In Chapter 6 you will learn more about the socialization process through a study of Erik Erikson's now classic view of development as a lifelong process. Erikson's theory, often called the "Eight Stages of Man," provides a nomothetic picture of development. In Chapter 7 you will encounter psychological perspectives that focus more on individual differences in development, i.e., an idiographic view. The remaining sections of the current chapter will give you a deeper understanding of the impact of each of the four socializing influences we have been examining—family, school, peers, and social context—upon your personal growth and the picture you have of yourself as a student.

You and Your Family

No two families are exactly alike. If each person is unique, imagine what happens when a group of unique individuals are joined together in a system. And that is just what a family is—a system in which a group of individuals interact and, to some degree, modify and mold one another. A great deal has been learned about families through the study of family interaction in family therapy. There the whole family is seen together by one or more therapists, with the goal being the improved mental health and communication of the family members both as individuals and as members of a social system.

Satir (1972) views the family as a sort of factory, in which people are made. She describes four important kinds of learning that children absorb in their families:

Self-worth—The feelings and ideas people have about themselves.

Communication—The ways people develop to share ideas and feelings with one another.

Rules—The guidelines that tell people in the family how they should feel and act.

Link to society—The way people relate to other people and institutions outside the family.

Self-Worth

The family is continually giving "messages" that strengthen or weaken a child's sense of worth. These messages are delivered by words, facial expressions, gestures, and actions. Consider how many times during the course of a single day someone in a child's family responds to something the child does. Each time this happens, something is added to the child's sense of self-worth or taken from it. Some homes seem to be filled with "good messages"; in others, a child may have to work very hard to get good messages. In still others, a child may simply give up, feeling unable to ever inspire good messages.

Try to focus back on your own growing-up years. Think about some situations in which your actions were judged, and remember how your family responded. You might think about:

Spilling things

Mispronouncing words

Disagreements with playmates or siblings

Sharing toys

Cleaning your room

Bad reports from school

Toilet-training accidents

Communication

Communication is the sharing of one self with another self. When communication between people is good, they are able to let others know what they are feeling or thinking and are able to hear and accept the feelings and thoughts of others in return.

In some homes communication is clear and direct; it is easy to understand what people are saying or feeling. In other homes, people develop various maneuvers that clutter up and confuse communication. For instance, imagine you are a 15-year-old boy, and you come home later than you were expected. Your mother looks rather unhappy. You say, "Is anything bothering you, Mother?" She says, "No, nothing," and walks away. What would it be like to live in a home where most communication was like this? If you picture this scene, you will see that the ways the mother looks, speaks, and feels don't match at all. When communication is going well, on the other hand, the body seems to match what the words are saying. Imagine the strain people feel when they must continually decode unclear messages. The young man in our anecdote might be thinking something like this: "Oh-oh! She says 'nothing,' but I can see by that way she has of kind of twisting her body away from me that I'd better watch my step."

People who grow up learning to decode these oblique communications tend to become very confused in the presence of clear com-

addition a family's intellectual level drops, as parents and older siblings must communicate at the new child's lower intellectual level.

There is much research information available today on qualities in parenting that promote optimal development in children. A good summary of that research is provided by Good and Brophy in Educational Psychology: A Realistic Approach *(1977), pp. 296–297.*

The late Haim Ginott was a psychologist whose books on communication in the family have been widely read. In Between Parent and Child *(1965) and* Between Parent and Teenager *(1969), Ginott argues that parents must learn to engage in "congruent communication"—to use words that fit feelings and that convey compassion and acceptance.*

As a follow-up to this chapter you may want to read either of Ginott's books on parent–child communication, or see how he applies his ideas about communication to the classroom in Teacher and Child *(1972).*

The family has a powerful influence on the development of a child's self-concept.

munications, probably because they always think that there is some hidden message they should be able to figure out.

Think about communication patterns in your home as you were growing up:

How did you know when your mother was annoyed with you?

How did you know when your father was annoyed with you?

Did you sometimes mistake parental concern for anger, or vice versa?

Did you or one of your brothers or sisters carry "messages" from one parent to another, from a sibling to a parent, or from one sibling to another?

Can you remember misunderstandings in your home that came about because people misread each other?

Rules

Any *should* that you learn in your family is a rule. Families tend to get organized by what people *should* do; often these rules are not so much stated as they are understood by the members of the family. In other words, they are what might be called unspoken rules.

Satir (1972) points out that angry parents will often say to a therapist, "He knows what the rules are!" Later they are amazed to find, once the situation is investigated, that in fact the child really doesn't. In still other instances, you may know the rules but not agree with or accept them. In many families there is no way of talking about, objecting to, or changing the rules. In some families, rules get outmoded, but are "kept on the books"—often with bad results. For example, many families cling to rules about socializing with others that may have been appropriate for a young child but are scarcely so for an adolescent.

Many family rules concern roles that people are expected to play in their families. Father is the breadwinner, mother is the housekeeper, the eldest child is super-responsible, and so on. Other rules relate to what you are "allowed" to feel or to say. For example: "Boys don't cry!" or "Girls don't play football!" What sorts of rules did your family make? How did you feel about the rules? Could they be changed? If so, how and by whom?

Consider your family's rules in situations such as these:

How were you supposed to handle anger?

How was affection shown?

Could sex be talked about?

Were there things you were not allowed to discuss about life at home even though you saw them with your own eyes (for example, an alcoholic parent or family arguments)?

Link to Society

Satir asks us to think of society as the sum of all existing families. She sees such institutions as schools, churches, businesses, and governments as "by and large, extensions of family forms to non-family forms." Families teach their children how to get along with the world beyond the family. Some families seem to make their children aware of things in the world that need improvement, whether in the physical environment, the government, or the neighborhood. Others seem to blind their children to the world about them, and these children often grow up with a "you can't fight city hall" attitude. Some families can demand such a degree of allegiance from their members that children have little left for the world at large. In still others the transition from family to the larger society is a natural and smooth one.

Think about what your family taught you about these links to society:

How closely should I associate with people of other racial, ethnic, religious, or social class groups?

What expectations have I developed about the roles men and women should play in business, in religious life, in the home?

To what extent have I been taught to feel responsible when I see injustice in the world, or to take a laissez faire attitude?

You and Your Schooling

You may have noticed in Exploration 2–3 that as you grew older you ranked the influence of family somewhat lower than you would have in earlier years. This is certainly understandable. In the early years our family is the only system we know intimately, and because

What rules in your family have been "kept on the books" even though they no longer may be appropriate?

What provisions are there for changing rules in your family?

To what extent were the rules for boys in your family different from the rules for girls? If there were differences in the rules for boys and girls, do you agree with them? Why or why not?

As you consider your family's teachings on these issues, reflect on what you learned from what your parents did, not simply from what they said. For example, if they spoke in favor of accepting people of other religions, to what extent did they associate with them? Or if they spoke against a double standard in sexual behavior, did they give their daughters the same freedoms and responsibilities they gave their sons?

James Coleman, in a now classic study, Equality of Educational Opportunity *(1966), found that the best predictors of how well children would achieve in school were their family's educational and social-class backgrounds. Children with better educated parents and those from middle- or upper-class homes did better in school than children from disadvantaged backgrounds.*

These results were basically supported by Christopher Jencks, who concluded a major study of U.S. efforts at equalizing educational opportunity with, "Our research suggests, however, that the characteristics of the school's output depend largely on a single input, namely the characteristics of the entering children. Everything else—the school budget, its policies, the characteristics of the teachers—is either secondary or completely irrelevant" (Jencks, 1972, p. 25).

we are so much a part of it and so little a part of society at large, we perceive our family as the world. It isn't unusual for kindergartners or first graders to tug at their teacher and call out "Mommy." But it isn't long before the children find that all the rules they learned at home don't necessarily go for school, and that teacher and mother or father may be quite different in both behavior and values.

Gearing into the school environment is, for most children, a major step in the socialization process. In Satir's sense, the school, like the home, may be thought of as a factory in each of the four areas of self-worth, communication, rules, and link to society. It has been pointed out by many writers (Jencks, 1972; Kozol, 1967; Silberman, 1970) that schools in America are institutions that reflect the middle-class, usually white, values of the teachers who teach in them and the community groups that control them. Consequently, for children who are black, economically disadvantaged, Spanish-speaking, American Indian, or in some other way "different," the transition from home to school can be very difficult.

Probably the greatest impact of the "official" school—that is, the school as defined by the teacher, the principal, and other officers of the school, such as the nurse, counselor, and school secretary—occurs in the early grades. The adults in the environment, as well as the physical arrangement of the school, play a great role in either reinforcing or diminishing the original learning the child received in the home. For example, children may be warmly praised for curiosity and liveliness at home; in school, they may be asked to curb these behaviors. Soon they may begin to wonder if it really is such a fine thing to be curious. Maybe it is better to be quiet; perhaps that's what school is about.

Look back at the rankings that you assigned to school in Exploration 2–3 as you moved through the early grades, to junior high school, senior high school, and finally college. Then consider these questions:

Do you think what you learned at school in Satir's four factors was consistent with what you learned at home?

Do some teachers stand out in your mind as especially helpful in your "becoming a person"?

Do you remember some teachers who had particularly negative effects on you?

What do you think your school's "ideal" student was supposed to be like?

How close do you think you came to this ideal?

How did you feel about the degree to which you did or didn't fit the model of the ideal student?

You and Your Peers

Just as the school begins to vie with the home's influence in the early grades, so does the role of peers in molding behavior grow stronger during the preadolescent and adolescent years. Once again, Satir's four factors come into play, but often the messages are very different as we pass from one social environment to another. For example, students who have received much praise at home and in class for maintaining consistently high grades may find that such behavior is distinctly "uncool" as far as their junior high school buddies are concerned. For teenagers who are seeking to establish their own identity and become less dependent on adults, it is very difficult to reject the norms and expectations of their peer group.

Think about your own teen years in terms of Satir's four factors—self-worth, communication, rules, and link to society. Chances are that you changed greatly during those years. To what degree was what you learned at home congruent with your peer group's expectations? How open was your family to the changes in your interests and behavior as you became more involved with your peers? You might consider some of the following:

How did your parents react to the kind of music you liked as a teenager?

If you experimented with smoking or drinking, how did your family respond? How did they talk about other young people who smoked or drank?

Chances are that there were times when your parents were "uptight" about how you and your friends dealt with drugs, sexual mores, or even political views. How were the differences on these subjects resolved between you and your parents?

Did your peer relationships strengthen or weaken your sense of self-worth? How?

Can you name some conflicts between the rules of your peers and those of your family?

Although we have been looking at the impact of peer-group influences particularly during adolescence, it should be clear that peer groups are important socializing influences throughout our lives. You can probably recall many things you learned from playmates—your peer group—in the earlier elementary grades. Adult peer groups—e.g., professional associations, country clubs, community action groups, athletic teams, women's groups, religious organizations, and political parties—exert pressures on our attitudes and behavior.

For further reading on the influence of the peer group on behavior read James Coleman, The Adolescent Society *(1961) or Ruth Newman,* Groups in Schools *(1974).*

You and Your Social Context

The events that swirl around us play a profound role in our development. Imagine growing up in a time of peace, a time of war, a time without television, a time of severe economic depression. The times in which we live contribute to our view of what the world is like, to our ambitions, to our system of values, to the way we perceive others, and even to the way we see ourselves. How many of the following events of the past 15 years can you recall either directly or through hearing parents and others discuss them? How do you think these events have affected your growing up? Can you add others that we didn't think of?

The assassination of President John F. Kennedy

The Viet Nam War

The landing of the first astronauts on the moon

Since the mid-1970s there has been a growing concern about the effects of television on the development of American children. With great numbers of children spending three or four hours a day in front of the "boob tube," television has become a powerful socializing force. Not only is the content, which includes great amounts of violence, being questioned, but critics are arguing increasingly that television promotes passivity and stifles critical thinking.

In forming your own opinion on this important issue, you may want to read Liebert, Neale, and Davidson, The Early Window: Effects of Television on Children and Youth *(1973) or Winn,* The Plug-In Drug *(1977).*

The Beatles

The civil rights movement

The murder of Dr. Martin Luther King

The unrest in high schools and colleges in the late 1960s

Woodstock

Watergate and the resignation of President Richard Nixon

Inflation and economic recession in the 1970s

Busing to achieve racial balance in public schools

The U.S. Bicentennial

On a less global level such things as the neighborhood you grow up in; your family's socioeconomic status; whether you live in an urban, suburban, or rural setting; and your racial, ethnic, and religious group all play an important part in forming your picture of the world. Some questions worth pondering regarding these aspects of your social context are:

What was your community like? Were most of the people from similar social-class, racial, religious, and ethnic backgrounds, or were there great variations?

Did you ever live in a neighborhood where you were a minority group member (e.g., a white living in a predominantly black community or a black living in a predominantly white community, a Jew living among Christians, a member of a working-class family in a suburban community of professionals, etc.)?

How did where you lived affect your attitudes toward people who were different from you?

Can you recall experiencing conflicts between the values you were learning in your family and those you encountered when you went to school or spent time with your neighbors? What were some of those conflicts?

Alvin Toffler has written a very provocative book on the psychological effects of living in the current period of tremendous technological and social change. You may find this book, Future Shock *(1971), helpful in understanding the world in which you have grown up.*

As you have been thinking about the times and environment in which you have grown up, you may have found yourself comparing your own growing-up years with those of your parents and grandparents. Try to imagine some ways you might be different had you grown up in your parents' or grandparents' world.

Putting It All Together

We have examined a number of the factors that play a role in the development of your concept of yourself as a person. Now let's consider your concept of yourself as a student. Each of the factors we have discussed has had an impact on this developing picture, which is further complicated by conflicting messages from home, school, peers, and society at large.

Look back over the questions you have considered in reading this chapter. Try to put them together now in the form of a brief description of yourself as a student. You might consider some of the following questions in organizing your statement, although we know you will think of others that are particularly relevant to you:

Do you think of yourself as an intelligent person?

In what academic areas do you feel most intelligent? Least intelligent?

Do you feel pleased with your work habits and level of productivity?

Do you feel that you have to be pushed or directed in order to achieve or that you are self-motivated?

Do you think of yourself as a creative person?

Has your view of the above factors changed through the school years? How and why?

After developing your picture of yourself, you might want to share it with a few of your classmates and learn their concepts of themselves.

Conclusions

In this chapter we have tried to help you understand your personal growth. We have focused on one important aspect of your growth, your concept of yourself as a student. By encouraging you to think about yourself as a student and about your schooling, we have tried to alert you to the ways some of your ideas about teaching and learning have developed. This background will be useful in Chapter 3 when we consider "Your Emerging Theory of Teaching" and in Chapter 4 when we provide an overview of some more formal theories of teaching.

The issues we have raised concerning the influences of family, schooling, peers, and social context apply to the question of socialization. In the process of learning more about yourself, you have also learned about the development of people in general.

Some Good Books

Bronfenbrenner, Urie. *Two Worlds of Childhood: U.S. and U.S.S.R.* New York: Simon and Schuster, 1970. Bronfenbrenner contrasts American and Soviet childrearing, pointing out that in the Soviet Union the socialization process is a careful preparation for life in society whereas in America socialization is largely an accidental process of development. Bronfenbrenner argues that we in America can learn from the U.S.S.R.'s concern for developing social responsibility in children.

Coleman, James S. *Youth: Transition to Adulthood.* Chicago: University of Chicago Press, 1974. This report prepared for the President's

Science Advisory Committee looks at growing into adulthood in the 1970s and recommends institutional changes that would respond to the needs of today's young people.

Combs, Arthur and Donald Snygg. *Individual Behavior: A Perceptual Approach to Behavior*. New York: Harper & Row, 1959. Snygg and Combs suggest that all human behavior is a function of the perceptions existing for any individual at the moment. They pay particular attention to the effects of individuals' self-concepts on their behavior.

Covington, Martin V. and Richard G. Beery. *Self-Worth and School Learning*. New York: Holt, Rinehart and Winston, 1976. Covington and Beery show very effectively the relationship between success or failure in school and a student's self-worth. Their book suggests many ways that teachers can reduce fear of failure and enhance the success and self-worth of students.

Erikson, Erik. *Childhood and Society*. 2nd ed. New York: Norton, 1963. A classic work suggesting that personality development continues throughout the whole life cycle from infancy to old age. Particularly important are Erikson's thoughts on the interaction between individuals and the society in which they develop.

Friedenberg, Edgar. *The Vanishing Adolescent*. New York: Dell, 1959. Friedenberg examines adolescence from an anthropological perspective, arguing that teenagers' social context must provide conflict in order for them to discover their own identity. Friedenberg believes that American culture no longer provides that conflict, and thus adolescence as a period of development is vanishing.

Hamachek, Don E. *Encounters with the Self*. New York: Holt, Rinehart and Winston, 1971. This book gives an excellent overview of the development of one's concept of self and is especially valuable in relating self-concept to teaching.

Maynard, Joyce. *Looking Back: Growing Old in the Sixties*. New York: Avon, 1972. Joyce Maynard wrote this book as a 19-year-old reflecting on her own growing up during the chaotic decade of the 1960s. As a personal statement on socialization, it is stimulating and deeply moving.

Mead, M. *Culture and Commitment: A Study of the Generation Gap*. New York: Natural History Press/Doubleday, 1970. This is a good synthesis of anthropologist Margaret Mead's thinking about contemporary culture in both primitive and advanced societies.

Rogers, Carl. *On Becoming a Person*. Boston: Houghton Mifflin, 1961. A collection of papers presenting and interpreting the conditions and goals of client-centered therapy. Rogers' focus on helping people better understand themselves is especially relevant to your thinking about your own growth.

Satir, Virginia. *Peoplemaking*. Palo Alto, Calif.: Science and Behavior Books, 1972. This book written by a noted family therapist describes in a very down-to-earth and informal manner the family as a "people-making factory." It provides a vivid view of the impact of the family in the socialization process.

Articles, Studies, and Other References

Bradley, Richard W. "Birth Order and School Related Behavior: A Heuristic Review." *Psychological Bulletin* 70 (1968): 45–51. Bradley summarizes a great deal of research showing that first-born children are more likely to attend college than their later born siblings. Particularly interesting are his attempts to draw upon psychological theory to explain these results.

Brookover, W., E. L. Erikson, and L. M. Joiner. "Self-Concept of Ability and School Achievement, III." *Final Report of Cooperative Research Project #2831, U.S. Office of Education.* East Lansing, Mich.: Human Learning Research Institute, Michigan State University, 1967, pp. 142–143. This extensive study of over 1000 students from the seventh through the twelfth grade shows that positive evaluations by others were very important in the formation of young people's positive concepts of themselves as students. The students' self-concepts also had a direct influence on their school performance (grade-point average).

Epstein, S. "The Self-Concept Revisited or A Theory of a Theory." *American Psychologist* 28 (1973): 404–416. An integration of a variety of theoretical perspectives on self-concept, all of which emphasize the human drive to enhance one's sense of worth and to avoid failure.

Henry, Jules. "In Suburban Classrooms." In Ronald Gross and Beatrice Gross (eds.), *Radical School Reform.* New York: Simon and Schuster, 1969, pp. 77–92. This condensed version of Henry's book *Culture Against Man* (1963) provides a view of public school education as a cultural indoctrination process whose goal is "to prevent the truly creative intellect from getting out of hand."

Jourard, Sidney. "Healthy Personality and Self-Disclosure." *Mental Hygiene* 43 (1959): 499–507. According to Jourard, the healthy personality exists within people who have been able to make themselves known to others and through this process have come to know themselves.

Suggestions for Action-Oriented Learning

1. Your parents and your grandparents grew up during times very different from those in which you have grown up. For example, your parents may have grown up during World War II and your grandparents during the 1920s, while you probably grew up in the 1960s during the Viet Nam War. Discuss with your parents and grandparents what it was like to be a student during those times. You might want to write up your findings and share them with members of your class.

2. Visit an elementary or secondary school in your community. Choose one of Satir's four types of learning in families—self-worth, communication, rules, or link to society—and observe how the school affects this type of learning. For example, you might consider how the class you observe affects the self-worth of its members.

3. Interview someone your own age who is different from you in racial, ethnic, or religious background. Discuss with that person how he felt his background affected the way he was viewed by students and by his teachers during his high school years. How did the way he was viewed by others affect his attitudes toward school and his performance? Compare your own experience with his.

4. Visit a class of "special students"—students who are grouped together because they are in some way different from other students and need special attention. Examples of classes for special students are those for the mentally retarded, emotionally disturbed, physically handicapped, gifted, blind, deaf, etc. By observing and talking with the students and teachers, try to determine how the students feel about themselves as students. Are their concepts of themselves as students similar to or different from those of students in "regular" classes? Report your findings to your class.

5. To become sensitive to the power of television as a socializing force in your life, try to go without watching any television for a week. Keep a diary of your thoughts and feelings.

3
Your Emerging
Theory of Teaching

In this chapter we want you to become better aware of, examine, and possibly reevaluate some of your own views about teaching. From Chapter 2 you can see the various influences that have made you the type of person, and more specifically the type of student, you are today. What you probably don't yet realize is that even though you may never have served as a teacher, you undoubtedly have the beginnings of an organized set of ideas about teaching—that is, an emerging theory of teaching.

The activity that follows will help you uncover some important aspects of your own theory of teaching.

Exploration 3–1: Toward Understanding Your Emerging Theory of Teaching

Imagine you are a teacher. You are teaching students in the subject, grade level, type of program, school, and community you would most prefer. First, provide the information below that describes you and your hypothetical teaching situation. Then read the letter written by the school superintendent to all of the teachers in your school and do what he requests.

Descriptive Information

Your School: Elem. _____ Jr. High _____ Sr. High _____

Your Grade and Subject: _____

Type of Class:

   Heterogeneous _____ Homogeneous _____

   Slow _____ Average _____ Bright _____

Type of Community:

   Urban _____ Suburban _____ Rural _____

Socioeconomic Status of Community:

   Lower Class _____ Middle Class _____

   Upper Class _____ Mixed _____

Heterogeneous—A class that includes students of a wide range of intellectual abilities.

Homogeneous—A class that includes students of approximately equal intellectual ability (e.g., slow, average, bright).

Letter

Aug. 30, 1980

Dear Colleague,

As you know, in recent months we in the administration have been working hard to give you classroom teachers more input in creating the type of classroom environment and curriculum that best meets your needs and, of course, the needs of your students. Toward this end I would like each of you to submit to your building principal a drawing of the way you would like your classroom to be set up. Within the limits imposed by architecture and physical facilities, we will have the custodial staff in your school arrange your room in any way you wish. Using the symbols below just fill in the floor plan—Form A—in the way you would like your room arranged, and we will see to it that each morning before classes begin your room is set up in that way. (Note: If on a particular day you want to make changes from the general plan you submit, you may do that on your own.)

Also, to allow more flexibility in your teaching, we are granting each of you a special budget of $600 to be used for any educational purposes you can justify in terms of your program for the coming year. You will be given your usual quantities of textbooks, reference books, supplies (paper, pencils, erasers, scissors, chalk, etc.) and laboratory materials as well as access to audio-visual and copying equipment. Your $600 is to be used for other things that you think would improve your program, so be creative as you make out your budget. Please complete Form B to indicate which items you feel you will need. Try to estimate the cost for each item and explain why it would be helpful in your teaching. Return Forms A and B to your building principal.

Sincerely,

Arthur P. Jones, Ed. D.
Superintendent
Snug Harbor Public Schools

Form A—Classroom Floor Plan

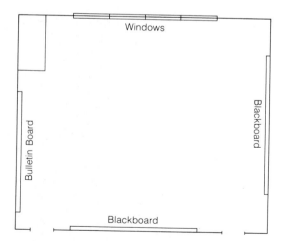

Using the following symbols, indicate on the floor plan where you would like each of the movable items placed. You will be provided with desks and chairs for 25 students.

Type of furniture	Quantity	Symbol
Teacher's desk and chair	1	⊠ (wide)
Student desk and chair*	25	⊠
Extra student chairs	8	✕
Book shelves	3	▭ (double line)
Work tables	4	▭

* If you choose to use student desks and chairs separately, you may represent the desk with ▢ and the chair with ✕ .

Form B—Special $600 Classroom Budget

Item	Brief Justification (regarding its value to your program)	Approximate Cost
1.		
2.		
3.		
4.		
5.		
6.		
7.		

8.

9.

10.   _____

                                       Total Cost
                                       (not to exceed $600)

After completing Exploration 3–1, please answer the following.

Questions regarding Form A—Classroom Floor Plan

1. Where did you put the teacher's desk?

   Is it in a position where all students face it or is it out of the way?

   Is the teacher's desk meant to be a symbol of the teacher's authority?

2. How did you arrange the students' desks?

   ___ In rows all facing the "front" of the room

   ___ In a circle

   ___ In a semicircle

   ___ In clusters (e.g., small groups of four, five, or six)

   ___ In some other way (explain)

3. To what extent can the students see each others' faces while sitting at their desks?

4. Is your classroom set up to allow much freedom of movement or is it set up for people to stay in their seats?

5. Where did you put the four work tables? What are you planning to use them for?

Questions regarding Form B—Special $600 Classroom Budget. Which of the following categories did you decide to spend money on? Check each category included in your budget.

____ 1. More textbooks

____ 2. More reference books

____ 3. Paperback books, fiction and/or nonfiction

____ 4. Individualized learning materials (those students can use on their own)

____ 5. Educational toys

____ 6. Educational games and simulations

____ 7. Magazines, periodicals, newspapers

____ 8. Supplies for creative projects (e.g., film, tape for recorders, etc.)

____ 9. Film rentals or purchases

____ 10. Furnishings for your classroom (e.g., a rug for sitting on the floor, some easy chairs)

____ 11. Food and/or cooking equipment

____ 12. Special equipment not normally provided by schools (cameras, calculators, slide rules, radio, typewriters, television set, etc.)

____ 13. Guest speakers

____ 14. Field trips

____ 15. Animals, aquariums, cages

____ 16. Maps, posters, pictures, wall decorations

____ 17. Printing or mimeograph equipment

____ 18. Other _____

____ 19. Other _____

____ 20. Other _____

Implicit Theories of Teaching

Implicit theory—*An implicit theory is part of our way of organizing our thinking about the world but has not been made explicit, that is, stated or expressed outwardly. Each of us has implicit theories about personality, childrearing, human relationships, politics, and many other areas, as well as about teaching. Since these theories exist in our minds and help*

You can probably see that your decisions for arranging your classroom and profitably spending your budget of $600 were not haphazard. They grew out of a set of ideas and general principles about what teaching is and what learning is. Having attended school and actively thought about education for at least 13 or 14 years, you have by now some rather strong feelings about teaching. This set of ideas, which has suggested to you ways of setting up your classroom and of using your budget money, is what we will call your *implicit theory* of teaching. While you may have never examined your own implicit theory of teaching in detail, it is now a very important part of you and affects your behavior. In fact, if you have ever tutored, taught a Sunday school class, coached a team, or engaged in any other teaching-type experience, you have already applied many of your ideas about teaching. In order to get a better picture of your implicit theory of teaching, let's look back to the actual classroom layout and budget you prepared for Exploration 3–1 and the questions you answered about your responses to that exploration.

Consider first the way you arranged your classroom. Did you place your students' desks and chairs in rows facing the teacher's desk? If you did, probably part of your theory of teaching is the view that the teacher is the primary source of knowledge and information in the class and that students learn primarily from her. If, on the other hand, you arranged the students' desks in a circle so that the students could easily see each other's faces, then you probably believe that students can learn a great deal from each other.

A classroom arrangement with all students facing the teacher's desk tends to emphasize the power, authority, and control of the teacher, while arrangements like a circle of student desks with the teacher sitting in the circle tend to play down the teacher's authority. In classrooms where the teacher sits with the students rather than in front of them, she is more a learning guide than a director.

How do you see your role as a teacher? As a learning guide or more as a director?

Do you feel that you would see your role differently if you had chosen to teach younger or older students? Why?

us organize our perceptions of the world, they continually influence our behavior. However, because we haven't thought through these theories carefully, articulated them, and tested them, they often mislead us by suggesting approaches that don't work.

As you read this material, you may realize that you have never thought about the relationship between the way a classroom is set up and the teaching that goes on in it. This, too, tells you something about your implicit theory of teaching. Think back to the physical environment of your classes in high school, junior high, and elementary school. What do those environments tell you about the implicit theories of your teachers? Were there certain types of classroom environments you felt increased your learning? Why?

The open classroom—what do you feel is this teacher's implicit theory?

If you would like to learn more about the physical environment and its effect on teaching and learning, you might look at Chapter 15, "The Physical Setting: Building a Psychological Context for Learning," in Good and Brophy, Educational Psychology: A Realistic Approach *(1977).*

As you are thinking about your responses in Exploration 3–1, it might be helpful to discuss your classroom and budget with classmates in pairs or groups of three or four.

As most of us who have spent any time in traditional schools can testify, student desks are not usually designed for physical comfort. How do you feel students' learning would be affected if desks were replaced by comfortable chairs and lounge furniture? Compare your ideas with those of other students in your class.

Another question worth considering is how you arranged your students' desks. Are they in clusters or groups, or did you try to keep the students as far from each other as possible? If you organized your students in clusters of five or six or had some students sitting at the work tables, you may feel that learning to cooperate, share, and work together are important educational goals. If, on the other hand you seated the students separately, you may be emphasizing learning as an individual experience in which people must rely on their own resources. Did you find yourself worried about distractions or fooling around if students sat together?

At this point look at how you chose to spend your $600 budget. Did you have trouble thinking of items to request as you filled out Form B? If you couldn't think of many things to buy, your view of teaching probably sees the primary learning resources as the teacher, textbooks, and reference books. If, however, you found that you had many more ideas for learning resources than your budget would allow, then you have a broad view of learning that sees the importance of a rich variety of materials from which students can choose.

Review your budget again, noticing the types of items you requested. This should help you identify patterns in your responses. Were you heavy on "book-type" materials or did you list such things as educational games, simulations, equipment, and materials—all of which might be used to promote more active, creative types of learning? Applying some of your budget to improving the furnishings and physical environment of your room suggests that you believe a classroom should be a comfortable, stimulating place. Were there any items in your budget that would provide opportunities for students to learn outside of school or for community people to come into the school? Attempting to provide a bridge between the school and community may mean you feel that schools should not be "ivory towers," separate and aloof from the larger society. Rather, you see the community as a wonderful resource for learning.

It should be apparent now that the way you completed the Classroom Floor Plan and $600 Budget in Exploration 3–1 was dictated by your implicit theory of teaching. Each of us has many implicit theories that influence our behavior in a variety of situations (e.g., how we interact with our parents, raise our children, work at our jobs, behave at parties, etc.). As N. L. Gage points out:

Yet, of course, all men, including graduate students, are theorists. They differ not in whether they use theory, but in the degree to which they are aware of the theory they use. The choice before the man in the street and the research worker alike is not whether to theorize, but whether to articulate his theory, to make it explicit, to get it out in the open where he can examine it. Implicit theories—of personality, of learning, and indeed of teaching—are used by all of us in our everyday affairs. Often such theories take the form of folk sayings, proverbs, slogans, the unquestioned wisdom of the race (Gage, 1963, pp. 94–95).

Making Implicit Theories of Teaching Explicit

Often we are not aware of our implicit theories, and so we don't understand how they influence our thinking and direct our behavior. Both prospective teachers and practicing teachers need to learn about their implicit theories of teaching in order to state them and test them against reality. In other words, each of us needs to make our implicit theories of teaching explicit.

Before reading any further, try the following exploration, which will help you see the value of making your theories on teaching explicit.

In Teachers for the Real World *(1969), B. O. Smith makes the point that theoretical knowledge is helpful to the teacher in understanding a particular problem and then in deciding how to deal with it. In short, a good theory is very practical in that it suggests a course of action.*

Exploration 3–2: Recommendations for Teaching That Are Products of Implicit Theories

The following are recommendations or words of advice for teaching. They are typical of the practical suggestions on how to teach passed on by experienced teachers to student teachers and first-year teachers.

Assume that you are just beginning your first semester of teaching. Decide for each suggestion whether you will accept it or reject it. Fill in the blank beside each number with an *A* for accept or *R* for reject. Jot down any notes on why you accepted or rejected the suggestion. Below each item explain in a sentence or two what implicit theory you think underlies that bit of advice.

A or R

____ 1. Don't become emotionally involved with your students. Your job is to teach, not play psychologist.

____ 2. Students who misbehave should be punished so that they will learn not to engage in that behavior again.

____ 3. Don't smile in the classroom until Christmas. This will help your students learn to respect the fact that you are the teacher and that there will be serious learning and no fooling around in your class.

____ 4. Start off right in the beginning letting the students know that you are the boss and won't tolerate any nonsense. Later on you'll be able to let up and be freer with them without discipline problems.

___ 5. For each lesson try to think of a way of capturing the interest of the students and making the learning fun. Then you won't have to be concerned about lack of attention.

___ 6. Don't set your expectations too high for students from economically disadvantaged homes. Many of them don't want to learn. They have too many other things to worry about.

___ 7. Don't be afraid to be demanding with your students. The hard teacher is the one the students come back to thank years later.

___ 8. If you want to avoid discipline problems, always be well prepared, have plenty of things to keep your students busy, and follow your lesson plans.

___ 9. Grades serve as motivators for students. Don't be too free with high grades or your students will slack off in their work.

___ 10. Always make sure that you present to the students the theory, the basics, and general principles before you move to the specifics and applications.

___ 11. If you make students feel good about themselves and happy in school, their learning will take care of itself.

___ 12. Allow your students a few minutes at the beginning of each period for talking about whatever is on their minds. Then they'll be ready to get down to business.

___ 13. Don't make exceptions to rules. If you make an exception for one student, you'll have to do it for everyone.

___ 14. If you want to be a good teacher, just stand back and let the kids go. They can learn a great deal on their own.

___ 15. Children like to compete. Build a spirit of competition into your classroom and you will be amazed at how much your students will learn.

Each of the above 15 suggestions to new teachers grows out of an implicit theory of teaching. Although some of the suggestions are contradictory, since they come from very different implicit theories, each of them seems to represent common sense and be quite logical. If you were to go into virtually any school, you would find varying degrees of support for most of them. Yet some current psychological research and theorizing could question each statement. Rather than a statement of psychological fact about teaching or learning, each recommendation is an opinion based upon a selective gathering of evidence to support it. Although there may seem to be some truth within each statement, for the most part the suggestions do not work; they simply do not have the effects that their advocates say they do.

Look back over your responses to recommendations 1–15. For each of the items you accepted, try to imagine the arguments rejecting it.

Or better yet, discuss each of your choices with another individual or a small group from your class. Try to understand their implicit assumptions and how they contrast with your own assumptions.

Our purpose in having you accept or reject the 15 recommendations about teaching has been to help you realize that many seemingly well-thought-out practical suggestions can and should be questioned. In teaching, as in all other fields, practices don't always have the results that proponents claim they have. In many cases what are passed on as truths or words of wisdom are at best half-truths or old wives' tales.

If we are to eliminate such "false advertising" in teaching and expose the teaching practices that don't work, we must make explicit and test out the theories underlying recommendations such as those in Exploration 3–2. In order to see what happens when implicit theories are kept implicit, and thus never tested, we will discuss in detail suggestions 2, 7, and 13.

Suggestion 2 states, "Students who misbehave should be punished so that they will learn not to engage in that behavior again." The implicit theory here is that if a particular human behavior is followed by a painful or psychologically unpleasant experience, that behavior is less likely to occur again. In fact, although the punished behavior may be eliminated for a few minutes, anyone who has been in schools knows that frequently the misbehavior returns; all you have to do is look at the number of repeat offenders. Obviously their behavior has not been eliminated by punishment. One explanation of what happens is that the attention and recognition the repeat offenders receive from being singled out more than compensates them for the unpleasantness of punishment. In other words, punishment may be increasing the likelihood of misbehavior rather than decreasing it, because it provides reinforcement. (See Chapter 4 for a further explanation of this behavioristic view of teaching and learning.)

There are many other psychological explanations for the failure of punishment to do what it is intended to do (e.g., Adams, 1973). While the explanations differ, there is widespread agreement among psychologists that punishment usually doesn't work and may have unfortunate side effects (hostility toward the punisher, aggression, emotional trauma, etc.). What we are suggesting, then, is that if teachers were to make explicit their theories about punishment and then systematically test them out, they would come to this same conclusion—punishment often doesn't work.

Looking now at suggestion 7, we see the following advice: "Don't be afraid to be demanding with your students. The hard teacher is the one the students come back to thank years later." The implicit theory here is that the proof that students learn more from a "hard" teacher is the number of students who recognize this years later. This theory could be made explicit and systematically checked out by keeping track over many years of the percentage of students who return to thank a particular hard teacher (which, of course, would have to be defined). Comparisons could then be made with the percentages of students who returned to thank teachers who were not hard. When their theory is not made explicit and tested, the hard teachers who give this advice often remember only the three or four students who return to thank them and forget about the many others who never would think of even returning to visit them let alone thank them.

A dramatic way to see how ineffective punishment can be is to visit a high school detention hall on a number of days and note the number of repeat offenders. Or check on many different days the lists of suspended students in one high school, again noting how many are repeat offenders.

Think back to the types of punishments used in your school experiences—e.g., low grades, poor conduct marks, detention, calls to parents, extra homework, teacher yelling, trips to the principal's office, standing in the corner, paddling. How effectively did they work for you? For your classmates?

To get some data on this question, get together with a group of other students and each prepare a list of 10 adjectives describing your "hardest" high school teacher. Then share your lists, compare what you feel you learned from that teacher, and discuss whether you have ever gone back to your old school to thank that teacher.

A traditional structured classroom—did any of your elementary or secondary school classrooms look like this one?

Recommendation 13 is: "Don't make exceptions to rules. If you make an exception for one student, you'll have to do it for everyone." The theory implicit in this statement is that rules should not have exceptions or they will no longer function as rules. As we make this theory explicit we can see the logical, as well as psychological, absurdity in the thinking it reflects. Logically it doesn't make any sense to say that if an exception to a rule or law is made for one person, it has to be made for all. The whole notion of an exception is that it is made only in certain justifiable circumstances. Thus a police officer can travel 100 miles an hour on the highway to pursue a bank robber, but most of us can't. Virtually no one would argue that because an exception is made for the officer it should be made for everyone.

All rules have exceptions (even murder is not against the law under certain circumstances, such as war or self-defense), and there is no reason school rules shouldn't have exceptions. For example, in a traditional classroom a child who has kidney problems should not have to conform to general rules about when to go to the bathroom. Or a student who has family problems ought to be able to turn in an assignment after the designated due date without being penalized. Just as our society does not fall apart when exceptions are made to laws, neither will our classroom environment disintegrate when exceptions are made. By granting legitimate exceptions to all rules, we are demonstrating that, while rules are necessary in social environments, exceptions that respect individual differences among people and circumstances are also necessary. With suggestion 13, as with the other two examples, until we make the implicit theory explicit and then test it, we will not know if that advice is worth listening to.

Can you recall rules in your elementary or high school experience for which you were told there were no exceptions? How effective were these rules?

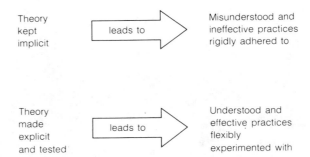

Figure 3–1. Improving Teaching Practices by Making Implicit Theories Explicit

In his popular text Educational Psychology in the Classroom *(5th ed., 1976), Henry C. Lindgren devotes a whole chapter to questioning common-sense principles that grow out of implicit theories. You may want to read this chapter, "Traditional/Conventional Views of Learning and Instruction," to better understand the problems of relying on untested beliefs in deciding how to teach.*

For each of the remaining 12 recommendations in Exploration 3–2, it is possible to carry out the same type of analysis we did with items 2, 7, and 13. When explicitly stated and systematically tested, each recommendation can be found wanting. Therefore, being aware of, making explicit, and ultimately testing out implicit theories of teaching will help us to be more effective in what we actually do in the classroom. Figure 3–1 illustrates this process.

Conclusions

Throughout this chapter we have sought to help you realize that you already have an emerging theory of teaching. We have encouraged you to do some activities designed to make you more aware of your own theory and some of its implications for teaching practices. Chapter 3 has focused on your personal theory to engage you in a type of prescientific thinking that we believe must precede the study of more formal scientific thinking.

Chapter 4 will help you understand the value of formal scientific theorizing to you as a prospective teacher. It will give you an overview of some of the major currently recognized theories of teaching. As you learn more about these more formal theoretical perspectives, you will be able to continually check and reevaluate your own emerging thoughts on teaching against viewpoints from beyond your experience.

Some Good Books

Bruner, Jerome. *Toward a Theory of Instruction.* New York: Norton, 1966. This collection of papers by a well-known psychologist provides a good discussion of the need for a theory of teaching that is integrated with a theory of learning. Bruner assists the reader in understanding how educational theory informs and dictates educational practice.

Curwin, Richard L. and Barbara S. Fuhrmann. *Discovering Your Teaching Self.* Englewood Cliffs, N.J.: Prentice-Hall, 1975. An activity-centered workbook for helping teachers (and prospective teachers) explore their own attitudes, values, feelings, and goals regarding teaching.

Gage, N. L., ed. *Handbook of Research on Teaching.* Chicago: Rand McNally, 1963. This now classic compilation of research on all aspects of teaching is an excellent source book. Chapter 3, "Paradigms for Research in Teaching," offers an informative perspective on the value of theory in teaching. (The second edition of this book is also an excellent resource: Travers, R. M. W., ed. *Second Handbook of Research on Teaching.* Chicago: Rand McNally, 1973).

Holt, John. *How Children Fail.* New York: Pitman, 1964. A well-known critic of public school education, John Holt argues in this book that schools teach children to fail and in general stifle their growth rather than facilitate it. His many examples of actual classroom situations illustrate that often teachers don't understand their implicit theories and thus employ ineffective practices.

Lindgren, Henry C. *Educational Psychology in the Classroom.* 5th ed. New York: Wiley, 1972. This widely read educational psychology text includes a chapter entitled "Traditional/Conventional Views of Learning and Instruction." Here Lindgren shows how many common-sense principles about teaching and learning grow out of implicit theories that, when systematically examined, are found to conflict with modern scientific views of education.

Postman, Neil and Charles Weingartner. *Teaching as a Subversive Activity.* New York: Delacourt, 1969. A radical criticism of teaching practices based upon poorly understood implicit theories that lead to fear, coercion, and rote-memory testing in the classroom. These authors make a case for teachers' better understanding themselves and their own views on education so that they might function as "subversives," committed to creating more open, student-centered learning.

Articles, Studies, and Other References

Broudy, Harry S. "How Can We Define Good Teaching?" *The Record* 70 (1969): 583–592. Broudy makes the distinction between *didactic teaching,* in which a teacher is primarily teaching skills and dispensing knowledge, and *encounter teaching,* which is primarily a person-to-person relationship. Each orientation grows out of very different assumptions about knowledge, teaching, and people.

Clifford, Geraldine J. "A History of the Impact of Research on Teaching." In R. M. W. Travers (ed.), *Second Handbook of Research on Teaching.* Chicago: Rand McNally, 1973, pp. 1–46. Although heavy reading, this chapter traces the history of the application of scientific thinking to education. It also explores the impact of educational research on educational practice.

Coladarci, Arthur P. "The Relevance of Educational Psychology." *Educational Leadership* 13 (1956): 489–492. Coladarci proposes that educational psychology can provide classroom teachers with information for formulating hypotheses about their teaching and testing those hypotheses to see if their techniques are working.

Rogers, Carl. "Forget You Are a Teacher." *Instructor,* August/September 1971: 65–66. Rogers makes explicit his theory of teaching as he asks his readers to forget they are teachers and see themselves as facilitators of learning. He emphasizes providing learners with the freedom to seek their own goals.

Stephens, J. M. "The Argument in Brief." In Stephens, *The Process of Schooling: A Psychological Examination.* New York: Holt, Rinehart and Winston, 1967. Stephens has reviewed a great deal of research on teaching in his book, and in this selection he concludes that there is no set of facts from which principles of teaching can be deduced. He recommends that teachers be spontaneous and use those approaches that fit their own styles and personalities. However, he does feel that teachers ought to try to understand teaching–learning through a scientific attitude.

Watson, Goodwin. "What Psychology Can We Feel Sure About?" *Teacher's College Record,* February 1960: 253–257. This article summarizes approximately 50 principles widely accepted by psychologists that have important implications for teaching practices.

Suggestions for Action-Oriented Learning

1. Go back to Chapter 1 and try to understand the implicit theory of one of the teachers whose autobiographical statement appeared there. Pay particular attention to the factors in that person's development that seem to have affected her implicit theory.

2. Visit a couple of junior high schools that have organized systems of punishment for undesirable behavior. Interview a number of teachers to learn how effective they feel their school's system is. Then interview a number of students (especially those who are frequent "behavior problems") to find out their views on the effectiveness of the school's system.

3. Take the 15 recommendations for teaching in Exploration 3–2 and ask a number of experienced teachers which ones they would pass on to a student teacher and why. Then tabulate your results and share them with your class.

4. You have done a great deal of thinking about your theory of teaching. Try now to create a picture (e.g., painting, collage, drawing, photograph, sculpture, etc.) that expresses your view of teaching.

5. Discuss with a group of students your responses to the questions on page 38 regarding the type of school and community and the subject, grade level, and type of students you want to teach. Explain your reasons for each choice and try to understand your classmates' reasons for their choices.

4
Teaching:
Four Theoretical Perspectives

The first three chapters of this book have been designed to help you understand your own emerging theory of teaching and some of the factors that have influenced its development—your family, school, peers, and social context. You have begun to make explicit and critically evaluate your personal ideas about teaching. However, it is not enough simply to be aware of your own views. Teachers (or helping professionals in any field) need to get beyond the subjectivity of their own experience and benefit from the thinking and research of others. This chapter will focus on the value of formal theories that have been made explicit, tested, and reevaluated. Our goal is to encourage you to become a "consumer of theories," whose personal views about teaching can be examined, checked, and supplemented by the research and theorizing of those who have systematically studied teaching.

The following anecdote, written in the form of a play, has been prepared to make you aware of the ways formal theories can generate important practical strategies for improving teaching. Described in the anecdote are the experiences of a new high school English teacher over a number of weeks. As you read through the anecdote try to imagine how you might have responded had you been teaching in that situation.

Miss Jane Bell's
First Semester as an English Teacher*

Scene I. *A few days before school opens—Thursday, September 2. Miss Bell walks into the principal's office in a large high school in a midwestern city of 50,000 people. She talks to the principal's secretary.*

Miss Bell: I came to pick up my supplies.

Secretary: Go right in. Mrs. Adams is handing them out right now.

(Miss Bell walks into a smaller inner office where the principal is handing out some supplies to another teacher. The other teacher leaves.)

Mrs. Adams: *(Looking up)* Oh, there you are, Jane. How are things going in preparation for your first day with us?

Miss Bell: Fine, I guess. I still have to think up something bright and cheery for our bulletin board display.

Mrs. Adams: You seem real enthusiastic. *(Smiling)* Well, most new teachers do. *(Handing Miss Bell some papers)* Oh, here's the information you wanted on your junior English classes: the

---

* Adapted from pp. 99–103 ("Half and Half") of *Problem Situations in Teaching* by Gordon E. Greenwood, Thomas L. Good, and Betty L. Siegel. Copyright © 1971 by Harper & Row, Publishers, Inc., by permission of the publisher.

I.Q.s, standardized English achievement test scores, and previous English grades of all the 175 students you will have. Don't tell the other teachers that I had Mary get all of these for you, or they will want her to do it for them too.

(Miss Bell sits at her desk in her classroom. The room is in disarray. There are potted plants set out on one desk, a pile of posters on another, and the bulletin board display is only partially completed. A stapler, some glue, some tape, and pencils are spread out in preparation for finishing the colorful display. Miss Bell is looking over the papers that she got from the principal.)

Miss Bell: *(Thinking to herself)* About half of these students are above average in I.Q., achievement test scores, and grades. Take William here. He's made almost straight As in English and has very high test scores. But then there is Mary. The other half are about on her level or a little lower. She's made Ds in English. Her I.Q. is 87 and some are lower than that. What a diversified class! I will really have to think of something to bridge these differences in ability. That won't be easy with 35 students in the class.

Scene II. *Several days later Miss Bell is lecturing about William Blake—Friday, September 10.*

Miss Bell: And so, this *Introduction to Songs of Innocence* by William Blake is Blake's account of how he came to write his poems. His "cloud child" commanded and he obeyed. It makes a lovely picture in reading.

Bob: I don't understand how a ghost could tell him what to do. *(Class laughs)*

Bill: It wasn't a ghost, dummy. The cloud child means inspiration.

Miss Bell: Yes, Bill, you could call it that.

Mary: But what does "stain the water clear" mean?

Bill: *(Retorting)* He made ink, duh!

(Mary blushes with embarrassment. Class laughs. Some students stare into space; some are flipping through the book looking at other selections. Some look at Miss Bell with confused faces.)

Bill: Miss Bell, can't we go on to another poem? I'm tired of this stuff and. . . .

Scene III. *Over a month later, Miss Bell's class is reading from* Romeo and Juliet—*Wednesday, October 20.*

Mary: Juliet: How camest thou hither, tell me, and wherefore? The orchard walls are high and hard to climb. And the place death, considering who thou art, if any of my kinsmen find thee here.

(Mary reads in a monotone, stumbling over the words, especially the old English. The class is fidgety. Two students have their heads down. One is openly reading a library book. There is a buzz in the back of the room which eventually breaks into laughter, interrupting the reading. Miss Bell walks to the back of the room.)

Miss Bell: What is all the laughter about? *(Earnestly)* Juliet is very serious here. Romeo could be killed by coming to see her. Do any of you remember why? *(Students exhibit blank faces; one boy tries to hide a motor magazine, but Miss Bell sees it)* Is this magazine part of our class literature?

James: No, ma'am. But I don't understand what Mary's trying to read up there, anyhow.

Miss Bell: But you have disrupted the whole class. I think the Dean of Boys will need an explanation of why you are reading that magazine in class. *(Other students show rebellious looks)*

James: But what about Susan up there reading a library book?

Class: *(Echoing)* Yeah!

Susan: *(Retorting quickly and cuttingly)* Well, I make As in this class; you're failing. *(Class breaks into a bedlam of comments)*

Miss Bell: Just a minute! This is a classroom, not a riot! Quiet down! *(The class quiets down as Miss Bell continues to speak)* Now, Mary, will you go on with your reading. You're doing fine.

Mary: *(Shyly)* But I don't understand a word I'm reading. . . .

(Bell rings to signal end of class. The students get up, slamming books about and talking loudly. They walk out into the hall talking about the incident in class.)

Scene IV. *In the hall immediately after English class—Wednesday, October 20.*

George: But, why can't she ever explain anything? She goes so fast you'd think we knew Shakespeare like we know basketball.

Sharon: Who cares about stupid old *Romeo and Juliet* anyway? My older sister and her boyfriend, Pete, went to see the movie and they said they couldn't understand a word. Shakespeare is such a drag!

Mary: *(Catches up with them)* Do you know what Bill just asked Miss Bell? *(They shake their heads)* He asked why we have to spend so much time on *Romeo and Juliet*. He wanted something harder like. . . . Oh, I can't think of the name of the play, but it was another one of Shakespeare's. Can you believe he would have the nerve? *(Disbelief on all faces)*

(Meanwhile Miss Bell sits in her classroom composing a letter to the parents of her slower students. She finishes the letter and reads it over for errors.)

Dear Parent,

Some of the students in my class are having difficulty with the material I present each day. Therefore, I am setting up a tutoring hour every afternoon from 3:20 to 4:20 for anyone who wants help. I hope that if your child is having difficulties he will take this opportunity to go over our day's assignment, classwork, and discussions. This way I can give individual help and the problems should be ironed out. Please urge your child to come. Thank you for your consideration.

Sincerely,
Miss Jane Bell
Junior English Class
Claremont-Sims High School

Miss Bell: *(Thinking to herself)* I hope this will clear up the problems I've been having.

Scene V. *After school over a week later—Monday, November 1. Miss Bell is in her empty classroom. She is sitting at her desk as two students enter.*

Miss Bell: Hi, girls, have a seat. We'll just wait a few minutes until more of the students arrive.

(The girls sit down and talk to each other. Two boys stand at the door. Miss Bell motions for them to come in.)

Miss Bell: Come on in, boys.

Jeff: No thanks, we just wanted to see if John and George were here. We're going to basketball practice.

(The boys leave as three other girls come into the room and sit down. Two boys come in a moment later. Miss Bell looks at the clock. It is 3:30.)

Miss Bell: It's time for us to begin. Do any of you have any questions? *(One girl raises her hand)*

Scene VI. *The afternoon of the next day at 3:30—Tuesday, November 2. Two students are there for the tutoring session.*

Miss Bell: Well, we must begin. We'll try to help stragglers catch up when they arrive.

Mary: Oh, the boys aren't coming today. They thought we were going to have Cokes at the last session and talk about something they were interested in like basketball. What did you think of that game last night?

Judy: Yeah, Gary Clark made 35 points!

Miss Bell: Well, that's fine. But let's get down to a discussion of any problems that you might have in English.

Scene VII. *The P.T.A. meeting—Tuesday, November 9. It is refreshment time at the monthly P.T.A. meeting and the teachers are socializing with the parents. Miss Bell is talking with one of the parents.*

Miss Bell: Why didn't Mary continue to come to my tutoring sessions? I know she is having problems and the sessions would have helped a lot.

Mother: *(Shaking her head)* I'm sorry. I told her she'd regret it, but she said she didn't want to spend another hour at school; and I couldn't make her stay. Kids need to relax too, you know!

Scene VIII. *The day after the P.T.A. meeting—Wednesday, November 10. Miss Bell visits the curriculum supervisor in his office. She sits across from him at his desk.*

In Chapter 3 we explored the concept of personal implicit theories. On the basis of this description of Miss Bell's approach, try to analyze her implicit theory.

Miss Bell: So you see, I've tried to help by having a tutoring session each afternoon. That didn't work. Then I changed the gearing of my teaching from the average–fast to the average–slow. But now the fast students are really bored and some discipline problems have developed. I've even tried putting them in discussion groups, both fast and slow together, but that just causes pandemonium. *(She pauses)* Isn't there any way some of the slower students can be transferred to an easier section?

Supervisor: We don't have fast or slow classes in the school, Jane. There just aren't enough facilities to do it or we would. Anyway, almost half the semester is over, and the adjustment to another class might cause even more problems.

Miss Bell: Well, then how can I gear my class to keep the fast students interested and not lose the slow ones? How do you teach a class like that?

This anecdote makes it obvious that Miss Bell needs help and doesn't know where to turn. Let's imagine that Miss Bell can present the information you just read to four different people for their advice, experienced educators who would serve as *consultants*. By having each one of them analyze what has transpired in her class sessions, Miss Bell will be able to get a number of reactions and suggestions on how she might more effectively teach her class.

A consultant is a professional who brings special training and expertise to a particular problem. When seeking advice or developing new ideas, businesses, governments, and educational institutions often call on consultants to work on a short-term basis.

Consultants usually are not regular full-time employees of the organization using their services. As a rule they are outsiders employed elsewhere. In their role as consultants they may work one day, a few days, or on a regular basis, such as one day each week or each month.

Exploration 4–1: Suggestions for Helping Miss Bell
Before reading any further try to offer Miss Bell three of your own suggestions for improving her teaching.

1.

2.

3.

Each of the following reports will present a written statement that describes from the perspective of each consultant what has occurred in Miss Bell's class, diagnoses the apparent problems, and prescribes steps toward solutions. As you read the four reports, try to get into the minds of the consultants and look at the problems as they perceive them.

For the sake of brevity, we will not go into great depth with any of the consultants' reports. The focus of the consultants' comments will be on Miss Bell's actual classroom teaching (Scenes II, III, and IV), even though Miss Bell's efforts in tutoring, meeting parents, etc. are also important.

The Reports of Four Educational Consultants

Report of Consultant 1—Ralph Thomas

To: Miss Jane Bell
From: Ralph Thomas, Educational Consultant
Subject: Teaching of Junior English Class, Claremont-Sims High School

From the information you have given me, I would like to call your attention to the responses of a number of your students to the study of *Romeo and Juliet*. The incident in which Mary was reading the part of Juliet (Scene III in the anecdote) is representative of other events that have happened in your classroom. In that incident I noted the following student behaviors as Mary read "in a monotone, stumbling over words":

Two students had their heads down.

One was openly reading a library book.

One boy was reading a motor magazine.

Several students were talking and laughing in the back of the room.

The whole class was "fidgety" as described by you.

The behaviors of many of your students indicate that they prefer activities other than reading, analyzing, and discussing *Romeo and Juliet*. Recall (in Scene III) that Mary and James told you (in one way or another) that they didn't understand the reading while Bill and Susan indicated that they found the material easy. In the way you have presented *Romeo and Juliet,* it appears that you have encouraged the bright students and those interested in the play; at the same time, however, you have discouraged the slower students and those who are not interested in the play.

Your objectives in having the students study *Romeo and Juliet* are not clear—especially to your slower students. What are you trying to accomplish? What can you do to make the study of *Romeo and Juliet* more responsive to the individual differences apparent in your class? Aren't there ways of giving your slow students more time and assistance in meeting your goals? Or why not adapt your expectations so that their study of *Romeo and Juliet* is more appropriate to their abilities and interests?

Some suggestions:

1. Think about and then write down your objectives as specifically as possible—what you want your students to learn from studying *Romeo and Juliet*. Try to spell out what it is you want students to *do* so that both you and they will be able to assess their progress accurately.

2. Communicate and justify your objectives to your students.

3. You might provide class time for advanced students to delve more deeply into some aspects of the play while your slower students use the same time for remedial work. Remember—it's not necessary for everyone in the class to be doing the same thing at the same time.

4. Make certain that the students know Elizabethan English well enough to read and understand Shakespeare. Identify 100 of the most common words within the play that are not used today. For each word select from the play a sentence in which the word appears. Prepare five alternative definitions (only one of which is correct) for the uncommon word as it is used within the context of each sentence. Organize the 100 sentences (and alternative definitions) into 10 lists of 10 sentences each. Give a copy to each of your students. Then, have each student work on one list until he or she can identify the correct definition for at least eight of the 10 uncommon words. In this way each student can learn to define the uncommon words within the context of real sentences taken from the play.

5. Have each class member be responsible for choosing and completing an individual project on some aspect of *Romeo and Juliet* (e.g., build a Shakespearean playhouse, report on the society and culture in which Romeo and Juliet lived, design and wear clothing that Juliet might have worn, etc.). Give each student the chance to share the project with the class, experiencing the rewards of his or her efforts. In this way every student—whether "fast" or "slow" intellectually—gets a chance to shine.

6. As a general rule, maintain control in your classroom by using ample praise and encouragement when your students do what you want them to do. Usually it is better to ignore an inattentive or disruptive student (giving attention will often strengthen the behavior). Then, when you notice the student paying attention or asking a question—no matter how simple it may seem—give praise for such involvement.

Report of Consultant 2—Barbara Stein

Dear Miss Bell,
      The information you have provided seems to indicate that neither you nor most of your students feel very positive about recent events in your Junior English class. You appear frustrated by the fact that your students represent such a wide range of abilities and interests. Some of the students feel confused when they try to read *Romeo and Juliet;* others are bored because they understand the play and would like to move on; still others feel alienated because they don't see the relevance of the play. The feelings generated are directed not only at you, but also from one group of students to another. Consequently, incidents occur such as in Scene III when Susan admitted to James before the whole class that she may have been reading a library book, but that she was receiving an A in the course while James was failing.

The problem, as I see it, is that your expectations regarding your students' learning and their responses to those expectations have created a variety of feelings in both you and them. Those feelings are influencing everything taking place in your classroom. The feelings will continue to interfere in your relationship with your students, and your effectiveness as a teacher will be curtailed until these feelings are brought out in the open where you can deal with them. You and your students have developed an adversary relationship with your classroom as a battleground.

My first suggestion is that you look at yourself and your own feelings about the class. You might want to think back to what kind of high school student you were and how you did when you were in Shakespeare class. Are you evaluating your students today in terms of the way you were as a student? Can you recall how you felt toward the teacher and your classmates in a course you were not particularly strong in? Perhaps some of your current students are experiencing that same feeling? It might be useful for you to talk with a few of your close friends about how they felt in courses in which they were "good" students or interested in the subject, versus how they felt in courses where they were "weak" or not interested.

Once you have examined your own feelings, try to "clear the air" by discussing with your students their feelings about the study of *Romeo and Juliet* as well as their feelings toward you and the other members of the class. Share as openly as possible some of your own feelings of frustration and ask for their ideas on how to make *Romeo and Juliet* more meaningful and how to eliminate the disputes between "fast" and "slow" students. By being honest and real with them, you will help them become more sensitive to your needs as the teacher and they may be able to help you improve the class.

Finally, why not attempt to relate the play to your students' own personal lives? For example, have a discussion of similarities and differences between their own dating relationships and those of Romeo and Juliet. Or you might ask them to compare the major themes of the play *Romeo and Juliet* with a more contemporary musical like *West Side Story*. Reassure them that you are more interested in their being able to express the emotions evoked by the play's passages than you are in their being able to translate the Elizabethan English directly.

Warmly,

Barbara Stein

P.S. There are some excellent references on values clarification that you can explore for ideas on how to "personalize" the study of *Romeo and Juliet*. These books offer a variety of teaching approaches for helping students to clarify and examine their feelings, attitudes, and values. Two that you might want to look for are:

Howe and Howe. *Personalizing Education: Values Clarification and Beyond.* New York: Hart, 1975.

Raths, Harmin, and Simon. *Values and Teaching.* Columbus, Ohio: Merrill, 1966.

Report of Consultant 3—William Kraus

Miss Jane Bell
English Department
Claremont-Sims High School

Dear Miss Bell:

Your students vary greatly in their intellectual readiness for and interest in reading and critically evaluating Shakespeare's *Romeo and Juliet*. When you direct your teaching to the brighter students, you frustrate and turn off the slower students. On the other hand, if you teach to the level of the slower students, you bore the brighter students. In short, there does not appear to be a good match between what you are doing in your classes and the level at which most of your eleventh-grade English students are functioning. This problem of match undoubtedly applies not only to the intellectual level of your students but also to the level of their experiences. Students who have done much reading (of Shakespeare and of other authors) will have more ideas to bring to their reading of *Romeo and Juliet* than those who haven't.

The central question is: What can you do in your class sessions to increase the match between the play *Romeo and Juliet* and the thinking levels and experiences of all of your students? Rather than simply assuming that your students will be able to analyze the meaning of *Romeo and Juliet* on their own, you need to help them learn to think critically about it. One of the most effective ways of doing this (and at the same time increasing their interest) is through provocative questioning on your part. If you ask *thought* questions as opposed to *information* questions, each student will be more motivated to enter the discussion at his or her own level of thinking since there can be more than one right answer to such questions. For example, following the passage that Mary was reading (Scene III in the anecdote), you might ask, "What do you think Shakespeare meant when he said, 'And the place death'?" The responses to that question could be followed by: "Can any of you describe a time when you were in a situation like the one Romeo was in, where you afraid of being discovered?"

Since the Elizabethan English frightens many students, help them discover that they already know most of the words in the play. You can do this by explaining that Elizabethan English is just a code in which they already know most of the words and can probably guess the meanings of the others. Then, have each student make a list of all the words on a randomly selected page of the play that he or she can't define. Ask one student to record all of these "new" words on the blackboard. Go through the new words asking for volunteers to define each word. If no one can define a particular word, ask your students to guess at the definitions, giving reasons for their guesses based upon the context in which the word appeared. Such an activity should help them realize that the words they don't know can easily be figured out if they use what they already know, examining the context within which the word appears.

Another activity that could be highly motivating to all the members of your class would be to give part of the dialogue between Romeo and Juliet to two black students and ask them to get together alone to translate it into black dialect. Then, during the next class period have them present their black dialect version of the dialogue to the whole class. After listening to the presentation each student should find the page where that dialogue occurred in the play and consider his or her response to the question: Is *Romeo and Juliet* a love story for all times or is it only relevant to the times Shakespeare was writing about? This activity would encourage your class to critically analyze what Shakespeare was saying and relate it to their own experiences.

Sincerely,

William Kraus

William Kraus
Educational Consultant

Report of Consultant 4—Margaret Olson

To: Miss Bell, English teacher
From: Margaret Olson, Educational Consultant

In describing your problems with your Junior English class, you have mentioned the existence of essentially two groups within the class—the students whom you characterize as "fast" and those whom you refer to as "slow." You have stressed that when trying to direct your lesson to the average student in one of the groups, you have not reached the other group. Also, much of the disruptive behavior that occurs during your class sessions involves disputes between these groups (e.g., Bill's retort to Bob in Scene II and the interchange between James and Susan in Scene III). It would seem, then, that the major problem you face involves the interactions taking place both between you and your students and among your students.

Your troubles may well have begun when in September, even before you had met your students, you read the class list that included their I.Q. scores, achievement test scores, and previous grades. By thinking of your students as essentially two separate groups—"fast" and "slow"—you have unwittingly emphasized the factors that divide them. You have created a self-fulfilling prophecy: Because you expected your students to be different, you treated them differently, and in so doing you have caused them to think of themselves as different and thus respond differently to you, your subject, and each other. Given such group dynamics, it is only logical that you would find it hard to involve many students in the study of *Romeo and Juliet*. To reach more of them, you must improve the "climate" in your classroom. Creating common experiences which bring together rather than divide your students will help them realize that they can learn from each other even though there are differences between them intellectually. Three suggestions you might use or adapt are:

1. Select a particular dialogue between Romeo and Juliet (e.g., the passage that Mary is beginning to read in Scene III of the anecdote) and have all the boys get together in one discussion group and all the girls in another. Have the girls discuss what they think Juliet's feelings are in that situation and the boys discuss what they believe Romeo's feelings are. Then, bring them back together to share and question each other regarding what came up in each of the groups. Not only will this activity generate

interest and thinking about the dialogue, but also it will allow both "fast" and "slow" students to come together and interact in a nonthreatening way.

2. Have the class actually produce a part of the play. To do this, committees could be organized—each with a different responsibility for some aspect of the production. There might be a committee for making the set, a committee of actors and actresses, a committee to direct the production, a committee to handle costuming and make-up, etc. Undoubtedly each student's choice would be determined more by interest and specific abilities (art, acting, carpentry, editing, etc.) than by general intellectual ability. In producing the play each student would have a contribution to make to his committee and would interact with many other students both within and outside his committee. Also, with the whole class working on the play, the students would learn that unity, cooperation, and at the same time diversity of talents are all necessary for a group to function effectively.

3. Continually seek new ways of encouraging students to communicate and work together. At times you might create dyads (pairs) or triads (groups of three) for discussion of their reactions to the play. On other occasions you might organize debates or large group discussions. You may even want to rearrange the furniture in the classroom so that students have a chance to become better acquainted with others they would not normally seek out.

Four Formal Theoretical Perspectives

As you read the reports of the consultants whose advice Miss Bell sought, you probably found that each of them looked at Miss Bell's situation in a different way, focusing upon different aspects of her teaching and making different recommendations. You may have noted some internal consistency in the ideas of each consultant even though there was some degree of overlap. This consistency arises from the fact that each consultant's suggestions reflect a particular theoretical perspective on how people learn and how teachers should teach. We will now examine in some depth each of those four theoretical perspectives. We will provide a brief description of the formal theory from which each consultant is operating as well as some of the key principles that led to each consultant's specific suggestions.

The Behavioristic Perspective—"Doing."
Consultant 1—Ralph Thomas

Ralph Thomas' theoretical perspective is *behavioristic*. A behavioristic psychological perspective concerns itself only with overt, observable behavior, in a scientific attempt to predict, modify, and control. Thus Mr. Thomas' focus in his consultation was on what Miss Bell and her students were doing, rather than on what they were thinking or feeling. Since neither thoughts nor feelings can be directly observed, they must be subjectively reported by the individuals experiencing them. The behavioristic view of the world suggests that all behavior, no matter how complex it may appear, is made up of very basic elements. This view, sometimes described as a molecular or additive approach, argues that if we want to understand a given behavior, we must analyze that behavior into its component parts, for the whole is simply the sum of its parts. All behavior, then, involves nothing more than *responses* to *stimuli* in the environment. And learning can be defined as a change in behavior that is the result of a connection or an association between a stimulus and a response.

Behaviorism is today a major school of thought in American psychology and is probably best exemplified in the work of B. F. Skinner. Skinner's theories have their roots in the research of John Watson in the early 1900s. Watson argued that the only legitimate scientific research method for psychology was the observation of overt behavior. His ideas have been expanded and adapted by many behaviorists; Skinner's major contributions have been in the development and articulation of what has come to be called *reinforcement theory*. Simply stated, this theory suggests that when a particular behavior (e.g., Ann's answering a question correctly) is followed by some reinforcing event (e.g., her teacher's saying, "Good, Ann"), then the likelihood of that behavior being repeated (Ann's answering another question) is increased. Both *primary reinforcers,* such as food and water, and *secondary reinforcers,* such as prestige, money, and praise, can function to reinforce human behavior.

Skinner's research in learning originated in the laboratory, where he manipulated and studied the learning of pigeons and rats. However, the principles of reinforcement he developed there have been extended and applied to human learning in the creation of programmed learning materials, teaching machines, and strategies for shaping and modifying human behavior. As you probably have already realized, much of Mr. Thomas' work as a consultant is based upon the principles of reinforcement that have emerged from Skinner's research. Let's return to Mr. Thomas' memo and try to understand how he utilized a behavioristic perspective and, more specifically, principles of reinforcement in the advice he gave Miss Bell.

As we pointed out earlier, in describing what he saw taking place in Miss Bell's classroom, Mr. Thomas spoke only about observable behavior—what the students were doing. He tried to help her see that the students' comments showed that they didn't understand her goals. He proposed that she specify her goals, explain them to her students, and then provide different learning activities for the faster and slower students. In this way students of all abilities would be able to receive reinforcement by succeeding at their own level.

Mr. Thomas also suggested that she break the Elizabethan English down into basics—10 lists of 10 sentences, with each sentence containing one of the 100 most commonly occurring difficult words. In this way students would learn new words in a step-by-step process and receive reinforcement as they mastered each new list. The proposal that each student complete and share with the class a project on some aspect of *Romeo and Juliet* was designed to reinforce every

Skinners' influence on both psychological research and educational practice in America has been tremendous. Not only are his explanations of how we learn widely accepted, but applications of his theories are used all over the world in schools, universities, clinical settings, and industry.

In Chapter 13 we will explore Skinner's work more deeply.

Primary reinforcers do not have to be learned, whereas secondary reinforcers do. For the most part the reinforcers used to promote learning in schools are secondary rather than primary. Most parents would not permit teachers to manipulate the food or water intake of students as psychologists do in studies of animal learning! However, there are some behavior-modification techniques that do utilize food as a reinforcer under carefully controlled circumstances, usually with seriously disturbed or retarded persons. More on this later.

An outgrowth of behavioristic psychology, with its concern for studying observable behavior, is the behavioral objective movement. Influenced by the thinking of De-Cecco (1968), Mager (1962), and Tyler (1964), advocates of the use of behavioral objectives argue that instructional goals must be stated as specifically as possible and in terms of observable behavior.

The behavioristic position does not advocate punishment, since it seldom reduces undesirable behavior and may actually reinforce it.

Can you recall any situations in which punishment actually strengthened an "undesirable" behavior?

The other major orientation within the phenomenological school of thought is the cognitive; we will speak of this approach shortly. While the affective orientation pays particular attention to feeling, the cognitive concerns itself with thinking.

Humanistic psychology *was called the third force by Maslow, since it provided a way of looking at psychology radically different from the two prevailing theories, behaviorism and psychoanalysis.*

student's participation. In his concluding remarks Mr. Thomas emphasized the need for Miss Bell to maintain control and promote learning by rewarding desirable behavior and not calling attention to undesirable behavior.

The Affective Perspective—"Feeling."
Consultant 2—Barbara Stein

The theoretical perspective underlying Barbara Stein's consultation is *affective*. The word *affective* comes from the German word *affekt*, which means feeling or emotion. An affective theory of teaching and learning concerns itself primarily with the feelings of both teacher and students in the classroom. Recall the heavy emphasis in Miss Stein's memo on openly examining and dealing with the feelings generated by both the classroom relationships and the content of *Romeo and Juliet*.

The affective position is one of two major orientations within the psychological school of thought known as *phenomenology*. Almost the opposite of behaviorism as a means of organizing our knowledge of human behavior, phenomenology focuses attention on what is "inside"—on our subjectivity not our outward behavior. This view proposes that human behavior is determined more by how people perceive the world than by how the world actually is. In other words, we are controlled primarily by our own *consciousness* (i.e., our feelings and thoughts) rather than by external events, as behaviorists argue.

The beginnings of the phenomenological movement in psychology took place in Germany around 1910, with the research of a group of psychologists led by Max Wertheimer. They disagreed with the behaviorist attempt to analyze all human behavior into its smallest elements. They maintained that any human behavior was a Gestalt—a total experience that was more than the simple sum of its parts—and therefore it needed to be examined in its totality. An experience often used by *Gestalt* psychologists to illustrate the limitations of behavioristic thinking is viewing a motion picture. If that experience is examined in terms of its elements—namely, a series of still pictures—the total phenomenon of perceived movement is lost, and the experience cannot be explained and understood. To the Gestalt psychologists learning involves not stimulus–response associations but the rearrangement of previous experience and ideas into new patterns of thought—a process they called insight.

The Gestalt tradition has provided important theoretical underpinnings for both the affective and the cognitive orientations within phenomenology. Two major theorists best articulate the affective phenomenological position—Abraham Maslow and Carl Rogers. Maslow (who died in 1970) was a psychologist who synthesized Gestalt psychology and his training in Freudian psychotherapy. His research and theorizing led him to found a movement in psychology today referred to as *humanistic psychology*. This view emphasizes our capacity for directing our own behavior and achieving self-actualization, the full realization of our unique potential. Rogers, probably the foremost living proponent of humanistic psychology, has built upon Maslow's thinking and applied concepts of humanistic psychology to the practice of psychotherapy and, more recently, to teaching.

Returning now to Miss Stein's memo to Miss Bell, we can see the extent to which she drew upon the affective theoretical perspective—and particularly the thinking of Carl Rogers—in formulating her suggestions. Because she was especially concerned with improving the emotional climate of the classroom, her first recommendations were that Miss Bell try to understand her own feelings about the class as well as those of her students. Rogers has discussed in great depth the open examination of feelings by both teacher and students, contending that only in an environment where there is trust, open communication, and positive feelings can genuine learning take place.

Miss Stein suggested that once the feelings of the students and teacher have been examined, the content of Shakespeare should be related to the personal lives of the students. Rogers would support this idea since be believes that real learning occurs only when it is personally significant, i.e., directly related to the needs and interests of the learners. Clarifying values in order to make Shakespeare more personal is a very practical approach to helping Miss Bell. Miss Stein's advice has pointed up the need to humanize both the relationships within the classroom and the English curriculum.

The Cognitive Perspective—"Thinking."
Consultant 3—William Kraus

William Kraus' advice to Miss Bell is based upon a *cognitive* theoretical perspective. The word *cognitive*, from the Latin verb *cognoscere*, refers to the mental process of knowing or thinking. A cognitive psychological perspective of teaching and learning pays particular attention to the thinking taking place within a classroom. As you reread Mr. Kraus' report to Miss Bell, you can see how he emphasized the need to relate her lessons to the previous knowledge and intellectual level of her students. He said that there was not a good match between the students' level of thinking and Miss Bell's expectations for their ability to read and critically examine *Romeo and Juliet*. In short, Mr. Kraus' primary focus was neither on what Miss Bell's students were doing nor on what they were feeling, but on what they were thinking.

Like the affective perspective, this cognitive perspective has its theoretical roots in phenomenology. Consequently, the emphasis is again on (1) what takes place within us rather than our overt behavior; (2) how we perceive the world as opposed to how it actually is; and (3) our capacity for controlling rather than being controlled by our environment. The major difference between the cognitive and affective orientations lies in the factors they stress as determining human behavior. The cognitive orientation stresses intellectual (thinking) processes; the affective orientation stresses emotional (feeling) processes.

Jerome Bruner is generally acknowledged as a leading contemporary spokesman for the cognitive position. Bruner has been heavily

You will learn more about Maslow's thinking in Chapter 9, on motivation.

Rogers' most comprehensive statement on education appears in his Freedom to Learn *(1969). It is there that he argues that good teachers are "facilitators of learning," not directors. Facilitators encourage students to learn rather than coerce them. They provide maximum freedom for students to direct their own learning. Rogers believes that all people possess both the desire and capacity for learning and therefore a nondirective approach by the teacher will allow learning to occur.*

Rogers draws many analogies between teaching and psychotherapy. He is the founder of nondirective— sometimes called client-centered— therapy. He views the therapist as a facilitator who listens rather than advises, always encouraging clients to make their own decisions. It is his success with this approach that has led Rogers to argue that teachers, too, ought to act as facilitators. Just as he uses a client-centered approach in psychotherapy, Rogers calls for a student-centered approach in education. For Rogers the qualities of both effective teachers and effective therapists include warmth, openness, self-awareness, and empathy.

Sometimes educators make the distinction between process *and content* in relation to subject matter. Process *refers to general concepts and principles, while* content *refers to facts and basic information. Two recent examples of process approaches to teaching are modern math, with its concern that students learn theory and not simply rote calculation; and history taught conceptually, in terms of major themes and issues rather than as a series of names, dates, and places to be learned chronologically.*

In expository teaching *the teacher directs the learning and does much of the speaking. A teacher who lectures most of the time is using expository teaching.*

One of the authors of this book remembers a professor's maxim that the purpose of education is to teach you where to look things up. How do you think Bruner would regard this goal? How about Ausubel?

influenced by the Gestalt tradition, and he has written extensively (1960; 1966), about the need for teachers to facilitate students' understanding of the *structure* of any subject. By structure he means the underlying principles and concepts rather than all the details and facts. He believes that the more teachers concentrate their efforts on helping the student to learn through the process of discovery, the more students will be able to learn new material independently. This type of learning, often called *process education,* can be transferred to subsequent learning.

Bruner's theories about the structure of knowledge and the nature of learning and thinking have important implications for the development of teaching approaches and curricular materials. Bruner's thinking implies approaches to teaching that encourage students' questioning, guessing, hypothesizing, and discovering. If students are to learn to think rather than simply to respond somewhat passively to stimuli, then new tests, films, learning games, and other materials must be developed to provoke questions and help students understand basic principles and concepts. Bruner argues that the students' experience and intellectual level must always be taken into account in the development and use of both curricular materials and teaching approaches.

Not all cognitive psychologists share Bruner's devotion to discovery learning. David Ausubel (1963; 1968; and with Robinson, 1969) is an exponent of expository teaching. Like Bruner, he is concerned with the development of cognitive structures, but unlike Bruner, he believes that the job of education is not so much to teach students how to think as it is to help them organize, master, and remember large amounts of information.

Ausubel proposed what he terms a *subsumption* theory of learning and forgetting. By subsumption he means that new learning fits into (is subsumed under) already existing frameworks of knowledge. Each intellectual discipline is seen as a set of hierarchically organized concepts. The most inclusive concepts are at the top, and subsumed under them are ever more specific subconcepts. In this respect Ausubel is directly opposed to Bruner. Bruner believes the learner builds a structure out of the mass of details, or data, through an inductive process; Ausubel believes the student begins with the large idea and then fits details into place. We could say that for Bruner learning moves from bottom to top; for Ausubel it moves from top to bottom.

Bruner's theories encourage students to guess, question, hypothesize, and discover. Ausubel's emphasize instead a lucid presentation by the teacher, beginning with a clear statement of the general nature of what is to be learned in the form of *advance organizers,* which are large concepts presented to the learner before the material to be learned is actually undertaken. These advance organizers create a kind of "scaffolding," to which more and more particular bits of information can be attached, until a structure is erected in the learner's brain that replicates the structure of the discipline itself.

Let us now see how William Kraus' suggestions to Miss Bell reflect a cognitive theoretical perspective. Mr. Kraus called attention to the students' lack of intellectual readiness for *Romeo and Juliet* and proposed, in his first suggestion, that Miss Bell use provocative questioning to get the students thinking critically about the play at their own levels. This approach, strongly advocated by Bruner as a means of helping students understand the structure of a discipline, is often called *inquiry* or *discovery teaching* in that it seeks to help students learn to inquire and discover answers to their own questions. The other activities—helping the students find out that they already know Elizabethan English and having two black students translate a passage of *Romeo and Juliet* into black dialect—also employ the discovery approach and provide opportunities for students to learn at their own level of readiness. In sum, Mr. Kraus has sought to help Miss Bell think of herself not as a presenter of information but as a questioner and learning guide whose primary goal is to help her students think, question, and direct their own learning.

In your school experiences have you had any teachers who used this approach? How effective do you feel it was?

This, of course, is a Brunerian position. Had Mr. Kraus been more Ausubelian in his cognitive viewpoint, he would have emphasized Miss Bell's organization and presentation of the intellectual tasks necessary to create a meaningful context to which students could anchor their growing understanding of the play. He might have suggested, for example, an advance organizer to help students understand changes in language since Shakespeare's time, the logic of these changes, and the necessity of understanding this changing language in order to grasp the play.

The Social Systems Perspective—"Interacting."
Consultant 4—Margaret Olson

Margaret Olson looks at the classroom as a complex social system within which all sorts of interpersonal relationships affect teaching and learning. This perspective focuses on the interactions among all the various groups and individuals in the class—between teacher and students, "fast" students and "slow" students, Bill and Bob, etc. You recall that Mrs. Olson was bothered by the hostility and lack of communication between the fast and slow students and proposed ways of bringing the two groups together.

The social systems perspective is not as well articulated a formal theory as are the other perspectives we have been considering. It is what might be called an emerging theoretical perspective, which is only beginning to synthesize a vast array of data and thought into a coherent and verifiable theory. Schmuck and Schmuck (1975) and Sprinthall and Sprinthall (1977) have pointed out that psychology in general and educational psychology in particular have tended to study individual behavior and have often ignored the complex interpersonal environments in which most human behavior takes place. They suggest that it's not surprising that teachers often complain that psychological theories are not very helpful since most of their work takes place within the complex system of the classroom, not on a one-to-one basis.

Few professionals are required to interact simultaneously with 25 or 30 people. Doctors, lawyers, social workers, and psychologists all have the "luxury" of working with clients on a one-to-one basis, although some of them may choose to work with families or groups.

The systems view of teaching and learning has implicit an *ecological* orientation, in that teaching and learning are affected by the social and physical environments in which they occur. The two major historical movements out of which the systems view has grown are

Ecology, from the Greek word for house, refers to the mutual relationship between organisms and their environment. A new movement in

psychology, referred to as human ecology or social ecology, has focused attention on the need to study individual and group behaviors in the complex environments in which they occur.

Two current books that view the classroom and the school in a systems perspective are Newman's Groups in Schools *(1974) and Schmuck and Schmuck,* Group Processes in the Classroom *(1975).*

What types of qualities do you feel are necessary for teachers to work effectively with many different individuals and groups within the classroom?

Teachers who share Mrs. Olson's concern for social learning in school are often critical of educational programs that place extreme emphasis on individualized instruction, in which students work alone at their own pace. They would challenge many of Ralph Thomas' suggestions on the grounds that students are not encouraged to work cooperatively.

What do you feel the school's role should be in encouraging children to learn from social interaction?

John Dewey's (1956) progressive education and the research on *group dynamics* initiated by Kurt Lewin (1936) and expanded by many other social psychologists. Dewey saw the classroom as a social environment within which children should learn to communicate, cooperate, and live together democratically. Dewey's view provides us with a philosophical rationale for a systems perspective. Group dynamics research—the study of how groups function and affect individual behavior—in the past has helped us understand general principles of social behavior and today is contributing much empirical evidence on teaching and learning in actual classroom groups.

Now that we have discussed systems theory, you should be able to understand Mrs. Olson's suggestions to Miss Bell. She saw the division between the fast and slow students as the central problem interfering with all of Miss Bell's efforts to promote learning. Therefore, she tried to alert Miss Bell to the fact that her own classroom behavior was furthering this division.

Mrs. Olson proposed that Miss Bell try to find ways of helping her students learn to communicate even though they differed intellectually. Her suggestions—that Miss Bell have the boys participate in one discussion group and the girls in another and that the students work in committees to produce the play—were designed to change the interaction patterns within the class and ultimately to promote cooperation and sharing among all students. John Dewey could well have given such advice in his desire to help students learn to work together and experience democratic living as well as learn to think.

Theories—Implicit, Personal, and Formal

As we discussed the major theoretical perspectives underlying the suggestions of Miss Bell's four consultants, we used the term *theory* in several different ways. In the final section of this chapter, we will examine the relationships between implicit, personal, and formal theories and their value in understanding learning and improving teaching. It was possible to use the word *theory* without first defining it because we all have used it at one time or another and, at least intuitively, assigned it a meaning, or perhaps several meanings. Here are some common uses of the word *theory*:

Can you think of any other ways you commonly use the word theory? *List a few here.*

That's *your* theory.

It works in theory but not in practice.

After all, it's just a theory.

I have my *own* theory about that.

The first and third statements suggest that a theory is a point of view—in the first case, someone else's and probably considered by the speaker to be rather stupid. In the fourth statement the point of view is the speaker's own, and therefore probably prized. The second implies that the theory may be a very logical explanation of some case (or cases), but that it does not fit the case at hand. The third simply dismisses theory outright, on the assumption that theory is useless, and only practice—doing something—has real meaning. The anti-theorist says: "Don't just stand there, do something." The protheorist replies: "Don't just do something—stand there for a while first and think about what you ought to do."

In fact, a theory is a contemplation of what is, what was, or what might be. The word *theory* derives from the Greek *theoria,* meaning looking at, contemplation, or speculation. We have already spoken about *implicit theory,* and you have seen that almost every act we perform is guided by some underlying assumptions about the nature of our world. To the degree that we become aware of our implicit theories, they cease to be implicit. We have chosen to apply the term *personal theory* to implicit theory that has been clarified sufficiently to be stated in spoken or written language. A personal theory, then, is an individual's attempt to make understandable to himself (and perhaps others) why or how something happened, or to decide upon some future course of action.

Formal theory is a broad concept, but it is useful to think of a formal theory as an attempt to make sense out of a large body of information. Your personal theory may take into account all your own experience in a given area but may exclude other relevant experience. An example would be the personal theory developed by a successful teacher in a white middle-class school. Over time she may develop a considerable body of personal theory about teaching, believing it applicable to all children. Suddenly she finds the neighborhood changing and, with it, the makeup of her class. Her theory may not be sufficient to cover this new situation. Some teachers react to challenge to their personal theory by becoming extremely defensive and clinging doggedly to practices that no longer work. Some revise their personal theory, and look for the relationship between the experiences that gave rise to their original theory and their new experience.

Many times crisis situations like the one just described push a teacher to look beyond personal theory and to seek more general theories to help generate new teaching behaviors or clarify personal theory. A formal theory has a power that no single personal theory can have because it is not limited to one person's experience. One of the factors that determines the "scope" of a theory is the kind of data with which it is concerned. By *data* we mean bits of information. Here are some examples of data:

The meter read 3.6.

The mean I.Q. of group A was 118.

Half the group had brown eyes.

This feels good.

Now I understand.

Try to recall some of the major principles of your personal theory of teaching that came out as you read and completed the activities in Chapter 3.

In reading the reports provided by the four consultants, did you come across suggestions that you wished you had thought of as you gave Miss Bell your own advice in Exploration 4–1? If you did, then you can begin to see the value of formal theory in helping to supplement and revise personal theories.

Each of these phrases describes a small fraction of what is happening at a given moment. In itself each phrase has no meaning, but each bit of information may be meaningful in the mind of a particular observer because they are part of some larger idea or some possibility worth exploring. In this sense a theorist is a sort of detective, and the data are clues. There are many reasons particular observations may be accepted or rejected as data in a given theory. An apple falling on Freud's head would probably have meant little to him; to Newton it suggested that the systematic observation of falling objects might clarify the nature of gravity. The first report that stones fell from the sky was dismissed as a foolish superstition; it was only after meteors were hypothesized that such data made sense. At that point, it became worthwhile to search for stones that might have fallen from the sky and to examine them exhaustively. The idea that dreams might tell us something about human behavior is useless to Skinner, but to Freud it was invaluable. Therefore, dreams were data for Freud but nonsense for Skinner. The theoretical frame, or point of view, tells us what data will be of use, and the data, in turn, further develop and clarify the theory.

Formal theory attempts to organize and make sense of as much data as can be found that fits the theory's criteria. In this sense no theory is "merely theoretical," that is, unconcerned with practice or reality. A *hypothesis* is a good guess or prediction, based on the principles that the theorist believes are inherent in the data. A hypothesis is a guess about how the theory might work in reality, stated in a form that can be tested. Winifred Hill (1963, p. 223) defines hypothesizing as "assuming for theoretical purposes that something is true although it has not been definitely shown to be true." The test of a hypothesis is "touching base" with reality, tying together theory and practice.

Theoretical frames may be essentially *descriptive*, that is, they explain how something comes to be; or essentially *prescriptive*, that is, they suggest what we should do in order to get something to happen. Theories of learning lean toward description; theories of teaching lean toward prescription.

Probably the greatest difference between the prescriptive and the descriptive orientations is that prescriptive theorists begin with some strongly held ideas about what people should be like, and look for logical and consistent ways of reaching that goal, while descriptive theorists are likely to reject what they consider such "moral" questions. While it is sometimes held that the study of human beings should be completely objective, our discussion of how we select data makes it clear that every theory is dictated by some underlying framework that reflects the theorist's values. If this is so, the major difference between the two approaches is not whether they contain values but whether the values are acknowledged as part of the theorizing or are ignored.

Imagine yourself in Miss Bell's position. How would you choose among the various suggestions offered? Would you feel bound by one suggestion or able to choose elements from several? What if new

Teaching is a continuous process of hypothesis testing. On the basis of her experience, her own educational philosophy, and her assessment of her students' needs, a good teacher forms hypotheses regarding what to do in the classroom. By observing the results of what she does, she can test her hypotheses and, if necessary, make revisions.

In this chapter, with our concern for helping Miss Bell, we have focused on prescriptive theories. Each of the four consultants provided prescriptions —suggestions of what to do —based on their own theoretical perspectives. However, their prescriptions for how Miss Bell should teach were influenced by different descriptions of how learning occurs. As we explore the characteristics of the learner in Chapters 5–9, we will go further into descriptive theories.

problems arose as you tried a particular suggestion? These are the issues that face a teacher as she attempts to make moment-to-moment decisions each day as well as long-term decisions. The teacher's dual role is often described as *practitioner–theorist*. That is, at the same time that the teacher engages in the practice of teaching she is theorizing, either out of some already articulated personal or formal theory or out of her own unarticulated implicit theory.

The term used to describe choosing elements of a number of theoretical positions rather than adhering to one is *eclecticism*. Eclectic thinkers are sometimes attacked as undisciplined, simply hopping willy-nilly from one theory to another. We would prefer to think of such unthinking eclecticism as atheoretical, that is, lacking any theoretical base. We use *eclecticism* to mean the responsible and knowledgeable use of many theories for the purpose of stimulating good, testable hypotheses in the classroom.

Moreover, skilled teachers are aware that there is probably no single correct approach to teaching. They have learned that some students respond wonderfully well to the discovery method, and others need the structure of clear expository teaching. For some students the open classroom is an ideal environment, encouraging great positive growth. For others, it does not provide sufficient structure, and they seem to flounder. Thus whatever their own predisposition, teachers are at pains to understand and respond to individual differences among their students. A broad acquaintance with many theoretical perspectives increases the likelihood that teachers will find a way of meeting the student's needs as a learner.

A final word about the nature of theories. Probably the best way to understand what *theory* means is to know many theories. As you grapple with some of the complexities of a number of theories, you will add to your understanding of what theory is. To help you we have listed at the end of this chapter a number of excellent books that attempt to define theory and to describe both learning and teaching theories.

As you read the suggestions of the four consultants, you probably found yourself agreeing with some and disagreeing with others simply because they coincided with or differed from your own values. Studying many theories can make you aware of inconsistencies and discrepancies in your own thinking.

We hope each teacher has a clear set of values about teaching—a personal philosophy. However, within this philosophy there is plenty of room for a teacher to be a "consumer of theories," one who is aware of and uses a variety of theories. As a practitioner of education, a teacher needs tools—ideas and resources for helping people learn. Theories, as we saw in the advice of Miss Bell's four consultants, can provide these tools. Thus theories can help teachers with the practical problems they face.

Conclusions

It has been the purpose of this chapter to introduce you to *formal theories of teaching*. Although there are many well-articulated theories about teaching, we have focused on four major points of view. Each of these theoretical perspectives examines teaching and learning from a different vantage point and thus suggests different educational practices.

The *behavioristic* perspective is concerned exclusively with observable behavior—doing—and uses principles of reinforcement as its primary tool. The *affective* perspective centers on feelings and suggests that teachers must deal openly with feelings both in classroom interpersonal relationships and in the curriculum. The *cognitive* perspective, which, like the affective perspective, grows out of a phenomenological view of human beings, calls attention to thinking

Table 4-1. Four Theoretical Perspectives

Theory	Focus	Major Proponents	Applications
Behavioristic	Behavior, as opposed to thoughts or feelings	Skinner	Behavior modification, programmed learning
Affective	Feelings	Rogers, Maslow	Humanistic psychology, values clarification, self-directed learning
Cognitive	Thinking	Bruner, Ausubel	Discovery learning (Bruner) Expository teaching (Ausubel)
Social systems	Group process	Dewey, Lewin, Schmuck and Schmuck	Group dynamics, communication and interaction

within the classroom and stresses matching learning experiences to the intellectual level of each student. Finally, the *social systems* perspective sees the classroom as a complex social environment and recommends an understanding of group dynamics to promote interaction and communication among all class members. Table 4–1 is a chart of the four theoretical perspectives we have explored in this chapter. You might find this chart helpful in integrating your learning.

We hope that you are beginning to see that formal theories not only help us describe and explain teaching but also provide us with important prescriptions for improving it. If you understand a variety of theories about teaching as well as the value of theorizing in general, you will be able to check your own views and experiences against the systematic thinking of others.

Some Good Books

Ausubel, David. *Educational Psychology: A Cognitive View*. New York: Holt, Rinehart and Winston, 1968. This general text is a useful introduction to Ausubel's cognitive theory.

Bruner, Jerome. *The Process of Education*. New York: Vintage, 1960. An excellent overview of Bruner's cognitive position regarding teaching, in which he discusses the role of structure in learning, readiness for learning, the nature of intuition, and motivation.

Bruner, Jerome. *Toward a Theory of Instruction*. New York: Norton, 1966. This book brings together a collection of Bruner's essays. Of particular relevance to the use of formal theory in teaching is the chapter "Notes on a Theory of Instruction."

Dewey, John. *Experience and Education*. New York: Collier, 1938. This concise book summarizes Dewey's concepts of progressive education and responds to questions raised by many of his critics.

Gorman, Alfred H. *Teachers and Learners: The Interactive Process of Education*. 2nd ed. Boston: Allyn and Bacon, 1974. One of the few books currently available that clearly articulates a systems perspective regarding teaching and learning in the classroom.

Hill, Winifred F. *Learning: A Survey of Psychological Interpretations*. San Francisco: Chandler, 1963. A classic survey of contemporary learning theories. Chapter 1 provides a good introduction to the nature and functions of theory. (A revised edition was published in 1971.)

Joyce, Bruce and Marsha Weil. *Models of Teaching*. Englewood Cliffs, N.J.: Prentice-Hall, 1972. If you would like to read further on formal theories of teaching, this book is a must. Joyce and Weil have brought together the models of Rogers, Skinner, and Bruner and more than a dozen lesser known but equally provocative theoretical perspectives.

Kaplan, Abraham. *The Conduct of Inquiry*. San Francisco: Chandler, 1964. In this work Kaplan develops a methodology for the behavioral sciences directed toward the scholar or advanced graduate student, but he also discusses the nature of formal theory and the role of values in theorizing.

Lyon, Harold C. *Learning to Feel—Feeling to Learn*. Columbus, Ohio: Merrill, 1971. Lyon provides a personal account of his own ideas, feelings, and experiences in humanizing teaching and learning within the classroom. The affective theoretical perspective of this book is supported by many strategies and techniques for bringing feelings into the curriculum.

Patterson, C. H. *Humanistic Education*. Englewood Cliffs, N.J.: Prentice-Hall, 1973. As a broad introduction to humanistic education, this book has few equals.

Raths, Louis, Merrill Harmin, and Sidney Simon. *Values and Teaching*. Columbus, Ohio: Merrill, 1966. This book presents the theoretical rationale for values clarification as an essential affective approach to teaching.

Rogers, Carl. *Freedom to Learn*. Columbus, Ohio: Merrill, 1969. This book has become a classic statement on the application of humanistic psychology to the realities of classroom teaching and learning.

Schmuck, Richard A. and Patricia A. Schmuck. *Group Processes in the Classroom*. 2nd ed. Dubuque, Iowa: William C. Brown, 1975. *Group Processes in the Classroom* provides an excellent overview of group dynamics theory as it applies to understanding the social psychology of the classroom.

Skinner, B. F. *Beyond Freedom and Dignity*. New York: Knopf, 1971. Here Skinner brings together much of his life's work in the creation of a behavioristic theory of psychology. He argues that this theory has profound implications for teaching, childrearing, and other socializing functions.

Skinner, B. F. *The Technology of Teaching.* New York: Appleton-Century-Crofts, 1968. This is Skinner's most specific statement on the application of his theories to teaching. He discusses why traditional approaches to teaching don't work and how behavioristic approaches can be utilized.

Skinner, B. F. *Walden Two.* New York: Macmillan, 1948. A controversial and best-selling novel in which Skinner shows how principles of reinforcement theory can be used to create a scientifically shaped utopia.

Articles, Studies, and Other References

Divoky, Diane. "Affective Education: Are We Going Too Far?" *Learning,* October 1975: 20–27. A critical view of the fadism and abuse within the affective education movement. At the same time Divoky shows some of the positive potentials of affective education.

Gordon, Ira J. "Affect and Cognition—A Reciprocal Relationship." *Educational Leadership*, April 1970: 661–664. Gordon emphasizes the importance of bringing together cognition and affect in teaching rather than treating them as mutually exclusive.

Hitt, William D. "Two Models of Man." *American Psychologist* 24 (1969): 651–658. Drawing heavily on the thinking of B. F. Skinner and Carl Rogers, this article provides one of the clearest statements of the contrast between behaviorism and phenomenology.

Krasner, Leonard. "The Classroom as a Planned Environment." *Educational Researcher* 5 (1976): 9–14. A model of teaching that integrates behavioristic views with the social systems (or group dynamics) orientations.

Lewin, Kurt. "Group Dynamics and Social Change." In G. E. Swanson, T. M. Newcomb, and E. L. Hartley (eds.), *Readings in Social Psychology.* 3rd ed. New York: Holt, Rinehart and Winston, 1952. A classic article in the literature of group dynamics, examining the impact of different types of leadership on group action.

Madsen, Clifford K. and Charles H. Madsen, Jr. "What Is Behavior Modification?" *Instructor,* October 1971: 47–56. A clear picture of the practical use of behavior modification in the classroom.

Rogers, Carl. "The Interpersonal Relationship in the Facilitation of Learning." In R. W. Leeper (ed.), *Humanizing Education: The Person in the Process.* Washington, D.C.: Association for Supervision and Curriculum Development, 1967, pp. 1–18. This article presents Rogers' classic statement on the role of the teacher as learning facilitator.

Thelen, Herbert. "Tutoring by Students." *School Review* 77 (1969): 229–244. A long-time advocate of a social systems perspective on teaching, Thelen argues persuasively for the academic and social benefits of students' tutoring students in the classroom.

Wilson, G. Terrence and Gerald C. Davison. "Behavior Therapy: A Road to Self-Control." *Psychology Today* 9 (1975): 54–60. The authors show how principles of behavior modification can be used to help seriously disturbed people toward self-direction and control of their own behavior.

Suggestions for Action-Oriented Learning

1. Arrange to observe in a classroom in the subject area and grade level of your own choice. Try to analyze and evaluate the teaching from one of the four theoretical perspectives presented in this chapter. If you and a friend do this together, you will be able to discuss your findings and see whether you agreed or disagreed in what you observed.

2. Identify the theoretical perspective closest to your personal theory of teaching and the one that is most dissimilar to your views. Discuss each with other members of your class.

3. Read Neill's *Summerhill* (1960) and contrast his views on education with the views of Skinner in *The Technology of Teaching*. Try to articulate the psychological perspective that underlies each book.

4. Present the anecdote describing Miss Bell's problems to an experienced teacher and ask the teacher to provide Miss Bell with suggestions. Then try to analyze that teacher's comments and determine if they fit any one of the four theoretical perspectives or if that teacher tends to be more eclectic. Share your findings with the members of your class.

Unit 2
The Learner

Unit 1 helped you as a prospective teacher to look into yourself and your development, to examine some of your own emerging ideas about teaching, and to begin thinking about the value of formal theoretical perspectives. Now in Unit 2 we would like to shift the focus from the teacher to the learner and the learning process. This unit will stress the distinction between the *internal environment* of the learner and the *external environment*. By internal environment we mean everything that is part of the learner—abilities, interests, feelings, motives, knowledge, ideas, physical characteristics, stages of development, self-concept, weaknesses, emotional difficulties, and so on. By external environment we mean all the factors outside the learner; in short, everything that is not part of the internal state but has the potential for influencing the learner. One's family, friends, teachers, physical environment, community, and culture, as well as books, the media, the school curriculum, rewards and punishments, are all part of the external environment.

We see the teacher's role in facilitating learning as *diagnosis* and *prescription*. Diagnosis involves finding out what the internal environment of the learner is; in other words, determining such things as abilities, weaknesses, past background, and interests. Once the teacher knows the learner's needs, she can establish goals of instruction and prescribe appropriate learning activities. Teaching, then, is a process of arranging circumstances so that the external environment is matched to the learner's internal environment. In this way external events, experiences, ideas, etc. are internalized, that is, learned, so that they can be called forth and used in the future.

Our goal in Chapters 5 through 9 is to help you understand important characteristics of the learner. We will concentrate on issues relevant to effective diagnosis, such as how people develop intellectually, socially, and emotionally; the relationship between thinking and feeling; the nature of intelligence and individual differences; and motivation.

5
The Learner's
Intellectual Growth

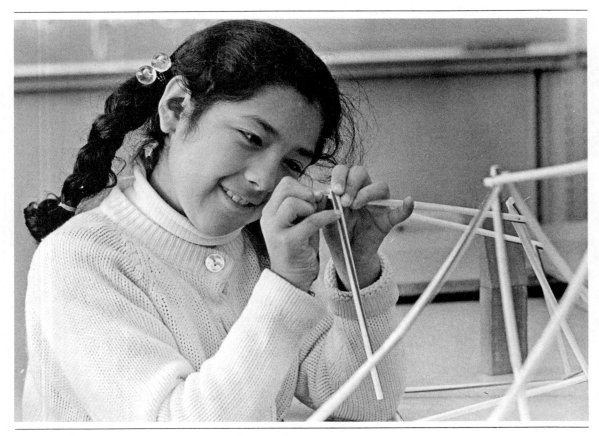

In this chapter we will explore the process of intellectual growth and its impact upon both students' learning and teachers' teaching. In Chapter 6 we will examine social–emotional growth. These two chapters will concentrate upon the work of two major theorists in American psychology, Jerome Bruner and Erik Erikson, who are concerned with the process of growth and have developed theories that help us facilitate learning. However, their perspectives on growth are very different, since Bruner (as we saw in Chapter 4) is primarily concerned with intellectual (cognitive) growth, and Erikson centers his attention on social–emotional (affective) growth. By devoting a separate chapter to each of these two types of growth we are giving equal emphasis to the development of thinking and feeling in the total person.

We have chosen to focus on Bruner and Erikson because their ideas have specific application to the classroom. However, no study of intellectual development would be complete without attention to the universally acclaimed research of Swiss psychologist Jean Piaget, and we will devote substantial effort to helping you understand Piaget. Freudian theory is central to any understanding of social–emotional development, and in Chapter 6 you will see how Erikson extended Freud's views. In that chapter you will also learn of Lawrence Kohlberg's research in another area of affective development—moral development.

Before reading the discussion of the theories of Jerome Bruner, try the following exploration. It is designed to raise some questions regarding your own thinking and problem-solving abilities and how they have affected some of your feelings about yourself.

Our purpose in these two chapters is not to teach you to teach, in either the cognitive or the affective area; that we will leave to your methods courses and student teaching. Our goal is to help you understand the way people develop intellectually, socially, and emotionally, and how educational programs can respond to that development.

Exploration 5–1: Dividing Fractions

Many elementary school students have little difficulty with mathematics until they come to fractions. Can you perform the following problem, which is usually taught in the later elementary years?

$$1/2 \div 1/3 = \underline{\quad}$$

How did you arrive at your answer to the problem?

The correct answer appears on page 82.

By using a rule?

By guessing?

By making a picture?

If you did not use a diagram to help you solve the problem, try making one in the margin to illustrate what it means to divide 1/2 by 1/3. Once you have made the diagram, use it to explain to another person how you arrived at the correct answer to this problem and what the answer means. Be sure that the person to whom you are explaining the problem understands your steps. If you can't find another person to work with, think through the questions you might be asked if you were explaining the problem.

If by now you are a little perplexed and having difficulty explaining what your answer means, you may be experiencing many of the thoughts and feelings of the authors of this book, who spent hours thinking and arguing about this problem. You may also feel that we are spending a lot of time with an activity that seems to have no relevance to educational psychology. Well, please bear with us; we'll explain shortly.

Probably you were able to figure out relatively easily that the answer to the problem is 1-1/2 by remembering the rule that when we divide fractions we invert the numbers we are dividing by and then multiply to get the answer. Thus the problem is solved as follows:

$$1/2 \div 1/3 = 1/2 \times 3/1 = 3/2 = 1\text{-}1/2$$

Before reading further make certain you have already attempted to explain what the answer 1-1/2 means.

Assuming that you came up with the correct answer, you may be puzzled by the question, What does the 1-1/2 mean? 1-1/2 what? In other words, what does it really mean to say we divide 1/2 by 1/3? How can two small amounts like 1/2 and 1/3 yield a larger number when we are supposedly breaking them apart?

Now compare your attempt to illustrate what this problem means with our diagram. One of the stumbling blocks in trying to diagram the division of fractions is imagining a fraction as what it really is—a part of a whole. The first diagrams we made led us to endless frustration:

1/2

1/3

However, once we realize that whenever we talk about fractions we are talking about parts of a whole, then the diagram can be shown as follows:

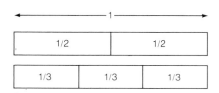

This problem also can be presented visually as a pie. We want to know how many pieces equal to 1/3 of the pie we can cut out of half the pie.

In other words, 1/2 of a pie = 1-1/2 thirds of a pie.

You can probably see that the problem $1/2 \div 1/3 = 1\text{-}1/2$ means that there are 1-1/2 thirds in 1/2. In other words, one half of a whole thing is equivalent to one and one-half thirds of that whole thing.

Now that you understand what the problem means, you might ask a second question. Why do we always invert when dividing fractions? While you may have used the inversion rule in solving the problem, we suspect that few of you *understand* why you used it. The answer is relatively simple and can be explained in the following steps:

1. $1/2 \div 1/3$ can be restated as a ratio:

$$\frac{1/2}{1/3}$$

2. This ratio is hard to work with, since a fraction in the denominator makes division difficult. Therefore, we must find a way to get rid of the fraction 1/3 in the denominator. This can be accomplished by multiplying 1/3 by its *reciprocal*—3. However, if we are to multiply the denominator by 3 and not change the problem, we must also multiply the numerator by 3. In this way all we are doing is changing the numerical values of the numerator and denominator without changing the relationship between them.

Reciprocal—That number which, when multiplied by another, yields 1 as its product. This simple manipulation of symbols is useful in helping us reconceptualize our problem.

3. Numerically the problem appears as

$$1/2 \div 1/3 = \frac{1/2}{1/3} = \frac{1/2 \times 3/1}{1/3 \times 3/1} = \frac{3/2}{3/3} = \frac{3/2}{1} = 3/2 = 1\text{-}1/2$$

4. Thus we can see that whenever we divide a number by a fraction we can shortcut the process shown in step 3 because the denominator multiplied by its reciprocal is always going to be 1, and the numerator is going to be multiplied by the reciprocal of the denominator. In other words, $1/2 \div 1/3$ $= 1/2 \times 3/1 = 3/2 = 1\text{-}1/2$

What does this math problem have to do with educational psychology in general and intellectual growth in particular? Maybe you are thinking that we have lost touch with reality. Let us explain. The problem involving the division of fractions has been presented here because it demonstrates that many of us don't understand either the answer or the explanation of the solution for a problem we supposedly "learned" in the fourth or fifth grade. You might argue that by remembering the rule of inversion we can solve this problem. But what happens when we come across a problem that is slightly different, or if we can't remember the rule? Then, unfortunately, most of us are stuck because we don't have an understanding of a process that will allow us to transfer our learning to new situations.

Can you recall other times in your schooling when you realized that you could not transfer your learning to new situations because you had relied on memorizing a rule or law or principle rather than understanding it? Have you ever:

We feel that many people have trouble solving this type of problem because the way they were taught did not match their stage of intellectual development. It might be informative for you to ask 10 of your friends to solve the problem, explain what their answers mean, and explain why inverting is necessary. Out of your sample of 10, how many people could demonstrate that they understand all aspects of this simple problem?

Done poorly on a geometry test because you were asked to do proofs you had never encountered in either your text or your homework assignments?

Found sight reading new music to be almost impossible because you could not recall having heard the music previously?

Been unable to conduct laboratory experiments in physics class other than those that had been demonstrated by the teacher or in the book?

Had difficulty analyzing a piece of literature that had not been discussed in class?

As you have responded to the questions above and the problem involving the division of fractions, you have probably begun to see that many of us have become better memorizers than thinkers. While there is undoubtedly a place for memorization in most types of learning, if we don't also have the capacity to think critically, we will not be able to transfer our learning to new situations. This can severely hamper us in our ability to solve all sorts of problems.

Although most of the discussion so far in this chapter has centered upon thinking, it is important to realize that feelings are always involved when we use our intellect to solve problems. Our feelings and our thoughts can never be separated. The questions below will help you examine some of the feelings you experienced in completing Exploration 5–1.

As you attempted to explain what 1-1/2 meant or why we invert when dividing fractions, did you feel embarrassed, stupid, angry, smart, frustrated, etc.?

Did the problem trigger memories of your feelings about yourself and your abilities in math classes in elementary and/or high school? Why or why not?

How do you feel about yourself today as a math student? In what ways do these feelings affect your performance in, solving mathematical problems?

Has your choice of a career in any way been affected by the concept you have of yourself as a math student? How?

Teachers frequently lose sight of the complexity of the educational process. Can you recall, for example, one of your teachers complaining, "I can't understand why you people didn't learn that material. I spent a great deal of time on it."

Helping people learn requires much more than time. Unless teachers understand the intellectual stage, personal interests, feelings, and background of their students, real learning that can be transferred is unlikely to occur.

Our purpose in presenting the fraction problem has been to illustrate that learning is a complex process. The capacity to recall information is at the simplest level of intellectual growth (Bloom, 1956). Recall alone certainly isn't sufficient to help us solve problems. We also must be able to understand, to apply our knowledge, to analyze, to synthesize, and to evaluate. As we saw in the fraction problem, most of us did not understand what we were doing. Our capacity to transfer our knowledge of fractions and solve new but related problems is limited.

Obviously, one of the justifications for having schools is to prepare people to solve problems of all kinds. Yet as the fraction problem illustrates, schools haven't been as successful as they should be in teaching young people to think and solve problems. We believe the reason is that most teachers don't understand how children develop intellectually and, therefore, the approaches they use are not effective in promoting students' capacity to think. The research and theories of

Jerome Bruner and Jean Piaget go a long way to addressing this issue.

Bruner's Theory of Cognitive Growth

Some educational theorists believe that no single theoretical approach can answer the question of how to structure successful learning environments. One author who has sought to pull many theories together is Jerome Bruner. Most psychological theories, says Bruner, are *descriptive,* "distilled from descriptions of behavior in situations where the environment has been arranged either for the convenience of observing learning behavior or out of a theoretical interest in some special aspect of learning" (Bruner, 1966, p. 37). While each theory may add something of value to our notion of how we learn, how we develop, how we remember, or how we forget, this knowledge is not sufficient. None of these theories tells us how to teach.

The purpose of theories of teaching is not to describe but to prescribe—to help us understand what to do in order to achieve a particular result. It is not that teaching theories have nothing to do with learning or developmental theories. The very opposite is true. A *theory of instruction* integrates descriptive theories in such a way that they pull together toward some stated instructional goal; in other words, a theory of instruction describes but also prescribes. In short, it can be called a *prescriptive* theory.

Furthermore, Bruner believes we need numerous theories of instruction. We may need different prescriptions for content areas as diverse as, say, mathematics and communications. Our ideas about the sort of people we hope our schools will produce may also lead us to create different prescriptions.

There is one general principle underlying Bruner's thinking. He believes that we must never forget that people are in a continual state of growth and change, and that theories of instruction should take developmental principles into account. One of the reasons most of us had trouble with the math problem that began this chapter is that our teachers undoubtedly didn't consider our level of intellectual development when they "taught" us how to divide fractions. They assumed that we could understand the process when, in fact, we needed a very concrete way of seeing what division of fractions actually meant.

Bruner's early work with students who had serious difficulties in learning led him to become interested in two types of learning behavior. One, which he calls *coping,* is growth behavior. When students are challenged, excited, unafraid of difficulty and newness, they are, in Bruner's sense, coping. Bruner's work on coping was published originally in French, and the word used in that article was *affrontement,* which is translated either as *confronting* or as *facing fearlessly.* Bruner contrasts this with *defending.* When students defend, they close out knowledge or experience. When students say, "I'll never understand

Recall that in our discussion of major theoretical perspectives in Chapter 4, we tried to illustrate how different theories can contribute different practical suggestions for promoting learning.

A criticism often leveled at the whole field of psychology is that psychologists spend too much time attempting to describe and explain behavior and not enough working on ways to solve human problems. Bruner has been concerned about this point in relation to teaching. In Toward a Theory of Instruction *(1966), Bruner draws upon his knowledge of how children learn and develop intellectually as he proposes approaches to promoting learning.*

As a means of understanding Bruner's concepts of coping and defending, try to think of a recent time when you pushed yourself to learn something new even though you were hesitant.

As Bruner would say, both the teacher and the student in this picture are "defending."

Can you recall a time recently when your fears got the better of you, and you defended by not trying or by giving up on a new activity?

this," "I'm too dumb," "I hate this," or similar statements, they are, in Bruner's sense, defending, or blocking their own growth.

A theory of instruction should help us to maximize coping behavior and minimize defending behavior. With this concept in mind, let us take a look at the four elements Bruner feels are necessary features of any theory of instruction: *predisposition, structure, sequence,* and *reinforcement.*

Predisposition

In its most general sense, predisposition describes all the factors that ready the student for learning. For example, the predisposition of a kindergarten child would be determined by the sort of home and family he comes from; his interactions with other children; his community and culture; and such elements in his environment as television, books, toys, and the like. In studying a preschooler's predisposition, we would want to know what "will tend to make the child willing and able to learn when he enters school" (Bruner, 1966, p. 40).

How do you think these factors might affect readiness for reading?

As the student moves from educational experience to educational experience, we want to find out what will cause him to be willing to explore alternatives or what will make him leery of taking chances. An investigation of predisposition might involve the social, intellectual, and developmental abilities needed to enter into a particular educational environment with some hope of success.

Application.   Skilled teachers keep in mind the student's entering level, and work to relate the material they wish to teach with the student's readiness. At times this may mean going back several steps because there is necessary information that the student does not yet possess, because necessary skills are not strong enough, or because

The whole justification for many of the recent federally supported programs for disadvantaged children lies in a concern for children's predispositions for learning. Operation Headstart was designed specifically to get preschoolers from economically disadvantaged areas "ready" for school learning. Likewise, Upward Bound has attempted to prepare disadvantaged high school students for college.

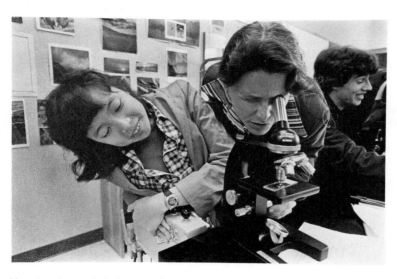

Here teacher and student are "coping"—happily learning together.

the student is not emotionally ready. At other times it may mean re-thinking the appropriateness of a teacher's goal for a given student. In short, teachers juggle two balls: "Is this student ready for what I am teaching?" and "Is what I am teaching appropriate at this time for this student?"

Structure

The structure of knowledge has two different but related mean-ings. In one sense it is the developing capacity of the mind to learn the environment; in another it is the way the teacher presents what is to be learned to the learner. It is a common-sense observation that 5-year-olds think differently from 10-year-olds, who think differently from 15-year-olds. All developmental theories agree that when we are younger, we tend to learn with our bodies. The term *concrete* is some-times used to describe the early modes of learning. At first we learn only what we directly experience. For example, babies have no name for crawling. They certainly don't think of it as "a type of locomotion," because they have no such abstract ideas. Crawling is something they do; it is an experience.

How does one learn to bat a ball, or tie a shoelace? This type of learning is bodily—we must do it and feel it. Bruner calls this *enactive* learning. It is only as children grow that they can cut themselves free of this very active type of learning. Psychological and intellectual growth, then, involves a move toward increasingly abstract learning. This learning is not rooted in the whole body, as is enactive learning; it seems to be more of a visual or perceptual process. Recall the old expression "One picture is worth a thousand words." Bruner uses the term *iconic* (from the Greek work *ikon,* or *image*) to describe this kind

Bruner has been heavily influenced by the Swiss psychologist Jean Piaget, who has devoted a life-time to the study of intellectual growth in children. Piaget's theoriz-ing, which tends to be descriptive rather than prescriptive, has made a tremendous contribution to our un-derstanding of how thinking pro-cesses develop as children mature.

Elementary school children could be helped to understand what the divi-sion of fractions actually means by giving them, for example, pizza pies or candy bars to divide enactively. Even the use of diagrams—an iconic approach—would be helpful.

of learning. In this sense learning that **o o o** represents three objects is iconic learning because **o o o** provides a *picture* or visual representation of the objects.

The most abstract learning process is *symbolic*. When we are ready for it, it is exciting; it enables us to go far beyond what our senses tell us. We can invent symbols for ideas that seem not even to exist, and these symbols may open whole new worlds to us. For example, the invention of the number *0,* which stands for nothing, opened up the whole world of mathematics. We would never have come upon the idea of zero by thinking enactively or iconically, because zero symbolized nothing.

A symbol for which we are not ready merely tends to confuse us. Therefore, the study of the structure of knowledge should explore how we use these three modes of learning and how an instructor can skillfully present us with information in the most appropriate mode for our developmental state.

Young children are limited by their stage of intellectual development to enactive learning. As they get older, they add iconic learning, and usually in adolescence they become capable of symbolic learning. However, adolescents (and adults) are often helped to learn by a teacher's involving them physically or providing them with pictures. In short, all of us need opportunities to learn by doing and seeing, not just by thinking.

Try to recall a course you had in high school or college in which you had difficulty because it was taught at a symbolic level above your head. How could the teacher have used enactive and iconic learning to promote your learning of the subject?

Application.   Teachers often become so accustomed to presenting information in a particular way that they are unaware of whether or not their presentation has any real meaning for their students. The fraction example at the beginning of this chapter demonstrates that many teachers present mathematical concepts at a symbolic level when the students may still be operating at the iconic or even the enactive level. Many students feel uncomfortable with algebra for this reason. Good teachers are sensitive to the learning needs of students, and search for inventive ways of "translating" from one Brunerian mode to another. For example, they may think: "I am not reaching this student or group—maybe a film would be a clearer presentation, or a diagram, or perhaps I ought to get them in touch with plastic models they can manipulate." This sort of continuing vigilance often leads to sudden new insights by the student.

Sequence

Every instructor faces the problem of where to begin, what to include, and in what sequence. Bruner suggests that there is probably no ideal sequence for a particular subject. This is because he sees the learner as inseparable from what is being learned. Decisions of sequence depend on students' developmental levels and other predispositional factors. In other words, Bruner believes that sequences should be determined *psychologically*—in response to the needs of the learner—rather than *logically*—as a step-by-step organization of the curriculum from simple to complex. An additional consideration is the goal of instruction—what kind of students we wish to produce. Bruner holds that it is most important to specify what we hope the students will be like as a result of our instruction. For example, do we hope that they will think like mathematicians or that they will be able to memorize theorems and pass examinations? An honest confrontation of our expectations may lead us to very different conclusions about what to include and when.

Bruner's views on sequence conflict sharply with the views of advocates of programmed learning, like B. F. Skinner (1968), who argue that there are "best" sequences for certain subjects. Bruner sees the sequence as varying with the learner. What is best for one student may not be best for another.

Application.   For many teachers sequence is tightly controlled by assigned textbooks or prepared curricula that must be rigidly followed. Until recently most curricula have been content-oriented. The goal of a typical social studies course, for example, might be learning a body of dates, names, and places; this orientation emphasizes content. Recently there has been a serious questioning of curricula built on content goals alone. This more psychological, process-oriented approach is less concerned with information and seeks to draw the students into activities that lead them to think, question, and discover. A good example is Bruner's (1966) "Man, A Course of Study" (MACOS)—an introduction to anthropology for elementary school students.

In the MACOS curriculum a fifth grader "discovers" what the development of tools meant to human history, not by being told what they do but by figuring out what they do. As the children try out tools, work with them, and picture their uses, they come to realize that tools act as amplifiers of human power. The teacher's job is not only to provide appropriate material and stimuli that lead the students toward discovery, but to alert them to their own power to think independently.

Effective teachers can take any curriculum, even the most content-bound, and develop meaningful process goals; but to do so successfully, they must always keep in mind their own underlying teaching objectives. They may find themselves wondering: "Is this activity helping my students to think something out, to grow intellectually, to make new connections for themselves, or are they merely obediently regurgitating for me?"

Reinforcement: Reward and Punishment

How teachers handle the issue of reward and punishment tells us a great deal about how they perceive the nature of learning. Bruner asks that we distinguish between, on the one hand, success and failure, and on the other, reward and punishment. He reminds us that success and failure are internal experiences for the learner. Failure need not be defeating. When people explore, they always risk failure, and they can learn to accept it as information: "I have tried this and it did not succeed; now let me try that."

Reward and punishment are external experiences, to a large degree in the hands of the teacher, whether in the form of stars and demerits, smiles and frowns, or As and Fs. Bruner believes that because rewards and punishments are extrinsic to the learner, they are unlikely to have the effect on promoting and maintaining learning that *intrinsic motives* will have. He feels that a theory of instruction must recognize and seek to capitalize upon the student's intrinsic interest in learning. This does not mean that Bruner dismisses the use of rewards by teachers. He says that rewards can be helpful in getting a type of learning going and in providing a student with an experience of success that will maintain the learning. However, he cautions us that unless a learning activity meets the intrinsic motives of the learner, genuine learning, which will allow transfer to new situations, is not likely to occur.

Application. It should be evident that a punitive classroom is a poor one. There is no question that many students perceive their

You can see here how a potentially very abstract subject—anthropology—is made enactive and iconic.

If you would like to learn more about the MACOS curriculum, a good overview of it is provided in Chapter 4 of Bruner's Toward a Theory of Instruction *(1966).*

Think back over your own years of schooling. How often did you encounter a teacher who was concerned as much with your learning to think and question as with your remembering course content?

According to Bruner an intrinsic motive does not depend on a reward outside the activity itself; rather, carrying out the activity is its own reward. If we say Sue is intrinsically motivated to read mystery books, we mean that the driving force in her reading such books is not praise, grades, or money, but simply the satisfaction she gets from her reading. For further discussion of the differences between intrinsic and extrinsic motivation, see Chapter 9.

In your school experience how often did you encounter teachers who were not punitive, i.e., didn't punish with low grades, keep people after school, publicly criticize, send people to the office, etc.? Why didn't more teachers rely on rewards rather than punishments to encourage desirable behavior?

As you have a chance to observe classrooms, try to use the four elements of Bruner's theory of instruction—predisposition, structure, sequence, and reinforcement—to analyze what you see.

teachers as "the enemy," and many teachers reciprocate as they see themselves in battle with their students. Good teachers know that an angry environment prevents high-level thinking, although it may promote a kind of sullen obedience. Understanding this, they try to anticipate management problems before they arise by setting clear, rational limits. When discipline problems do arise, they are more likely to look at the relationship between themselves and their students than to lash out angrily. They know that physical force or resorting to yelling, criticizing, or other forms of psychological punishment really will not work, and that order is best kept through mutual respect.

Effective teachers are careful to reward the kind of social and intellectual behavior they want. To a great degree, teachers get what they want through praise, positive attitude, and other types of positive reinforcement. Teachers may reward students for right answers but give little feedback for original or creative thinking; if they don't reward it, the behavior will probably "dry up." Good teachers are aware that their attention and praise are powerful tools, and they ask themselves often if they are using them to attain the ends they want.

Jean Piaget and Intellectual Development

If Bruner is a prime example of a prescriptive psychological theorist, Jean Piaget (born in 1896 in Switzerland) is as pure an example as we will find of the descriptive theorist. Piaget, who had a profound influence on Bruner's thinking, has carefully studied the development of concept formation in children for more than 40 years. His research has revolutionized our understanding of intellectual

Jean Piaget, throughout his life, has been an enthusiastic observer of children.

growth. Although his work was not widely recognized in the United States until the 1960s, today Piaget is probably the single most influential cognitive theorist in the world.

Piaget's original vocation was zoology. By his twenties his interests broadened to include philosophy and psychology. In his mid-twenties he worked in the laboratories of Alfred Binet, where he was fascinated not so much with a child's answers to standardized questions as with the fact that, by conversing with the child, he could begin to understand how the child arrived at the answers. Out of this realization, Piaget saw a way of combining his two deepest interests, psychobiology and philosophy, into the study of the development of thought from infancy to maturity. He called his study *genetic epistemology: genetic,* meaning developmental, and *epistemology,* referring to the acquisition of knowledge.

Piaget began his research by developing methods of clinical interviewing very much like those of a psychoanalyst. Soon he realized that thought grows out of action, and although he could interview older children to find out how they arrived at their answers, the basis of that process was laid even earlier, when words did not yet exist for the child. Therefore, he had to develop a new method of observation.

> I well knew that thought proceeds from action, but I believed then that language directly reflects acts, and to understand the logic of the child one had only to look for it in the domain of conversations or verbal interactions. It was only later, by studying the patterns of intelligent behavior of the first two years, that I learned that for a complete understanding of the genesis of intellectual operations, manipulation and experience with objects had first to be considered (Piaget, 1952).

Fortunately, just as Piaget began to think about cognitive development, his three children were born, providing him with an ideal opportunity to observe closely the earliest stages of intellectual development. By studying how his own infants manipulated objects presented to them, he was able to make inferences about the underlying process and growth of thought in infants. Over the last 50 years Piaget and his associates have devised many ingenious techniques for observing and interviewing children from infancy to about age 16, which they consider to be the age of intellectual maturity.

It is important to note that Piaget is not concerned with learning in the same sense as learning theorists such as Skinner, who focus on the impact of the environment upon the organism. Piaget's major concern is children's growing ability to make sense of their world, and to become increasingly independent of the distortions that the senses alone introduce. At first infants appear overwhelmed by information brought in by their senses, and are unable to give "adult" meaning to the information. Piaget's most basic theme is the development of logical thinking, which gradually releases children from their reliance on the senses and immediate experience alone.

Alfred Binet, a Frenchman, is recognized as the father of intelligence testing. The Stanford–Binet test, an adapted version of the I.Q. test originally developed by Binet, remains one of the two major individual I.Q. tests in use today. We'll be exploring Binet's work and the use of intelligence tests in Chapter 8.

This is very much the same position that Bruner takes when he argues that enactive learning—learning with one's body—provides the basis for later iconic and symbolic learning.

It should be pointed out that children do not move suddenly out of one stage and into the next. For example, as they are making the transition between concrete operations and formal operations, they will still employ concrete operations some of the time.

Piaget's Four Stages of Development

Piaget's research traces the development of autonomous thought through four stages:

Stage	Age (Approximate)
1. Sensorimotor	0–2
2. Preoperational	2–7
3. Concrete Operations	7–11
4. Formal Operations	11–16

We will discuss each of the stages briefly in the following paragraphs. Then in the final section of this chapter we will explore the implications of Piaget's research.

The Sensorimotor Stage (0–2). During the sensorimotor stage the infant at first seems, in Piaget's term, *autistic,* that is, utterly unaware of any distinction between her own body and her environment. The major accomplishment of this phase is the movement away from autism and toward the ability to act on the environment.

At first the infant is capable of nothing but reflex reactions, such as the sucking reflex in response to presentation of the nipple, or the grasping reflex when a finger is placed in her hand. Sometime during the second month, the child develops the ability to repeat something just to have the experience. This self-stimulation is probably the infant's first "discovery." Between the fourth and eighth month this ability reaches a new level—the baby intentionally performs an act but now for some goal—for example, shaking her body in order to make a rattle attached to the crib make a sound. It is probably at this point that the child begins to learn that there is a self, and an environment the self can affect. By the conclusion of the second year, the change from the reflex-bound infant is truly remarkable, as can be seen from Piaget's observation of his daughter at 18 months, 8 days:

Research by Harvard psychologist Burton White (1975) suggests that this sensorimotor period is very important in paving the way for the child's later intellectual development. White believes that the first eight months of life are heavily influenced by biological factors. However, from eight months to eighteen months, interaction with the environment is critical—especially interaction with other people. The Brookline (Massachusetts) Early Education Project has grown out of White's research. In it, parents of young babies are taught to interact more effectively with their babies and to design physical environments that stimulate their children's intellectual development.

> . . . Jacqueline sits on a bed beside her mother. I am at the foot of her bed on the side opposite Jacqueline, and she neither sees me nor knows I am in the room. I brandish over the bed a cane to which a brush is attached at one end, and I swing the whole thing. Jacqueline is very much interested; she says "Cane, cane" and examines the swinging most attentively. At a certain moment, she stops looking at the end of the cane and obviously tries to understand. She tries to perceive the other end of the cane, and to do so, leans in front of her mother, and then behind her, until she has seen me. She expresses no surprise, as though she knew I was the cause (Piaget, 1954, pp. 295–296).

Examples such as this illustrate the vast changes that occur over the first two years or so of life as the child moves through the sensorimotor stage. The helpless infant, completely at the mercy of her environment, has begun, by the close of the sensorimotor stage, to understand and control the environment. In Piaget's other three stages, changes of similar magnitude take place.

The Preoperational Stage (2–7). As the child enters the preoperational stage, the quality of her thinking begins to change. She is no longer bound to her sensorimotor environment. The beginnings of language allow the child to store information. With an average vocabulary of 200 or 300 words at age 2 and nearly 2000 by age 5, the child becomes more and more able to communicate her wishes and think about things that are not present. However, her thought and language are very egocentric; she cannot see things from another person's point of view. For example, a 3-year-old may close her eyes and insist that you can't see her. Or a 4-year-old may become very upset when he describes some situation or person and you don't know what he is talking about. The child at this stage incorrectly assumes that everyone perceives things as she does. Even when children are a little older, they are still very egocentric. Children of 5 and 6 talk *at* each other, not *with* each other. It is as if they talk to hear themselves talk; they have real difficulty listening. Piaget calls this *collective monologue.*

Children's spontaneous use of language in the early part of the preoperational stage is a source of continuous embarrassment to adults. Statements or questions like "Look at that man, he's so fat he can hardly walk," or "Mommy, why does that lady have a moustache?" are often expressed in a loud voice in public places. Children at this stage have not learned to monitor their language; they say what they think.

The preoperational child's limited thinking capacities are illustrated through her inability to *conserve,* that is, to recognize that the basic attributes of some object remain the same even when the object's appearance is altered. You can see this for yourself by showing a 4- or 5-year-old a ball of clay rolled out into a long "snake" and asking the child which is more, the snake or ball. Children at this stage usually say the snake has more clay, even though no clay has been added or subtracted. Similarly, children of this age will usually pick five pennies over one dime or a tall thin glass of milk over a short fat one that has the same volume. They judge things by appearance alone; if something looks bigger, it must have more.

Concrete Operations (7–11). As a child enters the concrete operations stage, she begins to question her senses. She learns to conserve and checks to see whether the tall glass really holds more milk or simply appears bigger. She learns that although 50 pennies cover a lot of space on a table, a dollar will buy more. The child is now developing *operations*—logical reasoning and problem-solving abilities that she can apply in new situations. Also during this period children are much less egocentric. They begin to carry on real dialogues and can relate to several people in their play. They play together rather than in "parallel play" (side-by-side, as preschoolers do, with only occasional interaction).

In this stage children begin to abandon much of the magical

In order to observe some of these characteristics it would be good for you to visit a day-care center or nursery school to watch young children at play.

Can you recall other examples of such spontaneous use of language by preschool-aged children you know?

An example of this lack of conservation recently happened at the dinner table of one of the authors of this book. My 4-year-old was not eating her hamburger, so we cut it up. With that my daughter began to cry and said, "I don't want it, you made more." To my daughter it appeared that there was more hamburger because one piece had been cut into many pieces!

To see these differences, try to observe children in a nursery school during free play and then observe the sophisticated games played by second or third graders during recess or after school.

Can you remember when you began to doubt the myths you were raised with? What were some of the questions you asked? How did your parents respond?

thinking and fantasy characteristic of the preoperational period. They ask a lot of questions about things they previously accepted—e.g., "How can Santa Claus deliver all those presents in one night?" "A lot of people don't have fireplaces, how does he get in their houses?" "Reindeers can't fly, can they?"

In the concrete operations stage children become very literal-minded. They see things in blacks and whites, not greys. They often become upset when a parent tries to help with homework and doesn't do things the exact way their teacher does, crying, "My teacher said to do it this way." They take things very literally, as one of the authors' 7-year-old daughter did when he was pulled over by a policeman for exceeding the speed limit on a recent family trip. She began to cry, saying that she didn't want her Daddy to go to jail. Even the humor that appeals to children at this age shows literal-mindedness, as they roar in laughter at slapstick, pie-throwing, cartoons, and bathroom jokes.

Formal Operations (11–16). The concrete operations stage prepares the child for the final stage—formal operations. This stage essentially parallels adolescence, as young people gradually learn to use abstract thinking. Now they can solve problems in their heads by visualizing solutions internally. They are able to organize information and reason scientifically by formulating hypotheses and then testing them. They understand symbolic meanings, metaphors, and similes. For example, they might reread *Alice in Wonderland* for its deeper meaning and watch cartoons for their social satire and puns. Adolescents are no longer bound to a literal interpretation of experience.

The thinking of the adolescent becomes more realistic as she is able to see shades of grey rather than simple blacks and whites. While in the concrete operations stage, she was very definite in what she liked or disliked and in her notions of right and wrong; she is now much less certain. Especially in the early parts of this stage, she becomes super-critical. It's almost as if she suddenly realizes she can think for herself and gets carried away with her new-found ability. She may criticize her mother's hair style, her father's clothes, her teacher's corny jokes, the hypocrisy of the members of her church or synagogue, etc. All of this is perfectly normal and healthy. If the teenager is to become a mature adult, she must be able to question the views of others and develop and articulate her own views.

In concluding our discussion of Piaget's stages of cognitive development, we would like to consider the following description by Gardner (1976) of all four Piagetian stages in terms of the child's gradual acquisition of the concept of water:

Can you recall how your views about right and wrong changed in your teenage years?

What were some of the issues on which you found yourself at odds with your parents as you passed through adolescence?

Although Piaget's formal operations stage ends with adulthood, it is important to note that cognitive growth goes on throughout life. The basic capacities for abstract reasoning emerge during adolescence, but they must be continually nourished with new experiences and new information if they are to be developed to their fullest.

> The first—that of *sensorimoter intelligence*—covers roughly the first two years of life. At this time the child "knows" the world exclusively through his own perceptions and actions upon it; for instance he knows water in that he can splash or drink it but he cannot conceive of it apart from such practical activities. The second stage—that of *intuitive** or *symbolic*

* We used the term *preoperational* for this stage.

thought—spans the preschool years. Now the child can talk about water and use water in his make-believe play even as he can form a static mental image of water "in his head." However, he cannot yet understand crucial physical laws governing the liquid—such as the fact that water can be poured into vessels of various dimensions while remaining the same in quantity. This ability to "conserve" properties of water only develops during the following or *concrete-operational stage,* characteristic of the elementary school years. The child capable of concrete operations can perform "mental actions" concerning physical entities: going beyond a static mental image of water, he can now "in his mind" pour the water back into its original container and verify that its quantity has not changed. Finally, during the period of *formal operations,* which begins in early adolescence, the child becomes able to perform mental actions upon symbols as well as upon physical entities. He can now write equations referring to H_2O and perform logical manipulations upon strings of such symbols; more generally, he becomes able to pose and solve scientific problems that require the manipulation of relevant variables.*

Implications of Piaget's Theory for Teachers

Jean Piaget is not a prescriptive theorist. Throughout his long career, he has maintained his fascination with the question he originally sought to investigate—the development of cognition. Piaget has not tried to provide teachers with more effective ways of teaching; nevertheless, his work offers many ideas for the teacher. Two ideas especially stand out—active knowing and sequential development.

For Piaget the mind is not a blank tablet waiting to be imprinted. Just the opposite; it is constantly at work, attempting to make ever more meaning of the bits of information the senses bring to it. At first this knowing is through physical action. As the child grows, internal mental ability begins to dominate, but always the mind is sorting, clarifying, and analyzing the flow of information and always attempting to make sense of the world. Each of the developmental steps is based upon prior development. Each new understanding serves as a base for further understanding. Children cannot truly "know" what they are not developmentally ready for, although they may give the impression of knowing it by repeating it parrot fashion.

If what Piaget says about active knowing and sequential development is true, then teachers must seek to recognize the child's stage of intellectual development and prepare learning activities appropriate to it. Children's thinking processes are very different from those of adults. Children do not learn well from listening to a teacher talk. There are concepts, ideas, and relationships they will not be ready to understand no matter how much a teacher goes over them. Especially for young children, learning must be as actively involving and as concrete as possible. Preschoolers and elementary schoolers learn with their whole bodies not just their minds. They need opportunities to play, to touch, to experience, not simply to listen or to read.

In Gardner's description we can see how children, as they mature, become less bound to concrete experience—what Bruner calls enactive learning. As they move toward adolescence, they become increasingly able to engage in iconic, and eventually symbolic, learning.

It might be helpful for you to observe a 1-year-old, a preschooler—age 3 or 4—a third or fourth grader, and an eighth or ninth grader, to see the tremendous differences in the thinking process at each of Piaget's four stages.

There are many examples of the limits of a child's reasoning. Have you ever tried to answer any children's questions such as:

What does God look like?

Is God married?

What does it feel like when you're dead?

How do all those people fit inside the television set?

---

* From H. Gardner's review of Piaget's *The Grasp of Consciousness, The New York Times,* August 1, 1976, p. 1. © 1976 by The New York Times Company. Reprinted by permission.

Both Piaget's and Bruner's views of intellectual development support active learning, what Dewey called learning by doing. The teacher's role becomes helping students think, question, and evaluate for themselves. Such an approach is often called discovery teaching *and is contrasted with* expository teaching.

Examples of such an approach at the elementary school level include learning math through running a school store, learning science through caring for classroom pets, or learning history through role-playing historical events.

Bruner's developmental concepts are closely related to Piaget's. It is easy to see the parallel between Bruner's three learning processes—the enactive, iconic, and symbolic—and Piaget's sensorimotor, preoperational, concrete operational, and formal operational stages of development.

However, differences in Bruner's and Piaget's views of intellectual development lead to different implications for teaching. Piaget holds that readiness results from an interaction between unfolding biological processes and appropriate experience. For that reason, he believes, to increase experience prematurely may be of little value. A teacher who adheres to Piaget's view would try to learn the child's level of development and teach at that level. Bruner, on the other hand, believes that good teaching nurtures biological readiness by providing appropriate experiences; in other words, readiness is taught rather than merely occurring. Bruner argues that teachers ought to provide experiences that are a little beyond the child's stage of development. Such experiences will stimulate the child to engage in higher levels of thinking.

Conclusions

In this chapter we have explored the processes of cognitive growth. The problem in which you were asked to divide fractions illustrated the fact that the development of one's intellectual skills is much more complicated than simply learning to recall or remember a rule for solving a problem. Memory is only one of a variety of cognitive processes. While most people have learned how to memorize, few of us have learned to think critically and utilize our intellectual potential to the fullest extent. Jerome Bruner's theory of cognitive growth has been presented here because it provides a theory of instruction—a prescriptive theory—that suggests what teachers can do to help students learn to think critically, or, as Bruner puts it, "to go beyond the information given."

According to Bruner, four elements of a theory of instruction must be taken into account in any learning situation if cognitive growth is to be fostered: *predisposition, structure, sequence,* and *reinforcement.* Predisposition is one's readiness for learning. In preparation for helping students learn, teachers must try to diagnose their current level of functioning and respond to their needs, interests, abilities, and weaknesses. Second is a consideration of the ways a body of knowledge can be structured so that it can be most easily learned. This involves determining which mode of learning—*enactive, iconic,* or *symbolic*—provides the best match with the intellectual readiness of the learner. For some students enactive learning—learning by doing—is most appropriate; other students will be prepared for operating at an abstract, symbolic level.

The sequencing of instruction makes up the third element in Bruner's theory of instruction. His concern is that sequence be determined by the needs of the learner rather than by the logic of the subject matter, as it is in programmed learning. Often, but not always, Bruner sees the best sequence as inductive—from the concrete to the abstract, from one's own experience to generalizations and concepts. Finally, Bruner discusses the role of rewards and punishments in fostering learning. He emphasizes rewards inherent in the task itself—intrinsic rewards—although he does not deny the place of extrinsic rewards (such as praise or good grades) in getting learning started. In sum, Bruner's theories offer suggestions for relating teaching to the cognitive growth of the learner in a way that promotes *coping*—an openness to new experiences—and minimizes defensive behavior.

The value of Piaget's research is the picture it gives us of intellectual development. Piaget has identified four major stages children go through as they mature. A clear understanding of the way children's minds work as they move from reliance on sensorimotor learning (ages 0–2) to the full capacity to abstract (age 12 and up) is invaluable for teachers. The better we understand the children's stage of development, the more likely we are to foster real learning, not the type of rote learning that led to our inabilities to explain the fraction problem that introduced this chapter. As we explore social–emotional development in Chapter 6, the importance of understanding development will become even clearer.

Some Good Books

Anglin, Jeremy, ed. *Beyond the Information Given.* New York: Norton, 1973. Included in this book is a collection of articles and papers written by Bruner throughout his career. The book provides an excellent resource for the student interested in a synthesis of Bruner's views on thinking.

Bruner, Jerome S., ed. *Play—Its Role in Development and Evolution.* New York: Basic Books, 1976. The articles collected in this book deal with the importance of play in the child's intellectual development.

Bruner, Jerome S. *The Process of Education.* Cambridge, Mass.: Harvard University Press, 1960. This book, already mentioned many times previously, introduces Bruner's concepts of readiness, structure, and motivation as they relate to the thinking process.

Bruner, Jerome S. *Toward a Theory of Instruction.* New York: Norton, 1966. Bruner's clearest statement on how children develop intellectually and the implications of that knowledge for teaching. If you are interested in the application of Piagetian–Brunerian thinking to the classroom, this is a good book to explore.

Elkind, David. *A Sympathetic Understanding of the Child from Six to Sixteen.* Boston: Allyn and Bacon, 1971. A former student of Piaget's,

Elkind brings a clearly articulated Piagetian orientation to this study of child and adolescent development.

Farnham-Diggory, Sylvia. *Cognitive Processes in Education.* New York: Harper & Row, 1972. This text in educational psychology brings together much of the current literature on cognitive growth. It is especially valuable as a supplement to this chapter since it emphasizes the implications of the thinking of both Piaget and Bruner for teaching.

Furth, Hans G. and Harry Wachs. *Thinking Goes to School: Piaget's Theory in Practice.* New York: Oxford University Press, 1975. In a follow-up to his book *Piaget for Teachers* (Englewood Cliffs, N.J.: Prentice-Hall, 1970), Furth has joined with Wachs in providing an overview of their two-year project in creating a "School for Thinking" in an elementary school in Charleston, West Virginia. Of special interest is the creation of educational experiences based upon Piagetian concepts.

Holt, John. *How Children Learn.* New York: Pitman, 1967. John Holt, the well-known critic of education who wrote *How Children Fail* (1967), provides here a highly readable collection of anecdotes illustrating children's natural curiosity and drive for learning.

Inhelder, Barbel and Jean Piaget. *The Growth of Logical Thinking from Childhood to Adolescence.* New York: Basic Books, 1958. While many of Piaget's writings are difficult to read, this book isn't. It examines the growth of logical thinking in the concrete operations and formal operations stages.

Piaget, Jean. *The Origins of Intelligence in Children.* New York: International Universities Press, 1952. For the ambitious reader who wants to tackle Piaget himself, this book develops in depth his theory of intellectual growth.

Piaget, Jean. *Science of Education and the Psychology of the Child.* New York: Viking, 1970. Here Piaget explores the implications of his theory of intellectual development for the teaching–learning process.

Wadsworth, Barry J. *Piaget's Theory of Cognitive Development.* New York: McKay, 1971. For the reader who wants a concise overview of Piaget's stages of intellectual development, this book will be quite helpful.

Articles, Studies, and Other References

Clarizio, Harvey F. "Natural vs. Accelerated Readiness." In H. F. Clarizio, R. C. Craig, and W. A. Mehrens (eds.), *Contemporary Issues in Educational Psychology.* Boston: Allyn and Bacon, 1974, pp. 107–118. An excellent article in which the views of the "environmentalists," who argue that schools can and should accelerate the child's intellectual readiness, are contrasted with the thinking of the "Piagetians," who advocate natural readiness.

Hunt, David E. and Edmund V. Sullivan. "Cognitive Developmental Approach: Piaget, Bruner, Gagné, Vygotsky." In Hunt and Sullivan, *Between Psychology and Education.* Hinsdale, Ill.: Dryden Press, 1974, ch. 6. This chapter provides an overview of Piaget's theory, relating it to other cognitive development theories.

Maier, Henry W. *Three Theories of Child Development.* Rev. ed. New York: Harper & Row, 1969. Chapter 3 of this book gives the reader a concise but comprehensive picture of Piaget's theory of cognitive development. In other parts of the book Piaget's theory is compared with the psychoanalytic theory of Erikson and the learning theory of Sears.

Strike, Kenneth. "The Logic of Learning by Discovery." *Review of Educational Research,* Summer 1975: 461. Strike has synthesized a great deal of research on discovery learning, an approach vigorously advocated by Bruner.

Suggestions for Action-Oriented Learning

1. Return to your old elementary school and observe a kindergarten or first-grade class. Pay particular attention to the learning activities and the types of materials being used. Why do you feel the learning is as enactive (using the whole body actively) as it is? Could junior high school and senior high school classes benefit, too, from emphasis on learning by doing? Why or why not?

2. Read one of the references suggested on Piaget (e.g., Wadsworth, 1971). Focus on the intellectual changes that occur during the stage of preoperational thought. Then with a 5- or 6-year-old relative or neighbor, try out some of the conservation tasks in order to better understand Piaget's ideas of intellectual development. Discuss your findings with other members of your class.

3. Visit two playgrounds—one in a well-to-do suburban community, one in an economically disadvantaged urban community. Prepare a report of the differences you notice in the type of play, language, social interaction, etc. What differences do you see in the predispositions for school learning (see pp. 86–87) of children from each of these environments?

4. A variation on activity 3 would be to contrast the leisure activities of junior and senior high school students in an affluent suburban community with those of students in a lower income city environment. Again think about the implications for teaching that grow out of the different predispositions for learning that each group brings to school.

6
The Learner's
Social–Emotional Growth

In recent years interest has been increasing among both researchers and practicing educators in social–emotional growth and development—the development of attitudes, values, feelings, social relationships, etc. It is becoming widely recognized that social–emotional factors are as important as intellectual factors in influencing learning. For example, many of the reasons for some students' poor performance in school seem to have little to do with ability or previous knowledge and much to do with the students' stage of development, motivation, emotional problems, or feelings toward teachers. An understanding of these influences is important for people who wish to work effectively as teachers.

In order to help you become more familiar with the social–emotional—the affective—nature of the learner, we have chosen to center our attention in this chapter around the work of Erik Erikson, a major figure in mid-twentieth-century American psychology. Erikson has articulated a theory of social–emotional development from birth through old age. In addition to exploring Erikson's theory and its implications for teaching, we will also introduce the research of Lawrence Kohlberg, which has enhanced our understanding of a more specific type of affective development, that of moral development. There are other theories and issues of social–emotional development that we could have explored in this chapter. However, as in other chapters in this book, we are selective in our coverage. The thinking of Erikson and Kohlberg provides a good overview of social–emotional development and offers many implications for teaching.

Erikson's Eight Ages of Man: A Theory of Social–Emotional Growth

Through his clinical work as a psychoanalyst and his research on growing up in a variety of cultural settings, Erik Erikson has evolved a theory that sees psychological development as continuing from birth to death, through eight stages. Erikson's early thinking was heavily influenced by the work of Sigmund Freud, whom he knew as an acquaintance, and through his study of Freudian psychology in Vienna with Anna Freud, Sigmund's daughter. However, Erikson has gone well beyond many of Freud's basic precepts to provide a theory of personality that is much more optimistic about human potential for healthy growth. And Erikson's ideas lend themselves more readily than Freud's to prescribing what teachers and other helping professionals can do to facilitate this growth.

Each of Erikson's stages of development (or *ages of man,* as he refers to them) centers around a crisis with both positive and negative dimensions. In order for healthy personality development to take place, individuals must face and deal with the crisis that becomes dominant at each stage before moving to the next stage. Social–emotional growth, then, involves moving forward as the individual confronts and surmounts the challenges of each new crisis, always trying to avoid getting stuck at a particular stage or reverting back to a previous stage.

For a comparison of Erikson's views on development with Freud's views, see Table 6–1.

If you would like to learn more about Freud's theory, you might read An Outline of Psychoanalysis *(1949).*

An excellent reference for further reading on Erikson is his classic statement on the social significance of childhood, Childhood and Society *(1963).*

Stage 1—Trust

Table 6–1. Development as Viewed by Erikson and Freud—A Comparison

Erikson's Psychosocial Stages	Years	Freud's Psychosexual Stages
Trust vs. Mistrust	0–1-1/2	*Oral Stage.* Attention and activity centered around mouth. Through satisfaction of oral needs dependent child learns trust.
Autonomy vs. Shame and Doubt	1-1/2–3	*Anal Stage.* Anal region becomes of dominant concern as child is expected to develop bowel (and bladder) control. First steps toward independence and self-direction.
Initiative vs. Guilt	3–6	*Phallic Stage.* Genital region provides satisfaction. Oedipus complex occurs with child seeking love and attention of parent of opposite sex.
Industry vs. Inferiority	6–11 or 12	*Latency Stage.* Period of diminished sexual interest. Oedipus complex is resolved by child's identifying with same-sex parent. Very little interaction between boys and girls.
Identity vs. Role Confusion	12–18	*Genital Stage.* Mature sexuality develops and with it psychological maturity and a search for close affectional ties.
Intimacy vs. Isolation	18–30	
Generativity vs. Stagnation	30–65	
Ego Integrity vs. Despair	Above 65	

Erikson's theory of development parallels Freud's theory for the first five stages and then adds three stages of adult development, thus emphasizing his view of development as a lifelong process. While Freud tends to see development as an interaction between the individual's unfolding biological nature and early family experiences, Erikson attaches much more significance to social influences throughout the lifespan. As you will see later in this chapter, Erikson's thinking on psychological development throughout the adult years has provided the basis for a great deal of research since the mid-1970s. If it's true that adults go through identifiable stages, as Erikson and many others now believe, then an understanding of those stages will be important to those helping professionals who work with adults and, of course, to adults themselves.

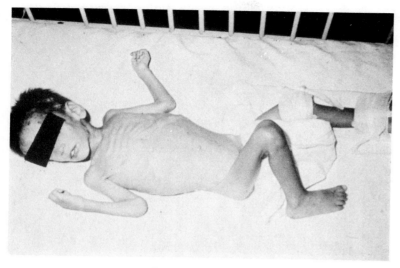

Stage 1—Mistrust

Another important aspect of Erikson's theory is his view of development as a psychosocial process, in which growing individuals interact with and are influenced by an ever widening social and cultural environment, beginning at birth with their parents (usually the mother) and gradually expanding outward.

On the following pages you will find an overview of Erikson's theory of affective growth that sketches in the eight stages of development. To help you better understand the key crisis around which each stage revolves, we have put together a photo essay designed to illustrate our discussion of each stage. Before reading the narrative try to get a feeling for the critical elements in each stage's crisis by contrasting the picture representing the positive dimension of the crisis with the one representing the negative dimension.

It's interesting to note that Erikson's notion of healthy personality development seems to incorporate Bruner's concepts of coping and defending.

1. Trust vs. Mistrust (Birth–18 months)—The Infant

At birth an infant whose needs have been taken care of automatically in its mother's uterus is thrust into a new world, in which it is totally dependent upon other people for its survival. Its needs for food, water, warmth, physical comfort, and human contact all must be met regularly if it is to remain healthy and physically comfortable. The quality of these early nurturing experiences seems to provide the basis for the development of a capacity to trust and depend upon others. An infant who spends much time hungry or who is in some other way poorly taken care of begins to learn mistrust—an inability to trust.

As the first major phase of a child's life, the trust vs. mistrust stage provides the foundations for the child's later development both

Stage 2—Autonomy

psychologically and socially. Erikson suggests that the feelings of physical comfort and security that come from being cared for in a loving way help a baby accept new experiences without fear. Such openness to new experiences is an important predisposition for later growth as a learner since, as Bruner might explain, the child is being prepared for coping behavior rather than defending behavior. Equally significant during the first year of life is the child's social learning. Through contact with his mother (and to a lesser degree his father and other family members) as he is fed and cared for, the infant begins to associate the pleasurable feelings he receives with the people who provide for him. A positive mother–child relationship in the early months of life paves the way for the child not only to identify with his mother but also to be open to identifying with and relating to other people.

Children whose needs are frequently not met or who are separated from their parents for a long time (especially after six months of age, when they have developed a close attachment and recognize the absence of their parents) are likely to become frustrated and fearful. Seemingly as a means of protecting themselves from further psychological harm, such children may well develop the beginnings of mistrust toward others. This undoubtedly makes their successful movement through later stages much more difficult.

The mothering (or parenting) function can be carried out by any person who meets the baby's physical and psychological needs. For the development of trust, it is not necessary that the child's biological mother be its primary caretaker.

Although Erikson believes that infancy is the critical period for the development of trust, he points out that all stages contribute to healthy development. In other words, people's social experience throughout life affects their sense of trust or mistrust even though infancy is the most important stage for this development.

2. Autonomy vs. Shame and Doubt (18 months–3 years)—The Toddler

As the infant learns to walk and talk, he is beginning to stand on his own two feet, not only in a literal sense. As his capacity to move around and to use language grows, he becomes less dependent on

Stage 2—Shame and Doubt

others for the satisfaction of his own needs. At this time he is moving out into his environment, exploring and doing things for himself. His parents want him to become more independent. It is during this toddler stage that most cultures expect children to begin to take care of their own bodily needs. In our culture toilet training is initiated at this stage. As you can see in Table 6–1, Freud pays special attention to this development and its psychological significance, calling it the *anal stage*.

The toddler's conflict revolves around his struggle for independence and self-mastery and his doubts about his own capacities and fear of separation from his parents, who have always taken care of him. He fluctuates rapidly and without warning between exploring and pulling back, not wanting to be held and clinging, laughing and crying. Thus Erikson's Stage 2 is a time of pushing and pulling back as the child strives toward autonomy and greater independence and yet clings to the security of dependence. Frequently the child finds himself caught between his own desires and those of his parents. Undoubtedly you can recall seeing a parent in a store attempting to deal with a 2-year-old who has made up his mind that he wants something his parent has told him he can't have. The resulting temper tantrum, no matter how the parent responds to the child, and the look of frustration on the parent's face give you a feeling as to why this stage is often called the "terrible two's."

Though it may be difficult for both parents and child, this period is important because it lays the groundwork for self-direction. The child's many "no's" and "me-do-it's" are indications of his recognition of himself as a person and of his first halting steps toward autonomy. He needs encouragement if he is to continue his quest for independence,

To understand the significance of this stage it might be helpful for you to observe a 2-year-old and discuss with the parents the conflicts they experience in trying to decide how best to respond to their child.

Freud emphasized the importance of toilet training in the child's psychological development during this stage. He believed that trying to force children to become toilet-trained before they were ready, and punishing them for "accidents," could lead to fears, anxieties, and the shame and doubt that Erikson discusses.

Stage 3—Initiative

yet he also needs restrictions to protect him from hurting himself or becoming overly frustrated. Too much restriction, however, can lead a child to doubt his abilities and feel ashamed when he can't do what some expect him to do. Achieving the right balance between permissiveness and firmness is the critical task for parents as they seek to promote the autonomy of their toddlers.

3. Initiative vs. Guilt (3–6)—The Preschooler

Erikson's third stage of development parallels the nursery school and kindergarten years, when the child who has developed a capacity for trust and a feeling of his own autonomy begins to initiate many new activities. His confidence in his increased ability to move around and to speak opens up a whole new world of experience. Now he really begins to detach himself from his dependence on parents. He has a sense of his own identity as a person, yet he carries his parents' expectations with him in his conscience (or, as Freud calls it, his *superego*). Although the preschool child is now able to be away from his parents for increasingly long periods of time, as he does in nursery school and kindergarten, his superego continually reminds him of their values regarding his behavior.

The initiative that the preschooler is developing is applied to an ever widening social circle and to an array of new activities. He becomes interested in peer relationships and spends much time in active play with other children. His movement away from home brings him into contact with new adults, such as his teachers and the parents of his friends, all of whom he tends to perceive as "parent figures." Initiative takes many forms, including making things; pretending and

In order to understand the world of the preschooler you might visit a nursery school and/or kindergarten. Note the ways children manifest initiative and how the teacher responds to the children's behavior.

Another interesting activity would be to watch a number of television shows designed for preschoolers, such as Sesame Street, Mr. Rogers, *or* Romper Room. *Try to analyze how the goals of each are relevant to Erikson's theory.*

Stage 3—Guilt

imagining; asking one question after another; and, for both boys and girls, masturbation, seeking pleasure through genital manipulation.

As the preschooler is encouraged to initiate and try out new things, he develops a sense of control over his environment as well as feedback about his own abilities. The child's success produces feelings of self-worth and a continued curiosity for learning. When a 3- or 4-year-old is criticized for such things as asking too many questions, not following directions, or playing with his genitals, he may develop feelings of guilt that can cause him to overly restrict his behavior. Overcontrol by parents or stifling of a child's desire to play and explore can lead to later difficulties in initiating.

Can you recall any times in your own life when guilt feelings led you to avoid experiences that only later you realized would have been good for you?

Erikson's view of the preschooler would support the idea of a "play-oriented" preschool rather than a very structured one. Such a school, Erikson might argue, would have lots of materials, which children could use to make things. It would encourage children to use their imagination and to interact with other children. Through play children would learn to initiate both in their thinking and in their socializing.

4. Industry vs. Inferiority (6–11 or 12)—The Elementary Schooler

The 6- or 7-year-olds in most cultures are expected to make a major transition from their previous development. It is at this time that children generally begin some more or less formal preparation for adult life, which usually includes learning to use the tools of the culture. In primitive societies boys may begin to learn to use weapons and hunt, while girls learn the use of food-preparing tools and ways of childrearing. In more technologically advanced cultures like ours, school is the formal means of providing the basic tools of the culture—capacities to read, write, and solve problems.

The school-aged child wants to learn to do and make new things

Stage 4—Industry

If you were to design an elementary school to promote industry and to keep children from developing strong feelings of inferiority, what would you emphasize most in the curriculum and in teacher–student relationships?

There is some evidence that sex segregation during the elementary school years is less profound today than it used to be. This may be the result of more open attitudes in our society toward childhood sexuality.

and continually seeks recognition from others for his efforts. He seems pushed by a drive toward mastery and success—toward competence. Erikson tells us that the young school child is especially ready to develop a sense of industry in which he perceives himself as a doer and producer. Yet at the same time the challenges and demands of this period can be ego-threatening and lead to feelings of inadequacy and inferiority if the child fails at many of the activities he attempts or if he is pushed too hard by parents and other adults. Negative feelings can lead him to avoid new learning experiences and even regress to earlier forms of behavior.

During the elementary school years the child's physical growth rate has slowed and he is in a stage Freud calls *latency,* when sexual concerns are less important than they were previously. The child's social world continues to expand as he comes under more peer influence in school, in community activities, and in play. However, sex segregation with boys and girls is fairly clear-cut—a fact Freud explains as part of the resolution of the Oedipus complex. The interaction between the elementary schooler's emerging abilities and the recognition these bring from peers and adults (especially teachers and parents) is important not only in his developing industry but also in his more general picture of himself as a competent and productive person.

> Try to think back to your own elementary school years. What were three things that you felt especially good at?
>
> What were three things that you felt inferior about?
>
> How did your teachers affect your feelings of competence and inferiority?

Stage 4—Inferiority

5. Identity vs. Role Confusion (12–18)—The Adolescent

Children enter adolescence with the onset of puberty, the beginning of the process that leads to adult physical maturity and the ability to reproduce. Adolescence is the transitional phase between childhood and adulthood, in which there are rapid bodily growth and new sexual drives. Accompanying these physical changes is a great deal of searching and questioning as the person seeks answers to such questions as "Who am I?" and "Where am I headed?" Erikson sees the adolescent period as centered around the conflict between the individual's beginning to know himself and have a sense of his own identity on the one hand, and his remaining confused and uncertain about who he is on the other. Erikson coined the term *identity crisis* to capture the psychological essence of this period.

As he changes physically and psychologically, the adolescent develops new social relationships, especially sexual relationships. His peers now become of great importance; he is very concerned with how he appears to them and with their acceptance of him. The feedback he receives from them helps him in forming his own picture of himself. In addition, peers serve as a source of emotional support, since they are experiencing many of the same conflicts. In their move toward adulthood, adolescents question the values and advice provided by parents and other adults. Such a challenging of adult authority is psychologically healthy because if adolescents are to make their own decisions and function independently as adults, they must know what they believe and why.

It should be pointed out here that establishing an identity is not limited to the adolescent period. Like each of the other conflicts Erikson discusses, the identity vs. role confusion conflict has its begin-

Adolescence is one of the most difficult stages an individual passes through. Rapid physical growth, new sexual feelings, self-doubts and self-consciousness, questions about the future, parental pressures, and concerns about being accepted by peers make life very difficult. Adults want adolescents to grow up, yet they often continue to treat them as children. Adolescents themselves want to be on their own, but at times they seem to prefer the security of letting adults make decisions for them. For these reasons many teachers describe junior high school students (who are in the early years of adolescence) as the most difficult to teach. Would you like to be a junior high teacher? Why or why not?

Stage 5—Identity

Stage 6—Intimacy

Erikson has written a book focusing specifically on adolescence and the issue of identity. If you are interested in this period, you might read Identity: Youth and Crisis *(1968).*

nings in the early stages of development and continues to some degree even for adults who have satisfactorily resolved the crisis during adolescence. For people who have not left adolescence with a sense of their own identity, independent decision making can be difficult and social relationships unsatisfactory in adulthood.

Stage 5—Role Confusion

Stage 6—Isolation

6. Intimacy vs. Isolation (18 or 19–30)—The Young Adult

The young adult years, which in our culture parallel the twenties, are years in which the individual is beginning to find his place in the adult world. The major developmental themes center around love and work. In order for a man or woman at this stage to establish an inti-

In her best-selling book Passages: Predictable Crises of Adult Life *(1976), Gail Sheehy has explored the years from 18 to 50. She sees the twenties as a trying period, in which young adults must determine how they will take hold in the adult world.*

Stage 7—Generativity

Another researcher who has studied this stage of life is Kenneth Keniston (1968). He argues that, especially for young people who go on to full-time higher education and don't move immediately into work and marriage, there is a transitional period between adolescence and full adulthood. He calls this the period of youth. Often they live in a prolonged state of adolescence, still dependent on others for their economic support.

Do you think Keniston's observations are accurate? Why or why not?

mate relationship with another person or to begin to contribute effectively to the working world, it is essential that he or she be able to share and cooperate. However, as Erikson points out, before a person can share or cooperate he must have a sense of his own identity. In other words, if one is to fuse his identity with that of another, as in marriage, or carry out a job in which he works with, not against, others, he must be secure in himself. He must be able at times to replace the *I* in his thinking with a *we*.

Socially, this first of Erikson's three adult stages calls for new types of relationships. Earlier relationships were primarily receiving rather than giving relationships, and thus they were unequal. On the other hand, the person who has satisfactorily passed into early adulthood is able to give as well as receive, to love as well as seek love, and to provide as well as be provided for. Such a capacity for cooperating and sharing as an equal—a peer—is a prerequisite to both effective childrearing and productive contributions to one's culture as a worker and citizen. The young adult who does not develop the sense of intimacy necessary for close and harmonious relationships with other adults is likely to feel isolated and excluded. Such feelings can lead to lashing out against others or withdrawing into oneself. Neither of these responses is psychologically healthy.

7. Generativity vs. Stagnation (30–65)—The Middle Adult

The years of middle adulthood make up the longest developmental period—approximately one half of the average person's life. Erikson sees these as the productive years, when people contribute to their culture and its future by raising children, working, and guiding its institutions. At this stage most people are finally relatively

Stage 7—Stagnation

independent both economically and emotionally. They are called upon to nurture and care for people both young and old who are less independent. Adults who raise families function in these years as parents of children who, over time, become increasingly less dependent upon them, and as children of their own parents, who become increasingly more dependent. Beyond their family roles, middle adults fulfill a multiplicity of roles, such as worker, citizen, and community leader. Each of these roles requires maturity and selflessness.

The major task facing the middle adult is developing a sense of "generativity." This comes as he contributes his knowledge, abilities, and values to guiding the next generation. For those adults who don't raise children of their own, productivity needs can be met through work with other people's children, through taking a serious role as citizen, or through contributions to a business, profession, or trade. An adult who does not feel productive may remain absorbed with himself as a means of defending against his feelings of uselessness, apathy, and stagnation.

The productive years of adulthood (approximately age 30–65) occupy half of the average person's life in the more technologically advanced countries. Yet less is known about psychological growth during this period than during any of the other periods from infancy to old age. As we mentioned earlier, the study of developmental changes during the adult years is just beginning (Gould, 1975; Sheehy, 1976). The causes of communication problems between parents and children, teachers and students, bosses and young workers, etc., may in part relate to conflicts in stage of development. As we discuss the helping relationship in Chapter 10, we will look into some of the problems brought on by differences in the life stages of "helpers" and "helpees."

Your parents and their close friends are most likely in this period of development. It might be interesting to talk with them about their feelings about this period. You could begin a conversation by asking them what they feel are the best things and worst things about being their age.

In Passages *(1976), Sheehy identifies a number of substages within this period. She explains the psychological changes people go through as they move from their thirties to their forties and fifties.*

Try to imagine how, at each age below, a teacher's stage of development would affect his view of teaching and his relationship with students and colleagues.

Age 22

Age 35

Age 44

Age 53

Age 63

Stage 8—Ego Integrity

The plight of elderly people in our society has become an important area of social concern. By separating our elderly from us in "adult communities," old-age homes, and geriatric hospitals, we lose the benefit of their experience and they feel alienated and rejected. The Gray Panthers is a militant group of mostly "senior citizens," working to help eliminate the injustices that elderly people in America encounter daily.

Getting old is a reality that many of us fear and all of us face. Yet, as Erikson points out, old age can be a stage of growth like the earlier stages. This view is shared by Elizabeth Kübler-Ross, a psychiatrist who has spent much of her professional life working with elderly and dying people. Her most recent book, Death: The Final Stage of Growth (1975), eloquently explains her point of view.

8. Ego Integrity vs. Despair (Above 65)—The Senior Citizen

As he moves through the final stage of life, the individual must maintain his own identity and sense of satisfaction in the face of increasing dependence upon others. By feeling that he has done his share in contributing to the growth of the next generation through childrearing, work, and service to the community, a person develops a fuller sense of trust as he must allow others to "carry the ball." The developmental theme of the first stage of life—trust—now comes together with the theme of the last stage—integrity. The older adult who feels pride and self-acceptance as he reflects on his own life can trust the future to others. During this stage the psychologically healthy adult achieves a philosophy of life and a wisdom that extend beyond his own life cycle, linking him with both the past and the future.

The extent to which the later years of life reflect integrity rather than despair is largely determined by the satisfactory resolution of the earlier developmental crises. The senior citizen who has developed trust, autonomy, initiative, and industry, and who has a positive identity, a capacity for intimacy, and a feeling of productivity, is less likely to experience old age as a period of despair than the person for whom the earlier life crises have not been resolved. As you think about people you know in their seventies or eighties, it is probably relatively easy to identify those who, by accepting themselves and their lives, are able to conquer their fear of death and to continue to live happily and productively. On the other hand, you undoubtedly also know people who give up an interest in life in their later years. They direct their despair at everything around them as they continually complain about their health, the youth of the day, the state of the world, and so on.

Stage 8—Despair

Implications of Erikson's Theory for Teaching

As we have seen, Erikson provides a view of growth as a lifelong process beginning at birth and continuing until death. The significance of his thinking is that it gives us a picture of healthy personality development, helping us realize that within each stage of life our experiences contribute to the person we become. The thrust for positive growth that underlies Erikson's theory can be compared with Bruner's concepts of coping and defending. As we successfully resolve each of Erikson's crises, we are, in Bruner's terms, coping—confronting life head-on. When we do not resolve a stage successfully—e.g., in the school years developing a sense of inferiority or in the young adult years a feeling of isolation—then, in order to protect our fragile ego, we must *defend* by closing out new experience.

If we take Erikson's theory seriously, we as teachers must concern ourselves with students' social–emotional development not simply their learning of information and academic skills. Advocates of humanistic education like Lyon (1971), Patterson (1973), and Rogers (1969) share Erikson's interest in social–emotional development. They agree that schools ought to help children to become more self-aware, to develop and clarify their own attitudes and values, and to get along with others. There are many movements in education today that reflect this concern. We will mention briefly three of the better known humanistic education movements and suggest references you can turn to if you would like to learn more about them.

Values Clarification. This approach is concerned with helping people clarify, better understand, and possibly reevaluate the values that guide their behavior (Raths, Harmin, and Simon, 1966). All sorts

Erikson's theory calls our attention to the importance of certain psychological qualities in an individual's growth. Trust, autonomy, initiative, industry, and identity, while especially critical at particular stages of development, are nevertheless influenced by experiences throughout life.

Try to indicate one thing a teacher might do to enhance the development of each quality below. Think in terms of the grade level you would most like to teach.

Trust

Autonomy

Initiative

Industry

Identity

Good practical references for each area are:

Values Clarification:

Canfield and Wells, 100 Ways to Enhance Self-Concept in the Classroom *(1976).*

Simon, Howe, and Kirschenbaum, Values Clarification: A Handbook of Practical Strategies for Teachers and Students *(1972).*

Confluent Education:

Brown, Human Teaching for Human Learning *(1971).*

Brown, The Live Classroom *(1975).*

Moral Education:

Mattox, Getting It Together: Dilemmas for the Classroom Based on Kohlberg's Approach *(1975).*

Today more and more adults are returning to school in evening high schools and in day and evening college programs.

With this increase in adult education, more teachers are finding themselves teaching students who are older than they are. How would you feel about teaching someone your parents' or grandparents' age?

Kohlberg's research on moral development and his concern for moral education have been well received by educators who are especially concerned with young people's learning of values and attitudes. In the post-Watergate years of public debate over immorality and unethical behavior by our leaders, some educators have seen in Kohlberg's work a means of promoting in children moral reasoning that will carry over into their adult lives.

of strategies have been developed for helping children and adults actively explore their values through discussions, rating scales, questionnaires, debates, role-playing, etc.

Confluent Education.   Heavily influenced by Gestalt psychology, confluent education (Brown, 1971) seeks to create a wholistic education in which cognitive (intellectual) learning and affective (emotional) learning flow together. This approach provides strategies for teaching English, social studies, science, etc., in a way that integrates thought and feeling.

Moral Education.   Stimulated by the research of Lawrence Kohlberg (Kohlberg and Turiel, 1971) on the stages people pass through as they develop a sense of right and wrong, many teachers today are helping children think through moral issues. In this approach students are presented with hypothetical moral dilemmas in which they must make decisions and explain their reasons. We will explore Kohlberg's thinking in depth later in this chapter.

In helping us as facilitators of learning, Erikson's theory not only tells us about the development of our students but also aids us in better understanding ourselves. Teachers who are just starting out at age 21 or 22 are in the early years of the young adulthood stage, whereas their principal and many of their fellow teachers are probably in Erikson's middle adulthood stage. At least a few of their colleagues are probably nearing the final stage of life as they approach retirement. The differences in background, interest, and outlook of these groups of adults in the school will have an impact on their relations with each other as well as with students. The way a 45-year-old teacher perceives and is perceived by ninth graders is not likely to be the same as a 22-year-old teacher. Erikson's theory implies that as we know more about both our own growth and the growth of our students, we will be able to more effectively diagnose the level at which a student is functioning and then prescribe the appropriate educational strategies.

Kohlberg's Theory of Moral Development

Another area of social–emotional development that has recently received a great deal of attention by educators is moral development—the processes of growth in moral reasoning and action. The work of Lawrence Kohlberg (1974) is central to our understanding of this important new area of study. Through the research he has conducted at the University of Chicago and, currently, at Harvard, Kohlberg has built upon Piaget's thinking (1932) regarding moral development. Like Piaget, Kohlberg sees a child's moral development as progressing in an unvarying and universal way through a series of stages, with the capacity for different levels of moral thinking paralleling the child's intellectual development.

In his research Kohlberg has presented to children and adults hypothetical situations he calls *moral dilemmas.* Each of these moral dilemmas calls for subjects to explain how they would resolve the dilemma and to discuss the reasoning behind their course of action. An analysis of their reasoning determines at which of Kohlberg's stages of moral development the person is functioning. In order to become familiar with Kohlberg's theory, give your response to the moral dilemma presented in Exploration 6-1.

Exploration 6-1: Woman Dying of Cancer— A Moral Dilemma Developed by Lawrence Kohlberg

Read through the following situation and answer the question at the end of the passage *yes* or *no,* explaining in a few sentences or a paragraph the reasoning behind your choice. Then try to determine which of Kohlberg's six stages is reflected in your response by reading the discussion on each of Kohlberg's stages. In determining your stage of moral reasoning, compare your response with the sample responses to this dilemma provided beside the description of each stage.

> In Europe, a woman was near death from a special kind of cancer. There was one drug that the doctors thought might save her. It was a form of radium that a druggist in the same town had recently discovered. The drug was expensive to make, but the druggist was charging ten times what the drug cost him to make. He paid $200.00 for the radium and charged $2000.00 for a small dose of the drug. The sick woman's husband, Heinz, went to everyone he knew to borrow the money, but he could only get together about $1000.00, which is half of what it cost. He told the druggist that his wife was dying and asked him to sell it cheaper or let him pay later. But the druggist said: "No, I discovered the drug and I'm going to make money from it." So Heinz got desperate and broke into the man's store to steal the drug for his wife.

Should the husband have done that? Why or why not?
Your response:

Level 1: Preconventional Moral Thought. Children are responsive to cultural labels of good and bad, right and wrong. However, they do what is right to avoid punishment, to get a reward, or out of deference to someone else's power.

Stage 1: The punishment and obedience orientation. Moral decisions are based on avoiding punishment or unquestioningly deferring to power. For example, a child might avoid taking another child's toy out of fear of being punished by his mother or father or out of a recognition of the other child's greater size.

Stage 2: The instrumental–relativist orientation. In this stage right is what satisfies one's own needs. "Look out for number 1" seems to be the watchword. Often this is done through exchanges of favors; thus, a 5-year-old says, "I'll give you one of my cookies if

Sample responses for Exploration 6-1: These brief responses are designed to highlight key elements in the reasoning that occurs at each of Kohlberg's stages. Note that the level of moral thinking is determined by the reason given for the decision, not whether the answer is yes or no.

Stage 1.

> Yes—"If he let his wife die, many people would blame him."

> No—"He would probably be caught by the police and be put in jail for stealing the drug."

Stage 2.

> Yes—"It's OK to take the drug because the druggist is charging too much for it."

No—*"His wife's probably going to die anyway. It's not worth taking the risk."*

Stage 3.

Yes—*"No one would condemn the man for stealing the drug to save his wife's life. But if he didn't, he wouldn't be able to face his family."*

No—*"Sure, some people might rationalize stealing the drug, but most would see the man as a criminal. How would he feel if someone stole something from him?"*

Stage 4.

Yes—*"If the man has any sense of honor, he will do what he must do to save his wife, even if that means stealing."*

No—*"Stealing is stealing, and it's against the law no matter what a person's good intentions may be."*

Stage 5.

Yes—*"He had no alternative for saving his wife's life. While there is no doubt that he broke the law, any court would recognize and accept the extenuating circumstances justifying his behavior."*

No—*"He should have made the druggist's immoral behavior known publicly so that social pressure would force the druggist to reconsider the price he was charging for the drug. Probably there is some legal principle by which the druggist could be compelled to lower his price."*

you give me some of your cake." Adult behavior at this stage might be having a traffic ticket fixed, paying off a waiter to get a better table, or not declaring all of one's income at tax time, rationalizing that the government takes too much tax money anyway.

Level 2: Conventional Moral Thought.   Living up to the expectations of one's family, group, or nation is seen as valuable in its own right regardless of immediate consequences. Concern exists not only for conforming to the existing social order but also for maintaining and supporting it.

Stage 3: The interpersonal concordance orientation ("good boy"–"good girl"). Good behavior is what pleases or helps others. Conforming to stereotyped images of what is good behavior, a child might say, "It's not nice to take things from other people." Or a parent might ask a 17-year-old, "What will your relatives think if they see you in that civil rights demonstration?" In either case moral decisions are based on conforming to social norms, without any real thinking on the individual's part.

Stage 4: The orientation toward authority and maintaining the social order ("law and order"). Moral behavior involves doing one's duty, obeying rules and laws, and respecting authority. Laws are viewed as fixed and unchanging, and the social order is seen as worth maintaining for its own sake. At Stage 4 a person might say, "Just because you disagree with a law doesn't give you the right to break it. What would happen if everyone did that?"

Level 3: Postconventional Moral Thought.   At this level there is an effort to define moral principles that have universal validity apart from the people holding them, and the individual's identification with those people.

Stage 5: The social-contract orientation. Right action at this stage is viewed in terms of general standards that have been agreed upon by the whole society. Other than what is constitutionally and democratically agreed upon, right or wrong is relative and a matter of personal values. Laws have been developed as a part of a social contract to which people agree for the common good, but which are always subject to change. This level of morality is the "official" morality of the U.S. government, as expressed in the Constitution.

Stage 6: The universal-ethical principle orientation. What is right according to an individual is defined by his or her conscience and is judged in relation to abstract, self-chosen ethical principles seen as universals. Such principles as the golden rule, a respect for the worth and dignity of all people, justice, and equality of human rights are examples. Martin Luther King's challenging of "unjust" laws that discriminated against blacks and his willingness to go to jail for his beliefs illustrate Stage 6 moral behavior. Another example is a conscientious objector's readiness to accept a prison sentence rather than be drafted to fight in a war. In both of these instances, laws are recognized as necessary for the common good but always subject to the dictates of one's conscience and higher ethical principles.

Implications of Kohlberg's Theory for Teaching

Through his research with children and adults, Kohlberg has given us a new picture of the process of moral growth. He sees the capacity for higher level moral thinking as developing as a person matures. The research stimulated by Kohlberg's theory suggests that moral development is an unvarying and universal process. In other words, the movement from lower level moral thinking to the higher levels always proceeds from preconventional, through conventional, to postconventional thought, with the process being the same for all cultures (Turiel, 1973). Until approximately age 9, most of a child's moral decisions are made at the preconventional level of thinking— Stages 1 and 2. Between ages 9 and 15, the typical child becomes more capable of Stage 3 and 4 decisions. Finally, beyond age 16 the child is increasingly able to operate at the postconventional level, making decisions based upon Stage 5 and Stage 6 thinking.

Although the potential for higher level moral thinking increases with a person's cognitive growth, Kohlberg has found that many adults do not get beyond the third and fourth stages. For such people most moral decisions grow out of their assessments of what others will accept ("What will the neighbors think?") or out of a rigid interpretation of rules, laws, and ways of responding to authority ("He's the boss and knows. You'd better do what he says.") This suggests that unless people have a chance to discuss with others how moral decisions are made, and thus evaluate their own moral thinking, they will probably not get to the highest levels. Recently Kohlberg and a number of his colleagues have become very interested in the implications of their research for schools. They would like to create programs designed to stimulate moral growth through social interaction and they want the programs to recognize the limits of stimulation imposed by the students' level of development.

It is now becoming clear why many of the old approaches used by schools to promote moral development (character building, as they were often called) through "preaching" at children and punishing them for infractions don't really work. First of all, they don't take into account the children's level of development and thus are usually over their heads. The children don't understand the "moral" or message because it is too abstract. Moreover, when they are always told by others how to behave, what is right and wrong, etc., children don't have to develop their own thinking processes. Therefore, if schools are to aid in promoting moral growth, opportunities for thinking about and discussing moral issues and making one's own moral decisions

Stage 6.

Yes—"The right of a human being to live transcends all human laws regarding property rights. While stealing certainly violates the rights of others, if there is no alternative for saving his wife's life, the man should steal the drug and face the consequences."

No—"Ultimately the man's decision must be consonant with his own moral principles. If, after weighing all the arguments pro and con, he felt that stealing the drug would violate not only the social contract but his own higher standards, then he would be right in not stealing the drug."

Some psychologists interested in moral development have commented on the Watergate scandal that led to the resignation of President Richard Nixon in 1974. They say that the moral behavior of many members of Nixon's Committee to Re-Elect the President (and indeed Nixon's own behavior) was at Stage 2—"Look out for yourself; the end justifies the means." The justification many of the young C.R.E.P. members gave for going along with the practices that were later found illegal was at Stage 3 or 4—"I had to do what I was told by my superiors."

Some social critics and educators have said that because so many well-educated adults don't operate at Stages 5 and 6, schools should develop programs in moral education. What do you think?

Some examples of moral dilemmas teachers could use for promoting higher level reasoning are given below:

Classroom problems:

Harry hit John for teasing him. Is John justified in hitting him back? Why or why not?

Bill sees Mary cheating on a math test. Should he report her? Why or why not?

Current events:

It is against the law in your city for teachers to strike. A local teachers' union organizes a strike to force a school district to hire more teachers and thus reduce class size. Should the chief of police order the arrest of all striking teachers? Why or why not?

Many good ideas for moral dilemmas to use with elementary, junior high, and high school students are presented in Beverly Mattox's Getting It Together *(1975).*

must begin in the early years of elementary school and continue through high school.

Between the ages of 9 and 12 children seem ready to move from Stage 1 and Stage 2 thinking to Stages 3 and 4 and, in a few cases, Stage 5. Teachers can respond to this readiness by bringing in appropriate newspaper articles, helping students explore the moral questions raised in their reading, and, most directly, by having the students analyze and decide upon ways of resolving the moral problems that occur in their day-to-day interactions in school. According to Kohlberg, the goal should always be to recognize each child's level of development and then try to stimulate thinking one stage above it. (Kohlberg believes that there are limits imposed on children's moral reasoning by their stage of development. A teacher should not expect a student or group to be able to reason at more than one stage beyond their level of development.) Young people should be given a chance to think and reach their own solutions to problems, with the teacher resisting the temptation to preach and moralize. The more practice children have in this process, the more effectively they will be able to employ moral thinking in the future.

Conclusions

This chapter has focused upon the process of social–emotional growth and its implications for facilitating learning. We chose to examine the theories of Erik Erikson and Lawrence Kohlberg because they integrate many concepts of development and research results; at the same time they lend themselves to a diagnostic approach to teaching. The essence of such a diagnostic approach is that it seeks to understand the learner before making any prescriptions for teaching.

Erik Erikson's view of life as a continuous process of development through eight major stages beginning with infancy and ending with old age is helpful in understanding the constant interplay between the growing individual and the social environment. As crises occur and are resolved positively at each of the major stages of life, the healthy individual develops personality characteristics such as trust, initiative, or a sense of identity that will help in coping with new experiences. On the other hand, when life crises are resolved unsatisfactorily, the individual develops such characteristics as shame or inferiority and is likely to be defensive in confronting new situations. The teacher who is aware of the crises most children confront as they develop, and the psychological and social factors influencing those crises, will undoubtedly be able to work more effectively with children. Teachers also can use Erikson's view of adult development to understand their own developmental level and help their relationships with students.

While Erikson's theory provides a broad view of many aspects of development, Lawrence Kohlberg has focused his attention particularly on moral development. Kohlberg sees moral development as proceeding through three levels, each of which is made up of two stages: preconventional—simply looking out for oneself; conventional—recognizing and conforming to the norms of one's group and community; and postconventional—being guided by a set of moral principles (a philosophy of life) that includes but transcends concern for the social order. Like Erikson's, Kohlberg's thinking encourages us to view development as a process of unfolding and maturing, in which experiences determine the extent to which growth potential is realized. The implications for teachers and other facilitators of growth are clear: Diagnose the student's level of development and create circumstances that will encourage taking the next step.

Some Good Books

Erikson, Erik. *Childhood and Society*. 2nd ed. New York: Norton, 1963. This is Erikson's major statement on psychosocial development. It provides an excellent discussion of the "Eight Ages of Man" and suggests how Erikson's psychological perspectives can be applied in the study of different cultures and historical developments.

Erikson, Erik. *Life History and the Historical Moment*. New York: Norton, 1975. A collection of nine essays written by Erikson from the 1950s to the 1970s. These essays examine the cultural and political upheavals of this period through Erikson's psychological concepts. Particularly interesting is an autobiographical essay that explores Erikson's own identity crisis.

Evans, Richard I. *Dialogue with Erik Erikson*. New York: Harper & Row, 1967. In this conversational dialogue with Erikson, Evans gives the reader not only a great deal of insight into Erikson's thinking but a portrait of him as a person.

Freud, Sigmund. *An Outline of Psychoanalysis*. New York: Norton, 1949. Freud's last book, this is a concise, easy to understand summary of the major concepts of psychoanalytic theory.

Kimmel, D. C. *Adulthood and Aging: An Interdisciplinary, Developmental View*. New York: Wiley, 1974. This book explores the psychology of adult development. Topics include identity and intimacy, work/retirement/leisure, families, and dying.

Lowenthal, M. F., M. Thurnher, and D. Chiriboga. *Four Stages of Life: A Comparative Study of Women and Men Facing Transitions*. San Francisco: Jossey-Bass, 1975. This study presents the results of interviews and questionnaires given to 216 people facing transitions—high school seniors, newlyweds, middle-aged parents, and pre-retirees.

Lyon, Harold. *Learning to Feel—Feeling to Learn*. Columbus, Ohio: Merrill, 1971. This book provides a rationale and a variety of suggestions for humanistic teaching that take into account students' social–emotional needs.

Raths, Louis E., Merrill Harmin, and Sidney Simon. *Values and Teaching*. Columbus, Ohio: Merrill, 1966. In contrast with Kohlberg's thinking regarding moral development, Raths, Harmin, and Simon present a theory of valuing designed to help teachers and other growth facilitators understand the process of valuing and ways of promoting "values clarification."

Sheehy, Gail. *Passages: Predictable Crises of Adult Life.* New York: Dutton, 1976. This is probably the best integration of current thought on the stages of adult development. Because of its readable style and its interest to great numbers of adults, it became a best-seller almost as soon as it was published.

Articles, Studies, and Other References

Elkind, David. "Erik Erikson's Eight Ages of Man." In R. F. Biehler, *Psychology Applied to Teaching: Selected Readings.* Boston: Houghton Mifflin, 1972, pp. 120–137. A brief overview of Erikson's theory, with ample explanation of its connections with Freudian psychoanalytic theory.

Gould, Roger. "Adult Life Stages: Growth toward Self-Tolerance." *Psychology Today* 8(1975): 74–78. Through his research on a sample of 524 men and women, Gould has identified important psychological changes that seem to indicate stages of adult development as people move from their twenties to their fifties.

Kohlberg, L. "The Cognitive–Developmental Approach to Moral Education." *Phi Delta Kappan* 56 (1975): 670–677. Here Kohlberg outlines and explains his views on cognitive development and their implications for promoting moral education.

Maier, Henry W. *Three Theories of Child Development.* Rev. ed. New York: Harper & Row, 1969. Chapter 2 of this book provides a comprehensive picture of Erikson's views on development. Especially valuable are the comparisons with the theories of Piaget and Sears.

Rest, James. "Developmental Psychology as a Guide to Value Education: A Review of Kohlbergian Programs." *Review of Educational Research* 44 (1974): 241–259. An excellent review of educational programs designed to promote moral education. Rest also makes some suggestions for further steps in the design of such Kohlbergian educational approaches.

Sprinthall, Richard C. and Norman A. Sprinthall. "Moral Education." In Sprinthall and Sprinthall, *Educational Psychology: A Developmental Approach.* Reading, Mass.: Addison-Wesley, 1974, ch. 9. This chapter provides a fine overview of Kohlberg's theory of moral development, its implications for teaching, and some of the most recent research.

Turiel, Elliot. "Stage Transitions in Moral Development." In R. M. W. Travers (ed.), *Second Handbook of Research on Teaching.* Chicago: Rand McNally, 1973, pp. 732–758. Turiel, a colleague of Kohlberg's, presents a synthesis of recent research on the process of movement through the different stages of Kohlberg's theory. Important implications can be drawn for fostering moral development.

Suggestions for Action-Oriented Learning

1. Interview the members of your family (parents, grandparents, high school–aged siblings, etc.), asking what are the best things and the worst things about being the age they are now. Compare and contrast their responses with your responses for your stage of development.

2. Volunteer to work a couple of hours a week in an old-age home and keep a log of your thoughts and feelings. Share your experiences with other students in your class.

3. Return to your old junior high school and spend a day watching the behavior of students both during and between classes. Note such things as differences in size and physical development of students, cliques, boy–girl relationships, clothing styles, things being discussed, etc. Then relate your observations to Erikson's views on identity and discuss them with other members of your class.

4. With another member of your class, visit a kindergarten or nursery school and observe the children. Notice what they are doing, how they relate to each other and the teacher, their emotional behavior, etc. Think about the stage of development they have recently left—the toddler stage—and the stage they are moving toward—the elementary schooler—as you reflect on their current level of development. After leaving the school compare your observations with those of your classmate.

5. Make copies of Kohlberg's moral dilemma as it is presented in this chapter and give them to a variety of people you know. Ask them to explain what the man whose wife is dying of cancer should do. After noting their responses, use Kohlberg's theory to try to determine their level of moral development.

7
Individual Differences

Are people basically the same? Or are people quite different from one another? The answers to these questions have been debated for centuries by ordinary people as well as by philosophers, psychologists, theologians, and others concerned with human nature and behavior. We believe that the answer to both of these questions is *yes*.

In Chapters 5 and 6 we explained some of the characteristics that people share. Although we are all very much like each other, we are each unique. We look like others, yet there is no one that we look exactly like. We think as others do, but our intellectual abilities and experiences lead us to different ideas. We pass through the same developmental stages as others do, yet some of us develop more quickly and others more slowly. We are able to feel what others feel because we have had similar experiences, but we can't help interpreting their feelings through our own experiences. We all have abilities, weaknesses, interests, and needs, yet no one shares our unique pattern of these qualities. In short, we are both the same as others and very different.

If a society is to function effectively, it must see the characteristics that people share and help them learn to live and work together. However, without recognizing and utilizing the unique contributions of each individual, no group can function for long. Similarly, in the classroom students of a particular age have many things in common, but they differ greatly in family background, intelligence, interests, personal characteristics, social maturity, etc. One of the things that makes teaching so difficult is that teachers must recognize what the students have in common and help them learn to work together, and, at the same time, accept differences among students and encourage each student toward self-actualization. This chapter will address itself to individual differences. Our goal is to help you see each individual as a total person with unique needs, abilities, and interests.

Special Education

The field of special education, probably more than any other area of public school education, has emphasized an individualized approach to education. Traditionally, special education teachers have taught children who were too "different" from other children to learn effectively in regular classes or schools. For years, the handicapped have been kept "out of sight and out of mind"—families hid their disabled children from sight. Few agencies developed appropriate services. Later, special agencies were developed for the blind, the physically handicapped, those with cerebral palsy, etc. These agencies were designed to help their clients to reach their full potential, but often they failed. In the 1960s and 1970s, the physically disabled began to compare their situation to that of blacks and other minorities. They came to believe that, at least in many cases, whatever gains could be achieved through special education could not make up for the deprivation caused by being segregated from "normal" students.

Throughout the United States today there is a trend toward "mainstreaming" children with special problems (blindness, deafness, other physical handicaps, emotional disturbances) back into regular classes. The theory behind this practice is that although these students need special attention, they will benefit from going to a school with "normal" children. However, such a movement places more of a burden on classroom teachers to respond to children as individuals.

What do you think would be the advantages and disadvantages for a blind child who attends a regular public school?

Sometimes teachers are extremely aware of handicapped students' potential and do their best to help them realize it, but they may struggle against negative parental or administrative attitudes. The very limited financial commitment that society has made to the handicapped also adds to their problems because of the difficulty in obtaining transportation and gaining access to buildings. With new federal laws being passed in Washington, this situation is finally beginning to change.

Further, many physically handicapped students found that they suffered by not learning effective social relationships as well as by inferior education.

More and more, we have come to realize that the limitations placed upon the handicapped are strongly related to the attitudes of those who help and teach them. An inability to move without a wheelchair, problems in speech, or visual difficulty are real handicaps, but these difficulties are surmountable. When teachers and other helping personnel have low expectations for their handicapped students, then students may accept these limited expectations and become less than they might otherwise be. A skilled teacher is aware of the physical limitations a disability imposes but helps students to move as far as they can toward a full and productive life.

Look for a moment at the photographs above. The only difference between the handicapped boy sitting outdoors in his wheelchair, alone and isolated, and the girl playing catch from her wheelchair is that she did not accept the wheelchair as a limitation. This attitude maximizes human potential. It accepts individual differences as real but then says, "Where do we go from here?"

The trend to bring the "different" back into society at large—whether they be physically handicapped, mentally retarded, or emotionally disturbed—has developed in the 1970s. Sometimes it is not possible to "mainstream" people completely, either because they lack necessary skills to function in an open society, or because there appear to be insurmountable limitations. For example, a blind child may need to master Braille or the use of tape recorders. The blind must even be taught to turn toward people who are speaking with them in order to put the sighted at ease. Where that training is started at a

young age, people can often be mainstreamed into regular elementary school classes.

On the other hand, people may be sufficiently mentally retarded that they cannot master living independently and holding down a job. Years ago such people would be confined to a large institution, perhaps containing thousands of people similarly afflicted. It has been shown that such treatment is frequently custodial at best, and often downright destructive. Today in some communities such people might be placed in a group home with perhaps six or seven other retardates, and a house mother and father who help the residents with daily living arrangements. It has been found that the same person who vegetated in an institutional setting can work in a sheltered workshop and live a much more productive and happy life in a group home.

The point at which it may be necessary to exclude a child from a "normal" class is imprecise. Often a judgment is made in behalf of a student that may not serve the student's best interests. For example, parents of a child confined to a wheelchair may be advised by the school district to place her in a special school. While the school officials may believe that they are acting in the child's best interests, they may be less aware of their own fear of facing some of the problems that a wheelchair poses, such as transportation, the need to build ramps or install elevators for accessibility, insurance problems, and the like. They may also fear that teachers will be unable to handle the special problems that the handicapped pose. Clearly, there may be a conflict of interest here between the rights of the child and the perceived needs of the school. The school may have a blanket policy toward the physically handicapped that ignores individual differences

A sheltered workshop is a working environment in which handicapped individuals are employed. People do jobs they are capable of, but with plenty of guidance and supervision.

Recent federal legislation gives the parents of the handicapped the right to choose their child's form of schooling. It is expected that such legislation will further the move toward mainstreaming.

such as emotional stability and stamina and thus groups all the handicapped under one label.

Labels are necessary but dangerous educational tools. The greatest danger is that a label may prevent us from perceiving a person as an individual. Most teachers have had the experience of being told "Watch out for Johnny—he's a real troublemaker," only to find that under their guidance Johnny becomes a valued member of the class. A student may be irrevocably typed with the label *underachiever, troublemaker, slow,* and the like.

Learning Disabilities

Sometimes labels seem extremely precise and "scientific," but in fact may add to the confusion rather than clarify it. In the 1970s, there has been an increasing interest in the field generally known as *learning disabilities.* Among the terms in common use are *hyperkinesis, hyperactivity, dyslexia, minimal brain dysfunction, visual–motor weakness,* and the like. All of these terms are designed to describe conditions that may prevent appropriate learning in children who appear to be of normal intelligence. The terms seem quite official and forbidding. Because they sound so precise, you may feel that they describe very specific disorders that have particular causes and should be treated in particular ways. *Dyslexia,* for example, is derived from the Greek *dys,* meaning difficult or defective, and *lexia,* meaning pertaining to words—in other words, difficulty in reading. Dyslexic children have difficulty discriminating among letters that have similarities in shape, such as *b* and *d* or *n* and *u.* They may also reverse words, such as *saw* and *was.* Some dyslexic children have difficulty making auditory discriminations; *pat* and *pot* may be indistinguishable for such a child. A number of hypotheses have been put forward to explain reading difficulty. Some experts, like Naomi Zigmond (1968) hold that auditory discrimination problems may underlie all dyslexia. Zigmond says that children first have difficulty in sorting out what they hear, and this is later reflected in reading and spelling errors.

No one knows for sure, however, whether reading problems are developmental or learned. It is possible, for example, that all children go through some difficulty in discriminating similar shapes. Perhaps some children do not get sufficient discriminatory training, or have not yet developed good enough eye–hand coordination or other skills when they first learn reading. In any event, today the term *dyslexia* is more a description of a particular problem than a statement of cause.

There seems little doubt, however, that some students do suffer letter-reversal problems that impede their educational careers. Often a sensitive teacher will spot such a child in the first or second grade. Sometimes the discovery is not made until well along in the students' career, even as late as high school or college. Once the observation is made, the teacher should seek the help of a specialist, such as the school psychologist or reading specialist, to help develop special activities for the student, to refer her for outside assistance, or both.

Hyperkinesis (or *hyperkinetic*) is another label we often hear to-

Two good basic texts that give an overall picture of learning disabilities are Johnson and Myklebust, Learning Disabilities *(1967), and Lerner,* Children with Learning Disabilities *(1975).*

day. It is used to describe children who are unable to sit still, are very easily distracted, and are often clumsy in gait. It usually means *moving around too much*. Here again, the label may suggest that we understand why the child is overactive. In truth, we have many hypotheses and no single answer. Among the theories are something wrong with the brain, nutritional problems, anxiety, or hyperactivity to hide depression. Recently physicians have become involved in the treatment of hyperactivity and have discovered that medications such as Ritalin, which acts as an energizer for adults, seem to quiet some hyperactive youngsters. However, some authorities feel that it is questionable to prescribe a drug when we do not fully understand how or why it works or whether it is essential. Another problem is that it may teach children that chemicals can solve their problems—a dangerous precedent in an age where so many people have come to believe that drugs are a way out of emotional difficulties. Once again, the teacher who observes hyperactive behavior would do well to work with other school personnel, such as the psychologist, nurse, social worker, and school physician, to try to define the problem carefully and prescribe a course of action.

Unfortunately, there is also the real possibility that some children are being "diagnosed" as hyperactive when they are reacting normally to oppressive classroom conditions. In these cases the problem may be the teacher whose expectations are out of line with the child's capabilities.

Individual Differences

While specialists can help teachers work more effectively with individual children, the primary responsibility for each child's learning remains with the classroom teacher. No two children are exactly alike. Even children who are the same age, who live in the same community, and who have been homogeneously grouped—placed in a particular class because their abilities are similar—will differ greatly. Consequently, if all students in a classroom are to learn, the teacher must try to respond to each student's unique pattern of strengths, weaknesses, needs, interests, and background. Developing such an individualized perspective and creating appropriate learning activities for each student is not easy. Yet there are always some teachers who manage to gear their instruction to individuals no matter how large their classes. These teachers are continually observing their students in order to obtain clues that will give them further insight into each child.

Have you ever known anyone who had normal intelligence but had real difficulties learning? How responsive was the school to that person's learning difficulties?

Some important categories of individual differences that any teacher can note and use in planning learning activities for children are intelligence or general intellectual ability, achievement, physical characteristics, stage of development, personality characteristics, social relationships, family and community background, and learning style. In the following paragraphs we will briefly explore each of these areas and its implications for teaching. Let's begin with intelligence and general intellectual ability.

How many classes in your years of schooling have you encountered where the teacher tried to gear the instruction to students as individuals?

How did you feel toward the teachers in those classes?

How effective were they in helping you to learn the subject?

Intelligence

For a long time schools have recognized that children differ greatly in their intelligence or general intellectual ability. Some children seem to be able to grasp ideas easily and to solve a variety of types of problems that other children the same age have great difficulty with. Simply by noting how students perform on tests, how they solve problems, and how they are able to apply their learning to new situations, teachers can make some good guesses about students' intelligence. In addition, when they have questions about an individual's intellectual potential, they can examine I.Q. (Intelligence Quotient) test scores and other measures of general ability recorded in the child's school records. We are not advocating "labeling" children by their I.Q. score. Rather, when problems arise teachers ought to check their own hunches against such scores and then adapt their teaching to students' intellectual needs.

It is important to remember that a standardized test may be a very inaccurate measure of a student's real potential. Where skilled teachers sense a discrepancy between their perceptions and reported information, they will observe more closely. They may discover that an apparently slow student is merely shy or uncertain, and that, questioned in privacy, the student shows good understanding. Such a student often tests poorly, perhaps because of a high test anxiety. Later in this chapter we will show how teachers and school psychologists can work together to develop a clearer picture of students and to develop better strategies to reach them. In Chapter 8 we will provide you with a more detailed picture of what intelligence is and the use and abuse of I.Q. scores by individual teachers and school systems.

Achievement

Another area teachers can draw upon in relating instruction to individuals is achievement. When they find a student isn't doing well in their course, good teachers try to learn about the student's past performance in that area. Questioning a student is one way of learning about the student's strengths and weaknesses. Another way is looking at previous grades and scores on standardized achievement tests. Talking with the student's previous teachers is yet another means of gaining insight into the student's problems. While, again, there are dangers of stereotyping if teachers are not careful, it is possible that such an exploration of the student's previous achievement may uncover reasons for difficulty and suggest new instructional approaches.

Physical characteristics very much affect a student's learning in school. It's important that teachers be on the lookout for serious physical problems that interfere with learning. Problems in seeing, hearing, speaking, eye–hand coordination, all show up in students' work. If teachers continually evaluate students' work and observe their classroom behavior, they are more likely to recognize such problems and can refer a student to a specialist for help. With students who have more serious physical handicaps, teachers must often adapt their teaching behavior and allow students to learn in alternative ways. For example, teachers may have to look directly at students with a serious hearing loss so that they can lip-read. Or they may have to give the students special written instructions for classwork. Even such

Unfortunately, students sometimes develop a "reputation" as word of their successes or failures is passed along from teacher to teacher. Effective teachers are conscious of the dangers of such stereotyping. They always question other people's opinions of their students and use their own method of diagnosis.

Did you have a reputation when you were in high school? If you did, how did it affect your learning?

physical characteristics as being tall or short, thin or fat, an early maturer or a late maturer, etc., can influence learning by affecting the way students feel about themselves. In short, teachers need to be sensitive to students' feelings about their bodies as well as to their actual physical capabilities.

Other Personal Differences

Awareness of the stages of development, personality characteristics, and social relationships of individual students contributes to more effective teaching. While the students in a class may be of approximately the same age, there will always be differences among them in stages of development. Some will be more mature than others, some will be able to do motor activities that others find difficult, and some will be further along in ability to think abstractly or work independently. Some students will be shy, some outgoing, anxious, aggressive, highly motivated, etc. By getting to know students individually, teachers can better understand the impact of these qualities on their school performance and then structure the learning experience accordingly. For example, shy students may need a great deal of encouragement and reassurance to help them learn to express ideas before the whole class, while more outgoing students may need to be pushed to listen to the views of others.

An especially effective way to establish a close working relationship with individual students is to know their interests. This not only makes the children feel that their teacher cares about them as people, it also gives the teacher additional insight in making learning experiences relevant to each child's life. For example, a third-grade teacher who knows a child is interested in dogs might have him select a library book on dogs when the class does independent reading. Or a high school English teacher who knows that a student plays on the tennis team might encourage her to center her composition on some aspect of tennis.

Family and community background have important effects on learning, too. The more sensitive teachers are about their students' background, the better they can understand the students' educational needs. A family's socioeconomic status, religious orientation, and ethnic background all have effects on the way children are raised and on their view of school. Even the number of children in the family, the child's place in the birth order, the marital relationship between the parents, and the type of home a child lives in (both its location and its "emotional atmosphere") are significant. Teachers must continually try to understand each student's situation even though their own family and community backgrounds may differ dramatically. Developing and maintaining this sensitivity is difficult, as is well illustrated by the frustrations of many middle-class teachers as they work with students from economically disadvantaged backgrounds, whose language, values, views about education, and lifestyle conflict with their own.

A final area of individual difference that is only beginning to be explored systematically is *learning style.* Researchers and educators

Have you ever had a physical problem that affected your learning? If so, how did your teachers respond to you, given that physical condition? How did you feel about their response?

If you were a teacher, what would you do to learn about the interests of students in your class? How might you relate the interests of your students to the curriculum?

What types of problems might teachers encounter if they taught in a community that was very different from the community in which they grew up? Try to imagine what it would be like being a:

White teacher in a mostly black school.

Black teacher in a white school.

Middle-class teacher in a very rich community.

Jewish teacher teaching mostly Protestant children in a small Southern town.

Teacher in an urban community with a great variety of religious, ethnic, and social-class backgrounds.

propose that people differ greatly in the ways they learn most effectively. If this is true, then children will probably learn best when their teachers use the approach that matches their learning styles. Psychologists call this area of emerging research *Aptitude Treatment Interaction (ATI)*. The research (Cronbach and Snow, 1975) on ATI seems to show that students who possess a high level of a given characteristic (aptitude) learn better when taught by one method (treatment), while students with a low level of the characteristic learn better with a different teaching approach. ATI researchers are currently studying two types of characteristics in their concern for improved understanding of differences in learning style: learning modality and field independence–field dependence.

How do you learn best?

Learning Modality.   This refers to the way a person takes in information and learns best. Some people seem to learn best through vision, others through hearing, and still others kinesthetically— through their whole bodies. For example, a visual learner may need to see something or read it before really understanding it, whereas an auditory learner may learn easily while listening to a lecture or a tape recording. By knowing the students we teach, we can use their individual learning modalities to help them much the way a teacher uses a blind child's sense of hearing and touch or a deaf child's capacity to "see" language through lip-reading.

Field Independence–Field Dependence.   It has been demonstrated that some people are better able than others to perceive items as discrete from their backgrounds; this characteristic is called *field independence*. Others seem to perceive information more wholistically and have difficulty separating items or elements of information from the context in which they occur; this is called *field dependence*. Field-independent people seem better able to think analytically and solve mathematical and scientific problems and are likely to enter careers in technical areas. Field-dependent people tend to be much more aware of their surroundings and have trouble focusing in on specific details; they move toward people-oriented careers such as teaching, counseling, sales, etc. Teachers who are aware of such differences in the ways students perceive things can adapt their teaching accordingly. For example, students who tend to be field-dependent might find group problem solving in mathematics helpful. On the other hand, students who tend to be field-independent might need more opportunities for independent study.

On the basis of the descriptions of field dependence and field independence, how would you characterize yourself? How does your field dependence or field independence affect your learning?

Research on aptitude treatment interaction shows a great deal of promise for improving education. People differ in many other areas besides learning modality and field independence–field dependence. Some people are impulsive, giving out many answers to problems in a short time; others are reflective, solving problems slowly and cautiously. Some people need a great deal of structure in order to learn, while others do best with minimal structure and freedom to do things their own ways. Our emerging knowledge of individual differences suggests that rather than one best method of teaching for all students, there may be many "bests," depending on the student.

If you would like to read further on this subject, an excellent article is David Hunt's "Learning Styles and Teaching Strategies" (1974).

In the following section we will acquaint you with one approach to dealing with individual differences—the *psychodiagnostic* approach. This approach, which involves careful observation and testing of a child by a school psychologist, can provide teachers with a great deal of help in understanding the child's strengths, weaknesses, and educational needs.

The Psychodiagnostic Approach

Good teachers recognize differences between individuals and are always informally diagnosing and prescribing for their students. Each time teachers try another approach, such as moving from the symbolic to the iconic level, they are presuming that, at least for the present, that mode may better fit the student's needs. Sometimes such informal diagnoses involve the student's concept of himself as a student. For example, a teacher might think, "Johnny is so discouraged about his math. I am going to try to bring him down a level or two so I can give him more successful experiences. But I'd better be careful that I don't discourage him further by making him feel he's been demoted."

Probably most such problems are handled well by an experienced teacher, but sometimes even the best teachers are stumped. Where can such a teacher turn? One possibility is to consult with members of the pupil personnel services department of the school. In most U.S. schools today, there is a team of nonteaching personnel who are concerned with the physical and mental health of students. This team may include the school nurse, attendance officer, speech therapist, school counselor, school psychologist, and a physician and dentist who consult with the team as needed. Some schools also include a social worker, a drug and alcohol abuse counselor, a learning disabilities teacher, and other related personnel. Such a team can be most helpful in enabling teachers to devise new strategies when they are having difficulty reaching a particular student.

For example, a teacher might observe some physical problem, such as a student's squinting to read or evidencing some difficulty in hearing. The teacher would probably turn to the school nurse to check out the source of difficulty. The nurse, in turn, might refer the child to the school physician. On the other hand, the apparent visual or auditory difficulty might turn out on examination to have no physical root. In that case, the nurse might well request the teacher to observe further. Could it be that the child is experiencing some anxiety about school work and that this is the cause of the squint? At this point the school counselor might be called to talk with the student. The counselor might suggest that the child be seen by the school psychologist for a series of diagnostic tests.

Sometimes the teacher may turn directly to the school counselor or school psychologist. For example, let's consider the case of Eliezer Cohen, a 12-year-old sixth grader in Mrs. O'Brien's class. Mrs. O'Brien

Most school districts employ a staff of school psychologists. These professionals usually possess at least a master's degree and frequently a doctoral degree. Generally, their job is to do all types of testing of children with special problems, some psychological counseling, and consulting with teachers, parents, and administrators to improve the teaching–learning process. Usually school psychologists have offices in the school district office where they see people who are referred to them. They also frequently travel from school to school to work with individual students and staff members.

Such a team approach can be invaluable in helping individual children. Unfortunately, such services are expensive, and in many areas these auxiliary personnel are the first to lose jobs in times of financial difficulties. Moreover, many schools in the United States still see a child's mental and physical health and individual needs as a secondary, not primary, concern of the school.

Counselors and school psychologists are important team members in any school.

An I.Q. score of 110 is considered slightly above average. You will learn more about the meaning of I.Q. scores in the next chapter. A group-administered test is one given to a large number of students at the same time. Students read questions and answer them on a machine-scorable answer sheet.

checked Eliezer's school records to find out why he was experiencing difficulty in the sixth grade even though he had repeated fifth grade a year earlier. When she consulted his records, she found that he had an I.Q. of 110 on a group-administered I.Q. test. Mrs. O'Brien concluded that he was an underachiever who was not working up to his potential, and she decided to push him harder.

Three months later Eliezer is not doing at all well. After discussing the matter, both Mrs. O'Brien and Eliezer's counselor agree that a consultation with the school psychologist would be in order. The psychologist, Dr. Rampullo, suggests that the teacher inform both the child and his parents that she is concerned, and that Dr. Rampullo may wish to see Eliezer at some future time. Meanwhile, Mrs. O'Brien is asked to observe Eliezer carefully during the next two weeks, so that if the psychologist decides to see Eliezer, she will have a clear picture of how he appears to Mrs. O'Brien. In this way Dr. Rampullo can tailor her examination to clarify the teacher's questions.

After two weeks Mrs. O'Brien sends the following note to the psychologist:

> I have been concerned with Eliezer's work all year. I knew he had repeated fifth grade last year, and he is now having difficulty in sixth grade. I checked his records and found that he had an I.Q. of 110. He does consistent low—C, D, or F—work. Because his I.Q. places him slightly above average, I felt that he was underachieving, and decided to push him harder. At first he seemed to be responding, especially in math, but soon he fell even further behind. Furthermore, he became unruly and disruptive in class. I had to send him to the office several times because he wandered around the room and provoked other students. As you suggested, I spoke with his parents. They seemed surprised to hear that he was unruly, and told me that he was exceptionally well-behaved at

home. They, too, were concerned with his poor school work, and also felt he could do better. They were pleased with the idea of his seeing you. Eliezer himself seems interested, but a bit apprehensive. I hope you will be able to see him soon.

Sincerely,

Mrs. J. O'Brien

Mrs. J. O'Brien

On the basis of Mrs. O'Brien's descriptions of Eliezer and his school behavior, what questions would you want to answer if you were the school psychologist?

On the basis of Mrs. O'Brien's note, Dr. Rampullo puts together a battery of tests, some individually administered and some paper-and-pencil tests. Of course, she will spend some time interviewing Eliezer in order to "loosen him up" and get a feel for what sort of youngster he is before she does any formal testing. She writes her first impressions:

Eliezer is a pleasant-looking, rather well-built 12-year-old boy. He is small for his age, so that he looks like the average sixth-grade boy, although chronologically he should be a seventh grader. He was quite polite with me, but seemed a bit standoffish. I asked him how he felt about his school work and he began to cry. He told me he felt stupid, and that "kids always tease me about being left back." I told him we would try to find out why he was having so much trouble, and figure out a way to help him out of it. He dried his tears, and then was most cooperative through the testing.

Dr. Rampullo administers the tests shown in Table 7–1. Some of the tests are reported in terms of scores (the WISC and the WRAT),

Table 7–1. Battery of Formal Tests

Test	Description	Purpose
Wechsler Intelligence Scale for Children (WISC)	Individually administered, yields three scores: Verbal I.Q., Performance I.Q., and Full-Scale I.Q. Broken down into 11 subtests, including general information, basic arithmetic, vocabulary, picture completions, object assembly, etc.	Tester can observe how the child functions in the testing situation so that she gets not only quantitative scores, but a wealth of qualitative information. This test will help to describe the child's intellectual strengths and weaknesses, and suggest hypotheses about the interaction of emotions and intellect.
Thematic Apperception Test (TAT)	Child makes up stories based on pictures. The pictures are ambiguous, and the child's story helps the psychologist make inferences about the child's feelings.	To help the psychologist get a sense of the student's inner world; depression, anger, motivation to succeed or fail can be determined in part by the TAT.
Bender-Gestalt	Child copies a set of simple geometric shapes.	Helps determine whether the student is having a problem in processing visual information or in reproducing what he sees.
Wide-Range Achievement Test (WRAT)	Achievement test yielding grade-level scores for reading, spelling, and mathematics	Shows academic achievement. Often differs somewhat from school grades.

but in each test the psychologist always looks not only at the scores but at how the child achieved them. In this way she can produce a clear statement about the child, showing how his feelings about himself relate to his level of performance. Even in the intelligence test, she begins to notice many things that were not evident in the group intelligence test. Let's begin by looking at the results of Eliezer's WISC test, shown in Table 7–2.

A word about the numerical scoring of the WISC. WISC scores are based on the comparison of the individual's scores with those of others his age. An average WISC total score would be around 100;

Table 7–2. Wechsler Intelligence Scale for Children (WISC)

Verbal I.Q. <u>99</u>

Performance I.Q. <u>97</u>

Full-Scale I.Q. <u>98</u>

Verbal Subtests*	Subtest Score	Brief Description
Information	8	General information acquired in our culture
Comprehension	12	Common sense
Arithmetic	7	Numerical skills and simple problem solving
Similarities	13	Seeing class relationships
Vocabulary	9	Word meanings
(Digit span, not included in total score)	(6) ── 49	Short-term memory; indicates possibility of anxiety

Performance Subtests*	Subtest Score	Brief Description
Picture completion	15	Pointing to missing part of picture
Coding	8	Learning and using new symbols
Picture arrangement	7	Putting out-of-place cartoons in sequence
Block design	10	Seeing and replicating abstract patterns
Object assembly	8 ── 48	Jigsaw type puzzles

* Subtests are sets of test items that measure different types of activities assumed to make up intelligence. On the WISC there are two major categories of subtests: *verbal*, which measure various types of abilities affected by language and schooling; and *performance*, which involve problem-solving abilities that depend very little on language.

roughly 68 percent of all those tested fall between 85 and 115 I.Q. points. An I.Q. of over 130, for example, places a student in the top 2½ percent of all students. Subtest scores have a mean of 10; roughly 68 percent of the population ranges between 7 and 13. A subtest score of over 16 places a student in the top 2½ percent of all students. There is an extended discussion of this type of scoring, called a *deviation I.Q.,* in Chapter 8.

Eliezer's scores on the WRAT (Wide-Range Achievement Test) were:

Spelling 4.6*

Reading 4.9

Arithmetic 8.1

In asking Eliezer the test questions on the WISC, Dr. Rampullo notices that Eliezer is frequently hesitant in giving a response. Often he will simply stare blankly when asked a question. If she pushes, he will say, "I don't know," or "I wasn't taught that." After she goes through the intelligence testing in the standardized manner, so that she gets accurate scores, she goes back to see if she can get a better understanding of his real capabilities. This is called *testing the limits;* the dialogue below illustrates the process. In the original testing Dr. Rampullo said, "Name four presidents of the United States since 1900." And Eliezer responded, "Kennedy, Roosevelt, Nixon . . ." When asked to think of a fourth, Eliezer said "I don't know," looking down. With the completion of the testing, the dialogue begins:

You will see in the dialogue how Dr. Rampullo tries to find out more than Eliezer's test scores tell her. This is a major advantage of having an individual psychodiagnostic session with a psychologist rather than simply relying on a child's score on a test administered to a whole group of children.

Dr. Rampullo: OK, Eliezer, now that we're done, let's just go back and look at a few questions again. Do you want to try?

Eliezer: OK, I guess so.

Dr. Rampullo: Name four presidents of the United States since 1900.

Eliezer: Kennedy, Nixon, Roosevelt . . . (*pause . . . Dr. Rampullo looks at him and smiles*) Oh! and Ford!

Dr. Rampullo: Hmm? Where was he last time?

Eliezer: It's funny, I thought about it, but I didn't know if it was OK to name the one right now.

---

* These achievement test scores are reported as grade equivalents. A spelling score of 4.6 means that Eliezer is spelling at a level equivalent to what an "average" child would be doing in the sixth month of the fourth grade. Thus on this test Eliezer's performance is below his own sixth-grade level for spelling and reading but above that grade level for arithmetic.

(From this, Dr. Rampullo begins to wonder if Eliezer's tentativeness has something to do with always needing reassurance that he won't be wrong before he takes a chance. She checks some other questions and gains some more evidence of this.)

Dr. Rampullo: What is the capital of France?

Eliezer: I don't know.

Dr. Rampullo: You probably know a lot about geography. Why don't you just take a guess?

Eliezer: Paris, maybe?

The Wechsler Intelligence Scale for Children (WISC) is designed to help assess a child's general capacity or potential for learning. However, while some of the tasks tap a child's general ability, others are heavily influenced by school experiences. The question on using the symbols in Figure 7-1 is probably not something a child will have learned in school; the question on presidents does more directly test school learning. As we will discuss in the next chapter, intelligence cannot be separated easily from achievement through experience.

Dr. Rampullo notices that the pressure of time is particularly hard on Eliezer. He loses credit on many items because he does not complete them within a time limit. For example, on one test he is asked to look at the set of symbols shown in Figure 7–1, each of which corresponds to a number.

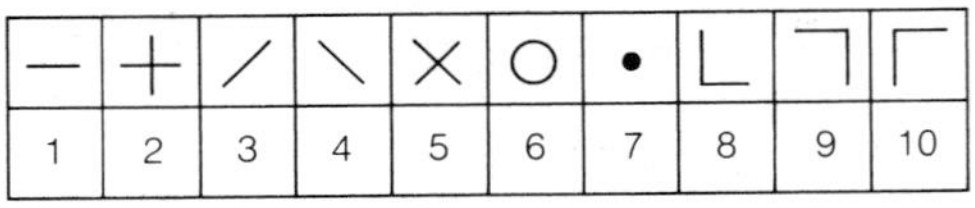

Figure 7–1. Sample Coding Test

Then Eliezer is shown a long series of random numbers and asked to put the proper symbol in the box over each number. Dr. Rampullo notes that he gets every one right but that he looks back each time and puts his finger on the example. He is very unsure of himself. It is as if he doesn't trust himself to remember the symbols, even with practice. He ends up making no errors, but he completes far fewer than the average child his age.

Dr. Rampullo now begins to wonder whether Eliezer has a perceptual problem, which slows him down when he is asked to perform certain tasks including eye–hand coordination. For this reason, she administers the Bender-Gestalt Test. Here Eliezer must look at a series of 10 cards, each with a single figure on it. She watches closely to see how well he can reproduce each figure, how he organizes the figures on a piece of paper, whether he has to tilt the cards around to figure out how to reproduce the symbol, and so forth. She notices the way he handles the task:

It's interesting to see how much more information about a child in addition to test results a good psychologist can gather through the right questions and activities.

Eliezer: Should I use a different page for each card?

Dr. Rampullo: You can do it any way you want.

Eliezer: Can I do them all on one page?

Dr. Rampullo: Whichever way you like.

Eliezer: *(Shrugs his shoulders and shakes his head)* OK.

Dr. Rampullo notes that Eliezer does each figure very well but has difficulty deciding where to put it on the page. Even though he asked before he started, he continues throughout the test to ask her where to put the next figure, if he can use another page, and similar questions. Nonetheless, each figure is carefully drawn. He makes very few mistakes, and when he does, he neatly erases and corrects himself, always looking back carefully at the card to check.

She administers another task to understand better how Eliezer feels about himself as a person. Dr. Rampullo is beginning to suspect that his problem has something to do with his feelings, and that an understanding of these feelings may help Mrs. O'Brien in her attempt to reach Eliezer. The Thematic Apperception Test (TAT) adds some useful information to her growing picture of Eliezer.

As Eliezer makes up a story for each card, Dr. Rampullo develops a sense of some of the feelings that may be holding back Eliezer's growth. However, she will not make up her mind on the basis of one TAT story. She is looking for repeated patterns that will help her sharpen her sense of what it must feel like to be Eliezer Cohen.

One of the many cards shows a young boy sitting alone and looking at a violin. She asks him to make up a story about the picture.

Dr. Rampullo: Make up a story about the picture. Give the story a beginning, a middle, and an end. Be sure to tell something about how the person in the story feels.

Eliezer: Oh! This boy is looking at the violin. He is taking lessons on it His father plays too. *(Pause)*

Dr. Rampullo: How does it turn out?

Eliezer: He will try and try, but he won't ever be great at it. *(Sighs)*

Gradually, Dr. Rampullo compiles a large amount of information about how Eliezer functions. Some of her information is in the form of *products*—how many questions he answered correctly on the WISC, how well his Bender-Gestalt forms matched those of the average child his age, how long he took to do this task compared with others. Still other information is *process* data—does he exhibit a great deal of anxiety as he performs some tasks, does he need constant reassurance, does he keep on going as a task gets harder or does he give up?

Dr. Rampullo does not accept a hunch or form a judgment on one bit of information. She builds a picture of Eliezer, testing for consistency in her findings. Then she tries to develop a report that will give a clear picture of his strengths and weaknesses and that, hopefully, will provide some new directions that Mrs. O'Brien may take in helping Eliezer experience greater success in school. Before you read her report, try to prepare your own brief report in the exploration below. Then compare your report with Dr. Rampullo's, which follows the exploration.

The TAT is a projective test. Such a test provides information about personality as individuals respond to stimuli (in this case pictures) that are presented to them. In other words, they "project" their own feelings and needs into their interpretation of the test items, and thus the psychologist gains insight. The Rorschach ink blot test is another widely used projective test with which you may be familiar.

Products refer to Eliezer's actual performance on the different tests. Process data, on the other hand, refer to the way he goes about answering— his behavior in the testing situation, his interaction with the psychologist, etc.

Exploration 7–1: A Psychodiagnostic Report on Eliezer Cohen
As you prepare your report, respond briefly to each of the questions below:

1. What picture of Eliezer's abilities emerges from the results of the WISC and the WRAT?

2. What did you learn from Dr. Rampullo's dialogues with Eliezer as she went over some of his responses to the WISC, gave him the Bender-Gestalt, and followed up with the TAT?

3. What recommendations or suggestions would you make to Mrs. O'Brien, Eliezer's teacher? Compare your suggestions for helping him in the classroom with Mrs. O'Brien's original plan (see p. 134) of "pushing him."

This means that Eliezer's score is equal to or better than the scores of 50 percent of the children in his age group.

To: Mrs. O'Brien   Subject: Psychodiagnostic Report
From: Dr. Rampullo   on Eliezer Cohen

Eliezer was seen for psychodiagnostic study because he is having difficulty with sixth-grade work. He repeated the fifth grade. His score on the WISC places him roughly at the *50th percentile* for children his age. However, further examination of his subscores suggests that his overall score is an underestimation of his potential. For example, although he is 12′5 (12 years and 5 months old), he functions in some areas like a considerably older child and in some like a considerably younger child. His score of 8 on the WISC arithmetic subtest indicates he is only functioning at the age level of a child who is 8′6. His vocabulary score is at an age level of 10′2, and his fund of information is 9′10. These three subtests are probably most closely related to school-learned skills, since they depend in part upon reading ability.

On the other hand, in those subtests that are most independent of school achievement, his scores are at an age level of 12′2 in comprehension, and 13′2 in similarities. This is strong evidence that he is considerably brighter than his full-scale I.Q. score would suggest. Further, these abilities are less dependent upon school-learned abilities such as reading, which suggests greater strength in aural than in visual learning. It also indicates that his poor grades and his low scores in the Wide-Range Achievement Tests do not accurately reflect Eliezer's abilities.

One interesting finding is the discrepancy between his low WISC score on the arithmetic subtest and his comparatively high WRAT arithmetic grade level. Since the WRAT is a written test of arithmetic skills and the WISC is orally administered, it is possible that his arithmetic skills are adequate if he sees what he is doing and is not pressed for time. In a one-to-one testing situation, such as the WISC, he may feel more pressured to perform well for the test administrator and thus his anxiety may interfere with his ability to answer the arithmetic questions.

What, then, accounts for Eliezer's poor school performance? In those areas where he is asked to perform, particularly under pressure of time, he tends to be extremely cautious. Given enough time and reassurance, he does well. There is no evidence at this time of any organic weakness, although it is possible that in the younger grades he did have some modest coordination problems that may have contributed to his original learning difficulties. Eliezer's major problem now appears to lie in his own feeling that he will not succeed, and his fear of taking chances. This problem is intensified by the fact that he does have low-level reading and spelling scores and arithmetic skills that, while reasonably intact, are interfered with by his reading difficulty. He is continually proving to himself how unsuccessful he is.

Here you can easily see how interrelated feelings about the self are with actual abilities. The more unsuccessful Eliezer is in his school work (due to his weaknesses in basic skills), the more likely he is to doubt his abilities and feel negative about himself as a student. This negative self-concept, in turn, further affects his ability to do his school work successfully.

To summarize, Eliezer's present strengths are· in the area of aural rather than visual reception. However, his high anxiety level and his high need for approval sometimes keep him from building upon these strengths.

Recommendations: Keep in mind that Eliezer's greatest strengths lie in his ability to grasp ideas presented verbally, rather than visually, and in his ability to understand relationships. At this point he is weak in the traditional skills of reading, writing, and arithmetic, although he can do basic arithmetic skills. He is afraid of taking risks, because he fears failure and consequent peer ridicule and parental and teacher disappointment.

I would recommend that you not push Eliezer at this time. Rather, try to find work at or slightly below his present level, so that he may experience a great deal of immediate success. Keep expectations for his written skills low; expectations for his verbal skills should be higher. Eliezer's arithmetic skills seem to be reasonably intact; it is possibly his inability to read the arithmetic problems that pulls him down in arithmetic.

Eliezer should be asked stimulating questions and encouraged to guess at the answers. He should be strongly praised for taking risks. It is suggested that you and Eliezer discuss these recommendations together so that he fully understands what you will be doing and why. Eliezer should be given frequent and, hopefully, positive feedback to help him see his growth. His outbursts of provocative behavior toward his peers are probably the result of his anger at his inability to meet his own high standards. It is expected that as his ability increases, his need to provoke will diminish.

M. Rampullo

M. Rampullo, Ph.D.
School Psychologist

When she receives Dr. Rampullo's report, Mrs. O'Brien will have a great deal of information to think about regarding Eliezer. Not only has she been given an assessment of Eliezer's present strengths and weaknesses, she has been provided with some recommendations on how to work with him. However, only Mrs. O'Brien can make the specific decisions about what approaches to try. She must add the psychologist's report to her own observations of Eliezer and then, given her curriculum and the needs of the rest of her class, decide how to best work with Eliezer. As she implements her plans for Eliezer, she will have to continually evaluate her progress and adapt her approach.

Conclusions

Teaching is a profession that places great demands on its practitioners. To be effective a teacher must be able to work simultaneously with a group of 25 or 30 people, each of whom has differing abilities, interests, and needs. This chapter has introduced you to some of the many individual differences that teachers encounter. We have tried to help you see the value of an individualized approach to education. Such a perspective sees a teacher as a diagnostician in the classroom. This perspective draws upon many of the insights gained in the field of special education, which has always concerned itself with the problems introduced by extreme individual differences such as blindness, deafness, emotional disturbance, mental retardation, and, more recently, learning disabilities.

In most school districts important support personnel can help teachers respond to the special needs of individual children. These professionals include nurses, counselors, physicians, speech therapists, social workers, and school psychologists. If children are having problems in learning and teachers are not sure how best to help them, they can be referred to a school psychologist who may administer a battery of tests called a *psychodiagnostic evaluation.* Such a testing procedure might include an individual I.Q. test, personality tests, achievement tests, and extensive observation and interviewing. As we saw with Eliezer Cohen, a psychodiagnostic by a highly trained and sensitive psychologist can provide a classroom teacher with many suggestions.

Although some students need the help of a specialist, the vast majority simply need to be seen as individuals and given some special attention. The more teachers know about each student's abilities, school background, personality characteristics, social relationships, family and community, and learning style, the more they can make the curriculum relevant to the student. By personalizing both the curriculum and their relationship with each student, teachers increase their effectiveness and, at the same time, make the teaching–learning process more enjoyable for themselves and their students.

Some Good Books

Axline, Virginia. *Dibs: In Search of Self.* New York: Ballantine, 1964. This case study of a seriously emotionally disturbed boy shows how a therapist worked with him and his parents.

Block, J. B., ed. *Mastery Learning: Theory and Practice*. New York: Holt, Rinehart and Winston, 1971. Block has put together one of the most concise statements on mastery learning, an approach to teaching that emphasizes learners' working individually at their own rates. As learners "master" a particular body of knowledge, they move on to more complex material.

Cronbach, L. J. and R. E. Snow. *Aptitude and Instructional Methods: A Handbook for Research on Interactions*. New York: Irvington Publishers/ Naiburg Publishing Corporation, 1975. This rather technical book brings together a great deal of discussion and research regarding aptitude treatment interactions.

Howe, Leland W. and Mary Martha Howe. *Personalizing Education: Values Clarification and Beyond*. New York: Hart, 1975. An excellent handbook of values clarification strategies for personalizing both the curriculum and human relationships within the school. The humanistic perspective on reaching individual students is very different from the behavioristic perspective such as B. F. Skinner's.

Kohl, Herbert. *The Open Classroom*. New York: Vintage, 1969. In this short, readable book Kohl provides a good rationale for open education as a means of making education relevant to the needs of each student.

Maslow, Abraham. *The Farther Reaches of Human Nature*. New York: Viking, 1971. This synthesis of Maslow's work compiled after his death includes some excellent chapters on his concept of self-actualization and his views on education. Maslow's thinking provides the psychological basis for many of our current conceptions of the uniqueness of each person.

Orem, R. C., ed. *Montessori Today*. New York: Putnam, 1971. Orem gives an overview of the Montessori approach to education in special schools throughout the United States. Montessori schools emphasize an individualized and rather structured approach to learning.

Skinner, B. F. *The Technology of Teaching*. New York: Appleton-Century-Crofts, 1968. *The Technology of Teaching* has become a classic statement on the application of behavioristic views of learning to the classroom. The book focuses on the use of programmed learning and teaching machines as ways of individualizing the educational process.

Articles, Studies, and Other References

Cronbach, Lee J. "How Can Instruction Be Adapted to Individual Differences?" In Robert Gagné (ed.), *Learning and Individual Differences*. Columbus, Ohio: Merrill, 1967. This article provides a useful rationale for adapting instruction to individual differences.

Fiske, Edward B. "Special Education Is Now a Matter of Civil Rights." The *New York Times Spring Survey of Education,* April 25, 1976. Fiske's article outlines the new federal laws that require that after 1978 states provide "free, appropriate educations for handicapped children." The whole *Spring Survey of Education* in which this article appears is devoted to new developments in the field of special education.

Gage, N. L. and David C. Berliner. "The Study of Individual Differences." In Gage and Berliner, *Educational Psychology*. Chicago: Rand McNally, 1975. Gage and Berliner have put together here an overview of the psychology of individual differences and its implications for teaching.

Hull, R. E. "Selecting an Approach to Individual Education." *Phi Delta Kappan* 55 (1973): 169–173. In this brief article Hull evaluates four of the most widely accepted patterns for individualized education in the United States. If you would like an overall picture of different approaches to individualized instruction, this is a good reference.

Sullivan, Patricia. "Suicide by Mistake." *Psychology Today* 10 (1976): 90–94. The true story that Sullivan reports depicts the tragedy of a young man whose individual differences and special needs were never really understood as he went through school. He became a dropout and ultimately committed suicide.

Suggestions for Action-Oriented Learning

1. Arrange to visit a number of different types of special education classes to learn more about the field and to develop a picture of some of the approaches that provide educationally for individual differences. Plan time to interview the teachers. You might choose from classes for the educable mentally retarded, the emotionally disturbed, the multiply physically handicapped, the hearing impaired, the learning disabled, or the blind.

2. Invite a school psychologist to come to your class to discuss his or her role in diagnosing and providing for the special needs of individual students.

3. Involve yourself in some type of helping relationship with a child or teenager who needs a great deal of special attention in school. As a class project keep notes on your work and develop a case study report based upon what you learn.

4. Get together with four or five students and explore the research or literature on learning style. Develop a questionnaire so that the members of your class can assess their own learning styles. Once everyone has completed the survey, summarize the results and discuss them with the other members of the class.

5. Visit a sample of about five elementary and five secondary schools to learn about any special efforts they are making to individualize instruction in regular (not special education)

classes. Interview the principals of the schools and try to visit any classes that they identify. Compare and contrast your findings and share them with your own class.

8
Intelligence

As teachers struggle to help young people learn, they often find themselves asking two questions: "What are the abilities of my students?" and "What do they already know?" The first of these questions is concerned with intelligence—the potential for learning; the second focuses on achievement—actual performance or acquired knowledge. By common sense most of us can agree that even at the same grade level people differ greatly from one another in both these qualities. Many everyday expressions convey this idea. We call people bright or dull, quick or slow, smart or dumb, as we speak about their intelligence. Or we say, "She really knows her math," or "He is an excellent English student" as we comment on achievement in school. Obviously, there is a close relationship between these two qualities, since intelligence will affect actual achievement in a particular subject. On the other hand, there is increasing evidence that the more people further their achievement, the more they will develop their intellectual capacity, i.e., their intelligence. In other words, intelligence and achievement are no longer viewed as the separate characteristics they were once thought to be.

In this chapter our focus is on intelligence, since it is probably the individual characteristic most widely used and at the same time most poorly understood in today's schools. Intelligence test scores are frequently used in conjunction with other data to place students into special classes, group students by ability, diagnose learning needs, and determine whether students are working up to their potential. On occasion they are even used to advise students whether to pursue certain careers or education beyond high school. With so much misinformation around and with so many decisions affecting students' lives made on the basis of intelligence testing, it is important that as a prospective teacher you understand intelligence and the controversy surrounding its measurement. As we discuss what intelligence is, and its use and abuse, we will continually examine its relationship to achievement in school. Exploration 8–1 will help you think through your own views on some important issues regarding intelligence that we will be discussing in this chapter.

Exploration 8–1: Examining Your Own
Views on Intelligence and Its Measurement

1. Do you know your own I.Q.? How has knowing it affected your picture of yourself, especially as a student?

2. If you don't know your I.Q., would you like to know it? Why or why not?

3. What do you feel is the value to teachers of knowing a child's I.Q.? Can you think of any dangers?

4. Do you think I.Q. can change as people go through life or does I.Q. remain relatively stable? Explain why you think as you do.

5. When you think of intelligence, do you think of it as a general characteristic; i.e., people who have high intelligence tend to

I.Q. is the abbreviation for intelligence quotient—the score that reflects a person's total performance on an intelligence test.

In most school districts children's intelligence is tested at least once on an individual intelligence test and a number of times on group tests.

be "smart" in many things? Or do you think that there are many specific types of intelligence; i.e., some people are "smart" in remembering things, some are "smart" in seeing spatial relationships, some are "smart" at working with abstractions, etc.? Explain your answer.

You may want to discuss your answers to the questions with some other people. You'll probably find that your answers differ since there are many conceptions of what intelligence is and a variety of opinions regarding its value as a tool for educators.

This chapter will help you better understand intelligence, its measurement, and the controversial issues surrounding the use of intelligence test scores in making educational decisions about children. We will explore the issues you began to consider in Exploration 8–1; you may want to refer back to those answers as you read.

Intelligence and Its Measurement

In our effort to understand current thinking about intelligence, a brief overview of the history of intelligence testing and the evolution of our concept of intelligence may prove useful. Given the great complexity and variability of the human body, there is little reason not to expect equally great variability in the functions of the brain. Just after the beginning of this century, the leaders of the Paris school system became interested in the question of intellectual differences. They had noticed, as teachers have through the ages, that some children seemed more able to benefit from instruction than others. Alfred Binet, a French physician and psychologist who had already done some research on mental traits, was invited to join a committee to develop ways of differentiating children who were ready to benefit from school from those who were not. The work of this committee led to the first formal attempt to measure intelligence through the individual's acquisition of knowledge.

Philosophers have long argued about whether man is the product of his environment or exists independent of it. This issue is sometimes called the *nature–nurture* conflict. It has been a central issue in the study of intelligence. Some theorists have argued that intelligence is primarily an inherited trait, like eye color, determined by one's "nature." Others insist it is mostly an acquired ability, influenced primarily by experiences of growing up, one's "nurture." There is some evidence to support each side. Most recent theories suggest an important interaction between the internal and external factors of heredity and environment. These differences of opinion on intelligence, and the value positions associated with them, have had profound effects on education in the twentieth century. As early as 1909 Binet himself expressed his concern about the negative effects of a strong "nature" position:

> . . . some recent philosophers appear to have given their moral support to the deplorable verdict that the intelligence of an individual is a fixed quantity. . . . We must protest and act against this brutal pessimism. . . .

What is your opinion on this question? Do you feel intelligence is something we are born with? Or do you believe that intelligence is very much affected by the experiences we encounter as we mature?

Why do you feel the way you do?

A child's mind is like a field for which an expert farmer has advised a change in the method of cultivating, with the result that in place of desert land, we now have a harvest. It is in this particular sense . . . that we say that the intelligence of children may be increased (Binet, 1909, pp. 54–55).

Let us take a moment to see how Binet and his associates first measured intelligence. They developed a set of simple tasks, such as identifying parts of the body, counting coins, naming colors, and defining words. These tasks were arranged in order of difficulty. *Norms* were developed for each age level by determining which tasks could be mastered by the majority of children in that age level. A child who could perform all the tasks that the average child of that age was capable of was described as having the same *mental age (M.A.)* and *chronological age (C.A.)*. In other words, a child whose C.A. was 8 and who could perform all the tasks that a typical 8-year-old could perform would be said to have an M.A. of 8. If, however, the child could do only what a 6-year-old was capable of, then we would say the M.A. was 6.

In testing the child, the examiner usually begins with the assumption that the child is average, and will start questioning about one year below the child's chronological age on the scale and continue asking questions until the point where no correct answers are given. Thus a 5-year-old who passed all items for age 6 and none for age 7 would have an M.A. of 6. Since it was awkward to refer to this data as the child got older, a simple way of describing this relationship, the *intelligence quotient,* usually referred to as I.Q., was devised. This is a ratio comparing M.A. with C.A., multiplied by 100. I.Q. = M.A./C.A. × 100. Using this formula, we can see that if a child is able to answer the questions that an "average" child her own age can answer, then her I.Q. will be 100. If she can answer questions that are more typical of older children, then her M.A. is higher than her C.A., and her I.Q. is over 100. If, however, she can only answer the questions that are typical of younger children, then her M.A. is lower than her C.A., and her I.Q. is less than 100.

Unfortunately, this seemingly convenient measurement probably strengthened the misunderstanding about the innateness of intelligence. There is something very permanent about giving a person a number. It seems to say, "This is the way she was and this is the way she'll always be."

From Binet's beginning in the early 1900s, a huge industry has grown. It has been estimated that several million intelligence tests are administered annually in the United States alone. Essentially, tests of intelligence can be divided into two major groups, individual intelligence tests and group intelligence tests.

Individual Intelligence Tests

Binet's test of intelligence was eventually used in research carried out in 1910 by an American, Lewis Terman, at Stanford University. Terman extended Binet's method to normal and superior children with the development of the Stanford Revision of the Binet Scale in

How do you feel about Binet's statement? Do you think advocates of a strong "nature" position are pessimistic?

In the context of testing, norms *are tables that indicate what is considered normal performance for different age levels. Norms are determined by administering the test to large numbers of people.*

To illustrate the use of this formula, let's take three different 8-year-olds. Tommy is capable of answering correctly questions that the average 10-year-old can answer. Bobby is able to answer questions that the average 8-year-old can answer. And Billy can only answer questions that the average 6-year-old can answer.

Before reading below try to figure out their I.Q. scores using the formula

$$I.Q. = \frac{M.A.}{C.A.} \times 100$$

Tommy:

$$\frac{10}{8} \times 100 = 1.25 \times 100 = 125$$

Bobby:

$$\frac{8}{8} \times 100 = 1 \times 100 = 100$$

Billy:

$$\frac{6}{8} \times 100 = 0.75 \times 100 = 75$$

Individual intelligence tests provide important diagnostic information on a child's strengths and weaknesses.

Individual intelligence tests are verbally administered by a trained test administrator (in schools this is usually the school psychologist) to one person at a time. Group intelligence tests are administered to many people at a time. Group tests are, of necessity, paper-and-pencil tests. On a group test each person must read questions in a test booklet and then code the responses on an answer sheet.

Here are some specific examples for different age levels on the Stanford-Binet test.

Age	Task
4	*Upon being shown a picture of an umbrella or gun, providing the correct name.*
6	*Defining orange, envelope. Giving the test administrator nine blocks.*
9	*Repeating 8–5–2–6 backwards. Figuring change from a purchase.*

1916. A new version of the Stanford-Binet was created by Terman and his coworkers in 1937. The most recent revision was published in 1960. The ratio I.Q., with its implication that there is some permanent relationship between mental and chronological age, was abandoned in favor of *deviation score,* which simply compares an individual score to a larger population. The Stanford-Binet Intelligence Scale remains one of the two major individual tests of intelligence currently in use in the United States. The other major individual test is the Wechsler, which has two versions—The Wechsler Intelligence Scale for Children (WISC) and The Wechsler Adult Intelligence Scale (WAIS). The Wechsler test was discussed in Chapter 7.

Both the Stanford-Binet and the Wechsler can only be given in a one-to-one relationship with a trained test administrator. Since the tests are given verbally, children's reading ability doesn't interfere with their being able to answer the questions, as it might on a group test. On the Stanford-Binet the test administrator begins by establishing rapport with the child to interest him in the games and tasks of the test. The tasks include such activities as giving the names of objects or pictures, defining words, following a maze, reproducing designs from memory, problem solving, explaining the meaning of a proverb, etc. No child is given all of the tasks. For example, a 10-year-old might begin with tasks at the 9-year-old level, and if he passed those, he would keep going until he reached the limit of his ability. Of course, some 10-year-olds would not get much beyond the 10-year-old level while a few might get to the level of a typical 15- or 16-year-old. The whole testing procedure usually takes about an hour. The scoring is then done according to a published scoring guide, and the child's total score—his raw score—is translated into an I.Q. score.

The Wechsler Intelligence Scale for Children is used more frequently than the Stanford-Binet with children age 6 and over. The primary reason seems to be that it gives not only a general I.Q. score, called a full-scale I.Q., as the Stanford-Binet does, but also two subscores. Each person taking the WISC receives three scores—a verbal I.Q., a performance I.Q., and a full-scale I.Q. The verbal I.Q. is determined by verbal responses to a series of five subtests: information, comprehension, arithmetic, similarities, and vocabulary. The performance I.Q. is based upon the response to five subtests that require problem solving only minimally influenced by language ability. The five performance subtests are picture completion, picture arrangement, block design, object assembly, and coding. By comparing a child's verbal I.Q. and performance I.Q., the tester can make inferences that are masked by simply looking at the full-scale I.Q. For example, a child with a verbal I.Q. of 90 and a performance I.Q. of 110 may have a language problem that interferes with his verbal communication and makes him appear slower intellectually than he really is. In testing him with the WISC, a psychologist would notice this difference, which might be less evident if the child were tested only on the Stanford-Binet.

Both the Stanford-Binet and the WISC have greater *reliability* and *validity* as measures of intelligence than do group tests. In other words, individual intelligence tests tend to give more accurate assessments of a person's intelligence than do group intelligence tests. Also, because they are given in a one-to-one relationship, individual tests are more valuable for diagnostic purposes. A school psychologist can use the data gathered on such a test to see a child's strengths and weaknesses in a number of areas; even the child's behavior during the testing session can be noted. On the other hand, individual tests are very expensive in terms of equipment and the test administrator's time. Each test takes an hour to give, can be given only by a trained professional, and requires hand scoring. For this reason group tests that can be administered and scored quickly and cheaply are often used to provide supplementary data on intelligence.

Group Intelligence Tests

The first group intelligence test was the Army Alpha. It was developed during World War I by a team of psychologists including Lewis Terman, who had been the primary figure in the development of the Stanford-Binet out of Binet's original scale. The Army Alpha was designed to provide a quick, efficient means of determining which Army inductees had the potential for officer training, which ought to be rejected as unfit, and how to classify the remainder. Because this test was practical and easy to administer, it wasn't long before schools and industry became interested in similar group tests. They believed that group tests would allow them to obtain useful information when large numbers of people had to be considered at once for employment or placement in a particular occupational category, or as a preliminary device to identify students for individual testing.

Age	Task
12	*Defining* skill. *Finding the absurdity in a picture.*
Average Adult	*Defining* regard, disproportionate. *Explaining how to measure 2 pints of water with a 5-pint and a 3-pint can.*

The concepts of reliability and validity are important in understanding any tests or psychological measures. Reliability refers to the extent to which a test is consistent in its measurement. If a student scored 115 on an I.Q. test one day and a few weeks later was retested and scored 85, we would question the reliability of the test. Validity refers to the extent to which a test measures what it was designed to measure. For example, if it was routinely found that I.Q. didn't accurately predict college success, we would say it had poor predictive validity. A test must have proven reliability before any judgment is made about its validity.

Statistical procedures are used to determine a test's reliability and validity.

An individual test tends to be more motivating to a child than a group test that involves reading from a test booklet. Because of the one-to-one relationship, the tester is able to develop rapport with the child and encourage her to do her best. The test materials also invite participation, since they are like games and puzzles.

Reading ability can interfere with doing well on such a test. Motivation can also be a problem. If children do not take the test seriously or are extremely slow workers, they might miss items that they would get right in a one-to-one testing situation.

Since the 1960s, roughly paralleling the growth of the civil rights movement, group intelligence tests have come under considerable fire. In fact, in 1965 the New York City school system, the largest in the United States, banned group I.Q. tests because teachers had come to believe that I.Q. truly represented a child's intellectual capacity and viewed it as an innate quality. This new policy became known as the Loretan Decision, named after Jacob Loretan, then assistant superintendent of the New York City school system.

In many instances an I.Q. score, based on, as a rule, less than an hour of testing in a group situation, followed a child throughout school. Loretan pointed out that teachers often "labeled" children who had low scores and expected them to perform poorly. In the next section we will further explore this issue and other controversies in intelligence testing.

You can see the potential diagnostic value of a multifactor group test, which reports subtest scores as well as a global I.Q., in the following hypothetical test.

On this test Jack and Len, who are 12 years old, each have a total score of

Since the Army Alpha, many group tests of intelligence have been developed. Of the millions of I.Q. tests given in schools each year, the majority are group tests generally administered by a teacher or counselor to many children at the same time. They are scored either by hand or sent to some central point to be scored by machine.

All group tests require that the student be able to follow directions, read, and make appropriate marks on an answer sheet. Usually the mark that the test taker makes represents a choice out of four or five possible answers to a given question. There are two basic types of group I.Q. tests. One type yields a single score, called a global I.Q.; the other yields a number of subscores as well as a total score. A well-known single-score test is the Otis-Lennon Mental Ability Test. This tests consists of 90 questions designed to assess a wide variety of aspects of thinking, including knowledge of vocabulary, ability to understand analogies, simple arithmetic skills, visual–spatial ability, etc. Figure 8–1 illustrates some of the sorts of items you might find in such a test at the elementary school age level.

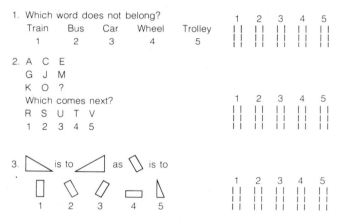

Figure 8–1: Sample I.Q. Test Items

As we mentioned above, the Otis-Lennon is an example of a single-score group intelligence test, often called a global test. The other major type is the multifactor test, in which test items have been chosen to represent different factors or abilities. A multifactor test gives a general I.Q. score based on the total number of correct items, but also gives subscores that reflect performance in different categories of response, such as language skills, numerical ability, spatial relationships, etc. It is possible, therefore, to obtain a picture of a person's overall performance and at the same time see the pattern reflected in the subtest scores.

As early as 1927 Charles Spearman, a British psychologist, suggested that intelligence was composed of a general factor, which he called *G*, and a large number of specific intellectual ability factors, which he called s. Two American psychologists, L. L. Thurstone and his wife Thelma Thurstone, developed many subtests they believed might represent s factors of the sort that Spearman had hypothesized. In one study they used 60 different subtests. They developed statistical methods showing the degree to which these subtests measured separate abilities, and concluded that there were six clearly defined abilities, which they named *primary mental abilities* (Thurstone, 1938). These were number (N), word fluency (W), verbal meaning (V), rote memory (M), reasoning (R), and spatial (S). Eventually L. L. Thurstone developed an intelligence test, the Primary Mental Abilities Test (PMA), which measured these abilities.

It would be quite valuable in counseling or developing educational programs for students with difficulties if we could accept the results of the research on primary mental abilities as highly reliable. Unfortunately, while the overall I.Q. score for the PMA tends to remain stable as students are retested over time, there is little stability for the subtests. One study (Wilson and Stier, 1962) showed that when the same students were tested in third grade and then again in sixth grade, they showed only about a two-point difference in overall I.Q. score on the PMA, but varied an average of 15 points on individual subtests. Perhaps this is because the number of questions on each subtest is so small compared to the number of questions on the entire test.

There are other group tests that yield subtest scores as well as overall I.Q. One example is the California Test of Mental Maturity, which gives subtest scores—a verbal score and a numerical score—and a total score. However, the stability of these subscores over time is questionable.

Scoring Intelligence Tests

In order to understand intelligence testing and interpret I.Q., it is important to have at least a basic awareness of how intelligence tests are scored. In both individual and group I.Q. tests, an answer key is used to mark correct answers. The total number of correct responses is called the *raw score*. Let us assume that there are 100 questions, and a given student receives a raw score of 67. By itself, this raw score tells us nothing. In order to convert the raw score to a meaningful number, the tester must consult a chart and compare the raw score with that of other students the same age. Most I.Q. tests in use today report I.Q. in terms of a *deviation I.Q.*, rather than the ratio I.Q. described earlier. In order to understand the concept of a deviation I.Q., we must first examine some aspects of the normal curve that provides the theoretical basis for this concept.

The *normal curve* is a mathematical concept depicting a hypothetical "ideal" distribution of any quality. For example, if we measured the height of all the adult men in a town, we would expect the greatest number of men to be somewhere around 5'8"—between 5'4" and 6'. A somewhat smaller number would be between 6' and 6'4" and between 5' and 5'4". Very few would be over 6'4" or

59, which gives them an I.Q. of 110. However, look at the differences in the patterns of their responses:

Subtest	Jack	Len
Language	38	21
Numerical	9	19
Spatial	8	17
Other	4	2
Total	59 = 110 I.Q.	59 = 110 I.Q.

What can you see from the pattern of Jack's and Len's subtest scores that you can't see by looking only at their total I.Q. scores?

Today most group tests are created so that they can be machine scored. Individual tests are scored by hand by a trained person using a scoring manual.

under 5'. If we were to express this distribution of height mathematically in the form of a graph, it would probably look something like Figure 8–2.

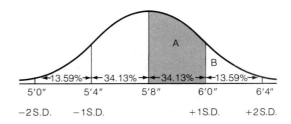

Figure 8–2: Height Distribution Curve

We read such a diagram in terms of the percentage of the data "under the curve." You will notice that the midpoint along the base of the curve is 5'8", and the base is marked off in equal units of 4 inches. Obviously, the number of men between 5'8" and 6'0" is much greater than the number of men between 6'0" and 6'4". Therefore, although the units of measurement (height) are equally spaced, the percentage of cases falling in each unit is different.

We can see this graphically in the curve. As the curve rises, a larger area lies beneath it; as it falls, a smaller area lies beneath it. A glance at areas A and B will show you that the area of A is much larger than that of B, because of the relative height of the curve. For convenience, we can describe these percentages in terms of *standard deviations,* often called S.D.s. A standard deviation is the average deviation from the mean in a large distribution of scores. In the example above the S.D. is 4". This means that in our hypothetical town the average deviation of the height of the men from 5'8"—the mean—is 4". In other words, the height of the average man will fall between 5'4" and 6'0". In terms of percentages, we see that 68.26 percent of men in the town will be between 5'4" tall and 6'0" tall. Note that the distribution is symmetrical; for the sake of convenience we consider those standard deviation units to the right as positive and those to the left as negative.

The discussion that follows refers to Figure 8–3, which shows an enlarged picture of the normal curve. It is marked off to the left and right of the midpoint in standard deviations. A score − 3 S.D.s below the mean is a percentile rank of 1; i.e., it exceeds only 1 percent of the scores in the distribution. A score at the mean, which is represented by the 0 point, has a percentile rank of 50; i.e., it exceeds 50 percent of the scores and is less than the other 50 percent.

What is the percentile rank of a score + 1 S.D.s above the mean?

What is the percentile rank of a score + 2 S.D.s above the mean?

In Figure 8–3 the axes below that for percentile rank show, respectively, the total scores for the WISC I.Q., the subscores on the

The mean is a statistical measure that represents the average score in a distribution of scores. It is found by adding all the scores and then dividing by the total number of scores.

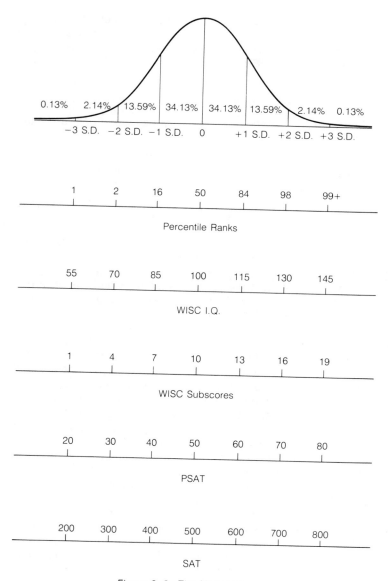

0.13%　　2.14%　13.59%　34.13%　34.13%　13.59%　2.14%　0.13%

−3 S.D.　−2 S.D.　−1 S.D.　0　　+1 S.D.　+2 S.D.　+3 S.D.

1　　2　　16　　50　　84　　98　　99+

Percentile Ranks

55　　70　　85　　100　　115　　130　　145

WISC I.Q.

1　　4　　7　　10　　13　　16　　19

WISC Subscores

20　　30　　40　　50　　60　　70　　80

PSAT

200　　300　　400　　500　　600　　700　　800

SAT

Figure 8–3. The Normal Curve

WISC, the total scores on the PSAT (Preliminary Scholastic Aptitude Test), and the SAT (Scholastic Aptitude Test). Many standardized test scores are reported in terms of the normal curve.

You may have taken both the PSAT and the SAT. Can you recall how you did?

The SAT has a mean of 500 for each of its two scores—the verbal and quantitative. The S.D. for the SAT is 100. Thus a little more than

The SAT (often called College Board Exams) is a test of verbal and quantitative (mathematical) aptitude used to predict the likelihood of success in college. Most U.S. colleges use the SAT scores along with high school grades, recommendations, interviews, etc., to decide whom to accept.

The PSAT is a "small" version of the SAT, usually given to high school juniors to prepare them for the SAT.

The field of special education has been concerned with helping people whose I.Q. (and other intellectual abilities) tends to place them at the extreme ends of the normal curve. Programs for the mentally retarded include the total institutional care of those whose intelligence is so limited that they can't feed themselves or become toilet trained; special schools for the trainable mentally retarded (I.Q. 30–50), who can achieve limited independence; and special classes for the educable mentally retarded (I.Q. approximately 50–75), who can live independently as adults but who require special help in learning to read at a basic level, to solve problems, etc.

It has also been argued that just as people who are significantly below average need special educational attention, so, too, do the bright and gifted. In some school districts there are programs and courses designed to challenge and extend the intellectual potential of children whose I.Q. places them in this group.

The dilemma remains in working with children whose I.Q.s are either very low or very high: How can we provide

two thirds of all people taking the test (68.26 percent) have scores between 400 and 600, and approximately 96 percent of all people score between 300 and 700. By looking at the percentile rank axis you can see that a score of 300 is at a percentile rank of 2; i.e., it exceeds only 2 percent of all the scores.

What is the percentile rank of a score of 700?

Where would your score on the verbal part of the SAT fall on the normal curve?

What was the approximate percentile rank of your verbal score? (Note: You won't be able to determine it exactly from the information we have presented.)

Which was higher, your verbal or quantitative SAT score? How great was the difference?

Now let's return to the normal curve as it relates to I.Q. Most I.Q. tests today are standardized so that they have a mean of 100 and an S.D. of approximately 15. Figure 8–3 shows that 98 percent of all people taking the WISC have scores between 55 and 145. Approximately 1 percent fall below 55 and 1 percent fall above 145. People whose I.Q. falls below 85 (i.e., at a percentile rank of 16 or below) usually require special education and attention. The lower their I.Q. the more special provisions they require and the less they are able to function independently. People whose I.Q.s range from 85 (− 1 S.D.) to 115 (+ 1 S.D.) fall within the average range and generally can function in regular school environments. People whose I.Q.s place them in the 115–130 range are above average and those with I.Q.s over 130 are considered to be "gifted" (i.e., superior) in their intellectual abilities. Only 14 percent of any age group fall between 115 and 130 and just 2 percent are above 130.

No matter how good a test may be, the reporting of the score always allows for some error, such as misscoring, incorrect directions, and other unpredictable factors that might affect the test taker. Thus the booklet explaining test scores also includes another aid to explaining the score: the standard error. For example, if the mean for a test is 100, the S.D. is 15, and the standard error is ±4, a score of 115 should be interpreted as falling within the band from 111 to 119. It should be clear then, that any individual's I.Q. score is understandable only when we know the mean, the S.D., and the standard error for the relevant age group.

Issues in Intelligence Testing

The measurement of intelligence and the use of I.Q. scores have been surrounded by controversy throughout the nearly three quarters of a century since the development of Alfred Binet's original intelligence scale. Today in the 1970s, there are no signs of this controversy abating; in fact, it may be increasing. Yet I.Q. testing remains widespread across the United States, and many decisions affecting the school experiences of individual children are based in part upon I.Q. test scores. It is important, therefore, for you as a prospective teacher to think through your views on this subject.

As you read the earlier sections of this chapter and encountered the use of I.Q. tests by Dr. Rampullo, the school psychologist in Chapter 7, you undoubtedly found yourself wondering about some of the following questions: Which is more important in determining a person's I.Q.—heredity or environment? Isn't it possible that someone's I.Q. can change? What is the value to a classroom teacher of knowing a child's I.Q.? Don't teachers and schools "label" kids when they know their I.Q.s? And won't kids who score high be pressured to perform well in school while kids who score low will be expected to do poorly? We would like to explore the issues underlying these questions in the next two sections of this chapter.

The Nature–Nurture Debate

We first mentioned the nature–nurture debate in relation to Binet's work in Paris in the early 1900s. Throughout the history of intelligence testing, some psychologists have emphasized the influence of environment on intelligence, while others have argued that heredity is the primary determinant. The environmentalists' position that one's nurture is the primary influence allows for the possibility of fairly large changes in I.Q. depending upon an individual's experiences. This position is often described as optimistic because it suggests that I.Q. may be increased by appropriate experiences. This "environmentalist" position helps teachers feel that what they do with children in school can make a positive difference in their intelligence.

By contrast, the position that sees heredity as the major determinant of I.Q. might be described as pessimistic, as Binet indicated in the quotation that appears earlier in this chapter. If I.Q. is primarily determined by heredity, then teachers can't hope to do much for students' I.Q.s. The genes we all are born with remain the same throughout our lives. Therefore, we should expect at best only very small changes in our intelligence from the very limited impact of our environment.

In the 1960s the predominant view on the nature–nurture debate seemed to favor nurture. The old popular idea that a person's I.Q. was essentially determined at birth was largely discredited and replaced by a view of intelligence as quite open to change, especially during the early years of a child's development. This view of the plasticity of intelligence evolved out of the research reported by many psychologists. Hunt (1961 and 1973) was probably its most widely regarded advocate. To support his position he cited evidence from three sources: studies of the effects of training on intelligence; repeated testing of the same children over a long period of time, which showed significant changes for many children; and studies of identical twins raised apart. Hunt reported a classic study in which seven pairs of identical twins raised apart had I.Q. differences of 10 points or more.

The environmentalist views of Hunt and others fit in well with the growing concern in the 1960s for civil rights and implementation of the

them with intellectual experiences at their own level and yet avoid isolating them from interaction with average students?

It should be noted here that virtually no one who has seriously studied intelligence believes that it is exclusively the result of either environment or heredity. What differentiates the "environmentalists" from the "hereditarians" is the relative importance each assigns to one influence over the other.

Studies consistently show a relationship between socioeconomic status and I.Q.—children from higher income groups tend to have higher I.Q.s than their peers from lower income groups. Hunt and others believe that the difference is the result of the higher level of cognitive stimulation found in more affluent homes.

American belief that "all men are created equal." It also tended to support the findings of the developmental psychologists whose research on critical periods suggested that early deprivation might result in a permanent handicap. Dennis and Najarian (1957) compared the development of children institutionalized in Crêche, an infant orphanage in Lebanon, with that of similar-aged children of the same socioeconomic background but raised in families. Crêche children received much less attention due to lack of sufficient staff. (For example, they were fed by a propped bottle rather than by hand, and adults seldom played with the infants.) On several different developmental tasks, Crêche children proved to be inferior to the noninstitutionalized children. Hunt (1961) and Bloom (1964) were not alone in arguing that if disadvantaged children were to increase in intelligence, they needed enriched early learning experiences. The U.S. government was persuaded to finance Project Head Start, a massive national effort to provide cognitive stimulation for preschoolers from poor families. Unfortunately, the initial I.Q. gains measured for many of the Head Start children disappeared as they went on to regular elementary schools and classes where there was no follow-up. Moreover, some researchers believe that even reaching disadvantaged children as early as age 3 or 4 might be too late, and they advocate help for parents in the home.

Recently psychologists in Boston have designed programs to teach the mothers of young children in disadvantaged families how to interact more effectively with their children and stimulate them intellectually. The early results seem to show a great deal of promise for the effects of such programs on children's I.Q.s (Reinhold, 1973; White and Watts, 1973).

In the winter of 1969 an article in the *Harvard Educational Review* aroused a storm of controversy over current thinking about intelligence. The article, "How Much Can We Boost I.Q. and Scholastic Achievement?" was written by Arthur Jensen, an educational psychologist at the University of California. Jensen argued that attempts at compensatory education (such as Head Start) had failed because they assumed that intelligence was primarily the result of environmental influences. Jensen cited a great deal of research to support the view that heredity plays a much larger role (80 percent) than environment in determining intelligence. Even more controversial was his statement that the I.Q. superiority of white children over black children was the result of genetic, not environmental, differences. Jensen suggested that since the racial differences in I.Q. were the result of heredity, blacks might benefit more from programs that stressed rote, associative learning rather than conceptual learning.

Studies in the United States have consistently shown that, on the average, blacks score lower than whites on I.Q. tests. However, before Jensen's article these differences were always attributed to the fact that whites were more affluent, had more educational opportunities, and in general had environmental advantages that enhanced their I.Q.s.

Jensen's article appeared at a time when many social programs had been developed to counteract the effects of poverty and racism and to equalize educational opportunities for blacks and other minority group members. His suggestion that blacks be taught through rote rather than conceptual approaches seemed to be a return to the second-class education minorities had traditionally received in segregated schools. Consequently, he was attacked by some as a racist and white supremacist. The reaction of academicians who had studied intelligence was swift in coming. The Spring 1969 issue of *Harvard Educational Review* published rebuttals to Jensen's article by seven leading scholars, who critiqued his research and challenged his conclusions. However, others (Eysenck, 1971; Herrnstein, 1971; Shockley, 1971) have drawn conclusions similar to Jensen's from analysis of the same sort of data.

In order to get a feeling for this debate, take a look at Jensen's article in the Winter 1969 issue of Harvard Educational Review *and the rebuttals to it in the Spring 1969 issue.*

More recent criticisms of "Jensenism" point out that I.Q. tests are culturally biased and discriminate against lower-class minority group children in many ways. First, they are made up by middle-class people (usually whites) and thus reflect their language and experiences, not the experiences of children growing up in the urban ghetto (or rural Appalachia). Second, minority group children have not developed the test-taking skills of middle-class children and have not been encouraged in their families to see the importance of such tests. Third, test administrators are virtually always white and middle class. They often don't understand the language and experience of children from different circumstances and often expect them to do poorly. In short, if it is true that I.Q. tests don't measure the true intelligence of minority group members and people who are not from the middle class, then Jensen's conclusions must be seriously questioned.

The nature–nurture debate regarding intelligence is likely to continue. In 1972, after the sharp criticism of Jensen's research, a group of 50 prominent psychologists signed a statement (*American Psychologist,* July 1972) deploring the attacks on Jensen's research. They argued that there was a place for a hereditarian view and that research exploring the biological basis of behavior ought to continue. Current prevailing opinion among psychologists leans toward environmentalism, with the views of Jensen, Shockley, and others remaining a minority position. Even the more environmental theories attribute between 20 and 30 percent of intelligence to heredity, while the most hereditarian allow for some environmental influence. Thus all agree that early experiences in the home, the community, and, later, the school have some potential for increasing a child's intelligence. By the same token, that potential can be stymied by such negative experiences as a family or school environment lacking in intellectual stimulation. Heredity may set the limits on a child's potential, but the extent to which he realizes that potential will be due to the experiences he has.

The Use and Abuse of I.Q. Testing and I.Q. Scores

As we have seen, intelligence testing in schools remains very controversial. Criticism has been directed at both the I.Q. tests themselves and the uses to which I.Q. test scores have been put. Critics of the tests themselves have stressed several points. First, I.Q. tests (both individual and group) do not measure intellectual potential or capacity directly since they are based upon knowledge of such things as vocabulary, general current events, and basic mathematics. In addition, group tests require learned skills like reading and paying attention to directions. Second, I.Q. tests reflect the cultural values and experiences of the dominant social class, i.e., the white middle class. Third, motivational factors cannot be separated from intellectual potential in contributing to I.Q. score. For example, a child who doesn't take a group test seriously will inevitably do poorly on it. As we saw with Eliezer Cohen in Chapter 7, even on an individual I.Q. test one's insecurities and fears can interfere with a demonstration of true intelligence.

Try to imagine what it would be like to take an I.Q. test in which you had to:

1. *Describe how to cook chitterlings.*

2. *Comprehend the following sentences (Morris, 1974):*

   This place was really together.

   The hostess was a stone fox who made sure everything was everything.

   The owner was a really down dude who kept the jive elements out.

Questions on I.Q. tests are frequently as foreign to black and minority group children as the above questions would be to most middle-class whites.

Someone once described intelligence by analogy with a rubber band. Heredity determines the length of the rubber band; however, environment can stretch it. With some effort even a very short rubber band can be stretched a long way. Our job as teachers, then, is to create circumstances that will stretch the rubber bands (LeFrancois, 1975).

Attempts made in the last few years to develop "culture-fair" I.Q. tests have not been too successful. Separating intelligence from cultural experience is not easy.

Have you ever been labeled by your I.Q. score?

How did this affect your attitude and school performance?

Research done by Rosenthal and Jacobson and reported in Pygmalion in the Classroom *(1968) explored the self-fulfilling prophesy phenomenon. They found that elementary school children labeled as potential high achievers on the basis of fictitious test scores showed significant gains in I.Q. They explained this finding by the fact that teachers had been deceived into believing these students had high potential and therefore expected more from them.*

While the research methodology of Rosenthal and Jacobson has been questioned (Elashoff and Snow, 1971), it seems quite plausible that other people's expectations affect the self-concepts and behavior of all of us.

Even more serious than the problems with the I.Q. tests themselves are the abuses of I.Q. test scores by school districts, individual schools, and classroom teachers. All too often children are labeled by their I.Q. scores as "smart" or "dumb." It doesn't take long for children who are seen by their teacher as dumb (or, to use a more common euphemism, "slow") and thus treated as dumb, to begin to see themselves as dumb and act dumb. This happens not only with individuals but with whole classes that have been grouped by ability. Very often classes made up of children with low I.Q.s come to see themselves as the "dummies" as they encounter teachers who don't expect much from them. In a sense the label becomes a *self-fulfilling prophesy.*

One of the unfortunate consequences of intelligence testing has been the trend toward grouping children in classes by ability. Such *tracking* (usually referred to by schools as *homogeneous grouping*) has deluded some teachers into thinking that all their students are at the same intellectual level and thus can be taught in the same way. However, even in a group of very bright or mentally retarded students, there are vast differences in ability. Furthermore, tracking tends to encourage students to label each other—the "brains," "retards," "eggheads," "regulars," etc. A status system even develops in many schools, with senior teachers given the more "advanced" classes while the new recruits must prove themselves with the "average" and "slow" classes.

Other problems in the use of I.Q. scores seem to stem from giving them too much importance. When they are used alone or seen as the most important measure of a child's intellectuality, then the possibility for misuse is great.

However, when intelligence tests are used within the context of a psychodiagnostic evaluation by a psychologist (such as Dr. Rampullo in Chapter 7), they can provide useful information. Even more important than the actual I.Q. score are the subscores and the patterns of abilities and weaknesses that emerge in individual intelligence testing. Especially for a child who is doing poorly in school, an intelligence test in combination with data on school achievement, personality characteristics, interests, etc., can suggest steps for help. The answer to the dilemma of intelligence testing lies not in the elimination of I.Q. tests but in the reeducation of professionals to recognize the limitations and utilize the strengths of these tools.

Another Way of Looking at Intelligence

The study of intelligence has tended to be empirical. Rather than beginning with a concept of what intelligence is and attempting to assess it, researchers have tried to decide what sorts of abilities and knowledge are evidence of intelligence and then devised tests to measure them. Anne Anastasi described the problems growing from the absence of a theory of intelligence:

An effort is made to arrive at ... an overall estimate of intellectual performance by "the sinking of shafts at critical points." In other words, a wide variety of tasks are presented to the subject in the expectation that an adequate sampling of all important intellectual functions will thus be covered. In actual practice, the tests are usually overloaded with certain functions . . . and completely omit others (Anastasi, 1954, p. 175).

J. P. Guilford (1959; 1967) looked at intelligence in a very different way. He tried to pull together all existing tests purporting to measure intelligence to derive the underlying structure of intelligence. This was a revolutionary step in conceptualizing intelligence. In essence, Guilford created a model of the mind, which he called the "structure of intellect." It was as if he spread before himself all of the already stated ideas about intelligence like the parts of some gigantic jigsaw puzzle and rearranged the pieces until patterns began to emerge. He realized that this was no ordinary puzzle; it did not lie flat on the table, so to speak. It was three-dimensional. Probably the realization that he needed three separate planes to fully describe the complexity of the mind's structure was his most important contribution to understanding intelligence. He conceived the mind as a set of *operations* (or processes) that organized the *contents* of the world around it into *products.*

Guilford was able to fit all of the known tests of intellectual functioning into these three dimensions and their subcategories. To understand his model, look first at the cube that represents the model in Figure 8–4. A cube, or cell, is formed for each intersection of the three subdivisions, as illustrated by cube *CFU* on the model. *CFU* refers to a test measuring the cognition of figural information at the simplest level (units).

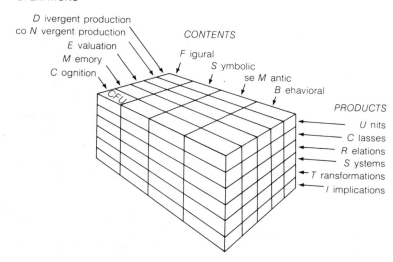

Figure 8–4. Guilford's Structure of the Intellect Model

Adapted from J. P. Guilford, The Nature of Human Intelligence. Copyright © 1967. Reprinted by permission of McGraw-Hill Book Company, Inc.

We can see that this model views intelligence as a collection of specific abilities —s—rather than as a general ability —G—as other I.Q. tests like the Stanford-Binet, the WISC, and WAIS do.

Theoretically, a test exists or could be devised for any intersection of the three planes. This would mean that, since there are five operations, four areas of content, and six types of products, there are $5 \times 4 \times 6 = 120$ different measurable aspects of intelligence. Any two people are unlikely to be identical in all 120 cells. Such a model makes us exceptionally aware of how unique each individual really is. As Guilford says, "There are 120 different ways of being intelligent."

Although Guilford's model seems quite complicated, it pulls a great deal of material together. Let us begin by defining Guilford's three dimensions. The operations are intellectual processes—the actions that the mind takes to digest the environment. The contents are all of the bits of information that make up the environment, such as sounds, sights, smells, words, numbers, etc. The products are the various ways that the mind has of organizing the environment by processing information leading to some end result.

If you image the mind as a computer, the structure of the intellect model would look something like Figure 8–5.

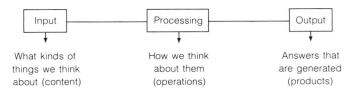

Figure 8–5. The Mind as Computer

Here is a brief description of each of the three major elements of the intellect and its subcategories, as shown in Figure 8–4.

Contents of Thought

These are the broad classes or types of information we take in from the environment.

How are you with figural content?

Are you able to complete a jigsaw puzzle quickly?

Do you tend to be good in many activities that involve your hands?

Figural (F). This content is the most concrete and has to do with tangible things. It probably combines what Bruner calls the enactive and iconic modes. The person who can fix a lawnmower just by the feel and sound of the machine is thinking figurally. So is a whittler who sees a new shape in a twig or branch, or a dressmaker who can visualize the way a piece of cloth will fold.

Symbolic (S). This content refers to marks or signs that have no real meaning but to which a meaning can be assigned. For example, *0* could be the letter O, the number zero, or, in Arabic, the symbol for the number 5.

Do you enjoy working with symbols as a mathematician or physicist might?

Being a teacher involves a great deal of semantic content. A teacher's professional life revolves around talking, listening, reading, and writing.

SeMantic (M). This content involves meanings to which words become attached. If a symbol evokes a meaning in our mind, at that point it is semantic content. If the word *house* simply conveyed the meaningless letters *h-o-u-s-e,* it would be symbolic but not semantic. If we heard the word, and pictured a house, without defining what house means, it would be figural. If we can think of *house* as an abstraction, it becomes semantic. For example, it might lead us to think of *house* as a noun and also as a verb, as in "to *house* someone."

Behavioral (B). This content is usually nonverbal information about the feelings and attitudes of others and of ourselves. Guilford sometimes called this *empathic* content. The ability to "read" someone else's facial expression or body language are examples of behavioral content.

Operations

If content is the *what* of thought, operations are the *how*. Each operation describes a particular way we process information.

Cognition (C). Guilford defines C as "immediate discovery, awareness, rediscovery, or recognition of information in various forms; comprehension or understanding." At this level, cognition refers to the information that the senses bring to the brain. These include visual, tactile, auditory, olfactory, and kinesthetic reception. If we imagine all the sensory apparatus conveying material to the brain for refined thinking, we have sensed the operation *cognition*. It is the basis of all other operations. It is the way information comes into the brain.

Memory (M). Memory is the retention or storage, with some degree of availability, of information in the same form it was committed to storage. Some information has entered the brain and can be easily gotten out. In the process of memory (or remembering), the mind is acting like a computer as it stores information. This information can be figural, symbolic, semantic, or behavioral.

CoNvergent Production (N). Convergent production involves generating new information from given information, leading to a single best answer. It is a logical process, in which lines of information narrow down and converge toward a single best answer. It is not simply remembering the best answer; it is important to differentiate it from memory. For example, "The capital of France is _____" is a memory retrieval (M). It could not be produced simply from internal logic. You could not figure out, without having learned it, that Paris is the answer. By contrast, the question "In what way are gasoline and wood alike?" is probably convergent. The mind searches through the various possibilities, and fixes on *fuel* as the single best answer. Of course, a student who had been carefully taught that gasoline and wood are both fuel, could answer simply from memory. In this instance, it would be an example not of convergent production but of memory.

Divergent Production (D). Here, too, information available from cognition is used to produce new information; but unlike convergent production, divergent thinking explores many paths. Divergent thinking is an important aspect of problem solving in that it permits the generation of numerous possible solutions. There is no one right answer. "Brainstorming" is a technique used to stimulate divergent thinking. Because this process emphasizes novelty and fluidity of production, it is very much a part of creativity.

A psychologist or counselor has to be very good at "reading" behavioral content. Teachers, too, must be capable of quickly noting and interpreting the nonverbal behavior of their students.

Some examples of cognition are:

Knowing that a baseball is white with stitching and quite hard. This is figural cognition.

Seeing a person crying and knowing that he is upset. This is behavioral cognition.

Which of these four types of content do you remember most easily— pictures, formulas, poetry, or faces?

For many people even social behavior involves convergent thinking. To do "what we are supposed to do" or "are expected to do" by others is to think convergently. Such behavior is influenced by a need to conform rather than deviate (or diverge).

Educational critics have argued that schools (from elementary to high school and often into college) emphasize memory and convergent thinking to the virtual exclusion of divergent thinking and evaluation.

Has this been true in your schooling?

To what extent have you been en-couraged to think creatively, e.g., write your own poetry or develop your own science projects or come up with your own explanations for histor-ical events?

Evaluation (E).   Evaluation is the intellectual process of judging the value of some information. Each time we process information, we check it through some evaluation process. For example, if we dip into our memory to retrieve information, we will then evaluate internally to check the correctness of what we have retrieved. If we see or think it is "wrong," we go back in for another try.

Products

Applying an operation to content yields a product. The mind seems to organize information into increasingly complex forms.

Try your hand at using the model in Figure 8–4. Can you locate the cell CMU?

Units (U).   The most basic building block is called a unit. For example, if we look at *CMU* in Figure 8–4, which presents Cognition of a SeMantic Unit, we are describing the perception of a single word. Other types of units can be words, ideas, figures, feelings, etc.

Classes (C).   Classes are groupings of units of information by common properties. For example, sparrows and parakeets are in the class *birds;* yellow and green are in the class *colors.*

Relations (R).   Relations involve ability to compare within a di-mension; for example, the opposite of high is low. A more complex relation is an analogy; boy is to girl as man is to woman. In all likeli-hood you cannot group relations without first understanding classes.

As you can see, we are moving to in-creasingly complex products. Being able to understand relationships re-quires much more intellectually than simply identifying a unit or being able to organize units into classes.

Auto mechanics who must remember how an engine they have just taken apart goes back together rely on a figural system.

Systems (S).   Systems are made up of internally consistent groupings of figural, symbolic, semantic, or behavioral contents. In order to understand a system, we must be able to perceive a set of interrelating parts. Examples of semantic systems would be the grammatical structure of a sentence and a psychologist's theory of human motivation.

Transformations (T).   Transformation requires the ability to see a new twist or a change in given information; for example, taking a story everyone knows and giving it a clever new ending. Punning is a good example of a semantic transformation. Like divergent produc-tion, transformation is highly related to creativity. Creative people are able to see new uses or possibilities for commonplace things.

Implications (I).   Implications involve the ability to see beyond the information given and extrapolate from it. It is the exact opposite of being literal-minded. As you read, you are jumping ahead in your mind, thinking, "Ah! If this is what he means, then. . . ."

Much of the work of educational psychologists involves perceiving the implications of various psychological theories for improving teaching and learning in the classroom.

The Value of Guilford's Model

Guilford's Structure of the Intellect (SOI) model has stimulated both educators and psychologists. Although at first glance it appears exceedingly complicated because of its 120 separate cells, it is economical because it organizes the complexity of mental processes into three simple areas, each of which is easily grasped by common sense. It is an information processing model. It is not based on pre-diction, nor is it rooted in any theory of innate ability. For this reason, information about students developed out of SOI testing does not suggest any limit to their capacity. It describes what their present abil-ity is. Therefore, it can be used for diagnostic purposes and, at the same time, can provide strong prescriptive implications. Mary N.

Meeker (1969), a student of Guilford, has developed a method whereby conventional diagnostic tests such as the WISC or the Stanford-Binet can be reanalyzed in terms of Guilfordian factors.

Here is one case presented by Meeker in which an SOI analysis resulted in a new "prescription" that proved quite helpful.

A boy in the fourth grade had been retained once and the school had recommended retention for the second time. The boy was so upset about another retention that his mother sought outside help. She felt he was very bright and something else was wrong.

His Binet was high, and Wide-Range Achievement Tests placed him at the seventh-grade level, except in spelling, which was low, yet he was unable to keep up with his work. He was not a real discipline problem, but the teachers felt he frequently showed poor judgment and could not be depended on to work independently or adequately, yet his verbal ability was so superior that it posed an enigma. (He showed strength in the "M," seMantic, columns except in evaluation.) His auditory problem solving in math was very high and when he was called on in class, he could be depended on to come up with correct answers in verbal solutions, although his written work was poor. (His SOI showed strength in symbols. The Binet, it must be remembered, is essentially an auditory test.)

The only SOI weaknesses were his failures in figural items, and this was a small sampling. School records showed two normal visual examinations, nevertheless we requested an *orthoptics* examination because of the figural and spelling deficits. The examination showed a most unusual visual defect, and corrective glasses were provided. On the basis of his high I.Q. score, the school principal agreed to let him go on with his class. Improvement was immediate in all written work, but especially so in spelling; in fact, he was soon taking "bonus" words in a month and making A's repeatedly. Similar results occurred in written math. His motivation was, of course, very high, as visual learning became easy.

Evaluation and judgment exercises were prescribed which parents were able to render. We asked his teacher to give him problem situations which depended on talking out alternate decisions, and to give him practice in committee leadership where he would have to make judgments. We felt sure his academic success would continue, and it has.*

Orthoptics is the study of the visual–perceptual process. Some psychologists and optometrists believe that perceptual problems can be remedied through retraining. Others believe that orthoptic training is not effective. Research is still inconclusive.

It is interesting to see how the comprehensive picture of this fourth grader's intellectual strengths and weaknesses provided by the SOI model led to the identification of a problem that no one knew existed.

The SOI model, with its emphasis on the three dimensions, also suggests novel ways of exploring important intellectual acts such as problem solving. Guilford reminds us that we have traditionally viewed problem solving as a series of orderly steps, such as those described by Dewey (1910)—seeing the problem, analyzing or structuring the problem, generating solutions, and judging or selecting one of the solutions. But, says Guilford, things are really much more complicated and dynamic. We perceive a problem, dip into our memory for possible ways of dealing with the problem, evaluate, reconsider, try another way, reevaluate, try still another operation such as convergent thinking or divergent thinking, reevaluate, and so on until we finally begin

Think about your own efforts at problem solving. Do they most closely fit Dewey's description or Guilford's?

* From M. N. Meeker, *The Structure of Intellect: Its Interpretation and Uses* (Columbus, Ohio: Merrill, 1969), pp. 158–159. Reprinted by permission.

Promoting divergent thinking and evaluation requires teachers to use good open-ended questioning techniques. Emphasis must be on the why and how rather than the what, who, when, and where, which all too often imply black or white, right or wrong.

Guilford's views on teaching strongly support the discovery approach we examined in Chapter 4. You might want to look back over the material presented on the cognitive theoretical perspective to see how it fits with Guilford's thinking.

to sense a "rightness" in our solution. This is a much more complex and chaotic process than Dewey's, but perhaps it more accurately describes the way many of us really think. It is not so much a logical explanation, like Dewey's, as it is a psychological description.

For the classroom teacher, probably the most important value of Guilford's model is its focus on operations, particularly convergent and divergent thinking. The distinction between convergence and mere memory helps the teacher to make clear for herself whether she wants students simply to memorize material or hopes they will develop greater reasoning power. For the same reason a teacher who understands the implications of Guilford's concept of divergent thinking may find herself asking, "Am I really helping my students to think for themselves and to generate new ideas, perhaps even ideas I had not thought of myself, or am I showing them what to think and then feeling disappointed when they don't come up with anything original?"

The model has shifted teacher attention to ways of releasing creativity in the classroom. In the same decade that Charles Silberman (1970) and others criticized American education as a wasteland of boring and repetitive practices, Guilford sounded a call for a new model of education, one in line with his conceptualization of the learner as an "agent for the processing of information," rather than mere memorizing. Guilford himself described what is perhaps the most important aspect of his model for educators when he said, "This conception of the learner leads us to the idea that learning is discovery of information, not merely the formation of associations . . ." (Guilford, 1959, p. 478).

Conclusions

In this chapter we have encouraged you to think about intelligence and its measurement. Our purpose has been to push you to think about your own concept of intelligence and your experiences with intelligence testing. We have explored the differences between individual and group tests as they have emerged over the history of intelligence testing.

Throughout our discussions we have been aware of the ongoing debate regarding which factor—nature (heredity) or nurture (environment)—is more important in determining a person's I.Q. Most current theories have a strong environmental component, and even the strongly hereditarian theories (such as Jensen's) recognize some environmental influence and thus the possibility for I.Q. change. Our approach to intelligence testing has been cautious; we have tried to show the potential limitations of intelligence tests brought on by their built-in cultural biases and potential misuse in labeling and stereotyping children.

Finally, we examined another way of looking at intelligence through Guilford's Structure of the Intellect. Here we focused on the value of thinking of the mind not as a blank tablet, waiting to be written on by the teacher, but instead as a kind of computer with a life of its own. The mind continually takes in the environment and creates its own internal organization. Guilford's model helps us to see the enormous variety of ways in which people differ in intellectual ability. It has brought us a giant step from the older notion of one global measure of intelligence toward the greatest possible respect for individual differences.

Some Good Books

Anastasi, Anne. *Psychological Testing.* 4th ed. New York: Macmillan, 1976. Although this book is practically an encyclopedia of tests and evaluative procedures, it is written with such clarity and style that it is a delight to read. It clearly describes each test and offers good criticism of its strengths and weaknesses.

Block, N. J. and Gerald Dworkin, eds. *The I.Q. Controversy.* New York: Pantheon, 1976. This book is probably the one best source of scholarly research and opinion on intelligence and the continuing controversy surrounding its measurement.

Hunt, J. Mc V. *Intelligence and Experience.* New York: Ronald Press, 1961. A far-ranging work on the history of the study of intelligence, emphasizing the turn away from viewing intelligence as fixed and immutable and toward the idea of an interaction between genetic endowment and environmental influence. Like Guilford, Hunt emphasizes the relationship between information processing and experience. He masterfully summarizes the relevance of Piaget's research (see Chapter 5) to the evaluation of intelligence.

Meeker, Mary N. *The Structure of Intellect: Its Interpretation and Uses.* Columbus, Ohio: Merrill, 1969. A complete description of Guilford's model, an examination of its educational value, and a technique for establishing tests like the WISC and the Binet in terms of Guilford's cube.

Articles, Studies, and Other References

Bogdan, Robert and Steven Taylor. "The Judged Not the Judges: An Insider's View of Mental Retardation." *American Psychologist* 31 (1976): 47–52. This is a report of an interview with a 26-year-old man who was labeled mentally retarded by his family, school teachers, and others. There is a great deal to learn from this passionate statement about the dangers of labels.

Jencks, Christopher and Mary Jo Bane. "Five Myths about Your I.Q." *Harper's* 246 (1973): 28. This easy to read article provides an environmentalist perspective on intelligence testing.

Jensen, Arthur. "How Much Can We Boost I.Q. and Scholastic Achievement?" *Harvard Educational Review.* Winter 1969, 39: pp. 1–123. This now classic statement presents Jensen's view on the heritability of I.Q., in which he makes the controversial claim that I.Q. is 80 percent determined by genetics and only 20 percent by environment. The other side of the picture is presented in the Spring 1969 issue of *Harvard Educational Review,* where seven leading scholars present their rebuttals to Jensen's theories.

Pines, Maya. "Head Head Start." *New York Times Magazine,* October 26, 1975, pp. 14 ff. Pines describes the Brookline Early Education Project in which teachers work directly with parents to help them more effectively stimulate the intelligence of their infants and toddlers (birth to age 2).

Suggestions for Action–Oriented Learning

1. Interview one or more teachers concerning their ideas about the nature of intelligence. Find out their school's position on group testing. What use do they make of the results of group tests?

2. Examine a school district's policy on the relationship between I.Q. score and class placement. If a group test is used, how aware is the school administration of the limitations of the test?

3. Examine Guilford's cube carefully. Try to rate your own education in terms of which cubes (e.g., *CFU*) have received the most stimulation and enrichment. Are there some that were all but ignored? Using Guilford's conception of intelligence, how might you have restructured your own education?

4. Survey a group of college students on their attitude toward intelligence testing. Do they have a general prejudice about such testing? How many are aware of the difference between group and individual intelligence evaluations?

5. Try to prepare a manual to help teachers present the pros and cons of intelligence testing to parents.

9
Motivation to Learn

Motivation and learning are intimately related. Try to recall how your motivation affected your learning when you took childhood lessons in dancing, music, art, or other activities.

Each of these statements looks at motivation in relation to a specific situation, but it is important to remember that human beings are always motivated, that is, pushed to behave in some way. Statements about motivating students are technically inaccurate since students are always doing something, and thus we must assume they are motivated. The teacher's problem is to encourage them to do something relevant to the lesson or subject.

In discussions about human behavior the subject of motivation comes up often. All of us use the word *motivation* in a variety of ways in our everyday language. We say, for example, "I feel motivated to learn how to ski." or "His motivation was good, but he just couldn't seem to get the idea of how to solve the problem." or "The teacher did a good job of motivating the class." While there are shades of difference in each of these uses of the term *motivation*, underlying them all is the notion of a driving force or an impulse that pushes us to behave in a particular way. What causes us to behave as we do has been of great concern to people since the beginning of our ability to think. Trying to understand what factors influence people to behave in particular ways is, of course, of special importance to those involved in helping others learn. For if people are to learn, they must be influenced to change their behavior in some way.

In the psychological literature motivation is seen as simultaneously functioning to (1) energize our behavior and get us moving, (2) direct our behavior toward some goal, and (3) maintain our behavior once it has been initiated (Bruner, 1966; Hamachek, 1975). The question of motivation, then, deals with the causes, or *why*, of behavior. Although the terms *needs, drives,* and *motives* are frequently used interchangeably, there are differences among them that can help us understand the nature of motivation. A *need* is a lack or deficiency in something that a person requires to function effectively. Needs can refer both to basic physiological deficiencies, e.g., a need for food or water, and to psychological deficiencies, e.g., wanting approval. The term *drive*, on the other hand, focuses on the energizing aspects of motivation. Drives are states of arousal or tension that are reduced by the satisfaction of needs. Finally, *motive* refers to the goal toward which the behavior is directed—e.g., "His motive was to do well on his project." Putting our three psychological terms for motivation together, we might say that a person's lack of something—her need—creates a state of arousal or tension within her—her drive—that is the source of her striving for a particular goal—her motive.

Now that we have formulated the beginnings of a concept of motivation, try the following exercise.

Exploration 9–1: Reflecting on Learning Situations That Involved "High" Motivation and Those That Involved "Low" Motivation

Think of one learning situation within the last year in which you were highly motivated and another in which you were not at all motivated—you were "turned off." These situations may have occurred within formal courses or in other circumstances, such as learning to fix your car or play tennis, or learning a part for a play. Describe each situation in a few sentences.

High Motivation Situation

Low Motivation Situation

Once you have completed your descriptions answer the following questions for each description:

1. Where did the idea to learn come from?

   High Motivation—

Low Motivation —

2. How much time did you devote to the activity?

High Motivation —

Low Motivation —

3. How intensively were you involved with the activity? In other words, did you find yourself absorbed in the activity or were you easily distracted?

High Motivation —

Low Motivation —

4. What emotions did you experience as you were carrying out the activity? Happiness, frustration, anger, etc?

High Motivation —

Low Motivation —

5. What would be the consequences if you did not learn what you were supposed to?

High Motivation —

Low Motivation —

6. Upon mastering the activity, what would you get?

Check as many items as are appropriate.

High Low

—— —— Food or water

—— —— Money, a prize, an award

—— —— A grade

—— —— Recognition from peers, parents, teachers, etc.

—— —— Feeling of accomplishment and satisfaction

—— —— Other (specify) _____

_____

Now that you have explored the two learning situations, you should be able to see differences in your motivation in each. It might be valuable for you to summarize what you learned about your motivation in a sentence or two. As we discuss various aspects of motivation we will ask you to refer to these data to clarify our discussion.

Motivation—why people behave as they do—has long occupied the attention of psychologists, who have carried out much research and developed many theories to help us understand the phenomenon. Some of the early views of motivation suggested that people were continually seeking to achieve pleasure and avoid pain. These *hedonistic* views were built upon by Sigmund Freud, who proposed that sources of pleasure and pain could be unconscious as well as conscious (Freud, 1960), originating in experiences of which the individual was no longer aware.

Today thinking about motivation can be represented best by two major theoretical orientations, one emphasizing the *extrinsic* nature of motivation and the other emphasizing the *intrinsic*. Extrinsically motivated behavior has a goal external to the act itself. Extrinsically motivated behavior can be striving to meet a *physiological need,* such as eating to alleviate hunger, or a *psychological* (learned) *need,* such as reading a book to pass a test. The common element in both cases is that the behavior is directed toward a goal extrinsic to the act itself— eating *in order to* reduce hunger and reading *in order to* pass the test. If, on the other hand, a person were to eat simply for the satisfaction of eating or read out of interest or curiosity without expecting a grade or a pat on the back, then we would say that the behavior was intrinsically motivated—the act was satisfying in itself. Many types of human behavior probably are motivated simultaneously by both extrinsic and intrinsic factors. However, we will examine each orientation separately since their implications for facilitating learning are quite different.

Did your high motivation situation in Exploration 9–1 involve extrinsic or intrinsic motivation? What about your low motivation situation?

Is your motivation to read primarily extrinsic or intrinsic?

Does your answer depend on the type of book—e.g., chemistry, extrinsic; sports, intrinsic?

Return to Chapter 4 if you need help in recalling behaviorism.

Extrinsic Motivation for Learning

The extrinsic orientation emerges from behavioristic psychology. Here all motivation is seen as arising from innate organic drives, such as hunger, thirst, sex, etc., or from learned drives that have developed through association with the satisfaction of organic drives. Thus as a baby's hunger drive is satisfied at his mother's breast (or as he is given his bottle), he learns to associate the pleasurable feelings he experiences with his caretaker. Gradually her attention to him and approval of what he does become a learned drive—something he seeks. This learning generalizes to other people, and the child develops a drive for social approval that can push him to behave in a variety of ways. Other learned drives develop in a similar manner; for example, the drive for money, high grades, success, etc.

Sometimes organic drives are called primary drives *and learned drives are called* secondary drives.

The extrinsic theory of motivation, therefore, emphasizes the importance of rewards in promoting learning. Rewards may be any objects or events that strengthen learning by reducing an organic or learned drive. For the most part, the rewards used in school settings are directed at learned drives since teachers have little control over the organic drives of their students. Most commonly teachers capitalize on students' learned drives for praise, good grades, and teacher and peer approval. The theory is that if we want people to learn certain things, then we must make their getting something they want contingent upon their first demonstrating learning. In essence, the teacher communicates to students either explicitly or implicitly the message "If you want a A on your report card, you'll have to. . . ." or "If you want my praise in front of the whole class you must. . . ."

Behavior modification is a means of promoting learning through the systematic use of extrinsic reinforcers to reward, and thus strengthen, desirable behavior (Madsen and Madsen, 1974).

With children who are severely retarded or severely emotionally disturbed, behaviorism advocates the use of food as rewards. In much the same way that dogs, bears, dolphins, and other animals are trained to do tricks, children are shaped toward certain behaviors. For instance, an autistic child who doesn't speak might be given an M & M each time she looks at her speech teacher. The goal is to help her learn to imitate sounds and eventually speak.

A useful extrinsic approach to motivation is the Premack Principle (Premack, 1965). This principle states that behavior that naturally occurs frequently may be used to reinforce behavior that occurs infrequently. Parents use this intuitively when they tell children that they can't go outside until they finish their supper. By observing children carefully during free periods, teachers can note the activities that they engage in often. Then they can use those activities as positive reinforcers for school work or other activities that children aren't likely to do on their own. For example, a fifth grader who likes to read science fiction could be given time to read after completing math problems he has difficulty with.

While there is no question that rewards work, there are some limitations to their value in promoting learning. Before reading our views, try to list below three weaknesses in relying on rewards such as grades, praise, and approval. You might want to consider your own school experience with various rewards.

How important were good grades to you while you were in high school? Can you recall any students who did not seem afraid of getting low grades?

1.

2.

3.

Critics of overreliance on rewards make a number of important points. First, they point out that many drives to learn are intrinsic, not extrinsic, and thus rewards are often not necessary. Second, when students are always rewarded for desirable behavior, they come to expect a reward. Teachers can get themselves in the same bind as parents who pay their children for doing family chores and find the children then may avoid doing anything to help unless they are paid. The third point was expressed by Haim Ginott (1972) who said constant praise loses its meaning and sincerity. It also makes the student dependent on the person giving the praise rather than developing self-reliance.

In discussing extrinsic aspects of motivation, we must deal with punishment since it is so widely threatened—and on occasion used—in schools. Whereas rewards are used to encourage people to do things that lead to learning, punishments are used to discourage people from doing things that are thought not to contribute to learning. The theory is that both the threat of punishment and its application will create a drive in the students—anxiety—which they will seek to reduce. In other words, Sue's anxiety about the upcoming history test will "motivate" her to read and study in order to lessen her anxiety. If she doesn't study and fails the test (the punishment for not studying), the next time she will know to study.

Can you recall how punishment or the threat of it affected you in high school and/or junior high school?

Techniques that threaten punishment and create anxiety are widely used in schools from the elementary to the doctoral level. However, psychological research raises serious questions about their value in promoting learning. Much evidence shows a negative relationship between anxiety and school achievement (Gaudrey and Spielberger, 1971.) A certain amount of anxiety is probably necessary to get us going when we have to face hard work (e.g., "I'd love to go skiing this week, but I've got to get this paper done"). On the other hand, high levels of anxiety can be so overwhelming that they become self-defeating, as in the case of children who are so frightened of parental or teacher retaliation that they become disorganized and unable to think clearly. Furthermore, the anxiety associated with both the threat and the use of punishment is often generalized to the teacher and the learning situation. Consequently, communication can be destroyed as students feel hostility toward the person who threatens or punishes them. The short-term benefit of temporarily stopping a behavior seems to be outweighed by punishment's creation of fearful, passive students.

The psychological literature is so negative about the effects of anxiety and punishment that practitioners of behavior modification argue strongly for using positive reinforcers—rewards—and ignoring, not punishing, undesirable behavior. Their position is that unreinforced behavior will gradually be eliminated (Joyce and Weil, 1972).

See Johnston (1972) for an excellent review of the literature on punishment and Holt, How Children Fail *(1964) on the effects of punishment.*

Intrinsic Motivation for Learning

The intrinsic view of motivation sees the impulse to behave as coming from within the individual rather than from external rewards. In other words, an intrinsically motivated behavior is one in which the goal is inherent in the behavior itself. Listed below are some examples of behaviors that are intrinsically motivated. As you read through the list, check those you have experienced and then add a couple of examples of other things you do that are intrinsically satisfying.

For these activities to be intrinsically motivated, you must have chosen them because of your own interest. Any rewards must come primarily from the act of doing them not from rewards or the praise of others.

___ Reading a novel and being so caught up in it that you can't put it down.

___ On a basketball court by yourself, trying to see how many foul shots you can make in a row without missing.

___ "People watching" as you sit in an airport.

___ Playing a particular musical piece until you get it to sound the way you want it to.

___ Keeping a diary or writing poetry with no plan to show it to anyone.

___ Solving a difficult math problem just for the fun of it.

___ Completing a jigsaw puzzle.

___ Riding a motorcycle.

___ Running long distances alone, with no plan to ever enter competition.

___ Teaching yourself a new language.

___ Visiting an art or historical museum.

___ _____

___ _____

At this point you might look back at the situations of high and low motivation that you described in Exploration 9–1 to see whether the motivation was primarily intrinsic or extrinsic.

You can see from your responses to the list that many of the things we do seem to be intrinsically motivated. A number of theories explain this type of motivation. We will focus here on one of those theories, that of Jerome Bruner, since it provides an overview of intrinsic motivation, especially in relation to learning.

Bruner, you will recall from Chapter 5, discusses predisposition for learning as encompassing all the factors that ready an individual to learn, including motivation. Bruner believes that people have a "will to learn" made up of powerful intrinsic motives. Although reinforcement or external reward is helpful in initiating certain actions or even in making their repetition more likely, Bruner feels that only through intrinsic motives is the will to learn sustained:

> The will to learn is an intrinsic motive, one that finds its source and its reward in its own exercise. The will to learn becomes a "problem" only under specialized circumstances like those of a school, where a curriculum is set, students confined, and a path fixed. The problem exists not so much in learning itself, but in the fact that what the school imposes often fails to enlist the natural energies that sustain spontaneous learning—curiosity, a desire for competence, aspiration to emulate a model, and a deep-sensed commitment to the web of social reciprocity. Our concern has been with how these energies may be cultivated in

support of school learning. If we know little firmly, at least we are not without reasonable hypotheses about how to proceed. The practice of education does, at least, produce interesting hypotheses. After all, the Great Age of Discovery was made possible by men whose hypotheses were formed before they had developed a decent technique for measuring longitude.

You will have noted by now a considerable de-emphasis of "extrinsic" rewards and punishments as factors in school learning. There has been in these pages a rather intentional neglect of the so-called *Law of Effect,* which holds that a reaction is more likely to be repeated if it has previously been followed by a "satisfying state of affairs." I am not unmindful of the notion of reinforcement. It is doubtful, only, that "satisfying states of affairs" are reliably to be found outside learning itself—in kind or harsh words from the teacher, in grades and gold stars, in the absurdly abstract assurance to the high school student that his lifetime earning will be better by 80 percent if he graduates. External reinforcement may indeed get a particular act going and may even lead to its repetition, but it does not nourish, reliably, the long course of learning by which man slowly builds in his own way a serviceable model of what the world is and what it can be (Bruner, 1966, pp. 127–128).*

The Law of Effect was first formulated by Edward L. Thorndike, probably America's most famous educational psychologist in the first half of the twentieth century. A behaviorist, Thorndike saw learning as simply a series of associations or connections between stimuli and responses. He emphasized the importance of extrinsic factors in motivating learning. As you can see from Bruner's statement, he and Thorndike are at opposite ends of the spectrum regarding motivation. In Chapter 13 you will read more about the differences between a behavioristic view of motivation and a cognitive or phenomenological view.

Bruner identifies four major intrinsic motives: curiosity, a desire for competence, aspiration to emulate a model, and a commitment to social reciprocity. The first of these, curiosity, is crucial to the child's learning about the world. Wanting to explore, seeking answers to questions, and continually asking *why*? are evidences of this motive in young children. Just watch a 2-year-old within a few minutes bang on a toy work bench, look at a book, run to look out the window, and talk to a favorite doll.

Although as adults we may have learned to focus our attention for longer periods of time, we too are motivated by curiosity. When was the last time you saw someone you didn't know and found yourself wondering what that person was like? When did you last browse in a bookstore or a record store for a long time without buying anything? Berlyne (1965), who has done a great deal of research on curiosity, sees it as a motive for learning that arises when conflicting responses to a situation are possible. If teachers want to capitalize on the curiosity of young people, they must see that their questions have alternate possibilities for answers rather than "right" answers and that the classroom has a variety of exciting learning materials.

The design of a classroom to tap a child's curiosity is something that advocates of open education, like Herbert Kohl (1969), make a strong case for.

Robert White (1959), in studying the desire to achieve competence, has shown that play is serious business. Through it children learn to cope with their environment and develop a sense of their own competence. Becoming good at something and being productive give a feeling of accomplishment that is its own reward, with praise, money, or other extrinsic incentives not required. In bed after the lights are out and parents are no longer present to be impressed and

Erikson also emphasized the importance of competence. The industry vs. inferiority conflict of the ages from 6 to 11 or 12 centers around the child's emerging need to feel capable and productive.

---

* J. S. Bruner, *Toward a Theory of Instruction.* The Belknap Press of Harvard University Press, copyright © 1966 by the President and Fellows of Harvard College. Reprinted by permission.

The drive for competence is well illustrated in children's games. Can you recall how you felt when you learned to jump rope or ride a bike?

Closely related to competence is what McClelland (1965) calls achievement motivation, the desire to excel or do well. However, McClelland differs from Bruner and Nardine in that he believes that this motive, which eventually becomes intrinsic, is learned. Parental influences are crucial in determining whether a child develops achievement motivation. However, children who have not learned this motive at home can be helped to develop it through special courses and training programs. A good discussion of this educational process appears in Alschuler, Tabor, and McIntyre, Teaching Achievement Motivation *(1971).*

Freud's theory of development heavily emphasizes the child's motivation to be like his parents. Particularly important is "identification," through which a child models himself after the parent of his own sex and learns behavior appropriate to his sex.

provide reinforcement, a 3-year-old may rehearse the language she is developing. In older children the drive for competence may take the form of a 5-year-old's practicing on her two-wheeler or a 17-year-old's struggling to master a piece of music on the guitar.

The third and fourth of Bruner's intrinsic motives for learning involve interaction with others. Aspiration to emulate a model refers to the process of identification, through which people model themselves after others, achieving pleasure by being like them. A commitment to social reciprocity involves a need to work with others cooperatively. As we think about a variety of social settings, including our homes, schools, religious institutions, communities, and work places, the importance of our *reference groups* can be seen. The astute teacher who recognizes the power of these social motives can promote learning by modeling the personal and intellectual qualities he would like his students to develop; i.e., he must practice what he preaches. In addition, he can humanize the classroom environment by giving students opportunities for interaction and cooperation in group activities and projects.

Our views about motivation have important implications for learning. If we agree with the extrinsic perspective, then we are concerned with providing rewards that respond to the various drives of our students. On the other hand, if we think of motivation for learning as primarily intrinsic, then we are likely to give students freedom so that their curiosity, competence, and social motives might flourish. In reality, most types of learning involve both extrinsic and intrinsic motivation. We will conclude our discussion of theories of motivation by acquainting you with Maslow's hierarchy of needs theory, which incorporates both extrinsic and intrinsic motives.

Maslow's Hierarchy of Needs Theory

Abraham Maslow's theories of human motivation, which can be applied to virtually any aspect of behavior, have made a major contribution to American psychology. You will recall that Maslow was identified in Chapter 4 as a leader of the school of thought called humanistic psychology or, as Maslow himself called it, third force psychology.

Maslow's book *Motivation and Personality,* published in 1954 when most psychologists identified themselves as Freudians or behaviorists, was the outgrowth of years of reading, thinking, and discussions with the major psychologists of the time. Although Maslow was educated at the University of Wisconsin as a behaviorist, his later reading in Gestalt and Freudian psychology and the birth of his first child were major factors in his move away from behaviorism. The shock and horror of World War II had a profound impact on Maslow, who resolved in the early days of the war to seek a comprehensive theory of human behavior that could become "a psychology for the peace-table." The theory Maslow developed and first presented in *Motivation and Personality* was a synthesis of much psychological thought. It was not a rejection of either behaviorism or Freudian psychology; rather, it built upon the strengths of each, incorporating them with many other psychological viewpoints.

Maslow believed that a theory of behavior had to include both internal and external determinants. With his emphasis on the importance of instinct and the subconscious, Freud had focused on the internal; the behaviorists (Watson, Skinner, and others) had focused on the external, one's experiences. Maslow said that to understand human motivation we must study both the external, objective world and the internal, subjective world. The hierarchy of needs theory brings together extrinsic and intrinsic influences on motivation. Included in the hierarchy are seven levels of needs, illustrated in the

Maslow wrote about the impact of the birth of his children on him: "Our first baby changed me as a psychologist. It made the behaviorism I had been so enthusiastic about look so foolish that I could not stomach it any more. It was impossible. Having a second baby, and learning how profoundly different people are even before birth, made it impossible for me to think in terms of the kind of learning psychology in which one can teach anybody anything. Or the John B. Watson theory of 'Give me two babies and I will make one into this and one into the other.' It is as if he never had any children. We know only too well that a parent cannot make his children into anything. Children make themselves into something" (Maslow, 1971, p. 169).

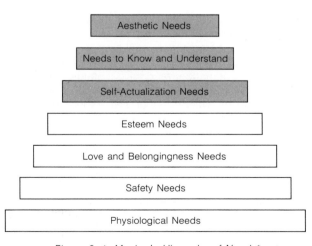

Figure 9–1. Maslow's Hierarchy of Needs*

*   The shading of the top three levels of needs indicates that they are *being needs.* The bottom four levels are *deficiency needs.*

chart in Figure 9–1. According to Maslow, individuals cannot move up the hierarchy to meet their higher level needs until their needs at the lower levels are satisfied.

The following descriptions provide examples of each category of needs Maslow has identified.

Physiological Needs.   These are the survival needs, including oxygen, food, water, temperature regulation, and physical comfort. Maslow points out that these needs are *prepotent;* that is, they must be satisfied before other higher level needs. These needs exert powerful influences on behavior only as long as they remain unfulfilled. For most of us who are fortunate enough to seldom be really hungry, the need for food is not generally a major influence on how we behave.

Because being hungry can so directly interfere with learning, the U.S. federal government has often provided school breakfast and lunch programs for children from economically disadvantaged homes who might not otherwise get enough to eat.

Safety Needs.   If physiological needs have been satisfied, then the needs for physical and psychological safety become important. These include the need for protection from danger and harm and the need for a secure, predictable social environment. For people living under conditions of war or in high-crime neighborhoods, these needs become major influences on behavior. In less dramatic but equally influential ways, people, especially children, living in homes where there is fighting, constant criticism, or sickness may feel threatened and spend much time trying to cope with that threat, whether it is physical or psychological. Schools in which children face destructive, negativistic teachers or chaotic classrooms also fail to meet the students' safety needs.

Think about how you felt in a class in which you were afraid of the teacher.

Love and Belongingness Needs.   When both the physiological and safety needs are reasonably well gratified, the love, affection, and belongingness needs emerge. The need to be loved and to give love motivates many of the things we do, such as seeking to please our family or our closest friends. Many things we do also are affected by our desire to be recognized, to be appreciated, and to feel we belong, whether to a fraternity, a women's liberation group, a neighborhood, or a professional association.

Maslow is talking about genuine emotional love not simply sexual love, which can be seen as a basic physiological need.

Esteem Needs.   The esteem needs include two closely related categories—self-respect and the respect of others. Self-respect derives from feelings of competence, achievement, independence, and confidence, all of which are influenced by the way others value us. As others accord us acceptance, recognition, status, and appreciation, we internalize these attitudes and become self-respecting.

Try to recall a few situations in high school classes or extracurricular activities in which your esteem needs were well taken care of.

Self-Actualization Needs.   Our self-actualization needs push us to fulfill our potential or, in other words, to become all that we are capable of becoming. Our lower needs for survival, safety, love, and esteem must be largely fulfilled if we are to achieve self-actualization. For one person an important aspect of self-actualization could be learning to write poetry, for another it could be improving as a football player, and for still another it could be becoming a better parent.

Maslow believes that because each human being is unique, the way one person works toward self-actualization will differ from the way another seeks it.

Needs to Know and Understand.   The needs to know and understand take the form of curiosity and a search for meaning. This quest to understand, to analyze, to look for relations, and to try to develop a system of values is self-motivated; it involves learning for its own sake.

It is interesting to see that for Maslow curiosity can't flower until one's lower level needs are met.

Aesthetic Needs. Once all of the other needs have been met, the needs for beauty and the appreciation of the order of life become important.

Maslow calls attention to the hierarchical nature of needs. That is, when our basic needs are not met, they draw attention away from the higher level needs. The lower level needs form barriers to the realization of the higher level needs and must be cleared away before we can move upward. An important distinction can be made between the first four levels—the physiological, safety, love and belongingness, and esteem needs—and the top three levels—the self-actualization, knowing and understanding, and aesthetic needs (see Figure 9–1). Maslow has called the four lower levels *deficiency needs* (D-needs) because each involves a lack of something that can be met only by factors external to the individual. The three higher levels he refers to as *being needs* (B-needs) because they spring from within the individual (Maslow, 1968). The deficiency needs provide extrinsic motivation since they are satisfied by external factors and involve dependence upon others; the being needs provide intrinsic motivation since they involve the self-satisfaction that comes from achieving one's potential or utilizing one's curiosity.

Underlying Maslow's view of human motivation is a concept of psychological growth that suggests we all have within us the capacity to change and to realize our inherent potential. However, also within us is a conflicting tendency to seek safety or security. As an illustration of this conflict, let's picture 8-year-old Sandra learning to jump off a diving board into the deep end of a swimming pool. Her growth needs push her to want to jump, but her safety needs cause her to pull back. Sandra gets up the nerve to venture out on the diving board, but then she walks back, away from the end. She returns to the end and looks down into the water below, maybe even curling her toes over the edge, but again hesitates and allows another person to go ahead of her. The conflict between her growth needs (being needs), on the one hand, and her safety needs (deficiency needs), on the other, seems to have caught her in a tug-of-war. If Sandra is to jump, and thus grow, in this situation, she must be open to the new experience, willing to take a risk, and able to transcend her fears. As we encounter many such new situations in life, we must "jump" if we are to grow.

The order of the needs within Maslow's hierarchy is not absolute. Some people can function at the level of self-actualization before their basic needs are met; for example, writers who get so wrapped up in their work that they forget hunger; or Martin Luther King, who would not allow his need for safety to interfere with his work in the civil rights movement.

You will recall from Chapter 5 that Bruner discusses this same conflict. He uses the word coping *to describe the desire to be open to new experiences on the one hand, and* defending *to describe the tendency toward safety and security.*

Educational Implications of Maslow's Theory

Maslow's theory of motivation suggests many implications for education. Maslow sees a teacher as a growth facilitator or, in his own words, a *Taoistic helper,* in contrast to the traditional view of a teacher as a boss, lecturer, and reinforcer. Maslow's ideal teacher is receptive rather than intrusive and helps all students to learn what kind of people they are. The teacher's goal is always to take students from where they are toward self-actualization. This humanistic teacher's method involves asking rather than telling, nudging rather than push-

Taoism is a Chinese philosophical system that advocates selflessness and emphasizes human oneness with the world. Many of Maslow's basic concepts are drawn from this and other areas of Eastern philosophy.

Maslow writes: "Taoistic means asking rather than telling. It means nonintruding, noncontrolling. It stresses noninterfering observation rather than a controlling manipulation. It is receptive and passive rather than active and forceful. It is like saying that if you want to learn about ducks, then you had better ask the ducks instead of telling them. So also for human children. In prescribing 'what is best for them' it looks as if the best technique for finding out what is best for them is to develop techniques for getting them to tell us what is best for them" (1971, p. 15).

As you think of suggestions for more actively involving these tenth graders in the learning process, reflect on the extent to which you express yourself verbally in your own classes. Do you tend to be a participant or a nonparticipant in class discussions? To what extent does your participation vary with the type of teacher you have? In what ways do your growth needs conflict with your safety needs as you participate or avoid participating?

ing, encouraging rather than threatening, and supporting rather than criticizing.

The following activity will help you consider the types of things a teacher might do to help a person grow. On the basis of your own thoughts or your reading of Maslow's ideas, respond as honestly as possible to the questions.

Exploration 9–2: Promoting Growth by Helping Nonparticipants Become Participants in Class Discussion

Imagine that you are teaching a tenth-grade English course. Five of the students have told you that they like the class discussions you frequently hold but they just can't seem to participate verbally even though they want to. They have many thoughts about the issue being discussed but have trouble in getting up the nerve to speak.

What could you do to increase their participation?

1.

2.

3.

4.

5.

6.

Having responded to the above questions, you may want to compare your suggestions with the following implications for teaching that can be drawn from Maslow's views on motivation.

1. It is essential to know each student as an individual and establish an open, trusting relationship in which genuine two-way communication can occur. Since each human being is unique and has different abilities, interests, weaknesses, etc., teachers can promote self-actualization only when they are aware of individual differences.

2. A continuous process of diagnosis is important in suggesting which types of learning experiences are most appropriate for which students. Asking students to describe their own interests, abilities, weaknesses, and needs can be most helpful in developing appropriate prescriptions for learning.

How might a teacher get to know students as individuals?

3. A teacher should do everything she can to see that the lower level needs of her students are met. For example, she might recommend that a child who frequently comes to school tired be seen by a school nurse and possibly by a counselor in order to determine the source of the problem and eliminate it. Or she might note that a student who is seen as an outsider by his peers continually disrupts the class out of a need for recognition. By giving such a student a more socially acceptable way of gaining recognition—for example, allowing him to help another student in a subject he is more skilled in—she might lessen his disruptive behavior.

Obviously a teacher cannot take care of all of the lower level needs of her pupils. Just by being aware of them, however, she should be able to plan lessons more realistically.

4. Students whose deficiency needs are not met will be reached more effectively through extrinsic reinforcements for learning. In order to feel secure, see themselves as belonging, and experience some esteem in the classroom, they may require structured learning experiences, more direction by the teacher, and more praise, encouragement, and possibly tangible rewards for learning.

5. On the other hand, students who are functioning at the levels of Maslow's being needs can benefit from a freer, more student-directed learning experience. These students are able to function independently since their deficiency needs have been met and their behavior is influenced primarily by intrinsic motives such as curiosity, competence, the drive for self-actualization, etc.

6. Helping students to grow and learn is not easy. There is virtually always some conflict between their need to be open to new experience and to change and their need to remain comfortable and secure at their present level of functioning. Consequently, a teacher must simultaneously respond to both sets of needs—the growth needs and the safety needs. If the teacher pushes a student too hard, the student may become anxious and threatened, only to retreat from the learning experience. On the other hand, if the teacher doesn't encourage the student enough, no growth may occur. It is critical to know the student well enough to know how and when "to nudge without pushing."

Can you describe one of your teachers who had a gift for nudging you to try something you were fearful of without pushing you?

Responding to Motivational Differences: Open Education, Traditional Education, and Alternatives in Education

The views of motivation we have been discussing can be applied in different types of learning environments. In recent years in the

All five of the books referred to here make excellent reading for anyone interested in understanding the issues discussed by these critics. They also will help you to clarify many of your own views about teachers and the teaching and learning process.

The wave of educational criticism of the middle and late 1960s was part of a much larger social phenomenon in the United States. During the time of the Viet Nam War and many civil disturbances, virtually all American social institutions were being attacked as unresponsive to the needs of the people.

In the works referred to here, the early critics present their own solutions to the problems of American education. It might be fun to read one or two of these books after having read the author's previous book.

Any attempt to place most approaches to formal education into one of two categories is obviously an oversimplification. Yet by focusing on two quite different educational approaches, we can help you better understand how views of motivation relate to educational practice.

In his most detailed statement on education, The Technology of Teaching *(1968), B. F. Skinner emphasizes the importance of the teacher in structuring the curriculum and reinforcing learning.*

United States a great deal of often heated discussion has asked what types of schools and classrooms most effectively promote learning. Beginning in the late 1960s, many critics claimed that schools have frequently inhibited rather than promoted growth and learning. Jonathan Kozol (1967) spoke of the psychological destruction of black children he encountered as he taught in the Boston ghetto; Herbert Kohl (1967) chronicled similar experiences as a teacher in New York's Harlem. George Leonard (1968) charged that formal education stifled the potential of children; John Holt (1964) described how schools teach children to fail; and Charles Silberman (1970), after a 3-1/2-year study of more than 100 schools, concluded that, for the most part, schools were joyless, dehumanizing places that mutilated love of learning and spontaneity. These authors represented just the vanguard in a period of intense questioning of traditional approaches to education. Soon to join them were other critics from the ranks of high school and college students, parents, school teachers and administrators, teacher educators, the media, and local, state, and national government.

Initially, the flood of books and discussion focused more on the problems than on possible solutions. However, proposals gradually began to suggest new approaches to teaching and learning. Some of the first and most outspoken critics put forth their solutions, with Kohl (1969) writing a guide for an open classroom, Kozol (1972) describing a type of free school relevant to the needs of disadvantaged children, Holt (1967) writing about how children learn, and Silberman (1973) collecting articles on the theory and practice of open education.

The discussion of what types of educational environments most effectively promote learning continues today. This discussion centers around two approaches to teaching and learning, which we shall refer to as *traditional education* and *open education*. Open education was advocated by many of the critics writing in the late 1960s and early 1970s. Since the mid-1970s there has been a growing backlash against open education, with many educators and parents supporting a return to traditional education, which is sometimes called the Back-to-Basics Movement. Underlying these two orientations are two very different philosophical and psychological perspectives on human nature and motivation.

Let's consider first the traditional approach, which remains the prevailing approach in American schools. This approach sees motivation to learn as primarily extrinsic, i.e., we do things essentially to gain rewards and avoid punishments, both of which come to us from beyond ourselves. If we believe that the primary motivation for learning is extrinsic, then a number of implications for teaching necessarily follow. First, the class must be teacher-centered in order to make certain that students use their time wisely. Second, the curriculum should be fairly tightly planned and structured so that new experience builds upon old and reinforcements occur to strengthen learning. Third, the teacher must continually be on the lookout for new reinforcers, both rewards and punishments, that will motivate students.

In contrast with traditional education, open education grows out of a view of the motives for learning as primarily intrinsic. Critics of traditional education like A. S. Neill (1960), who founded and directed the Summerhill School in England until his death in 1973, believe that we have within us a powerful drive to learn, which must be allowed to flourish. Consequently, rather than being structured, the educational environment must be as "open" as possible to allow students the freedom to learn. Advocates of open education see children as innately curious about virtually everything and they try to create classrooms that have a multitude of resources for learning. The reinforcement students receive will come from satisfying their own curiosity or achieving a new competence rather than from extrinsic rewards or punishment. In an open classroom the teacher becomes a facilitator or guide, not a director of learning. Because it is assumed that children are genuinely motivated to learn for learning's sake, they can be given much latitude in directing their own educational experience.

There is certainly evidence to support both traditional education and open education. We suggest that the needs of students should determine which approach is utilized. Some students may be ready for and comfortable with an educational experience that gives them maximum freedom and many opportunities for self-directed learning. Others whose basic needs have not been met (and who are operating at the lower levels of Maslow's hierarchy) may require much direction and extrinsic reinforcement as they learn. If we are to respond to individual differences among learners, we must provide many alternative types of learning environments, including both open and traditional approaches.

A. S. Neill's Summerhill: A Radical Approach to Child-Rearing *(1960) describes his school and its educational philosophy. Some people love his book, yet others charge that his school is naively utopian, allows children to choose to learn nothing, and does not prepare people to live in the real world of laws, restrictions, etc. A balanced presentation of the pros and cons of Summerhill is the collection of articles by educators, psychologists, and sociologists entitled* Summerhill For and Against *(1970).*

In Freedom to Learn *(1969) Carl Rogers provides further psychological underpinnings for open education. Rogers was the first to use the term* learning facilitator *to replace* teacher *and to stress the importance of student-directed learning.*

If you would like to learn more about open education and how it has been influenced by the British primary schools, you might look for Roland Barth's Open Education and the American School *(1972).*

Conclusions

This chapter has tried to help you understand the differences between extrinsic motivation and intrinsic motivation. As you have seen, there is ample support in the psychological literature for each viewpoint. Probably you can recall times when you learned things primarily out of a desire for some reward, and other times when the satisfaction of learning itself seemed to be the major force pushing you forward.

As a synthesis of many of the different viewpoints on motivation, Maslow's hierarchy of needs theory is useful. By suggesting that each human being is unique, possesses tremendous potential for self-actualization, and at any given time may be operating at a different level of needs, Maslow gives us a model for better understanding ourselves and ultimately others. Maslow's theory can assist teachers in diagnosing motivational differences in students and prescribing either traditional or open approaches.

What type of student are you?

Do you tend to learn better when you have a great deal of freedom or do you do better with more structure and extrinsic rewards?

Which approach do you think you would prefer as a teacher—open or traditional? Why?

Some Good Books

Barth, Roland S. *Open Education and the American School.* New York: Agathon, 1972. Barth has put forth an analysis of the history of open education, its basic assumptions, and the problems frequently encountered by those committed to implementing it.

Fantini, Mario. *Alternative Education: A Sourcebook for Parents, Teachers, Students, and Administrators.* Garden City, N.Y.: Doubleday, 1976. This collection of articles is an excellent resource for anyone interested in alternative schools and programs.

Goble, Frank G. *The Third Force: The Psychology of Abraham Maslow.* New York: Grossman, 1970. This book is a sensitive presentation of Maslow's theories of humanistic psychology that gives insight into Maslow the man.

Kohl, Herbert R. *The Open Classroom.* New York: New York Review Books, 1969. In this concise paperback Kohl offers practical suggestions for creating an open classroom and so provides his readers with a good introduction to the concept of open education.

Kozol, Jonathan. *Free Schools.* Boston: Houghton Mifflin, 1972. In his follow-up to *Death at an Early Age,* Kozol discusses the problems unique to creating an urban free school. He also challenges the "do your own thing" ethic and laissez faire approach of some rural and suburban free schools.

Maslow, Abraham M. *The Farther Reaches of Human Nature.* New York: Viking, 1971. This book, published after Maslow's death, is a wide-ranging synthesis of his life's work on motivation and humanistic psychology. Especially valuable are the chapters on "Education and Peak Experiences" and "Goals and Implications of Humanistic Education."

Maslow, Abraham. *Toward a Psychology of Being.* 2nd ed. Princeton, N.J.: Van Nostrand, 1968. Here Maslow elaborates on his hierarchy of needs theory, focusing especially on the higher level needs, the being needs.

Neill, A. S. *Summerhill: A Radical Approach to Child Rearing.* New York: Hart, 1960. This best-seller describes the English private school that Neill directed until his recent death. This book is an important statement on the philosophy and practice of education that provides students with a great deal of freedom and is concerned with both their emotional needs and their intellectual needs.

Skinner, B. F. *Walden Two.* New York: Macmillan, 1948. As Skinner describes his fictional utopian community based upon principles of operant conditioning, he illustrates the psychological perspective that sees human motivation as primarily extrinsic.

Summerhill: For and Against. New York: Hart, 1970. This book brings together the views on *Summerhill* of a wide spectrum of educators, sociologists, and psychologists. The articles imply a variety of views on motivation.

Articles, Studies, and Other References

Deci, Edward L. *Intrinsic Motivation.* New York: Plenum, 1975. This volume is an integration of much that is known regarding intrinsically motivated behavior.

Greene, David and Mark R. Lepper. "Intrinsic Motivation: How to Turn Play into Work." *Psychology Today* 8 (1974): 49–52. In an article with profound implications for teachers, the authors discuss their research, which indicates that extrinsic rewards can undermine interest in activities that were previously intrinsically motivated.

Hamachek, Don E. "Motivational Processes and Human Learning." In Hamachek, *Behavior Dynamics in Teaching, Learning, and Growth.* Boston: Allyn and Bacon, 1975, Ch. 11. If you are looking for a general discussion of motivational theory as it applies to the classroom, this chapter will be quite useful.

McGregor, D. *Leadership and Motivation.* Cambridge, Mass.: M.I.T. Press, 1966. McGregor has developed a view of industrial organization that grows out of basic views of human motivation. He suggests that many companies emphasize the need for extrinsic motivation but some emphasize intrinsic motivation and give employees more freedom and equality in decision making.

Miller, L. K. and R. Schneider. "The Use of a Token System in Project Head Start." *Journal of Applied Behavior Analysis* (1970): 213–220. In this research study preschool children in a Head Start program were taught handwriting using a "token economy," in which they received tokens (which could be exchanged for snacks, movies, etc.) each time they did something correct. In contrast with a control group, these children showed great improvement in their writing.

Suggestions for Action-Oriented Learning

1. Visit an open classroom in an elementary school and discuss with the teacher his or her assessment of the strengths and weaknesses of such an approach. Contrast this type of teaching with your elementary school experience.

2. Read Skinner's *Walden Two* and Neill's *Summerhill* and contrast the views of motivation implicit in each of their utopian communities.

3. With a few of the other students from your class, design a questionnaire to assess the pros and cons of grades as extrinsic motivators. Have your teacher help you put it into final form. Then have a sample of college or high school students complete the questionnaire. Discuss the results with your class.

4. Try to locate a number of alternative programs within high schools in your area. Visit a few of those that sound most interesting and prepare a report based upon the reactions of students in the programs, your own observations, and any information you receive from teachers.

5. Make arrangements to help out two hours a week in an elementary or secondary school classroom with an approach to education different from your own school experience. Keep a log of your thoughts and feelings about each weekly visit.

Unit 3
The Teaching–Learning Process

Unit 3 provides a social-psychological view of teaching and learning. We see teaching as an interactive process, which always takes place within a complex social environment. As any teacher knows, helping others learn is no easy job; it requires a rare combination of personal, intellectual, and social knowledge and skills.

What makes teaching different from most other professions is that, in order to be effective, a teacher must interact spontaneously and differently with individual students, with groups of students, and with whole classes; with other teachers, administrators, counselors, and other colleagues; and with parents, community members, and the school board. As the history of American education documents, in their concern for the future of their culture all citizens have an interest in schooling. And most people feel they know something about teaching because they teach their own children or their friends, albeit informally.

In Unit 2 we introduced you to our concept of teaching as a diagnostic–prescriptive process. We tried to help you understand the learner and his development, his uniqueness, and his motivation. Such an understanding of the learner is a prerequisite to effective diagnosis. In this unit we will focus our attention on the more prescriptive aspects of our model as we consider teaching as a communication process. We will use an *ecological* perspective—that is, one that emphasizes the influences of the social and physical environments upon human behavior. In Chapters 10, 11, and 12 we will view teaching as a helping relationship. This will enable us to draw analogies between teaching and other helping professions such as medicine, social work, counseling, and the ministry, where the goals and the prescriptive strategies may differ, but where the communication problems are similar.

As teachers help children or adults learn, they must work within at least three types of social settings: (1) the one-to-one relationship, (2) the group and classroom environment, and (3) the school and community. We will devote a chapter to each of these settings.

All teachers must spend some of their time helping students on a one-to-one basis. Within any class there are always individuals whose special abilities or problems require special attention—e.g., the student whose reading level is far below the class, the aggressive–disruptive student, the gifted student, or the one with a physical handicap. Today it is argued increasingly that all students should be treated differently and given some *individualized instruction*. Each student has unique strengths, weaknesses, personal qualities, etc., and thus requires different educational experiences.

While teachers can certainly work individually with students some of the time, virtually all the time they are working in an environment that includes other students. Unlike other helping workers, teachers seldom have the luxury of working with their students alone. Even when helping one child, the teacher remains in the same room with and responsible for as many as 25 or 30 other students. If teachers are to be effective, they must interact spontaneously, and often simultaneously, with a variety of groups within the class as well as with the class as a whole.

A teacher needs support for doing what he believes in and sharing his ideas with other educators. He must understand the school as a social organization and develop effective human-relations skills if he hopes to serve as a change agent within his own school or the larger community. It is our purpose in this third unit to address the social-psychological problems encountered by teachers as they seek to help others learn in one-to-one settings (Chapter 10), in classroom groups (Chapter 11), and within the organizational context of schools (Chapter 12).

10
The Teacher and the Learner: Helping the Individual Student

In this chapter we will view teaching as a process of communication. We will explore teaching as a dynamic social relationship in which both the learner and the teacher are involved both intellectually and emotionally.

As we begin to consider some of the problems teachers face as they interact with students, we would like to introduce you to four anecdotes. Each of these anecdotes describes a relationship between a teacher and an individual student in which some difficulties have arisen. Let us assume that the teachers are well-meaning and working hard to help their students. However, each teacher feels that things are not going as smoothly as they might. The statements that follow present each situation in the words of the teacher.

As you read each statement, place yourself in the role of the teacher and try to feel what the teacher is experiencing.

Situation 1—Mr. Jackson and Tommy

I can't for the life of me seem to help Tommy learn to read. When I've had the chance throughout this school year, I've worked with him individually. Yet I feel like I've made almost no progress. He is finishing third grade and is still only able to recognize a few three- or four-letter words. You would think that I had ignored him. But I know that I have given him more special attention than any one else in the class. I go over and over the exercises in a very basic first-grade level book with him, but he just guesses rather than trying to sound out the words he doesn't know. I've even had him checked by the school psychologist and the results of the tests confirm my own assessment that he is average in intelligence. His ability to carry on conversations both with me and his classmates is good. Yet he keeps telling me that he is "dumb" and doesn't care if he ever learns to read.

Other than in class discussions, when he often perks up, Tommy shows little interest in school. He often talks about playing basketball or baseball with his older brothers when he gets home. Sports seem to be his major interest in life! I try to tell him that he has to learn to read well if he is going to be successful in later life, but he just shrugs his shoulders and says "I don't care." I try to be patient with Tommy, but his negative attitude and wild guessing drive me crazy. And the result is that I end up getting angry and yelling at him.

What do you feel is the primary problem in the relationship between Mr. Jackson and Tommy?

Situation 2—Mrs. Vitale and Melinda

Melinda is one of the nicest, most well-behaved girls I have ever had the pleasure of teaching. While she is not the brightest person in the junior class, she is certainly one of the hardest workers. As a result she receives As in all of her courses other than science and math, in which she usually gets Bs. My concern is with her extreme shyness in class. She will never volunteer an answer in a discussion in U.S. history. If I call on her to respond to even the easiest question, frequently she will blush and say in almost a whisper, "I don't know." I'm sure she knows the material because she is always paying attention and does so well on tests and papers. She doesn't seem to be shy outside class; I have noticed that she comes to class with two or three other girls.

I often try to joke with Melinda and tell her she needs to be more aggressive and outgoing if she's going to prepare herself to compete at one of the universities she hopes to enter after she graduates. However,

Have you known students like Melinda who were very hesitant about speaking up in class? Why do you feel that Melinda doesn't participate verbally?

her response is often a meek "I can't!" I sense that she feels very hostile toward me when I'm trying to get her to participate verbally in our class sessions. The more I try to involve her in the class the more she seems to "clam up" and the more frustrated I become. I don't know why she can't see that I'm trying to help her.

On the basis of your knowledge of students like Melinda, why do you feel Mrs. Vitale wasn't making much headway?

What would you do to help Melinda?

Situation 3—Miss McFarland and Brad

I've been teaching elementary school for 25 years and I've never encountered a boy like Brad. He has to be by far the worst discipline problem I've ever had. I knew from the day he entered my sixth-grade class in September that I was going to have trouble with him. Before school started, when I was briefing myself on the backgrounds of my students, I noticed that other teachers had indicated that he was "hostile" and "continually getting into fights" with the other children. Sure enough, he seemed to have a chip on his shoulder from practically the first day of class, and ever since working with him has been a real battle.

Try to suggest three or four possible reasons that Brad behaves as he does.

Bradley seems to have average intelligence, but he sure doesn't put it to good use. He does almost nothing in class and never completes his homework. It wouldn't be so bad if he would just sit quietly, but he bothers the other children who are trying to work and as a result is pretty much ostracized by the rest of the class. I've tried every type of punishment, from keeping him after school to sending him to the principal's office to sitting him in the corner in the classroom. But nothing has any effect.

Why do you feel the punishments didn't "work" for Brad?

Once after one of his fights I called Brad's mother and asked her to come in with him to speak with me. When I told her about Brad's behavior, she hit him so hard across the mouth that I was sure he would lose some teeth. I resolved then to try to straighten things out on my own, but I've just about had it. He makes me feel so inadequate as a teacher that I find myself hoping each day that he will be absent and wishing that he were old enough to quit school, as he often says he is going to do at age 16.

How are Miss McFarland's feelings about herself affecting her relationship with Brad?

Situation 4—Mr. Bachman and Emily

My first year of teaching has been going pretty well. I find I enjoy working with the students. Maybe it's because I'm only 22, but I tend to identify more with the students than with many of the older teachers. I dress in a casual way and never hang out in the teachers' room with the other teachers. I really like teaching and spend a lot of time after school just rapping with students.

I haven't had too many problems so far, considering this is my first year of teaching. However, there was an incident this winter in my third-period biology class that I know I mishandled, but I still haven't quite figured it out. In that ninth-grade class is a girl named Emily, who is a very mature-looking, attractive 15-year-old. She is an above-average student who, until the incident I'm about to describe, was one of my most serious biology students. She was a member of the biology club, which I sponsor, and frequently helped me put away equipment and feed the animals after school. I found her to be fun to talk to and I guess saw her not just as a student but as a friend.

One day last winter it started to snow just as Emily and I were finishing cleaning up the lab, so I offered to give her a ride home. As we were nearing her house we passed two of the girls from her biology class who looked surprised upon seeing her with me in my car. I never thought

As you think about being a teacher, have you ever wondered about how close you should get to your students?

What do you think Mr. Bachman was feeling as he saw the heart on the blackboard?

What might Emily have felt when Mr. Bachman told the story of his fiancée?

anything of their reaction until the next day when I entered my third-period class and noticed some giggling. On the blackboard was a heart in which was written "Mr. B. and Emily." I didn't know quite what to do or what to say, but somehow I blurted out, "My fianceé's name is not Emily, it's Cathy. Some time I'll have her come to school with me so you can all meet her." The truth is I was not engaged and at that time didn't even have a girl friend. The story just seemed like a convenient way of getting off the hook in that situation. The problem is, though, that after that day Emily dropped out of the biology club, stopped coming by to help me after school, and seemed to turn off to biology. She still won't speak with me and her grades in my course have dropped to barely passing.

Exploration 10–1: Responding to Problems in Teacher-Student Interactions

Having read the four anecdotes presented above, consider your reactions to the following questions. It might be helpful to jot down your responses and then compare them with those of another student.

1. For each of the four anecdotes, specify what you feel was the *major* problem in the relationship between teacher and student. Then offer one suggestion for improving each relationship.

   a. Mr. Jackson and Tommy.

   b. Mrs. Vitale and Melinda.

   c. Miss McFarland and Brad.

   d. Mr. Bachman and Emily.

2. If you were a teacher today, which one of the situations would you feel *most* comfortable with? Why?

Which situation would you feel *least* comfortable dealing with? Why?

3. What do the teacher–student relationships in the anecdotes have in common?

Later in this chapter we will introduce you to psychological concepts that will help you understand the dynamics in the four anecdotes.

Teaching as a Helping Relationship

The anecdotes that you have just been thinking about provide illustrations of some of the problems teachers face as they try to help students grow and learn. As we move through the subsequent sections of this chapter, we will return to those situations to clarify various psychological concepts in the helping process. You have probably noted that our notion of helping is not limited to learning subject matter. We see teaching as a helping relationship that views the learner as a total person. Of necessity, teachers must concern themselves with students' social, emotional, and even physical nature, not only their intellectual nature.

None of the difficulties encountered above by Mr. Jackson, Mrs. Vitale, Miss McFarland, and Mr. Bachman are primarily academic problems. For example, Tommy's inability to read at his grade level undoubtedly affected his self-concept, and his low self-concept probably influenced his guessing and made him more likely to make mistakes and continue to feel dumb. Melinda's fears in social settings were a direct impediment to communicating verbally what she knew and thus interfered with her academic learning. Teachers must understand the interlocking of the different aspects of each student if they are to foster the growth of the total person. Let us now look in greater depth at the psychological thinking that underlies the helping process in teaching.

We have been using the term *helping relationship* somewhat loosely and would like to explore it a little more closely. Carl Rogers, the humanistic psychologist who has been a leader in counseling and psychotherapy, first spoke of a helping relationship in an address he gave to a convention of professional counselors in 1958. His own words provide the best sense of his meaning:

Maybe you can recall some examples from your own school experience where academic problems might have led to emotional or social problems, or where social or emotional problems affected your academic performance.

In our perspective a teacher is concerned not only with knowledge but also with the growth of the child as a person. To become a teacher of children rather than simply a teacher of a subject (e.g., math, English, or third grade) requires a great deal of knowledge, commitment, self-awareness, skill, and hard work. This process is never ending; even a teacher with 30 years of experience has much to learn.

In Chapter 4 we acquainted you with Carl Rogers and his humanistic psychology as we discussed the affective theoretical perspective, with

> My interest in psychotherapy has brought about in me an interest in every kind of helping relationship. By this term I mean a relationship in which at least one of the parties has the intent of promoting the growth, development, maturity, improved functioning, improved coping with life of the other. The other, in this sense, may be one individual or a group. To put it in another way, a helping relationship might be defined as one in which one of the participants intends that there should come about, in

*its emphasis on feelings. You might
want to read over that discussion as
background for this section on helping relationships.*

*Rogers argues very persuasively that
the psychological elements that
make up a good teacher–student relationship, counselor–client relationship, or physician-patient relationship are basically the same.*

*If you would like to learn more about
perceptual psychology, which forms
the theoretical basis for much of the
work of Combs, Avila, and Purkey,
see Combs and Snygg,* Individual
Behavior *(1959).*

*An update of this thinking is pre-
sented in Combs, Richards, and
Richards,* Perceptual Psychology: A
Humanistic Approach to the Study of
Persons *(1976).*

*Have you ever thought about how
much continuous change is built into
a teacher's job? To be effective,
teachers must adapt what they do to
the student, the class, the community
in which they teach, the day of the
week, etc.*

*How does Combs' concept of teach-
ing compare with the philosophy of
the teacher education program you
are currently going through?*

one or both parties, more appreciation of, more expression of, more functional use of the latent inner resources of the individual (Rogers, 1958, p. 6).

Rogers points out that his definition of helping includes a variety of human relationships in which the primary goal is facilitating another person's growth. Relationships between counselors and clients, teachers and students, physicians and patients, and parents and children are all helping relationships. Rogers encourages us to view not only one-to-one relationships but individual–group interactions (such as a teacher's work with a class) as helping relationships. However, in this chapter we are concentrating on the one-to-one relationship between a teacher and a student as a basis for the discussion of the more complex dynamics of teacher–class relationships in Chapter 11.

Rogers' ideas on helping are supported and extended by the thinking of another well-known psychologist, Arthur Combs, and his coauthors at the University of Florida, Donald Avila and William Purkey. Although originally trained as behaviorists, Combs, Avila, and Purkey have become increasingly involved in the application of humanistic psychology to such helping professions as education, counseling, nursing, social work, and the ministry. Their interest in "helping helpers help" has led them to a great deal of research on the dynamics of helping and the factors related to its effectiveness. Through their writing they provide helping professionals with a clearer understanding of themselves, their clients, and the helping process (Combs, Avila, and Purkey, 1971).

Central to the work of Combs, Avila, and Purkey is their concept of the "self as instrument." They believe any effective helping person is not a technician who mechanically applies learned methods but a creative, thinking, and sensitive person who uses himself, his knowl-edge, and any other appropriate resources to aid in solving the prob-lems he encounters. In speaking of the application of the concept of self as instrument to teaching, Combs has said:

> If we adapt this "self as instrument" concept of the professional worker to teaching, it means that teachers' colleges must concern themselves with persons rather than competencies. It means the individualization of instruction we have sought for the public school must be applied to the teachers' colleges as well. It calls for the production of creative individuals, capable of shifting and changing to meet the demands and opportunities afforded in daily tasks. Such a teacher will not behave in a set way. His behavior will change from moment to moment, from day to day, rapidly adjusting to the needs of his students, the situations he is in, the purposes he seeks to fulfill and the methods and materials he has at hand.
>
> The good teacher is no carbon copy but stands out as a unique and effective personality, sometimes for one reason, sometimes for another, but always for something intensely and personally his own. He has found ways of using himself, his talents and his environment in a fashion that aids both his students and himself to achieve satisfaction—their own and

society's too. Artists sometimes refer to "the discovery of one's personal idiom" and the expression seems very apt applied to teaching as well. We may define the effective teacher as a unique human being who has learned to use his self effectively and efficiently for carrying out his own and society's purposes.*

As you reflect upon what Combs is saying, it probably occurs to you that good teaching involves much more than knowledge of one's subject. While it can't be denied that it is necessary to know what one is trying to teach, a teacher's subject matter knowledge is not sufficient to promote learning in students. Just as physicians must be able to apply their knowledge at a moment's notice as they are called upon to make a diagnosis or carry out an operation, so too must teachers be able to use their knowledge spontaneously in their ever unpredictable relationships with students. A teacher who knows her subject but whose students don't learn is analogous to a doctor whose medical knowledge is strong but whose patients seldom get better—neither is helping. Most teachers, of course, mean well and only intend to help their students; yet as you saw in the four anecdotes, some students are hurt by the most conscientious teachers. Let us now identify some of the factors that distinguish effective teachers from those who are not so effective.

The importance of teachers' knowing more than just their subject was clear in the four anecdotes presented at the beginning of this chapter. The major difficulties were problems in teacher–student communication.

Characteristics of Effective Teachers

The question of which characteristics set good teachers apart from poor teachers has been debated with much emotion in teachers' rooms, at family dinner tables, and in the offices of education professors. Researchers have begun to provide us with some helpful information, although their findings are by no means clear cut. Before reading about some of the research, why not compare your own views on teaching effectiveness with those of others by carrying out the activity below?

Exploration 10–2: Best and Worst Teachers

Ask three or four people what they think are the characteristics of good teachers and of poor teachers. In order to structure your interviews (which can involve parents, brothers and sisters, fellow students, former teachers, acquaintances, etc.), read each person the directions below. Before doing this activity with others, try it yourself so that you will be able to contrast your results with theirs.

Directions

1. Try to recall one teacher you had (at any level of your schooling) whom you would call your very best teacher.

* From A. W. Combs, "The Personal Approach to Good Teaching," *Educational Leadership* 21:6 (1964), 373. Reprinted by permission.

2. Use one side of a 3 × 5 card to convey in a paragraph what that teacher was like.

3. After completing your paragraph, reread it and circle the five adjectives you feel best describe this person. If you did not use five adjectives, think of five that provide an accurate picture.

4. Now try to recall one teacher whom you would characterize as your very worst teacher and repeat steps 2 and 3 above for that person.

Be sure the answers are clear and complete. If you are unsure of what your interviewee meant, probe until it becomes clear. Once you have completed all of your interviews, make a list of all the adjectives used to describe best teachers and those chosen for worst teachers. Reflect on the words that recur and look back at your results as you read the research findings reported below.

Studies of teaching effectiveness have paid particular attention to three dimensions: (1) personal characteristics; (2) perceptions regarding self, others, and teaching; and (3) instructional procedures and styles of interaction. We will provide a summary of some of the major results for each of these dimensions.

Personal Characteristics

In summarizing the literature on cognitive characteristics of teachers, Klausmeier (1975, pp. 175–176) has reported: "Intellectual ability, total grade-point average in college, subject matter preparation, student-teaching grade, and information about child development and learning have been found to be related to teaching effectiveness. However, the relationship is so low that evaluations of teachers on these characteristics have limited usefulness for predicting the effectiveness of individual teachers."

Recently much attention has been directed toward assessing the *affective* characteristics of teachers. Klausmeier, who is a cognitive psychologist, states that affective differences among teachers are probably more important in determining teaching success than are cognitive differences.

One of the most extensive studies of teaching ever done (Ryans, 1960) seems to support Klausmeier's statements. This study, which included both high school and elementary school teachers, found important differences in personal characteristics between teachers rated "high" in effectiveness and those rated "low" by trained observers. The "high" teachers were more likely to be extremely generous in appraising the behavior and motives of others, had strong interests in reading, and enjoyed relationships with pupils and participated in many social groups. They were above average in emotional adjustment, had superior verbal intelligence, and preferred nondirective teaching. On the other hand, "low" teachers tended to be critical of others, especially their students, preferred activities that did not involve close personal contacts, and were judged to be less well adjusted emotionally than the teachers who were high in effectiveness.

Any definition of best *is OK.*

If you don't have the time to interview three or four people for this exploration, just do it youself. Then compare your results with those of other students in your class.

Were there any characteristics that came up over and over as you discussed best teachers or worst teachers? Or did each person's notion of the qualities of good teaching and poor teaching differ considerably?

You will recall that affective *refers to emotions and feelings. The affective characteristics of teachers include their self-concepts, feelings about teaching and children, interests, attitudes, values, etc. Cognitive characteristics, on the other hand, would include intelligence, general knowledge, knowledge of one's subject, performance in school, etc.*

To what extent are the characteristics of "high" teachers in Ryans' research similar to the qualities of the "best" teachers you identified in Exploration 10–2?

E. Paul Torrance, who has spent a lifetime studying creativity, has argued that "great" teachers share with great people in other fields three essential characteristics. They perform miracles; they inspire their students, stimulating them to creative thinking; and, because they encourage students to question established values and practices, they are often viewed as "dangerous" and may have conflicts with both colleagues and superiors.

> In different ages, this problem has been handled in different ways. Socrates was made to drink hemlock. Jesus was crucified on a cross. Later, such teachers were imprisoned, stoned, burned as witches, or the like. Today, they are fired, discredited, and isolated, or their funds are withdrawn. These things happen even when the learners being taught are children, if these children do things that get out of hand and threaten the establishment. For example, Jonathan Kozol (1967) was fired when his ghetto students started reciting Langston Hughes' "Ballad of the Landlord." His book, *Death At An Early Age,* has won national awards, but there are plenty of elementary schools which will not employ him. Such cases have abounded in the news of the 1960's and 1970's (Torrance, 1975, p. 459).

Do you agree with Torrance's statement that "great" teachers are often considered dangerous? Why or why not?

Can you recall any teachers in your own past who were seen as good by students but who had conflicts with their colleagues and superiors?

Another psychologist who has given much thought to the personal qualities that go into good teaching is Carl Rogers. His long career as both psychotherapist and teacher has led Rogers to see effective teachers as being very similar to effective therapists. He feels that in their relations with learners, good teachers exhibit an *authenticity* and a capacity to *empathize.* They not only accept others as unique but they prize others and have a great degree of trust in their capabilities and potential for growth.

An authentic *teacher, according to Rogers, is one whose teaching personality is congruent with his or her "real" self. To empathize is to show empathy, to "feel with" another person. A teacher who has a capacity to empathize really understands the feelings of students.*

Perceptions of Self, Others, and Teaching

The research of Combs and his colleagues provides some useful findings regarding the way effective teachers see themselves, other people, and the actual task of teaching. Table 10–1 summarizes those findings. As you read each of the 16 characteristics described, consider the extent to which you possess that quality.

In your opinion which two of the 16 characteristics listed are the most important?

Why?

The data presented here were gathered from a study of a large number of effective teachers. For any one individual to possess all 16 characteristics would be rare indeed. So don't feel frustrated if you find yourself to be lacking in a number of categories.

Table 10–1: Perceptual Characteristics of Good Teachers

Perceptions of Self

1. Good teachers feel identified with, rather than apart from, others. They are close to others, part of all humanity.

2. Good teachers feel basically adequate rather than inadequate. They are able to cope with problems, competent.

3. Good teachers feel trustworthy rather than untrustworthy. They are dependable, reliable, confident.

4. Good teachers see themselves as wanted rather than unwanted. They are likeable, accepted by others, sought after.

5. Good teachers see themselves as worthy rather than unworthy. They are respected, possessing integrity.

Perceptions of Others

6. Good teachers perceive others as able rather than unable. They believe people are capable of solving their own problems.

7. Good teachers tend to see others as friendly rather than unfriendly. They feel others are well intentioned.

8. Good teachers perceive others as worthy rather than unworthy. They see them as possessing dignity and integrity.

9. Good teachers see people as internally motivated rather than externally motivated. They see people as creative, dynamic, and motivated from within.

10. Good teachers see others as trustworthy and dependable rather than unpredictable or undependable.

11. Good teachers see people as being helpful rather than impeding or threatening. They see them as sources of satisfaction rather than sources of frustration.

Perceptions of Teaching

12. Good teachers are concerned with freeing rather than controlling students. They see their purpose as releasing or facilitating behavior rather than controlling or inhibiting it.

13. Good teachers tend to be more concerned with larger issues than with smaller issues. They seem to have a global or molar [holistic] perspective and see relationships rather than specifics.

14. Good teachers are more likely to be self-revealing rather than self-concealing. They are willing to disclose their own feelings and be themselves rather than hide behind their role.

15. Good teachers tend to be personally involved rather than alienated in their helping relationships. They tend not to remain aloof or remote.

16. Good teachers focus their attention on furthering processes rather than on achieving goals. They see their role as helping others learn to search and discover rather than simply find a preconceived solution.

Adapted from Chapters 5, 6, and 7 of Arthur Combs, Robert Blume, Arthur Newman, and Hannelore Wass, *The Professional Education of Teachers: A Humanistic Approach to Teacher Preparation.* 2nd ed. Boston: Allyn and Bacon, 1974. Used by permission.

Methods of Teaching, Teacher Behavior, and Styles of Interaction

In studying teaching effectiveness, many researchers look at what teachers do in the classroom as they interact with students. They have tried to find out if the methods teachers use or the way they relate to students leads to improved learning. A number of the studies of teaching methods have compared the effects of lecture-type approaches with discussion-oriented approaches. In a review of nearly 100 studies, Dubin and Taveggia (1968) found that half the time the discussion method appeared better and half the time the lecture method was more effective. Such studies show little difference between the amount of information acquired in either type of class. However, discussions seem to have a greater impact on ability to apply concepts and think critically, on changing attitudes, and on improving motivation to learn (McKeachie and Kulik, 1975).

On the basis of your own experiences in high school and college, what do you feel are the pros and cons of lecture approaches and discussion approaches?

Research has also examined the relationship between teacher behavior in the classroom and various measures of student performance. In reviewing the results of 50 such studies, Rosenshine and Furst (1973) have concluded that the following factors are most consistently related to improved student learning:

Clarity of presentation.

Variability, i.e., use of a variety of activities, materials, etc.

Enthusiasm of instructor.

Extent to which instructor is task-oriented (concerned with "staying on track").

Teacher indirectness—encouraging students to initiate and participate actively rather than doing most of the talking.

Use of structuring comments—providing an overview for what has happened or is about to happen.

Providing for multiple levels of questions, i.e., questions that test judgment and evaluation as well as memory.

The studies reported here looked at teaching effectiveness in terms of students' academic achievement. They did not study the relationship between teaching behaviors and such noncognitive factors as students' self-concept, attitude toward school, or relationships with other students.

The research of Brophy and Evertson (1976) and Tikunoff, Berliner, and Rist (1975) appears to confirm Rosenshine and Furst's findings. However, Good and Brophy (1977) argue that it makes more sense to talk about patterns of teaching behavior rather than single behaviors. As children and situations differ, some behaviors will be more effective than others.

Although these and other studies show that the way teachers relate to students in the classroom affects student performance, more research is necessary before we can rely on these results with certainty. As both Combs et al. (1974) and Rogers (1969) point out, looking only at methods of teaching or teacher behaviors fails to take into account other important influences, such as who is doing the teaching, what his purposes are, or how the students perceive the teacher.

The research on teaching effectiveness that we have presented has focused on both the personal qualities of teachers and their teaching methods. These results do not provide a clear-cut picture of which aspect is more important.

What is your own opinion on this much debated issue? Why do you feel the way you do?

The Process of Teaching

Having looked at the characteristics of teachers, we will now focus on the communication process between teacher and student (or helping professional and client). Any helping process involves both

Before you read further, it might be helpful to look back over the four anecdotes presented at the beginning of this chapter. We will relate our discussion to them.

thoughts and feelings, which are communicated back and forth between the participants through words, gestures, and other more subtle forms of body language. If teaching is to work smoothly and promote growth in the student, a comfortable psychological climate must exist.

I–Thou Relationship

The existentialist philosopher Martin Buber (1958) provides a perspective on human relationships that is important in creating the psychological atmosphere for genuine communication. Buber calls for *I–thou* relationships between people rather than *I– it* relationships. In an I–thou relationship people encounter each other on an equal basis, with each person recognizing and respecting the qualities found in the other. In an I–it relationship, on the other hand, there is no mutuality or true meeting. Rather each person relates to the other as an object or thing, in terms of a category or function—e.g., teacher–student, boss–employee, adult–child, etc. A good illustration of an I–it relationship is Miss McFarland's relationship with Brad (situation 3). She saw him not as a person, but as a discipline problem. Undoubtedly, her perception of him helped Brad to see her not as a "thou" but as an "it"—another teacher who was on his back.

Can you recall any times when you were given a label by a teacher; e.g., underachiever, troublemaker, jock, class clown, or hippie?

How did you feel toward the teacher who treated you as an "it" rather than as a "thou"?

In what ways did that relationship affect your growth?

The stereotyping that develops within organizations when people seldom communicate is basically the same that occurs between racial and ethnic groups. Only when people have a chance to get to know each other do their inaccurate generalizations and misperceptions have a chance to break down.

Can you recall one of your teachers who treated you as a "thou" not an "it"? How did you feel about that teacher's class?

Buber points out that it is difficult to avoid I–it relationships in schools, institutions, and large organizations. In such settings the specialization of roles and functions tends to keep people from getting to know each other, and consequently stereotypes develop. In schools we find teachers who say "all administrators are uncaring paper-pushers," administrators who complain "teachers are resistant to any change," students who state "teachers get their kicks by pushing kids around," teachers who grumble "today's students don't want to learn," etc. Of course, as such stereotyped perceptions are acted upon, adversary relationships develop, feelings get hurt, and no one benefits. However, even in the most dehumanizing setting there are always some people who maintain I–thou relationships with others. And usually those people react in kind. A teacher who treats students as people worthy of respect is likely to create a more cooperative atmosphere and, as a result, be treated as a "thou" rather than as an "it."

One way of establishing such positive relationships between teacher and students is by using what Thomas Gordon (1970) and Haim Ginott (1972) have called *I messages* rather than *you messages* in situations that call for criticism. An I message expresses the speaker's feelings and tries to avoid blaming, humiliating, or threatening the person at whom it is directed. Mr. Jackson in situation 1 could have used such an I message with Johnny. Instead of yelling at him for guessing and saying to him, as he probably did, "Tommy, your guessing is going to get *you* nowhere. Why don't *you* try to sound out the words as the other boys and girls do?" he might have said *"I find myself getting upset and at times even angry when you guess at words without sounding them out."* Rather than escalating conflict, the I message expresses the speaker's feelings, maintains dialogue, and encourages the other person to take responsibility for himself.

Transference and Countertransference

Effective helping requires an openness in communication between teacher and student, helper and client. Helping people must be continually aware not only of the client's feelings but also of their own feelings and how they promote or interfere with their work. Two phenomena—*transference* and *countertransference*—that have been observed, studied, and written about in the literature of psychotherapy can be useful in understanding the dynamics in any helping relationship. Sigmund Freud was the first to study these phenomena. He found that in therapy his clients often directed feelings they once had toward a significant person in their life (mother, father, husband, wife, etc.) toward him. This *transference* of feelings could be either positive or negative. When it led to an identification with the therapist and thus cooperation, it was positive. The client brought out and directed at the therapist many of the feelings that needed to be examined in therapy. On the other hand, negative transference occurred when the client transferred "bad feelings" to the therapist. This could make communication difficult unless it was talked through carefully.

Just as the client's feelings can be passed on to the therapist, so too can the therapist's feelings be directed at the client. This is called *countertransference*. The practitioner, like the client, is human and has a variety of feelings toward the client—positive or negative. For example, as a therapist encounters a client who is very dependent and who reacts to her as a mother figure, she may be drawn into that role and try to direct the client and discourage independence. With other patients she might be sexually attracted, repulsed, not demanding enough, etc. In any helping relationship (especially in a one-to-one situation) countertransference is likely. The problem becomes not to try to eliminate the countertransference, but to make the helping person aware enough of her own psychological needs and feelings that she can recognize them and, if necessary, talk with her client about them. It is for this reason that clinical psychologists and psychiatrists are required, as part of their training, to undergo therapy themselves.

Although we have introduced the concepts of transference and countertransference in clinical settings, they also occur in the classroom, the guidance office, the tutoring session, or even in the

If you would like to learn more about effective communication, you ought to read Haim Ginott's Teacher and Child *(1972). In a very conversational style and with a multitude of anecdotes, Ginott provides many suggestions for improving teacher–student relationships.*

Thomas Gordon's P.E.T.: Parent Effectiveness Training *(1970), although written primarily about parent–child communication, has many implications for the classroom.*

Gordon's more recent book T.E.T.: Teacher Effectiveness Training *(1974) deals specifically with ways of improving communication in the classroom.*

A very popular offshoot of Freudian psychology is Transactional Analysis (T.A.). Developed by Eric Berne and popularized in his best-seller Games People Play *(1964), T.A. has become widely used by both therapists and lay people in improving human communication. Harris's* I'm O.K., You're O.K. *(1967) extends Berne's thinking by providing many illustrations of effective and ineffective communication.*

Psychotherapy and counseling involve very close relationships between people, and consequently they generate strong feelings between the parties involved. Such feelings are communicated back and forth, and if they are not understood, they can create problems in the relationship.

As psychologists or psychiatrists go through therapy and enhance their own self-understanding, they become more aware of their own feelings and needs and are less likely to impose their needs on their patients.

An excellent reference for further
reading on the application of transference and countertransference to
communication in the classroom is
W. J. Kirman, Modern
Psychoanalysis in the Schools
(1977).

medicine or law office. We will illustrate how transference and countertransference worked in two of the school situations presented at the
beginning of this chapter.

First let's take Mrs. Vitale and Melinda (situation 2). Mrs. Vitale
perceives Melinda as bright but very shy about contributing verbally
to class sessions. The more she attempts to get her involved, the
more Melinda pulls back and won't even try. While we haven't heard
Melinda's side of the story, it's possible that Mrs. Vitale's directive
behavior makes her feel anxious and hostile toward her. In turn,
Melinda's behavior seems to trigger feelings of frustration in Mrs. Vitale. When she says, "I don't know why she can't see that I'm only
trying to help her," Mrs. Vitale seems to be telling us that she feels
hurt and inadequate because she can't reach Melinda. Why she is
so frustrated is something we can only speculate about. Maybe
Melinda reminds her of her daughter who is also very shy, maybe she
brings back memories of the way she was as a student, or maybe
Melinda's passivity calls attention to her own aggressiveness. Obviously, we don't know what is behind Melinda's transference and Mrs.
Vitale's countertransference. However, the more self-aware Mrs. Vitale
is as a teacher, the more likely she will be able to see how her own
needs may interfere with reaching her student. Then, as she begins to
see the "problem" from Melinda's perspective, she may develop alternative strategies.

Try to recall a situation in which you
were attempting to teach someone
and felt you were not making much
progress. Which of your own needs
might have interfered with your relationship with your student? How did
you feel about your lack of success?
As you think about your feelings,
you may gain a better understanding
of your own "teaching self."

Mr. Bachman and Emily (situation 4) also had some transference
and countertransference problems. From the situation it appears that
Emily liked Mr. Bachman and probably had a "crush" on him. This
transference of feelings was undoubtedly pleasing to Mr. Bachman
and something that he encouraged, whether he was aware of it or not.
We don't know whether he was sexually aroused by her, but whatever
the case he did direct much positive feeling toward her. When others
teased about the emerging relationship, he became threatened (possibly out of his own insecurities as a new teacher). It would seem that
the intensity of Mr. Bachman's own feelings kept him from considering
Emily's feelings when he spoke in class of his fictitious fiancée, Cathy.
Again we have seen how transference and countertransference occur
in the classroom. Just as students can become defensive and not
function effectively, so can teachers.

Just as Emily undoubtedly liked the
attention she received from Mr.
Bachman, he in turn enjoyed her
company.

What advice would you give Mr.
Bachman for resolving his communication problem with Emily?

Each of the four anecdotes shows how feelings are communicated back and forth and how, without any deliberate efforts on the
part of either the teacher or the student, adversary relationships can
occur. As Bruner would suggest (see Chapter 5), both parties are
defending rather than coping; i.e., each person is feeling threatened
and takes out hurt feelings on the other. This can be further illustrated
by Miss McFarland and Brad (situation 3). Miss McFarland admits
feeling inadequate when she works with Brad. The more she feels this
way, the more she will unconsciously try to hurt Brad—all of which
builds up the adversary relationship between them. If this battle is to
end and cooperation is to begin, someone must pull out. Pulling out
requires both the psychological insight to see what is going on and
the capacity for admitting one's own contributions to the problem. The

Some professional educators and
psychologists have argued that
teachers need much more training in
psychology and human relations in

person who should be able to step back, analyze what is happening, and then work to change things must be the teacher.

In conclusion, teachers are helping professionals who must be able to use themselves as instruments. While there should be an equality of feelings between teacher and student—an I–thou relationship—there is an inequality between the psychological skill of the teacher and that of the student. The teacher is the professional hired to make the learning process work. In order to be effective, the teacher must be able to recognize and cope with both transference and countertransference.

order to improve their communication with students. A few have even supported the idea of psychological screening, and possibly required psychotherapy, for all teachers as a prerequisite to getting or holding a teaching position.

How do you feel about these proposals? Do you see any possible dangers in them?

Conclusions

The focus of this chapter has been on the helping relationship. The anecdotes describing four problems in teacher–student interactions were designed to stimulate your thinking about the complexities of helping another person learn. The studies of effective teaching place less emphasis on teaching methods and more emphasis on the personal qualities of teachers and the ways they perceive themselves, their students, and the teaching task.

The concepts of transference and countertransference are useful in understanding how feelings are communicated between students and teachers. As you become aware of these phenomena in your own helping relationships, you will be better able to avoid the types of problems experienced by Mr. Jackson, Mrs. Vitale, Miss McFarland, and Mr. Bachman. Establishing a comfortable psychological atmosphere for learning, in which your relationships with students are cooperative rather than adversary, will require a continuing effort at understanding not only your students' feelings but your own.

Some Good Books

Avila, Donald L., Arthur W. Combs, and William W. Purkey, eds. *The Helping Relationship Sourcebook.* Boston: Allyn and Bacon, 1971. This book provides a collection of articles about the psychology of the helping relationship written by a variety of professionals.

Brammer, Lawrence M. *The Helping Relationship: Process and Skills.* Englewood Cliffs, N.J.: Prentice-Hall, 1973. Written at a level appropriate for "lay helpers," this book focuses on the use of self in helping and the development of specific skills, such as listening, reflecting, interpreting, and confronting.

Buber, Martin. *I and Thou.* 2nd ed. New York: Scribner's, 1958. This classic book develops Buber's notion of I and thou. Buber gives us an excellent philosophical basis for humanism and improving relationships between people.

Combs, Arthur W., Donald L. Avila, and William W. Purkey. *Helping Relationships: Basic Concepts for the Helping Professions.* Boston: Allyn and Bacon, 1971. As an integration of many of the basic concepts of humanistic psychology and perceptual psychology, this book is a major statement on the psychological principles involved in helping.

Combs, Arthur W., Robert A. Blume, Arthur J. Newman, and Hanne-lore L. Wass. *The Professional Education of Teachers.* 2nd ed. Boston: Allyn and Bacon, 1974. This research done at the University of Florida on teaching effectiveness is presented in a way that stimulates the reader's thinking about the perceptual characteristics of good teachers.

Ginott, Haim. *Teacher and Child.* New York: Macmillan, 1972. Haim Ginott was a psychotherapist who applied his clinical expertise in parent–child communication to the educational process. He suggests many practical ways of dealing with virtually any classroom problem as a problem in communication.

Gordon, Thomas. *T. E. T.: Teacher Effectiveness Training.* New York: McKay, 1974. Gordon's *P.E.T.: Parent Effectiveness Training* (1970) has become a good resource for improving communication in the family. His later book, *T.E.T.,* offers teachers many ways of improving classroom communication.

Greenberg, Herbert. *Teaching with Feeling.* New York: Pegasus, 1969. Greenberg has written a fine book on the feelings of teachers and how they promote or interfere with communication in the classroom.

Kirman, W. J. *Modern Psychoanalysis in the Schools.* Dubuque, Iowa: Kendall Hunt, 1977. This book applies concepts of modern psycho-analysis to such school problems as dealing with students who have trouble learning, evaluating, and communicating with parents.

Rogers, Carl. *Client-Centered Therapy.* Boston: Houghton Mifflin, 1951. *Client-Centered Therapy* is a basic source for much of the psychological thinking on human relationships we have explored in this chapter.

Articles, Studies, and Other References

Dunkin, Michael J. and Bruce J. Biddle. *The Study of Teaching.* New York: Holt, Rinehart and Winston, 1974. This book provides a major synthesis of research on classroom teaching. The findings presented cause one to question many established educational practices.

English, Fanita, "T.A.'s Disney World." *Psychology Today* 6: 45–50, 98. A very thoughtful article on the contribution of Transactional Analysis to our understanding of human communication.

Rogers, Carl. "The Characteristics of a Helping Relationship." *Personnel and Guidance Journal* 37 (1958): 6–16. In this paper, which is now a classic, Rogers draws upon his experience in counseling and psychotherapy to explain the dynamics of virtually any helping relationship.

Rosenshine, Barak and Norma Furst. "The Use of Direct Observation to Study Teaching." In R. M. W. Travers (ed.), *Second Handbook of Research on Teaching.* Chicago: Rand McNally, 1973. These authors have put together another integration of a great deal of research on teaching effectiveness.

Suggestions for Action–Oriented Learning

1. As we pointed out in Chapter 1, one of the best ways to learn about helping is to do it. Try to make arrangements to work on a weekly basis in a one-to-one relationship—as a tutor, peer counselor, coach, social-work aide, hospital volunteer, etc. Keep a log that focuses on your own countertransference.

2. Interview individually a number of teachers (or helping professionals in another field) you know regarding their own countertransference—feelings toward their students—and how they cope with it. Ask them to describe some of the strong feelings (anger, happiness, sadness, etc.) they have experienced in their work with individual students. Encourage them to discuss with you their perceptions of the feelings their students direct toward them.

3. Visit a number of different classes. Then write a description and analysis of the extent to which an I–thou relationship exists between teacher and students in each class. Discuss your results with other members of your class who have done similar work.

4. Survey a number of students from a range of grade levels regarding the qualities they feel make a good teacher. Look for similarities and differences in their points of view. Try to determine whether they emphasize methods or personal qualities as most important.

5. Debate in your class the pros and cons of required psychotherapy in all teacher training.

11
The Teacher and the Class: Fostering Learning in Group Settings

If there is one thing that distinguishes a teacher's work from that of other helping professionals, it is the teacher's responsibility for working with groups. While all good teachers spend some time relating to students on a one-to-one basis, most of the time they will be interacting simultaneously with many people. It is not easy to create an atmosphere in which 25 or 30 individuals, each with different abilities, interests, and needs, will grow. Consequently, many of the major problems teachers encounter, such as how to explain concepts, which teaching methods to use, and understanding student "misbehavior," are primarily group dynamics problems. Even though they may complain to their superiors, teachers generally receive little help in improving their effectiveness as group leaders.

Psychologists and teacher educators, in particular, receive their share of criticism from classroom teachers, who argue that the principles of learning and development operating in a laboratory or in a one-to-one learning experience are quite different from those operating in a classroom. Bridging the gap between educational psychological theory—with its traditional emphasis on the individual student—and educational practice—with its focus on the interaction between a teacher and a group of students—remains a problem. However, within the field of social psychology a movement has emerged that has promise for addressing classroom realities more directly. As you may recall from Chapter 4, we call the psychological perspective that explores the interactive aspects of the teaching–learning process a *social systems* perspective. It views the classroom as a complex social system in which the behavior of the teacher and each student is affected by many dynamic social forces. These include friendships, communication patterns, power and influence, leadership styles, peer-group norms, and even the physical environment. In this chapter we will examine the implications of this social systems perspective for improving teaching in group settings.

Perhaps you have heard teachers say things like "Johnny is fine alone but when he is with his friends in class he is almost impossible to deal with" or "I can't understand the difference between my third-period class and my fourth-period class. The subject is the same and the range of abilities is the same, but the two classes are as different as night and day in the way they work together."

Each of these statements illustrates the fact that individuals behave quite differently in groups than they do alone. The influences on group behavior are complex and in continuous flux.

It might be helpful to return to Chapter 4 and reread the section on the social systems perspective to refresh your thinking.

The Classroom as a Social Environment

A typical classroom group consists of a teacher and a number of students, let's say around 30. A classroom group might be viewed as a work group. It is organized into a formal structure so that the students will achieve learning. As with other work groups, appropriate strategies must be developed for promoting smooth operation and achieving goals. Open communication must take place if students are to grow and feel positive about their time spent in class.

There are also some important ways in which classroom groups differ from other work groups. First, the expected outcome in a class is learning, not a tangible goal. A factory's goal of making cars or a hospital's goal of helping a sick patient get well is easier to evaluate. Second, participation is mandatory. Neither students nor teacher can very easily leave the group once they are assigned to it. Third, teachers' roles require a great variety of functions. Fourth, teachers work mainly with children and adolescents, while leaders of most

As we will see later in this chapter, groups work most effectively when they meet the social and emotional needs of their members as well as accomplish the specific tasks they are designed for.

Try to make a list of all the different roles a teacher is expected to play in the course of a day.

other work groups spend their time working with adults. Since school children are not fully mature and ready for totally independent thinking and decision making, parents and other community members expect teachers to serve as "parent figures" and models.

Another way that classrooms differ from other work groups is the extent to which they must be responsive to views in the community beyond their own walls. Because education is designed to preserve the culture by preparing young people for adult citizenship, everyone has a stake in the effectiveness of teaching. Many citizens, not just students and their parents, want input into the goals for schools. For this reason, teachers must be sensitive not only to the views of students. They must also understand the objectives of their fellow teachers, the administrators of the school and district, the school board, the students' parents, other community members, and government at the local, state, and federal levels.

Each student comes to a class with some expectations, strengths, weaknesses, feelings, and needs that are unique and some that are shared with other students. To be effective, therefore, a teacher must respond to each student individually and still provide for the common needs of groups of students and for the class as a whole. The creation of an I–thou relationship in the classroom is essential if teachers are to help their students. Establishing such a relationship requires a great deal of self-awareness, trust, and emotional security on the part of the teacher. How the teacher behaves will set the tone as early as the first day of class for a cooperative relationship or an adversary relationship.

The teacher's impact on classroom atmosphere is illustrated in the two anecdotes that follow. The anecdotes present the introductory remarks made by Mrs. Reilly and Mr. Morton, two science teachers in the same junior high school, to their seventh-grade general science classes on the first day of school.

Although popular opinion has it that teaching is an easy job with 9–3 hours and long vacations, anyone who knows good teachers realizes that teaching is tremendously demanding intellectually, emotionally, and even physically.

As you read the two anecdotes think about the first days of some of your college courses. How did you feel about these classes and their teachers after the first day?

Mrs. Reilly: I'm pleased to meet each of you. I know that we'll get along fine this year if you are willing to work hard. You may have already heard from former seventh graders that I'm strict and I don't tolerate any nonsense. Well, that's true. You're no longer in elementary school. This is junior high. My job is to help prepare you for high school science and that's why I have to expect a lot from you and can't waste time.

As long as you do what you are told, turn in your homework, get to class on time, and avoid talking and fooling around with your classmates, you won't have any worries. On the other hand, if you do in any way cause trouble, watch out. . . .

Mr. Morton: I'm really happy to see each of you. I hope you didn't have too many problems in finding this room. Changing classes each day is a new experience for most of you, but you'll be used to it before long. At the end of this period I'll give anyone who needs them directions to your next class.

By now probably some of you have decided you like science and others of you are convinced you don't. I have a feeling that more of you will see how enjoyable science can be as we all do experiments, raise plants and animals, and go on field trips. Before we begin talking about some of the things we'll be learning in this course, I would like to suggest that we play a game designed to help us get to know each other a little better.

Having read each of the anecdotes, try to describe in a sentence or two how you might have felt if you had been a seventh grader hearing Mrs. Reilly's remarks.

How would this first experience have affected your attitude toward Mrs. Reilly and your behavior in subsequent classes?

How would you have felt if you were a student in Mr. Morton's class? In what ways would his first day introduction have affected you and your reaction to him?

It appears that Mrs. Reilly came into her class expecting her students not to take either her or their course work seriously. She tried to anticipate problems and scare students into behaving through the use of threats and warnings. She had her seventh graders stereotyped and began the class in an adversary manner. Mr. Morton, on the other hand, showed his concern for the feelings of his students as he reassured them about finding their way around the school. He tried to deal with their attitudes toward science. By continually emphasizing the *we* in his relationship with the seventh graders, Mr. Morton was working at creating a cooperative, I–thou relationship.

In each of the anecdotes, the teacher took the first steps in establishing the classroom climate. A positive, supportive attitude by the teacher and a willingness for open communication are necessary for

Have you ever imagined yourself on your first day of teaching? How do you think you will behave toward your students?

successful work with groups, but they are certainly not sufficient. An understanding of group dynamics and a repertoire of communication skills are also required for effective functioning with groups.

Properties of Classroom Groups

To understand how classroom groups function, why they function as they do, and ultimately how to make them work more successfully, we need to be aware of their main characteristics. Here our focus will be on four characteristics, which we call properties—membership, norms, structure, and goals. These characteristics all affect the thinking, feelings, and behavior of both the teacher and the students in the classroom.

Membership

Membership (i.e., who belongs to the group) in school groups, as in other formal groups, is clear-cut: A student is either a member of a particular class or not. Membership in most school groups from kindergarten to high school is involuntary. Students generally cannot choose which group of students or which teacher they would like to be with. However, as they move into junior and senior high school they have more options open to them in the curriculum. While they can't choose the people they will be with, students do have some choice of the subjects they will take.

In departmentalized schools students and teacher may be members of five or six different groups, or classes. It is understandable that the behavior of both teacher and students will vary in each social setting. Even when the same group of students "travels together" (moves from teacher to teacher), their behavior will change with each different teacher. What seems to account for such differences is the teachers and the classroom atmosphere they create.

More dramatic illustrations of the teacher's impact on student learning and behavior can be seen with tracking, or as it is called officially, *homogeneous grouping.* Secondary school teachers are often assigned subject classes in which students are supposedly grouped by ability. For example, a tenth-grade social studies teacher might be given one advanced placement class, two regular college prep. classes, and two general classes (students with average or less-than-average abilities), all for the same subject.

It is not uncommon to hear a teacher remark, "Well you can't expect too much from them; they're my lower track kids" as he comments on teaching his general classes. Or in reference to the advanced placement class, the same teacher might say, "That's my good class. They're a real pleasure to work with." Such perceptions are likely to affect not only the way the teacher relates to those classes and the students' academic learning but also the students' feelings toward the teacher. Even the feelings of the students toward each other are influenced by the teacher's perceptions. In short, the way a teacher perceives his students affects his expectations of them and may create a *self-fulfilling prophecy.*

Some educational critics argue that because schooling is compulsory, it can never promote learning for some students because they attend against their will. If you would like to learn more about this "deschooling" viewpoint, you might read John Holt, Instead of Education *(1976), or Ivan Illich,* Deschooling Society *(1971).*

Within any classroom group there are also subgroups with their own properties and behavior. Some teachers unwittingly create an atmosphere that sets these subgroups against each other, while other teachers are effective in getting them to cooperate.

Did your secondary school use "tracking"? If so, what track were you in? How did you feel about being in that track? How was your academic learning affected by being in that track?

A self-fulfilling prophesy *is an expectation about an individual or group*

Norms

Norms are among the most powerful influences on the behavior of individuals in a group. Norms are behavioral rules that are accepted, at least to some extent, by the members of a group. They grow out of shared expectations as to what is appropriate and are generally unwritten and unspoken. Deviation from the norms of a group can lead to criticism by other group members and, if the deviation is too great, possibly to the member's expulsion from the group. Norms may exist in dress, language, hair style, whom one speaks to, what one speaks about, how much work one should do, etc. Rules or guidelines that are imposed by a group leader or teacher are not norms; such official expectations become norms only if the majority of members of a group see them as proper, accept them, and follow them.

In any classroom norms influence the behavior of students and teacher. Norms also dictate school behavior outside the classroom. These norms can either facilitate or interfere with the achievement of educational objectives. If a teacher is to promote learning, she must be aware of the norms operating in her class (and its subgroups) and in the students' out-of-school peer groups.

The following exploration will help you reflect on some of the norms that operated when you were in high school:

Exploration 11–1: Peer Group Norms

Think about your experiences as a high school senior in relation to each of the following categories. Check those areas in which there were norms in your peer group that affected your behavior, and provide a brief description of the norms. Then answer the questions that follow the checklist and discuss your responses with some of your classmates.

The peer group's influence on the behavior of individuals, especially during adolescence, is great.

that comes true, i.e., fulfills itself. (We explored this idea in relation to I.Q. in Chapter 8.) Evidence suggests that our expectations of the behavior of others can actually affect what they do (Braun, 1976; Brophy and Good, 1974). For example, Mrs. Reilly expects her students to misbehave, and they probably will. Mr. Morton expects his students to cooperate with him, and probably he will get cooperation.

Norms exist in any group setting and may vary greatly from one group to another. Try to think of the norms that might exist in the following groups:

Men working on an auto assembly line.

Members of a country club for the extremely rich.

Middle-class women in a Wednesday morning bowling group.

College professors of business.

Inner-city teenagers in a street gang.

Members of a college fraternity or sorority.

Members of a teachers' union.

Within each of the groups listed there are probably general norms and norms for the subgroups that exist within the larger groups.

Example: ___ Clothing—casual look, jeans and T-shirts; no coats, ties, or dresses

___ 1. Clothing—

___ 2. Hair style—

___ 3. Amount of homework completed—

___ 4. Cutting classes—

___ 5. Drinking—

___ 6. Asking questions in class—

___ 7. Smoking—

___ 8. Getting high grades—

Although we are focusing on student norms, adult behavior in the school is also influenced by norms.

___ 9. Talking with a teacher before or after class—

___ 10. Volunteering answers to a teacher's questions—

Imagine a teachers' room when a group of teachers are sitting together during a free period. They are then governed by norms that are different from the norms that influence their behavior in the classroom or in meetings with parents or administrators.

___ 11. Drug use—

___ 12. Participation in athletics—

___ 13. Cheating on tests—

___ 14. Amount of studying for tests—

___ 15. Talking or fooling around in class—

___ 16. Other _____

—— 17. Other _____

—— 18. Other _____

Discussion Questions

1. On the basis of the information you provided above, describe the basic values and views on appropriate behavior of your peer group as a high school senior.

2. Did your peer group generally work closely with teachers or did it encourage you to not go along with the expectations of teachers?

3. What could a teacher do to create a good working relationship with the members of your peer group?

As you can see from examining your own school behavior, norms affect the way all of us behave and may counteract or impede a teacher's goals. In a national study of adolescents, Coleman (1961) learned that peer-group norms emphasized athletic ability for boys and popularity as a date for girls rather than academic achievement. Similarly, Hughes, Becker, and Geer (1962) found that peer-group norms in medical school supported behavior contrary to faculty values. Norms influenced such things as which lectures were attended, how much students studied, and which faculty members were considered most knowledgeable. The message for teachers from this research is that attempts to impose unilateral guidelines for behavior and learning upon students will not work. The student peer group will modify them. The answer seems to lie in enlisting the students' cooperation in establishing guidelines for behavior, topics to be studied, and even the types of assignments to be completed.

Students, like any group of people, are more likely to cooperate with decisions in which they have some say. Teachers who have the power of the peer group working for them rather than against them have a tremendous asset. For example, in a junior high school class in which the students participated in making up classroom rules, one might hear such comments as "Hey John, how about cutting out the talking, the rest of us can't hear the discussion." Third graders who have discussed with their teacher conflicts that have arisen may say, "You know it's not fair to laugh at what someone says. How would you like to have someone make fun of your ideas?"

Structure

A group's effectiveness is also influenced by its *structure*—the patterns of relationships that develop out of the positions individual members occupy within the group. We will discuss three aspects that affect group structure—*roles*, *status*, and *attraction*.

Because of their inadequate understanding of group behavior, many teachers get themselves into battles with students as they try to impose rules or guidelines that conflict with existing group norms. Even elementary school–aged children can outmaneuver teachers whose expectations they don't understand or disagree with. In such a battle everyone loses—teacher and students alike—and educational objectives go unmet as a power struggle ensues.

For an excellent discussion of norms and their impact in the classroom, look for Schmuck and Schmuck, Group Processes in the Classroom (1975).

A peer group has much more influence over its members than does an authority figure outside the group, like a teacher. This is especially true as children move into the adolescent years. The more teachers enlist the aid of the student peer group in dealing with classroom problems, the more likely they are to resolve those problems.

How do you think teachers might effectively work with the student peer group rather than against it?

After just a few years in school, children form a mental picture of what a teacher is "supposed to be" like. Teachers who choose to differ from the prevailing view of their role may find themselves in conflicts. We will see this more clearly in Chapter 12 in a number of the anecdotes describing teachers who see themselves as change agents.

Can you recall classes in which your teachers saw their role differently than the way you and your classmates saw it? What happened?

While teachers influence the status of students in groups, the peer group itself awards varying amounts of status to different individuals. For example, an eighth-grade boy who is bigger, taller, and stronger than his classmates may be well liked and given high status. Or a high-school girl who is bright, friendly, and athletic may be very popular and perhaps be elected class president.

Teachers must be very sensitive to how their relationships with individual students are perceived by other class members. Divisiveness occurs very quickly when some students feel that the teacher "favors" a particular student or group.

Can you recall any examples of this from your own school experiences?

Any group has expectations for what is acceptable behavior in a particular position. In other words, a *role* suggests what a person is supposed to do in a group. The two major roles in a classroom are teacher and student. Both are culturally defined, but they are adapted according to the views of the members within a particular class.

One first-grade teacher may interpret her role as director of learning and disciplinarian. Another first-grade teacher in the same school may see herself as a facilitator of learning and a friend and counselor to boys and girls. If the students' perceptions of the teacher's role and the teacher's perception of her role are quite different, problems can result. For example, if the first graders expect their teacher to be very strict and directive (like their kindergarten teacher was), but the teacher sees herself as permissive and nondirective, the teacher may be disappointed as her students apparently "take advantage" of the freedom she allows. If she is committed to a more nondirective approach, she may have to adjust her teaching strategy, keeping a tighter control at first and only gradually granting more autonomy. Otherwise, the teacher may find herself locked in a power struggle with a class that sees her as a pushover in comparison with their previous teacher. The primary responsibility for recognizing such conflicts in role perceptions and dealing with them rests with the teacher.

Status is another aspect of class structure. There is often a hierarchy of positions in a classroom. Different individuals have different levels of status; that is, the ideas and behavior of some members carry more weight than those of others. Such a situation gives rise to differences in relative power in influencing the group.

The teacher has the greatest formal status in a class and is most likely to be accepted as the leader. However, different degrees of status exist among the students. Teachers both consciously and unconsciously influence the status of individuals and groups in the classroom. When elementary teachers place children in reading groups or when high schools organize students into tracks, status systems are created. Such well-meaning administrative arrangements can lead to lack of communication, name calling, and, on occasion, fighting between students from these differing ability groups.

Did students in your school use any of the following names to refer to members of other groups: hoods, collegiates, retards, know-it-alls, geniuses, dummies, generals, smart-asses, greasers? Can you recall other names that implied status?

If a teacher grants one student a great deal of recognition, other students might be resentful and call him teacher's pet, brownnose, or goody-goody. Similarly, if a teacher communicates an extremely negative evaluation of a student, his classmates may also reject him. The teacher should be aware that teacher recognition of a student—whether positive or negative—may affect that student's peer relationships.

A final aspect of structure is *attraction,* the extent to which members of a group like each other. In any organization friendship patterns have an impact on communication and thus on the accomplishment of objectives. All classes have friendship pairings, cliques, and some students who are not members of any subgroup. Schmuck and Schmuck (1975) suggest that physical appearance and proximity in seating trigger classroom friendships. Then, if there are no major threats to the students' needs for status and security, communication continues. Discussions of common attitudes, values, and interests deepen these relationships among students and often carry them beyond the classroom.

Hostilities and negative feelings among students (or between the students and the teacher) usually lead to defensive behavior by everyone. When this happens, people close off communication and, as a result, don't grow. Such conflict interferes with the learning of course content. Although no teacher can ensure that everyone likes everyone else, an awareness of existing friendship patterns can be useful as the teacher develops learning activities. There are strategies teachers can use for promoting positive feelings among students and building a more cohesive class. We will discuss those strategies in more depth later in this chapter.

Overemphasis on competition in the classroom can generate such negative feelings. In Learning Together and Alone *(1975), Johnson and Johnson provide many suggestions for promoting cooperation.*

An excellent book, which provides many ideas for improving relationships in the classroom, is Howe and Howe, Personalizing Education *(1975).*

Goals

Goals are outcomes, or the places a group would like to end up. In a classroom a number of different types of goals exist simultaneously. There are definite goals that school officials, especially at the state and local levels, expect a class as a formal work group to accomplish. In addition, teachers have their own goals for a particular class. As the class meets together over a period of time, the student group itself develops its own goals. And finally, the individuals within the student group have definite expectations for the outcome of their experiences in the class. While these four constituencies have some expectations in common, they also have some very different aims. For example, the state or school district may expect a teacher to deal with some topic areas that he feels are not important. One student may want a course to be taught from a lecture approach, while other students may prefer a discussion approach. Or parents may want the school to deal only with subject learning, while a teacher may be concerned with helping students explore their own feelings as well.

Harmonizing different goals is one thing that makes teaching so difficult. If each class member is concerned only with personal goals, then there is no sense of group and continual arguments and hostility may become the behavioral norm. On the other hand, if the teacher uses her power to force students to accept her goals, or if the group pursues only goals upon which there is consensus, then the needs of individual students are unsatisfied. In Chapter 15 we will explore further the difficulty of establishing an educational environment that both respects the individual differences and transcends them.

As you begin to formulate your own goals as a teacher, do you anticipate problems with any of the following groups: students, other teachers, the administration, parents, etc.?

Why or why not?

It might be useful to describe one of your classes in which there were good working relationships between teacher and students and among the students themselves. What made that class such an effective group?

Leadership in the Classroom

To see the teacher's leadership role in perspective, we will first describe two types of functions that must be performed if a classroom group is to accomplish its objectives. *Task functions* in a learning group involve furthering the work-oriented, subject matter requirements, i.e., seeing that progress is made in the curriculum. Examples of task functions in the classroom are initiating discussion, providing information, raising questions, giving assignments, and evaluating learning. On the other hand, *social–emotional functions,* which are sometimes called *maintenance functions,* focus on the feelings and interpersonal relationships of the class members. Examples of social–emotional functions are encouraging participation, reducing anxiety, handling conflict, promoting cooperation, and clarifying feelings. Ideally, both teacher and students can share the task and social–emotional functions necessary to keep a group working. Usually, however, because teachers have more experience than students do, they have primary responsibility for group leadership. For that reason our focus in this part of the chapter will be on the teacher's leadership role.

The task functions and social–emotional functions in a group are often referred to as content and process, respectively. Most teachers have a reasonably good grasp of their role in promoting learning of content. However, very few have all the process skills they need to be effective in dealing with group dynamics problems. Teachers themselves are quick to state that their major problems are not in teaching content but in human relations, i.e., discipline, breaking through to alienated children, individual differences, etc.

Power, Influence, and the Teacher

To create a positive climate for learning, a teacher must influence students to behave productively. French and Raven (1959) saw teacher influence in terms of five types of power.

Referent Power.   This kind of influence is not usually thought of as power. People who possess referent power are those others tend to like, identify with, and feel close to. Their power comes not through any direct control but through others' voluntary choice to accept their influence. A teacher may have referent power for a student because that student identifies with her, perceives her as a model, and generally feels close to her.

Referent power, which comes through the relationship one person has with another, is easily seen in our friendships. Even though our friends have no direct control over what we do, we are very influenced by them as we seek their acceptance and recognition.

Legitimate Power.   People with legitimate power are given the right, through their position, to make decisions for others. This power may be granted by a higher level of authority in an organization, may be established by law, or may be agreed upon by the members of a group. Members of Congress have legitimate power to represent their constituents in Washington, physicians have legitimate power to make certain medical decisions, parents have legitimate power in raising their children. Teachers are designated as the official authorities in the classroom and thus have legitimate power to make decisions for student learning.

Expert Power.   People acquire expert power when others recognize that they possess some specialized knowledge or skills. While expert power and legitimate power often go together, it is possible to have either one without the other. Some people have legitimate power but are unable to influence others because their expertise is questioned—e.g., a boss whose employees feel he is not competent and have no confidence in him. Some people have expert power but

Traditionally, teachers have had legitimate power over children as our society has expected them to act in loco parentis—in place of parents. Throughout our society today, legitimate power is being questioned and decreased—in religion, in government, in business, in the family, and in schools. Power is being more democratically distributed among the people affected by decisions. Since teachers have less legitimate power than they used to, they must rely more heavily on other sources of power.

no legitimate power—e.g., a woman to whom many people turn for counseling yet who is not state-certified as a psychologist.

A classroom teacher is hired to use specialized knowledge and teaching abilities to help students learn. However, if students don't perceive that teacher as being an expert, then his capacity to influence them (and so promote their learning) is limited.

Reward Power. A leader who has reward power is able to influence others because he has something they would like, whether it be praise, a promotion, a gold star, money, greater responsibility, free time, or even a nod of approval. However, when people don't consider a reward desirable, the leader has no reward power. For example, a teacher may be able to dispense high grades, but if a particular student doesn't care whether he gets high grades, the teacher has no reward power.

Coercive Power. Leaders who have coercive power are seen as able to punish those who don't comply with their wishes. For example, an employer may threaten to dock a person a full hour's pay each time he is late to work, a parent may warn that the next repetition of a child's misbehavior will result in a spanking, or a committee may inform a member that she will be replaced if she doesn't start carrying her share of the load.

In the classroom some teachers use coercive threats such as low grades, a call to parents, detention hall, or a visit to the principal's office. As with reward power, the effectiveness of coercive power in influencing desirable behavior depends totally on the student's reaction to the threat. If the student doesn't fear low grades, then an F on her report card won't encourage her to change her behavior.

At some point almost any teacher will probably be called upon to use each of the five types of power discussed here. However, there is some indication that legitimate, reward, and coercive powers are less effective in influencing students in the classroom than are referent and expert power (Schmuck and Schmuck, 1975). The teacher who is using himself as instrument (see Chapter 10) and who is developing an I–thou relationship with his students is utilizing both expert power—his special abilities as a helping person—and referent power—his concern for a cooperative teacher–student relationship. Continually emphasizing his legitimate power or using coercion seems to mark a teacher as insecure about his authority and not competent in engaging students in learning. Heavy reliance on legitimate authority and coercion makes students defensive and leads to adversary relationships. Reward power is always available to a teacher and, if used wisely and with respect for individual differences between students, it can be helpful.

Leadership Style

In a classic study Lewin, Lippitt, and White (1939) studied three styles of leadership in boys' clubs—autocratic, democratic, and laissez faire. The *autocratic leader's* major sources of influence were legitimate power and coercion and, to a limited extent, his capacity to

How do you feel about the breakdown of the teacher's legitimate power?

Good teachers find quickly that no one reward works for all students. Students differ tremendously in terms of the rewards that will reinforce their learning. For some verbal praise is most important, for others recognition by classmates is primary, still others require tangible rewards like grades, etc.

Although coercive power can be effective, it has potentially destructive side effects, such as hostility, fear, and anxiety. Teachers who rely on coercive power usually find themselves in battle with their students.

Unfortunately, many schools have relied primarily on coercive power to promote learning and encourage desirable behavior. To what extent has this been true of the schools you have attended?

We believe that the most effective leadership style in the classroom is democratic. If students participate in the decisions, they are more likely to take them seriously. At the same time students are learning how to make responsible decisions and are actively preparing for their role as citizens in a democracy.

How many of your college teachers have used democratic leadership styles? What have been the effects of their leadership style on you and the other students?

In Schools Without Failure *(1969), William Glasser argues persuasively for a democratic classroom environment. Glasser sees group discussion as a valuable teaching technique and he describes the use of classroom meetings to promote learning and resolve conflicts.*

Two other books that provide much practical information on creating more effective group learning environments are Gazda et al., Human Relations Development—A Manual for Educators *(1977), and Shaw,* Group Dynamics: The Psychology of Small Group Behavior *(1976).*

Teachers, like therapists, need to improve their ability to read nonverbal behavior. Videotaping lessons can alert teachers to the rich variety of nonverbal behavior that goes on in the class. The more aware teachers become of that nonverbal behavior, the more they can use it to improve class sessions.

reward. He made most of his group's decisions and gave directions for accomplishing work. The *democratic leader* used referent power, encouraging the boys in his group to identify with him, and expert power. He involved his group members in the decision-making process and encouraged them to share the various group functions. *The laissez faire leader* abdicated his authority and provided no real leadership, allowing his group members to do whatever they wanted.

The effects of each type of leadership on the group members were very different. The authoritarian group was most productive, but the boys were very hostile toward one another. The democratic group was somewhat less productive but showed marked improvement in social behavior; some aggressiveness was evident, but interactions were mostly friendly. The boys in this group offered constructive advice to each other, assumed individual responsibility, and most important, kept working when the leader was absent. The laissez faire group showed the lowest morale, lowest productivity, and a great deal of aggression.

The pioneering research of Lewin, Lippitt, and White (1939) has led to many other studies on authoritarian vs. democratic leadership. In reviewing many of these studies, Anderson (1963) concluded that neither democratic nor autocratic styles were consistently associated with high group productivity. However, democratic leadership usually led to higher morale. Any decision as to which style to use must vary with the situation.

Toward Improved Communication

Any educational process is essentially a communication* process, in which both teacher and students give and receive messages. These messages are either verbal or nonverbal. The verbal and nonverbal aspects of communication usually compliment each other, but on occasion, the two provide conflicting messages, as when a child who is visibly upset says "I'm fine," when asked if anything is bothering him. Words may be our principal means of communication, but the verbal message is always supplemented by such nonverbal cues as facial expressions, body posture, and gestures. Sometimes no talking is taking place, but messages are communicated through nonverbal behavior. For example, a student who is not verbally participating in a discussion may be sitting on the edge of his chair with his hand raised, and another student in the same class is looking down at his desk with a frown on his face. Each of these nonverbal behaviors communicates important messages about the student's interest, involvement, and feelings regarding the lesson.

As we consider ways of improving classroom communication, it will be helpful to examine the model of communication presented in Figure 11–1.

---

* Our focus here is on direct communication through talking or nonverbal behavior. We are not going to discuss communication through print or other media such as film, radio, television, etc.

Figure 11–1. A Model of the Elements of Communication

From M. Bany and L. Johnson, Educational Social Psychology, p. 299. Copyright © 1975 by Macmillan Publishing Co., Inc. Reprinted by permission.

According to Figure 11–1 the person who initiates communication is called the sender. A message is created, which is spoken to another person or a group. Upon hearing the message, the receiver(s) must interpret it and decide how to respond. *Encoding* refers to the process of putting an idea into words. *Decoding* refers to the process of determining what the words of a message mean, i.e., figuring out what the message is. In a classroom situation a teacher is a sender some times and a receiver at other times. In teacher-centered classes teachers do most of the sending and students do most of the receiving. However, in student-centered classes teachers encourage students to do a great deal of the sending of messages and minimize their own role as senders.

Whatever the type of classroom, maintaining effective communication is difficult. Even the best of teachers find that the communication process can easily break down and miscommunication can occur. As we discuss Figure 11–1 further, places where problems in the communication process can occur become more obvious. First, each sender's encoding is influenced not only by the thoughts she wants to put into words, but also by her feelings, attitudes, values, and even her language skills. Similar factors influence the receiver in decoding the sender's message. Communication problems can result when a sender doesn't accurately express verbally what she really means to say or when a receiver doesn't interpret a sender's message correctly.

Moreover, nonverbal behavior can cause confusion if one message is spoken and another comes through in gestures or facial expressions. A teacher must be able to recognize when effective communication is not taking place and then make adjustments so that messages—whether from teacher to student, student to teacher, or student to student—are interpreted by the receiver(s) as the sender intended them.

Promoting effective communication requires that a teacher be both a good sender and a good receiver. She must be very aware of both the verbal and the nonverbal messages she is sending and be able to determine how they are received by students. She must also become expert at interpreting the verbal and nonverbal messages she is sent. Good communication requires special abilities not only in speaking but in listening. Such listening requires empathic skills through which the teacher "gets inside" and "feels with" the person who is speaking so that she can understand what the speaker is saying without misperceiving it. A good teacher also learns to read body

In any classroom the potential for miscommunication is great. Often conflicts arise not out of real issues but out of one person's misunderstanding what another was trying to say. This is why it is so important to help students of all ages develop their capacities to accurately convey their ideas and to listen and understand the ideas of others.

For some practical suggestions on improving teacher–student communication, you might consult Ginott, Teacher and Child (1972), and Gordon, T.E.T.: Teacher Effectiveness Training (1974).

Why not try to visit a number of classrooms and note the extent to which teachers really listen to their students?

language, which provides further cues as to whether students understand what's being said, agree or disagree, wish to say something, etc.

Some examples of the types of communication problems that develop as teachers work with groups are misunderstandings about the teacher's expectations for academic assignments, bad feelings between students or between teacher and students, students' inadequate understanding of information covered in the course, and students' feelings that course material is irrelevant and meaningless. Working through such problems in communication requires first, recognizing their existence; second, trying to find out what caused them; and finally, proposing alternatives to respond to them. The key to identifying, explaining, and resolving communication problems, then, is the teacher's effort in seeking continuous feedback from students.

Of course, all of these suggestions are easier said than done. Teachers must possess a great deal of personal security in order to open themselves to the possibility of criticism. Teachers who are not succeeding can usually sense it in their relationships with students. By talking about it openly, they can clarify their feelings and develop steps toward improvement.

Students, too, have to be helped to communicate openly since most of their teachers probably have not encouraged them to do so.

Teachers can gain feedback in many ways. Asking students to paraphrase something they heard or explain it in their own words can help a teacher learn whether students received a message. Encouraging students to express their feelings about a lesson, an assignment, another student, or even the teacher's behavior can be useful. Having students complete anonymous course evaluations a number of times during a semester provides the teacher with suggestions for adaptations in the course. Being on the lookout for nonverbal cues indicating interest, boredom, frustration, hostility, etc., is always necessary. Such an ongoing attempt to keep the lines of communication open is vital to effective group functioning. We will discuss process evaluation in greater depth in Chapter 13.

Another way to improve communication in the classroom is to change the physical environment. Studies (Sommer, 1967) have shown that participation is affected by seating arrangements in the classroom. The four seating arrangements shown in Exploration 11–2 (on page 223) have different effects on communication. Before reading our discussion, study the diagrams and provide your own answers to the following questions.

Exploration 11–2: Classroom Seating Arrangements

If none of the four arrangements provided is close to your most common seating arrangement, draw in yours.

1. Which one of these seating patterns was most common in your schooling? ___ Least common? ___

2. a. Which arrangement would you feel most comfortable in as a student? ___ Why?

    b. Which arrangement would you feel least comfortable in as a student? ___ Why?

Discuss your responses to these questions with other members of your class.

3. a. Which arrangement would you feel most comfortable in as a teacher? ___ Why?

    b. Which arrangement would you feel least comfortable in as a teacher? ___ Why?

It might be interesting to do a survey on the seating arrangements in a number of classes in different schools.

4. Which arrangement most emphasizes the teacher's authority? ___ Why?

5. Which arrangement least emphasizes the teacher's authority? ___ Why?

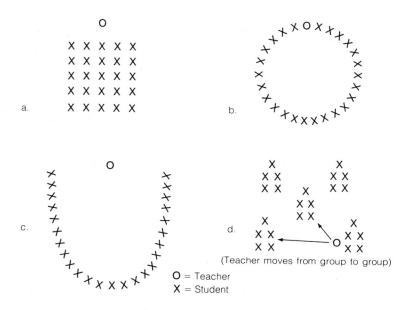

(Teacher moves from group to group)

O = Teacher
X = Student

As you thought about your own experiences as you completed this activity, you probably realized how seating arrangements in a class affect people's feelings and the ways they communicate. If a teacher desires student–to–student communication, a traditional classroom seating arrangement like *a* is counterproductive. When students can't see each other and when all desks are faced toward the teacher, students have no eye contact with each other and teacher power and control are emphasized. By contrast, in the circle in diagram *b*, all students do have eye contact and student–to–student communication is facilitated and teacher power played down. If intensive contact among a few students is desirable, then a small-group arrangement in which the teacher moves from group to group, as in diagram *d*, is beneficial. Clearly, different physical environments will lead to different communication patterns—a factor no teacher should ignore in attempts to improve classroom communication.

When students are given a chance to choose their own seats in a traditional classroom like a, they often repeat old patterns (Good and Brophy, 1977). Where do you tend to sit in a traditional classroom? In the front row? In the back row? Near a window?

Why do you think people make such choices?

Conclusions

Our goal in this chapter has been to help you understand the dynamics that affect both teacher and student behavior in the classroom as a prerequisite to effective group leadership. Teachers must be aware of the effects of various types of power and leadership styles. They must be knowledgeable about the process of communication and be able to create an atmosphere that encourages open, friendly relationships between group members. In such a classroom miscommunications can be recognized and resolved constructively.

The primary responsibility of any group leader is to see that the group accomplishes its objectives. For this to happen, the individual members of the group must feel they are satisfying their own interests, values, and needs by being a part of the group. If task and social-emotional functions are carried out effectively in a classroom, individual students will have a sense of group progress and positive feelings toward their peers and the teacher. Such feelings lead to cohesiveness and cooperation in the group and promote everyone's growth and fulfillment.

In concluding, we would like to present a model (Figure 11–2) that we feel brings together in a novel way the essence of our focus on the teacher and the class. Look the model over before you finish reading the conclusions.

TEACHER

	Coping	Defending
Coping	1. Teacher coping, class coping: Open communication Cohesiveness Good feelings Growth	3. Teacher defending, class coping: Teacher is not leading. Class is trying to make group work. Will probably lead to 4.
Defending	2. Teacher coping, class defending: Teacher is confronting problems openly and nondefensively. With skill and patience, this can lead to 1.	4. Teacher defending, class defending: Adversary relationships Bad feelings No growth

CLASS

Figure 11–2. Defending and Coping in the Classroom

The model we have created in Figure 11–2 is based upon Jerome Bruner's concept of coping and defending. As you will recall from Chapter 5, coping is behavior in which a person is growing and moving forward; defending is behavior characterized by lack of growth and resistance to change. Coping involves an openness to new experience, i.e., learning. Defending involves stagnation and so blocks learning. In the classroom the ideal relationship is one in which both teacher and students are coping, in other words, cooperating and growing together. This relationship is shown in Figure 11–2 in cell 1. Throughout this chapter we have tried to illustrate how important what a teacher does and says is to establishing such a positive atmosphere for learning.

Cell 2 in the chart represents a situation in which the teacher is coping, but the class is defending. With self-awareness, understanding of the group's dynamics, strategies designed to open up communication, and patience, a teacher can gradually move the group

In your school experience how common were classes in which both students and teachers were coping?

___ *a. Very common*

___ *b. Somewhat common*

___ *c. Somewhat rare*

___ *d. Very rare*

An insecure teacher in the situation illustrated in cell 2 of Figure 11–2

toward coping. In cell 3 the teacher is defending and the group is coping. It is very likely that the teacher's defensive behavior will lead to defensive behavior by the class since there is no real leadership. The teacher in this situation needs help, but unless group members can initiate outside intervention, they usually do not have the skills or time necessary to get things moving constructively. Finally, in cell 4 we see the classic illustration of an adversary relationship between teacher and class. In this type of relationship both the teacher and the class are defending and a battle, not genuine learning, is going on. Discipline problems take up most of the class time and both teacher and students can't wait for the class to be over.

Although it always takes two (or more) to cooperate or to fight, we believe that the teacher is the key to whether coping or defending occurs in a classroom group. As we saw with Mrs. Reilly and Mr. Morton at the beginning of this chapter, the teacher's behavior sets the stage for development of an I–thou relationship. The teacher's knowledge, communication skills, self-awareness, and emotional security all help to perpetuate that type of relationship. To promote learning a teacher must be able to turn students' defensive behavior into coping. And that difficult task demands coping on the teacher's part!

may become defensive himself as he confronts students who are defending. Then, of course, "the battle has begun."

In your school experience how common were classes in which both students and teacher were defending?

____ *a. Very common*

____ *b. Somewhat common*

____ *c. Somewhat rare*

____ *d. Very rare*

Some Good Books

Bany, Mary A. and Lois V. Johnson. *Educational Social Psychology.* New York: Macmillan, 1975. This text looks at many areas of educational psychology from a social-psychological perspective. As a general overview of the social psychology of education and its application, it is very good.

Dreikurs, Rudolf, Bernice Grunwald, and Floy Pepper. *Maintaining Sanity in the Classroom.* New York: Harper & Row, 1971. The focus of this book is on classroom problems, with special emphasis on group dynamics. It provides many suggestions for dealing with discipline problems through group discussion.

Glasser, William. *Schools Without Failure.* New York: Harper & Row, 1969. Glasser emphasizes that schools are failure-oriented and shows how classes can be used as counseling groups for resolving behavior problems as well as educational problems.

Gorman, Alfred H. *Teachers and Learners: The Interactive Process of Education.* 2nd ed. Boston: Allyn and Bacon, 1973. A brief, clearly written view of student–teacher interaction in the classroom.

Jackson, Philip. *Life in Classrooms.* New York: Holt, Rinehart and Winston, 1968. This book has become a classic statement on the "inside world" of the elementary school classroom. Reporting his own visits to a number of different classes, Jackson provides a thought-provoking view of what school is really like for teachers and students.

Morrison, Donald W. *Personal Problem Solving in the Classroom.* New York: Wiley, 1977. Morrison provides a method for helping young people in a classroom group work together in solving their emotional and behavioral problems.

Napier, Rodney W. and Matti K. Gershenfeld. *Groups: Theory and Experience.* Boston: Houghton Mifflin, 1973. This book is useful as a source of information and strategies for understanding and improving group functioning.

Napier, R., J. Hayman, and G. Moskowitz. *Classroom Dynamics: Viewing the Classroom as a Social System.* Monterey, Calif.: Brooks/Cole, 1976. This book discusses theories and research on group cohesiveness, warmth, and other variables of group dynamics.

Newman, Ruth G. *Groups in Schools.* New York: Simon and Schuster, 1974. By using many real situations and anecdotes, Newman has done a nice job of showing how groups function within school settings.

Schmuck, Richard A. and Patricia A. Schmuck. *Group Processes in the Classroom.* 2nd. ed. Dubuque, Iowa: William C. Brown, 1975. As a synthesis of current theory and research on the dynamics that affect classroom behavior of students and teachers, this book has no peers.

Suggestions for Action-Oriented Learning

1. Visit a junior high school a number of times and try to note as many norms as you can that influence the behavior of students. You might pay special attention to norms regarding clothing, hair, shoes, language, and ways of behaving, especially in class as opposed to in the halls, cafeteria, etc. Share your observations with members of your class.

2. Visit a number of elementary school (or high school) classes. Try to analyze student–teacher coping and defending according to Figure 11–2. Consider what factors might have led to the type of teacher–student relationship you observed.

3. Discuss with your classmates the extent to which task functions and social–emotional functions are being fulfilled in the class. Make suggestions for improvements.

4. Observe leaders operating in a variety of social settings within the school; e.g., in different academic classes, in gym, at a faculty meeting, at a P.T.A. meeting, at an assembly, in the cafeteria, etc. Try to analyze their leadership behavior and rank how frequently each leader uses each of the five types of power discussed in this chapter.

12
The Teacher and the School: Promoting Educational Change

Throughout this book we have viewed learning as a process of continuing growth for each individual that is always influenced by the social environment—the family, classroom, school, peer group, society, etc. Each individual also has the potential for influencing and changing this environment. The process of growth or change is reciprocal—groups change individuals, and at the same time, individuals change groups.

What do you feel should be the school's role in its society?

Do you see yourself as a conservative, a progressive, or a reconstructionist? Why?

You might like to read a little more about the three views of the schools' role in society. The references below, which are now classics, should help.

On conservatism:

Jacques Barzun, Teacher in America *(1955).*

Robert M. Hutchins, The Conflict in Education *(1953).*

On progressivism:

John Dewey, Experience and Education *(1938).*

On reconstructionism:

Theodore Brameld, Toward a Reconstructed Philosophy of Education *(1956).*

George S. Counts, Dare the School Build a New Social Order? *(1932).*

Learning is a process of growth, or change. Change is necessary for an individual's survival and self-realization. Moreover, the continued existence and improvement of society demands change. The members of a society collectively must benefit from the experiences of their predecessors, respond effectively to the problems of the present, and develop new resources and strategies for anticipating and creating the future.

As societies have become more complex socially and technologically, the family and the community have become increasingly less able to provide the young with the learning necessary to make the transition from the past to the present and toward the future. Consequently, schools have been established (and the number of years of formal schooling required by law has been increased) to prepare young people for life and work, i.e., to perpetuate the culture. Teachers—hired on the basis of their special knowledge, skills, and training—are expected to change people by helping them learn. As individuals change, the institutions they create eventually change. A teacher, therefore, is always a potential catalyst for changes that extend well beyond the walls of a classroom.

There is general agreement that an important function of schools is the preparation of young people to enter and carry on the existing culture. However, there are different opinions among both educators and citizens about the role of the school in changing the culture. Some see the school as primarily a conservative institution, which passes on the tested knowledge and skills the young will need to fit into the existing culture and maintain it. Others view the school as a progressive institution, which seeks to prepare youth for active participation in an ever changing culture. And a few argue that the school must take the lead in reconstructing the social order. The advocates of these three viewpoints on the purpose of schools are often called, respectively, *conservatives, progressives,* and *reconstructionists.*

Although this book attempts to provide many perspectives on the role of the school in society, we definitely write from a progressive–reconstructionist orientation. As both teachers and writers we believe that education must seek to transform the future. We are convinced that the world as a whole, and the United States in particular, are in deep trouble. The problems of war and conflict, overpopulation, poverty, pollution, depletion of our natural resources, and injustice threaten the very continuation of life on earth. Unless the educational process alerts people to the seriousness of these problems and helps them develop the personal and institutional resources for confronting them, there is little hope for the future.

If social changes are to be influenced by formal education, a new breed of teachers who see themselves as change agents is required. As we have suggested earlier in this book, teachers must understand themselves in order to understand students and help them change. Teachers must also have a knowledge of the structure of the school in order to implement the changes in curriculum, teaching strategies, and educational environments that will stimulate changes in students and, eventually, in society.

In this chapter we will focus on the role of the individual teacher in bringing about educational change. We want to present a realistic picture of the teacher's power to operate as a change agent within the educational system and the system's power to resist change. We believe that by understanding some of the complexities of the social environment of schooling, you will be better able to implement your own ideas to help children learn.

Through a series of six anecdotes we will describe the successes and failures, hope and despair of teachers as they struggle to bring about change. By providing real situations, we hope to help you understand not only the change process but also the structure of the school as an organization and social environment.

Let us first look in on the efforts of two teachers who decided to make rather substantial changes within their own classrooms. Later, we will explore the problems of some teachers who tried to introduce changes that would also affect other teachers and students outside their own classes. Following each anecdote are questions for you to think about in preparation for our discussion of the anecdote.

Being a Change Agent in the Classroom

Change Agent 1—Linda Simmons, U.S. History Teacher, Eleventh Grade

As Linda Simmons explained the oral history project to the students in her junior U.S. history class, she noted that a few of the students sitting in the circle were whispering, and others had frowns or questions on their faces. She had sensed from the beginning of the school year two months ago that some of her students didn't understand her goals or why she was using such different teaching methods. However, she felt that she had adequately explained why, over the past few years, she had changed dramatically from the ways she taught during the first twenty years of her career. Consequently, she found herself getting more and more irritated with the lack of response to the oral history assignment. Finally, in utter frustration, she called on Ken, generally a serious student. She wanted to learn why he was reacting so negatively to her proposal. The dialogue proceeded as follows:

Miss Simmons: Ken, what is it that is bothering you? All I want you and the other members of this class to do is carry out an oral history project. It involves interviewing your parents, grandparents, relatives, or other adults about their recollections of life in the United States during World War II. Don't you think that through interviews with people who remember World War II you will improve your understanding about that period?

Ken: Well, maybe. But that just doesn't sound like history to me. In all my previous history classes we read books, heard lectures by the teacher, asked questions if we had any, and took tests.

To what extent is your decision to become a teacher based upon a desire to be a change agent?

If you do see yourself as a change agent, what are three changes that you would like to implement when you become a teacher?

1.

2.

3.

Try to recall how many teachers you had who, after many years of teaching, still experimented with new approaches.

What did you feel about their classes?

Have you ever experienced the feeling Ken is discussing?

This is a big problem for teachers who choose to be innovative. It's all too easy to fall into the trap of doing only what other teachers do because that's what students are most comfortable with.

How can a teacher introduce students to an unfamiliar approach without causing them to turn off or become hostile?

Miss Simmons: But don't you understand? I'm trying to make history real and have you learn it actively as well as from books. By doing oral history you are acting as a historian instead of just learning history second-hand from a text. Doesn't that make history more fun?

Ken: Yeah, but how do I know I'm learning anything? I have almost no notes in this course. And all we do in class is sit around in a circle and hear each other's opinions about things we've been reading.

Miss Simmons: My reason for eliminating lecturing and for encouraging discussion is to get us all thinking historically rather than simply copying down bits of information. Role-playing historical events and discussing our feelings about historical issues help us see how relevant history can be. As we try to solve today's problems, history can be a valuable resource.

Ken: I know you really want us to understand history not just memorize it as we do in our other classes, and I like that. It's just that your whole approach is so different from what we've had before that it's really hard to get used to. Doing projects and being prepared for good discussions take a lot of maturity on our part. At times I think it would be easier on all of us if you just did what our other history teachers have done. But then again, I really didn't "learn" history in those classes. . . .

The discussion continued until the end of the period with input from other students that basically supported Ken's observations. It was then that Linda Simmons began to reflect on what her students were telling her. Maybe she would have to take things more slowly and help her students learn how to learn more actively. After all, it had taken her many years as a teacher to change from her nonstop lectures, classrooms set up in rows, rote homework assignments, and multiple-choice tests. Why should she expect all of her students to adjust quickly to a new teaching approach that she had taken years to feel comfortable with?

Have you ever been in a class in which a well-meaning teacher like Miss Simmons became frustrated because the students weren't ready for a new way of teaching? What eventually happened?

What advice would you offer Miss Simmons in her predicament?

The dialogue between Miss Simmons and Ken provides a picture of a dedicated teacher who, even after years of teaching, continued to question what she was doing. Often when people experience something new or develop novel ideas, they become "true believers" and try to help others see the light. Such was the case with Miss Simmons, but fortunately she was self-aware enough to get beyond her own defensiveness and hear what Ken was saying. She realized that she had been trying to convert many of her students to her own changing views of education. However, as Ken explained, neither he nor most of the other students were ready for such major changes. Consequently, Linda Simmons saw that she would have to devote much more time and effort to understanding her students. She would have to help them learn to do oral history and to try other innovative ways of learning.

The next anecdote describes the work of an elementary school teacher who decided to create an open classroom. The difficulties she encountered came, as you will see, from an unexpected source.

We can see here that being effective as a change agent requires the same diagnostic perspective that we discussed in Chapter 7. The more feedback a teacher gets from her students, the more she can modify her expectations and genuinely reach her students.

Change Agent 2—Carol Worthington, Open Classroom Teacher, Third Grade

Carol Worthington is one of three third-grade teachers in an elementary school in suburban Chicago. At 38 she is in her eighth year of full-time teaching. She had two years of teaching experience before the first of her two children was born. At that time she left teaching and only returned when her second child entered school, when she was 32.

At the beginning of the current school year, Carol decided that she would like to develop an *open classroom* approach in her teaching. This decision was prompted by a number of factors. She felt that she had begun to teach subject matter rather than children, losing much of the fun of getting to know her students as individuals. She seemed to be getting bored with the sound of her own voice, and was finding it increasingly hard to motivate her students to be active thinkers and participants in class. During the summer she had taken an open education workshop at a local university, where she had a chance to share her concerns about changing her teaching with other teachers. Reading Neill's *Summerhill* (1960) and Kohl's *The Open Classroom* (1969) further stimulated her thinking.

In August before the school year began, Carol Worthington started planning for her open classroom. She decided to reorganize her room by placing the desks in clusters of four or five and by using tables and bookshelves to create a reading center, a math center, a science center, and a creative activity center. She also began to collect all sorts of materials that before her summer workshop she would never have thought useful in teaching—old magazines, plastic food containers, newspapers, even an old square of carpeting for students to sit on in the reading corner. Carol was fortunate to have ordered new reading and mathematics books that lent themselves to individualized teaching and independent study. However, becoming familiar with the new books and deciding how to use them took time.

You probably recall the concept of the open classroom *discussed in Chapter 9. An open classroom provides greater freedom for students than a traditional classroom. Open often means more student-centered learning through discussion, projects, etc., and less teacher-centered learning. Frequently students work at their own rate on projects of their choice. There may even be a more open physical environment, which allows for movement and interaction between students.*

As you can see, becoming a good open classroom teacher requires a great deal of planning.

When the first day of school came, Carol was excited about trying her new ideas. She was also a little nervous about how her students would respond. As the semester went along, Carol became more and more involved in her new approach to teaching. She was not only giving students opportunities to work at their own rate; she was also providing choices of assignments and projects for each child. She

*How many teachers do you know
who put in the amount of time outside
school that Carol puts in?*

*Do you expect to do a lot of work at
home when you become a teacher?*

had to diagnose each child's strengths and weaknesses in a particular area, prescribe appropriate learning experiences, and then evaluate what had been accomplished. Just keeping track of each child's progress was a big job. Carol found herself spending more and more time at home developing materials, planning lessons, and thinking about her class.

The students' progress and their enthusiasm for the open classroom brought Carol great satisfaction and helped compensate for her frustrations as she realized how much "homework" she was doing. However, one evening Carol's 12-year-old daughter took her by complete surprise when she said, "Gee, Mom, I wish you would spend as much time with me as you do in planning for your third graders." This comment triggered a worry about neglecting her family that Carol usually managed to push out of her consciousness.

*Have you ever wondered how you will
balance your work and home life
when you become a teacher?*

Later that evening, after telling her daughter that she would have more time once she got her classroom organized, Carol mentioned the comment to her husband. Rather than reassuring her, he agreed with their daughter's comment, adding that he wished Carol could talk more with him about things other than her class. Carol had felt herself becoming more and more preoccupied with her teaching, and now she began to wonder whether she was neglecting her family as she became increasingly wrapped up in her teaching.

*It might be helpful to interview a
number of teachers you know to find
out how they feel about taking work
home.*

Some teachers, social workers, physicians, and other helping professionals feel that professionals should not take their work home with them. Others argue that it is normal for dedicated helping professionals to work at home and to continually think about their efforts. How do you feel about this question? Why?

As we can see from Carol Worthington's conflicts, being a change agent is physically and emotionally demanding. Even making changes within one's own classroom, where a teacher usually has legitimate power and a fair degree of latitude, is hard work. Resources are often limited and there are seldom enough people available to help out. Therefore, changes must be preceded by much planning in order to anticipate problems and help the people affected by the change understand it and adjust to it.

*Struggling to implement any type of
change is hard work that takes its toll
not only on the change agent herself
but also on her relationships with family, close friends, and colleagues.
The personal feelings generated by
the strong commitments and
the long hours need to be discussed
openly with those who are affected
by them.*

Leaving the status quo and trying something new creates anxiety for those affected by a change, especially for the change agent. Doubts, fears, and insecurities are raised as a change agent encounters resistance and faces the possibility of failure. Yet as we learned from the thinking of Abraham Maslow (Chapter 9), opening oneself to new experiences can foster personal growth and provide tremendous satisfaction. The problem for the change agent seems to be maximizing the positive aspects of the change and minimizing the frustrations and difficulties. For Carol Worthington this may mean discussing with her family whether she should devote less time at home to preparation for school or whether her family should accept her need to work at home. Do you have any ideas as to how Carol should resolve her problem?

Promoting Change in a School

Change Agent 3—Bob Jennings,
High School Physical Education Teacher

As he sat at the Physical Education Department meeting, Bob Jennings felt his pulse increasing, his face reddening, and his anger building. It was February of his second year teaching physical education in Memorial High School, and once again the meeting had gotten sidetracked into a discussion of the various strengths and weaknesses of the athletic teams and how to improve their records. Even on the few occasions when the teaching of the physical education classes was discussed, most of the time was spent on questions Bob felt were trivial, such as the amount of time it took many of the kids to get dressed, the number of students cutting gym class, or the problems of getting students to wear the proper gym clothes. Bob could remain quiet no longer and exploded:

Do you think meetings like this one went on in your high school physical education department? Why or why not?

"Why the hell do we always spend our time talking about the athletic teams and never about improving the physical education program? Aren't we hired here as full-time teachers who are supposed to devote ourselves to all the students? Athletics are extracurricular activities for a few students and we should see them as extracurricular. Isn't that why we're paid extra for coaching and why the teams practice after school?"

There was complete silence in the room as Bob went on, his voice shaking. "Maybe the reasons so many kids cut our physical education classes, try to skip showering, and spend most of their time complaining have something to do with us. Couldn't it be that they see us as more concerned with the 'jocks' on our teams and with our won–loss records than we are with them? We don't really teach them unless you call dividing them up into teams to play football or refereeing a basketball game teaching. Every year it's the same old thing, football and soccer in the fall, basketball and gymnastics (which many kids dread) in the winter, and softball and volleyball in the spring. No wonder the kids are bored!

How did you feel about physical education classes when you were in high school?

Were your phys. ed. courses taught the way they were in Bob's school?

"Why don't we stop wasting our time talking nonsense and discuss ways we can make our program more attractive? What about giving students more choices of different types of activities, especially individual activities they might continue as adults? If we were less hung up with military-type discipline and punishing students for misbehavior by making them do exercises or run laps, we might find that more of them would like gym class. De-emphasizing competition and maybe even bringing the boys' and girls' classes together might make gym more fun for both groups. And isn't that our goal—to help young people find physical activities that they can both enjoy and use to keep their bodies in shape?"

How do you feel today's high school students would react to the type of physical education program Bob is proposing?

As Bob searched for other ideas to bolster his arguments, his department chairman spoke up. "Well, Mr. Jennings. Are you finished?" "I guess so," stammered Bob.

What do you think Bob's department chairman would say to Bob's remarks?

How effective do you think Bob Jennings will be as a change agent within his department? Why?

If you need to refresh your thinking on different kinds of power, return to Chapter 11.

As a new member in the Physical Education Department, Bob Jennings has neither seniority nor a position of authority. He has no legitimate power and no official power to either reward or punish the other members of his department. His two potential resources are referent power—through the positive relationships he might establish with his colleagues—and expert power if he can demonstrate that he has skills and knowledge that other department members don't have.

Have you ever wondered how effective you will be as a young teacher in trying to initiate changes in your department or school?

Unfortunately, although his strongly worded speech helped him work through many of his own feelings, it probably antagonized many of his colleagues. It would be only normal for them to become defensive when listening to such a direct attack on their own behavior as teachers and coaches. And since they may well perceive Bob as still young, naive, and idealistic, they may simply dismiss what he says and resent the "holier-than-thou" tone of his remarks.

Many young teachers find themselves questioning established practices within a school or department. Sometimes it is very difficult to remain true to one's beliefs and still avoid threatening the establishment to the point that one's advancement or job is jeopardized. New teachers with strong commitments at times feel as if they are walking a tightrope.

Bob might accomplish more by carefully analyzing which members of his department are most open to his ideas and then developing a relationship with them. If some of his colleagues trust him, they may support some of his proposals even though they don't totally agree with them. If there aren't other teachers who feel the way Bob does, he might propose a trial project to allow him to try out some of his ideas with a small group from a large class or with a class that he teaches alone. If the other members of the department don't feel coerced into something they don't believe in or aren't ready for, they will probably not spend their time blocking Bob's efforts. And if Bob's ideas prove effective, some of the original skeptics might even ask him what he was doing and how they might try something similar themselves.

A good book for learning ways to pursue change within the educational system is Postman and Weingartner, Teaching as a Subversive Activity *(1969).*

Change Agent 4—Karl Pulaski, Elementary Teacher in a First-, Second-, and Third-Grade Interage Class

Karl Pulaski entered the teachers' room and sat down to have a cup of coffee. It felt good to have a few minutes to rest away from the class. As he was beginning to daydream about summer vacation, the silence in the room was broken by Sue Johnson, a fifth-grade teacher who had begun teaching at the same time as Karl, four years ago. Looking up from her lesson plans she asked, "How's your teaching going this year Karl? You look worn out." "Oh, it's pretty good, but a lot more work than I expected," responded Karl. "I really like the idea of having *interage grouping* so that first, second, and third graders are all together in the same room with three of us as teachers. But 75 kids and three teachers is rough no matter how you look at it." "Well, don't you also have a full-time teacher's aide?" questioned Sue.

Interage grouping is a way of organizing classes across age levels. The example provided here is a class that includes children ranging in age from

"Yes we do, and she helps a lot, especially with the clerical work and with supervising the students working independently," Karl answered.

"And you also have more preparation time than the rest of us who are teaching alone," Sue continued with a slight hint of jealousy. "That's true," Karl said, "but we need the extra time to plan appropriate activities for our 75 students and especially just to learn to work together. When I agreed to participate in this new approach, I never anticipated that it would be so hard for three experienced teachers to cooperate. Each of use is enthusiastic about this project and our views about education are similar. But our styles of teaching and the things we feel should be covered differ. We've found that if we don't have time to talk things through, it's very easy for us to have our feelings hurt when either our colleagues or our students reject something we feel is important. At times I really believe that the kids are adjusting much faster to this change than we are."

"I guess you know that the local teachers' union is not too happy about the extra preparation time you three are getting or about the special attention you receive from our principal," Sue mentioned with some hesitation. "Yea, we're concerned about that and try to keep the lines of communication open with the other teachers," Karl responded. "We try to reassure them that we chose to try this new arrangement and that no one is going to push them into interage grouping. But some teachers still seem fearful and a few are even outwardly hostile to us."

"How do you feel the class is working for the students? Are they learning? And what about having little first graders in with second and third graders? Don't they get lost in the shuffle?" asked Sue. "No, the kids seem to have adjusted to each other well," answered Karl. "They not only work together and help each other in the classroom, but they even play together at recess. As for whether they're learning more than they would in regular classes, I'm not sure. I'll be anxious to see the comparisons between the progress of our students and the first, second, and third graders in regular classrooms. Our kids seem to me to be happier with school, and they act as if they like being in an interage group."

Karl went on, "As far as my own feelings go, I have both highs and lows. There are days I love the team teaching and feel like I would never want to teach in any other way. And there are other days when I'm ready to go back to working by myself with 25 students." "Well, I have to give you credit for trying," Sue concluded with a sigh. "As you might have guessed, I'm kind of skeptical about the whole thing. I can't imagine myself in a room with 75 children and trying to work together with two other teachers!"

Why do you suppose there is tension in Karl's school between the other teachers and his team? What could Karl and his team members do to reduce this tension?

What do you feel would be two major strengths and two major

6 to 9. Proponents of interage grouping argue that it gives children a chance to learn from each other and allows the possibility of tailoring instructional groups to children's levels of ability irrespective of age.

Have you ever been a student in a class that was taught by a team of teachers?

How did the team teaching work out?

There is always the potential of "bad vibrations" developing when a few teachers in a new program appear to their colleagues to be given special attention and/or resources. Only careful groundwork will prevent confrontations growing out of such projects.

Interage grouping allows children to teach each other. Studies show that children learn a great deal from helping other children learn.

Two excellent references on this subject are Vernon Allen (ed.), Children as Teachers (1976), and Gartner, Kohler, and Riessman, Children Teach Children: Learning by Teaching (1971).

"Highs" in teaching are often followed by "lows," as Karl has seen. Even the best new programs run into snags that must be analyzed and resolved.

weaknesses of a team-teaching approach compared to the more common self-contained classroom in an elementary school?

The conversation between Karl Pulaski and Sue Johnson illustrates some of the communications problems that can develop when a small number of people become involved in a project that does not fit within established organizational patterns. It is clear that Sue is skeptical about the change that Karl and his two colleagues are making in their teaching. It is also clear that she is not alone in her views; apparently other teachers feel that the three members of the "interage team" are receiving special treatment, especially from the principal. The other teachers seem to fear that they may be pushed toward interage grouping.

Such skepticism and fear could lead the teachers, through their union, to put pressure on the principal to limit the special support granted the interage classroom. And this could seriously hamper its effectiveness. Consequently, Karl and his two team-teaching colleagues must be careful not to isolate themselves from the other faculty. They must be open to explaining what they are doing and showing why they require special support. Allaying the jealousy and doubts of the other faculty members will probably require a great deal of time and effort. And if Karl hopes eventually to convince other teachers to try interage grouping and team teaching, an even bigger educational task lies ahead of him.

The Community and Educational Change

Change Agent 5—Mark Greenberg, Health Teacher, Eighth Grade

On his way back to his classroom from lunch, Mark Greenberg stopped at the office to pick up his mail. Mixed in with the usual assortment of memos and brochures from textbook and instructional materials companies was a letter that caught his eye. The return address indicated that it was from Mrs. Shirley Tucker, the mother of Darlene Tucker, a student in his eighth-grade health class. As he opened the letter, Mark wondered why Mrs. Tucker was writing to him. The letter, it turned out, was not to him directly; Mrs. Tucker had sent him a copy of a letter she had sent to Mr. DeCarlo, the principal of his junior high school. The letter read as follows:

11/9

Dear Mr. DeCarlo,

I am writing to you to demand that my daughter Darlene be transferred out of Mr. Greenberg's eighth-grade health class at once. When I signed the letter approving her taking that course, I never in my wildest dreams would have expected what seems to be going on in that class. Last Wednesday Darlene came home from school saying that her class was not only learning about the actual physical act of sexual intercourse, but that they had discussed premarital sex. She said that in the discussion one of the boys said that his brother had told him that

Many good projects designed to improve the educational process become divisive because teachers and administrators committed to them don't adequately explain their purposes. Change agents must not only justify what they are doing but "politic" for support.

The American socioeconomic and political system with its emphasis on individualism and competition, has not prepared teachers or students for working cooperatively. Team teaching and interage grouping will require a great deal of reeducation of both children and adults in schools.

As you read this letter, try to recall what you learned in health class (if you had one) in junior high school.

How do you feel about teaching human sexuality and discussing issues like premarital sex in junior high?

many of the boys in the sophomore class had engaged in sexual intercourse with their girl friends. What really upset me was her comment that Mr. Greenberg had responded to the boy's remark by saying that there was nothing wrong with sexual intercourse between a boy and a girl if they really cared for each other.

My Darlene is only 13 years old and is very impressionable. She has recently become interested in boys, and I do not want her being indoctrinated into permissive sexual values that I find personally repugnant and that are contrary to the teachings of our church. Some of my friends tried to warn me before I agreed to let Darlene take this course that this sort of thing might happen. I guess I should have listened to their advice.

I'm too upset to write any more at this time. I would like to speak with you about this matter as well as with Mr. Greenberg to whom, as you will note, I have sent a copy of this letter. I assume you will call me at your earliest convenience.

Mrs. Shirley Tucker

Sometimes students misperceive things their teachers say and then report their misperceptions to parents, who become upset at what they hear. Do you think this could have happened here?

As Mark finished reading his copy of the letter, his head was spinning. Why hadn't Darlene recalled accurately what he had said in class? He had told the students that any sexual relationship between two people would affect them not only physically but, especially, emotionally, so both people should weigh the pros and cons of sexual intercourse carefully. Mark had tried to help his students consider their own views and those of their families, churches, friends, etc., and had not expressed a personal opinion either in favor of or in opposition to premarital intercourse. He felt his students had to come to their own decisions.

Mark was worried about his principal's reaction to Mrs. Tucker's letter. He knew how hard it had been to get the health course established even as an option for eighth graders whose parents approved their taking such a course. If Mrs. Tucker's letter became public, there were conservative community groups that would love to use it to rally more people in support of their anti–sex-education movement. Mark was certain that it wouldn't take much public controversy to bring about the elimination of the whole eighth-grade health curriculum that he had worked so hard to develop and implement. Mark also was concerned how this issue might affect his principal's evaluation of him for tenure.

However, the more he thought about the letter and what had transpired in Darlene's class, the more Mark was convinced that he could explain to Mrs. Tucker what had happened and justify his approach. He believed in what he was doing and felt that if he and Mr. DeCarlo saw Mrs. Tucker together, they might even be able to convince her to leave Darlene in the class.

The next step was to talk with Mr. DeCarlo. . . .

How do you think Mr. DeCarlo ought to respond to Mark, given his responsibilities to both his staff and the students and their

Mark is apparently one of a growing number of teachers who believe that schools should deal with the real, personal issues that young people confront as they grow up. He does not see health as just another subject that provides information. He believes that it should concern itself with the feelings, attitudes, and values of students as well. He is committed to humanistic education, the education of the total person.

Values clarification is one of the teaching approaches Mark was using in his class. Values clarification is a means of helping students reflect on, state, and compare their values with those of others. When used as its designers (Raths, Harmin, and Simon, 1966) intended, this approach does not advocate any one value over another. It encourages students to make up their own minds on values issues.

No matter what the merits of their own views on education, teachers and administrators cannot ignore the feelings of the community in which they work. The more they try to understand the values of their students' parents, the more likely that major confrontations will be avoided, and more important, the more successful they may be in introducing valuable innovations. Many new programs die because they were poorly presented to the community. When this happens, the community alone should not be blamed. The educator must question and review his own planning.

Herbert Kohl has written an excellent book that, in part, explores the politics of teaching. In his book, On Teaching *(1976), Kohl offers many suggestions for gaining support for new ideas both within the school and in the community.*

parents? Try to imagine what you would say to Mark if you were Mr. DeCarlo.

If you were Mark Greenberg, how would you approach Mrs. Tucker and what would you say to her?

The anecdote presented here illustrates the fact that teachers must be sensitive not only to the attitudes and values of their students but also to those of their students' parents and of the community at large. In a controversial subject area like human sexuality, the potential for misunderstanding the best-intentioned lesson is always great. People who see themselves as change agents, and who are committed to exposing students to new and often unpopular points of view are in a risky position. Mark's principal, even more than Mark himself, will end up in the "hot seat" if Mrs. Tucker decides to publicize her complaints in the community. It is important that Mark appreciate the precarious position his principal may be in and try to work with him rather than against him. Otherwise the easy response in the face of community pressure might be for the principal to eliminate Mark (who is as yet untenured) or his health program, and possibly both.

Change Agents 6—Jeff Noland, English Teacher, and Maria Rivera, Science Teacher, High School

The idea for the community school had been discussed among a small group of the Eastern High School faculty for a couple of years. Both students and the administration of the school, which was located in a large northeastern city, had been involved in the planning sessions. Although other teachers had resisted, the principal had hesitated, and the planning committee had some disagreements, a written proposal was developed and was approved by the faculty and student government of the school. Jeff Noland, an English teacher, and Maria Rivera, a science teacher, were then designated by the planning committee to present the written proposal at a school board meeting. They were chosen because they had been two of the prime movers behind the concept of the community school.

Jeff and Maria were anxious about what would happen at the board meeting. They knew that the board had been especially cost-conscious in recent years, voting down a number of seemingly good, innovative proposals. Their proposal would require some expense in renovating one wing of classrooms to create the community school within the high school building. Maria and Jeff also knew that the educational philosophies of the five board members were quite varied, leading to many 3–2 split decisions. They expected that one of the board members would surely support their proposal, and another would almost certainly vote against it. How the other three would vote was by no means clear. Consequently, if the community school was to become a reality, two of the three undecided board members needed to see its educational value.

Have you ever attended a school board meeting? If you haven't, you ought to try to attend a meeting of the school board in your area to get a clearer picture of how school policy is made. Generally, school board meetings are open to the public.

Another factor complicating the situation was the high school principal. While she would attend the board meeting with Jeff and

Maria, they knew they couldn't expect her to be an enthusiastic supporter. She was worried about the negative reactions to the idea of a community school expressed by a small but powerful minority of the high school faculty. In short, she couldn't be counted on for any heroic efforts beyond the call of duty.

When the day of the school board meeting finally arrived, Jeff and Maria were both anxious. They would be trying to convince the board to support a proposal that was not only their dream but the dream of a number of other teachers and students. When asked to provide a brief verbal overview of the written proposal, Maria addressed the meeting:

"What we hope to do, with your support, is to provide an alternative learning experience for a group of approximately 200 students, 100 juniors and 100 seniors. Those students would participate in a community school with eight regular teachers who have volunteered to teach in the school and who represent all of the major subject areas. The school would be housed in the north wing of Eastern High School. The central mission of the community school would be to connect the academic learning of the students with experiences outside the school.

"Each student would carry out some sort of volunteer work in a field placement of his or her own choice. Examples of field work settings in which students might work five or six hours each week are hospitals, scientific labs, day-care centers, schools, businesses, social work agencies, engineering firms, nursing homes, law offices, etc. Jeff will now tell you a little about the relationship between the field work and the students' academic learning."

Jeff began: "All field experiences will be supervised by the person under whom the student is working. Our teachers will help the students reflect on their experiences by expecting them to keep written logs and evaluations of their field work. Students involved in similar field work experiences will participate in teacher-led groups in which they will carry out readings, research, and discussion relevant to their field work. In addition, to see to it that students get a breadth of learning, the field work and teacher-led groups will be supplemented by a variety of mini-courses. The mini-courses will provide informal learning experiences that cut across the traditional disciplines of literature, history, art, science, and math."

As Jeff prepared to go on, he was interrupted by Mr. Barton, a board member who he had been warned would be skeptical. Mr. Barton said, "Your ideas sound interesting, but very idealistic. Have you considered all the problems this school will create? For example, are today's students mature enough to shoulder the freedom and responsibility you seek to give them? Have you thought about how our community will react to 200 students traveling unsupervised from school to their field work? And what about the reaction of the other teachers in the high school if we provide extra support to get your community school going? . . .

Try to put yourself in the place of Jeff and Maria and respond to each of Mr. Barton's questions.

This principal, like most principals, probably feels pushed and pulled by the many different constituencies she must respond to and try to keep happy —students, parents, other administrators, teachers, the school board, the superintendent, etc.

What do you feel would be the educational value of volunteer work to high school juniors and seniors?

Why not try to visit an alternative high school in your area? Ask the students and teachers what they feel their school provides that young people could not get in a regular high school?

Mario Fantini has compiled a good collection of articles and reports on alternative learning experiences in Alternative Education (1976).

The questions Mr. Barton is asking are the real nitty-gritty questions that must be faced if the community school is to receive support from the board members.

As Mr. Barton's questions indicate, there are many issues in addition to educational questions that must be considered if changes such as the community school are to become a reality. While Maria and Jeff have spent a lot of time developing the educational concept of the school, they also must be able to respond to questions regarding the administrative, financial, and political viability of the school. The school board is charged with overseeing both the philosophy and the actual day-to-day operation of the school district as a whole. If they perceive that the community school is going to be administratively complicated or financially costly, or if they sense that it will create divisions among teachers, students, parents, etc., they will hesitate to approve it whatever its educational merits.

Teachers who choose to work for changes that go beyond the walls of their own classrooms must always be certain to do their homework in order to anticipate roadblocks. Being a change agent requires not only commitment, creativity, patience, and hard work, but also a sophisticated understanding of the social structure of a school and the district.

An excellent handbook that presents both a theory of educational change and many practical suggestions for implementing it is Ronald Havelock, The Change Agent's Guide to Innovation in Education *(1973).*

Conclusions

In this chapter we have tried to give you a sense of the highs and lows, the excitement and frustration experienced by teachers who see themselves as change agents. Schools are extremely complex social environments with many groups and subgroups, each of which comes to function as a political constituency with its own norms, power relationships, communication patterns, leadership, status system, etc. Resistance to change, therefore, is built into any school setting and is a reality that change agents must face. Students, teachers, administrators, parents, school board members, etc., all develop habits and secure ways of behaving as they function day-to-day in an institutional environment. The power of such groups to perpetuate the status quo is great. Therefore, change agents must not only suggest alternatives to existing practices, they must diagnose where the resistance to change exists, determine why it exists, and develop ways of overcoming it.

Struggling against tendencies toward inactivity and inertia is always emotionally trying. Calling attention to what is wrong and needs to be changed often is not pleasant. In the face of what at times seem insurmountable odds, it is normal for a teacher–change agent to feel like giving up. Yet the personal feelings of satisfaction we receive as we act on our values and help educational institutions to change can more than compensate for our pain and frustration. If we as helping professionals don't stand up against the educational practices with which we disagree and advocate what we believe in, what models are we providing for our students?

Some Good Books

Boyer, William. *Alternative Futures: Designing Social Change.* Dubuque, Iowa; Kendall Hunt, 1975. Boyer makes a strong case for transforming public school education in order to prepare young people to actively confront such major world problems as overpopulation, pollution, poverty, injustice, and war.

Brameld, T. *The Teacher as World Citizen—A Scenario of the 21st Century*. Palm Springs, Calif.: ETC Publications, 1976. Brameld argues eloquently that teachers and others must see themselves as world citizens and work toward world community if there is to be any hope for the future.

Carnoy, M. and H. M. Levin. *The Limits of Educational Reform*. New York: McKay, 1976. Carnoy and Levin argue that the work of change agents must be directed at the economic and political institutions of America rather than at the school. They disagree with many educational reformers who believe that changes in the schools can indeed lead to social change.

Conrad, D. *Education for Transformation*. Palm Springs, Calif.: ETC Publications, 1976. This book explores the thinking of Lewis Mumford, an important twentieth-century humanist, and its implications for an educational process committed to social justice, peace, world community, and ecological harmony.

Freire, Paulo. *Pedagogy of the Oppressed*. New York: Seabury, 1970. Freire has written about his work as a change agent with illiterate Brazilian peasants. He helps them take control of their own lives through what Carl Rogers would call a student-centered approach to teaching, emphasizing their strengths and shifting power from the teacher to them.

Hapgood, Marilyn, ed. *Supporting the Learning Teacher: A Source Book for Teacher Centers*. New York: Agathon Press, 1975. This collection of articles suggests that teacher centers can be places that stimulate, facilitate, and support innovative approaches to teaching. Teachers interested in becoming change agents in their own schools will find this book quite useful. Note: A teacher center is a place where teachers gather to further their own growth as teachers by attending workshops, developing new curricular materials, etc.

Kohl, Herbert. *On Teaching*. New York: Schocken, 1976. This book offers many practical suggestions for influencing educational changes.

Kozol, Jonathan. *The Night is Dark and I Am Far from Home*. Boston: Houghton Mifflin, 1975. In this book, a radical critique of the public schools in America, Kozol argues that American schools imprison, indoctrinate, and dehumanize. He calls for educators to commit themselves to revolutionary action to confront such oppression.

Postman, Neil and Charles Weingartner. *The Soft Revolution*. New York: Delacorte, 1971. This is a handbook for students who wish to influence progressive changes in school and university settings.

Postman, Neil and Charles Weingartner. *Teaching as a Subversive Activity*. New York: Delacorte, 1969. In this classic Postman and Weingartner argue that all teachers have more power to influence change than they realize. They make many suggestions to help teachers operate as "subversives" within their own classrooms.

Rogers, Carl. *On Personal Power: Inner Strength and Its Revolutionary Impact.* New York: Delacorte, 1977. Here Rogers emphasizes that as people are helped to grow personally and see themselves differently, they increase their potential for political and social change.

Toffler, Alvin, ed. *Learning for Tomorrow: The Role of the Future in Education.* New York: Random House, 1974. Toffler, the author of *Future Shock,* has brought together a collection of writings that present a strong case for educational reforms that both anticipate and create the future.

Articles, Studies, and Other References

Havelock, Ronald G. *The Change Agent's Guide to Innovation in Education.* Englewood Cliffs, N.J.: Educational Technology Publications, 1973. A synthesis of a vast amount of research on the social psychology of educational change, this book gives educators an almost step-by-step guide for implementing new ideas.

Sarason, Seymour. *The Creation of Settings and the Future Societies.* San Francisco: Jossey-Bass, 1972. Through a social psychological perspective on the process of change, Sarason explores the reasons why some settings—e.g., new schools, clinics, community agencies, or even marriages—succeed and others fail.

Shimahara, Nobuo, ed. *Educational Reconstruction: Promise and Challenge.* Columbus, Ohio: Merrill, 1973. Shimahara has brought together a collection of original essays that present the reconstructionist's goals of radical personal and cultural change through the process of education.

Suggestions for Action–Oriented Learning

1. Interview a number of student teachers to find out how they perceive their own capacities for effecting change in the classroom.

2. Jonathan Kozol has written three books—*Death at an Early Age* (1967), *Free Schools* (1972), and *The Night Is Dark and I Am Far from Home* (1975). Read the books in the order Kozol wrote them and try to see how his ideas about education developed over almost a decade and how his own growth as a change agent occurred.

3. Visit two elementary or high schools. Through careful observation and interviews of teachers, administrators, and students, try to gain a sense of each school's responsiveness to change. Summarize your comparisons and contrasts in writing.

4. Try to identify four or five innovative educational programs in your area (e.g., an alternative high school, an open elementary classroom, a new media program for junior high school students). Spend some time at each place. Try to get a picture of the problems each program encountered as it was developing and how the originators of the program overcame those problems.

5. Interview a sample of administrators, teachers, and parents in a school district in which teachers are represented in collective bargaining by a teachers' union or professional organization. Ask your interviewees to discuss the pros and cons of unionization of teachers.

Unit 4
The Teacher as
Learning Facilitator

In this final unit we build on many of the concepts and implications for teaching that we have explored earlier in this book. Here we are looking at the teacher's role as a learning facilitator, a person who makes the learning process easier. He is a guide rather than a director. In his relationships with students, a facilitator nudges rather than pushes, encourages rather than criticizes, and frees rather than controls.

In Chapter 13 we will explore with you ways teachers can create conditions to facilitate learning. Sometimes before we can promote learning we have to eliminate barriers that inhibit learning. We will present a model of four types of teaching behaviors that promote learning—enhancing positive feelings, reinforcing desired behavior, promoting cognitive clarification, and modeling desired behavior. This chapter calls upon you to consider the value of each of these orientations rather than rigidly adhering to one. Although each of the four elements of our model grows out of a different theoretical perspective, you will see that they all contribute to the whole. As we have said earlier, we are trying to help you become a wise consumer of theories so that you can most effectively create your own environment for learning and change it when necessary.

Chapter 14 focuses on evaluating learning and teaching. There we will raise questions about evaluation practices currently used in schools and introduce a concept of evaluation that advocates continually gathering feedback on both the actual subject matter learning of students and communications process in the classroom. Learning facilitators must evaluate both the students' learning and their own teaching if they are to make modifications that will improve learning.

Finally, the epilogue is our personal statement to you as we conclude the book and wish you well in your journey toward becoming a teacher.

13
Facilitating Learning

Almost every teacher has had the experience of reaching an "unreachable" child. It is as if a great flow of energy that had been dammed up is suddenly released. A student who was sullen and resistant now seems driven to know and to grow. Carl Rogers calls the teacher's role in releasing this energy *facilitation,* or making easy. Unfortunately, the teacher who helps a student reach this magical moment of learning often cannot reconstruct or analyze what she has done, and so she can't count on her ability to accomplish the same thing the next time a similar problem arises. By the same token, a teacher may sense that she is somehow inhibiting growth, generating sullen, listless, unwilling, or downright hostile attitudes in her students. She may be equally in the dark about what she has done and how to change.

In Chapter 4 we explored theories of teaching and the nature of learning. Our focus there was on how theories are developed and tested. Through the anecdote of Miss Bell and her group of eleventh graders, we described the teacher as a consumer of theory. Theoreticians are committed to their own particular theories, but practitioners can choose among theoretical frames, seeking the theory or collection of theories that will dictate or clarify their own strategies. In this chapter we will present some important principles from four major theoretical perspectives on learning and the ways each can improve teaching.

Our primary concern is to help you understand in psychological terms what you can do to create conditions that facilitate learning,and to recognize teaching behaviors that inhibit learning. The concepts we present are so well accepted that they may be considered "laws" of learning. Teachers are either masters of these laws or their victims.

The first psychological principle we will explore is *emotional conditioning,* an aspect of Pavlovian conditioning. An understanding of what causes and controls good and bad feelings can help the teacher to create a more positive and productive classroom environment. The second principle is *operant conditioning,* pioneered by B. F. Skinner. A knowledge of operant conditioning helps the teacher to strengthen desirable behavior and reduce undesirable behavior (through reinforcement) and to evaluate his own teaching behavior and develop more control over his own actions. Third, we will examine *modeling,* or the power of imitation in developing new behaviors. Finally, we will consider the importance of *cogniton,* or understanding, in bringing about change in behavior or in feelings and in developing and structuring knowledge.

We do not claim that the four areas we explore here are the only "laws" of learning; there are certainly many others. However, we have chosen to focus on these because we feel they are especially helpful in promoting learning.

A Model of Learning Facilitation

A number of years ago one of the authors of this book was a graduate student in a very intense four-week summer course in statistics, a subject designed to strike fear into the hearts of many psychology students. The 50 or so class members were divided equally into undergraduate and graduate students. It was a hot summer. The room was bare and the seats uncomfortable. The teacher was young, gifted, and new to her job. She had high hopes of covering a great deal of material in a very short time, and class consisted primarily of rapid-fire lectures.

Our teacher told us to feel free to ask questions if we felt lost, and, in fact, she encouraged these, answering courteously and clearly. Nonetheless, by the end of the first week, it was apparent that something was terribly wrong. When one student would ask a question, other students would begin talking among themselves. There was an angry undertone in the class.

One day during the second week, our instructor was trying to answer a question. She was at the blackboard with her back turned. Suddenly she wheeled around and confronted the class: "I don't understand what's happening here . . . but I can't stand it for another minute. What is going on?"

Here is an all-too-common classroom situation, in which both teacher and class are defending. Return to Chapter 11 if you need to refresh your memory on this type of teacher–student relationship.

It didn't take long for the class to quiet down. Two hours of discussion followed, some of it angry, some reasoned. Almost every student spoke. At first it was difficult to understand what all the anger was about. As the air cleared, the problems began to emerge. First of all, most of the class had entered with very negative feelings about statistics. Students were anxious, and many had a feeling that they were doomed to fail. Furthermore, a great rift had developed between the graduates and the undergraduates over the issue of questions. The undergraduates resented the kinds of questions the graduates raised and felt the graduates were trying to show off and "gain points" with the teacher. The graduates, in turn, felt that the undergraduates were not doing their homework and were asking questions that had been answered in the readings. Both groups were angry with the teacher because they felt she was drawn into answering unnecessary questions. Some felt that she was sometimes involved in lengthy conversations with the more advanced graduate students, perhaps because she felt competitive with them.

Have you ever been in a class like this? If so, how did you feel? Why?

The session concluded with a number of agreements. The teacher agreed to slow down the pace a bit in order to release some of the tension and, hopefully, to lower the anxiety level. But in order to slow down, it was necessary for her to spend less time answering questions. The more advanced students agreed to ask themselves before asking a question: "Does this question really add to the class, or am I ego-tripping?" Other students agreed to say to themselves: "Is this question really necessary, or am I asking it because I didn't do my own studying?" The teacher admitted that perhaps she did feel a little competitive with some of the top students and promised to watch this in herself.

Here we see the teacher and the students together trying to determine what they can do to improve the class. Such open communication makes it possible for defending behavior to turn into coping behavior, which constructively confronts and seeks to change the classroom atmosphere.

The change was dramatic. By the next class period the behavior in the class had already begun to change. Occasionally people slipped, and then the teacher or one of the students would ask, "Is this question necessary?" Generally this was enough to stop irrelevant questioning. When good questions were raised, the teacher praised the student, sometimes adding a brief explanation of why she felt the question was valuable. One day the teacher did get drawn into an "ego trip" with a particularly bright student. Just as the class was becoming restless, she stopped and said to herself "Oh, wow—there I go again," and added to the student, "Your question is a really good one. Why don't we talk about it after class?" At the end of the semester, the class seemed to have learned a great deal and almost everyone felt positive about the experience.

This story may seem somewhat utopian, yet it is true. In all likelihood, the intensity of a summer session, with its short duration and highly motivated students, was helpful in maintaining the change. Over a full semester, some backsliding would be likely. A teacher must be prepared for regression. When it occurs, a fresh look and a refusal to feel defeated often enable the teacher to get her bearings again and make necessary changes in teaching strategy to get things back on course.

This anecdote is valuable because it illustrates the four key psychological principles that we described. Figure 13-1 represents four aspects of learning facilitation derived from those principles.

Even the best teachers have days when everything seems to go wrong. A particular class session is influenced by many factors, and a teacher can never be certain that her plans will work. What distinguishes good teachers from not-so-good teachers is not being a "star" every day; it is their ability to evaluate what is occurring, rethink their plans, and make changes.

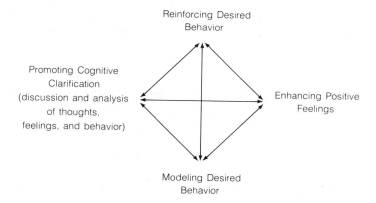

Figure 13-1. A Model of Learning Facilitation

Our model includes four different types of behaviors—or tools—that teachers can use to promote learning. There is no one "best" starting point; a teacher may begin by modeling desired behavior and then enhancing positive feelings, or she might begin with cognitive clarification and then reinforce desirable behavior. By learning to use all four tools, a teacher has more resources to help her cope rather than defend as she works with students.

The model can be useful in diagnosing classroom difficulties and prescribing appropriate teaching interventions. Often nothing more than a hunch gets a teacher thinking about a particular aspect of the model. For example, the teacher of the statistics course first sensed a problem by the angry undertone in the classroom, which could be viewed as an undesired behavior or feeling. The teacher's hunch was to discuss and analyze what was happening (cognitive clarification). Once the air was cleared, both students and teacher had a better idea of what was wrong and what could be done to right it. As students exhibited more of the desired behavior, both the teacher and other students could reinforce it. There was also a modeling effect; as students saw others asking productive questions and receiving praise for them, they were motivated to do the same. The teacher, too, modeled better behavior when she publicly admitted that she may have been "ego-tripping" and stopped it. Finally, by slowing the class pace and offering more reassurance, the teacher created a more positive emotional environment.

There is no single best sequence. For example, the teacher might have figured out the problem on her own and simply started rewarding pertinent questions and rejecting unnecessary ones, perhaps with a brief explanation. She could have relaxed the pace by providing a half-time break or by offering more reassurance. The advantage of the model is that it provides the teacher with a checklist, both to create a facilitating environment and to use for diagnosing problems.

The model is concerned with the teacher's role in eliminating conditions that inhibit learning and creating circumstances that promote learning. Listed below are some questions teachers might ask themselves as they consider each of the four aspects of the model.

What seems to be most important in the anecdote is the teacher's recognition that something was wrong and her willingness to confront the problem as nondefensively as possible. As she became less defensive, her students, too, felt less defensive and could help her work out a solution.

1. Enhancing positive feelings:

   What feelings have my students brought with them from previous classes or teachers? How can I deal with these feelings?

   How do they feel about me? About my subject?

   How do they feel toward each other?

   Do they have fears, anxieties, or frustrations that are hindering their learning?

   What can I do to make them feel more comfortable and open to learning?

2. Reinforcing desired behavior:

   Are my students doing the kinds of things they must do in order to learn well?

   Am I unintentionally rewarding (and thus strengthening) undesirable behavior?

   What are some effective ways of rewarding desirable behavior?

   What can I do to help my students positively reinforce each others' desirable behavior?

3. Modeling desired behavior:

   How do my students see me? Do they see me the way I want them to?

   Is my own behavior a model of what I want from my students? Am I practicing what I preach?

Am I unconsciously allowing students who exhibit poor behavior to serve as models for other students?

4. Promoting cognitive clarification:

Do my students know what I expect of them? What can I do
to state my expectations more clearly?

How can I encourage the students to ask more questions
when they need help?

What can I do to help my students talk about and analyze
their own thoughts and feelings about the course, my effectiveness as a teacher, what they are learning, etc.?

In the remaining sections of this chapter we will explore in some
depth the four aspects of learning facilitation and the psychological
laws underlying them.

Enhancing Positive Feelings

We will begin by examining the work of Ivan Petrovich Pavlov,
which is now called *classical conditioning*. His work is of interest to us
because it helps us understand how feelings are learned. A simple
anecdote may help you understand the relationship between Pavlovian conditioning and feelings. Laura has little reason to fear a spelling test if she has never had one. After all, it is just a collection of
words. But let her fail her first few tests, and it will not be long before
the mere announcement of a spelling test will arouse her feelings of
fear and anxiety. In psychological terms, we would say that the child
has associated fear and spelling tests and now has a fear response,
which may generalize to spelling itself and perhaps to anything connected with words. Pavlovian theory helps us understand how this
conditioning occurs and how it may be eliminated.

Pavlov (1849–1936) was a Russian physiologist who became interested in the digestive process early in his career. In 1904 he won
the Nobel Prize for his work with digestive glands. One day while
working in his laboratory, Pavlov noticed that his experimental dogs
showed gastric secretions before their food arrived. In fact, as soon
as the dogs heard the attendants come into the room with their food
trays, the secretions would begin. Pavlov reasoned that the dogs must
have learned from previous experience that the attendants' sounds
meant food was on its way. In other words, those sounds became a
signal to which the dogs responded. Pavlov became so interested in
this phenomenon that he turned his attention to the study of salivation,
which was easier to measure than gastric secretion. G.V. Anrep
(1920), an early collaborator of Pavlov, described one typical Pavlovian study:

Think back to your own schooling. Did you learn to fear any subjects? What were the experiences you had that led to such learned fears?

In order to permit the recording of the magnitude of the salivary
response, the dog was first subjected to a minor operation in which the
duct of the parotid gland was diverted so that the saliva flowed through

Here we see that the "association" between the sound of the tuning fork and salivation became stronger the more often the tuning fork and the food were presented together.

Referring back to Laura's fear of spelling tests, we can see that failure has become associated with, or conditioned to, spelling tests. The mere words spelling test *probably arouse unpleasant physical responses in Laura, such as sweating, increased heart rate, or muscle tension.*

Example: *A child is* conditioned *to fear the school principal because the*

an opening on the outside of the cheek. A small glass funnel was firmly cemented over the opening to collect the saliva, which could be measured with an accuracy of one-tenth drop by suitable devices. The dog was trained to stand quietly in a loose harness on a table in a room which was insulated against any distracting noises or vibrations. The experimenter occupied an adjoining room, observing the dog through a small window and presenting the stimuli by means of automatic devices. A tuning fork was sounded, and 7 or 8 seconds after the beginning of this stimulus, a plate containing a small measured quantity of dry powdered food was moved within reach of the dog's mouth. No salivation was evoked by the tone, but during the eating there was a copious flow of saliva. Combinations of the tone and food were presented three times during a daily session, separated by intervals of from 5 to 35 minutes. The strength of the conditioned response was determined by presenting the tone alone for 30 seconds and measuring the amount of salivation. After ten double stimulations there was a slight conditioned salivation, and after thirty combinations the tone evoked a salivation of sixty drops. On the early tests the conditioned salivation did not occur until the tone had sounded for 18 seconds; on later tests the salivation began after only 1 or 2 seconds. Both measures indicate an increase in the strength of the conditioned response with training.

Pavlov (1927) developed a useful set of terms to describe his investigations:

Unconditioned Stimulus. The stimulus that automatically elicits the unconditioned response, i.e., the powdered food.

Unconditioned Response. Previously called unconditioned reflex; an innate response, regularly elicited by an external stimulus, i.e., the salivation at the presence of the food powder.

Conditioned Stimulus. The new stimulus, presented prior to, or together with, the unconditioned stimulus; in Anrep's example, the sound of the tuning fork.

Conditioned Response. The response elicited by the new, or conditioned, stimulus. It is similar, although not identical, to the unconditioned response. For example, in Anrep's experiment the tuning fork elicits salivation, but not as much as the meat powder does.

Note that the conditioned stimulus precedes the unconditioned stimulus. It may stop just before the unconditioned stimulus is presented, or as it is being presented, but it always begins first. If the conditioned stimulus does not begin before the unconditioned stimulus, no conditioning occurs. Another interesting observation is that often a conditioned stimulus evokes an unconditioned response. For example, when the dog hears the tuning fork, even before it is paired with the meat powder, it lifts its ear in what Pavlov called an investigatory or "what-is-it" reflex. It may be that the conditioned stimulus has a warning, or alerting, value and gives a signal to the animal that the conditioned stimulus is about to be presented.

Some more terms Pavlov used to identify the phenomena he studied are:

Conditioning. The repeated association between an unconditioned stimulus (UCS) and a conditioned stimulus (CS), so that the CS comes to evoke a response that previously occurred only to the

UCS. We study such variables as the number of pairings necessary before the conditioned stimulus alone will elicit the conditioned response (CR) and the effect of varying the interval between conditioned stimulus and unconditioned stimulus.

Extinction. As a rule, the power of the conditioned stimulus to elicit the conditioned response is not permanent. After a time the ringing of the tuning fork alone without the food powder no longer leads to salivation. The loss of CS strength is called *extinction*.

Reinforcement. If we wish to maintain the CS–CR bond, we must "re-pair" the CS and the UCS occasionally to reinforce the link between the two. *Reinforcement* has a somewhat different meaning for Skinner than for Pavlov. For Pavlov reinforcement meant a strengthening of the CS–UCS bond through reassociation. For Skinner reinforcement has to do with the strengthening of a behavior through some consequence, such as a reward.

Generalization. As a conditioned stimulus develops the strength to elicit the conditioned response, related stimuli also develop some power to elicit the response. A famous example is psychologist John B. Watson's "little Albert." Watson became interested in the learning of fears. He had noticed that a loud sound elicited an automatic fear response in a young boy named Albert. He showed Albert a white rat, but this caused no fear response. He then made a loud sound by striking a steel bar as he showed Albert the rat. After repeated pairings of the loud sound with the rat, Watson found that the rat alone would evoke fear in Albert. Once Albert was conditioned to fear the rat, he began to fear similar things, such as a white coat, a Santa Claus mask, a white rabbit, etc. In other words, Albert's fear had *generalized* to other stimuli that he saw as similar to the rat. In Anrep's experiment, tuning forks pitched higher and lower elicited a salivary response in the dogs, although it was not as strong as the response to the original tone.

Discrimination. If little Albert remained frightened of anything furry or anything white, his life would become quite difficult. Imagine being restricted to your home in order to isolate yourself from all possibly dangerous stimuli. The ability to differentiate among related stimuli is called *discrimination*. When a response is too generalized, we may want to help the responder to discriminate among stimuli. The example that follows will give a clearer picture of discrimination.

Robert has had very happy experiences with women teachers in the early elementary grades. In grade four he has his first male teacher, and, unfortunately, they hit it off very badly. The following year he has another woman teacher and does well. The next year his new sixth-grade teacher, Mr. Brown, is quite puzzled. He reads the previous year's reports and finds that Mrs. Jones, Robert's fifth-grade teacher, described Robert as a likable, willing student and a good achiever. His own experience with Robert is very different. Robert looks away from Mr. Brown when he speaks, does poorly in classwork, and seems to scurry away whenever Mr. Brown tries to approach him. Robert has generalized his feelings about his male fourth-grade teacher to Mr. Brown, the only other male teacher he has

only time the principal talks to him is to punish him for misbehavior.

Can you think of any other examples?

Example: *The principal can extinguish the child's fear response by talking to the child when he is behaving well and by avoiding punishing the child. Of course, this will take much time and patience on the principal's part.*

Example: *Earlier we spoke of Laura who, after failing a number of spelling tests, became fearful and anxious each time one was announced. It is quite likely that her fears would not remain limited to spelling, but if unchecked could generalize to writing, to her class, and even to her teacher because of their association with her experiences of failure.*

Can you think of any examples of the generalization of fears in your own school experiences?

Fortunately, Watson worked on extinguishing Albert's fear response by gradually letting him see the rat without making the loud sound. This experiment raises many ethical questions, since Albert could have been emotionally scarred by the experience.

Joseph Wolpe is a psychiatrist who has devoted a great deal of research to the application of Pavlovian theory to reversing the effects of phobias and anxieties. Through a step-by-step procedure Wolpe helps patients to gradually extinguish fears and anxieties as they increasingly confront a situation that previously triggered strong negative emotional responses.

A swimming teacher might employ Wolpe's techniques with an adult who had an extreme fear of swimming. First, the instructor might just talk with the person and help him relax, while sitting 100 feet from the side of a swimming pool. At the next lesson both teacher and student might stand at the side of the pool. Next they might dangle their legs in the pool while sitting on the side. Then they might stand together in shallow water, get wet up to their shoulders, etc. Gradually, with a lot of reassurance from the teacher, the student would work his way into learning strokes, going into deeper water, and ultimately swimming.

If you would like to learn more about Wolpe's work, you might look for his book The Practice of Behavior Therapy *(1969).*

encountered. Mr. Brown's job is to help Robert make a better discrimination. If he succeeds, Robert will give his next male teacher a chance. If he fails, the next male teacher's job will be even harder.

Many psychologists today believe that Pavlov's studies have taught us the most about how we learn emotional responses. They point out that in the typical Pavlovian experiment what is conditioned is some internal response to a particular stimulus. Basically, a good feeling or a bad feeling is aroused. These feelings have potent effects on our behavior. If we are afraid, or angry, or tense, it is hard to concentrate on learning anything at a high cognitive level. If we are happy and relaxed, we are usually ready to learn.

Probably the most important message of Pavlovian conditioning for the teacher is that it is remarkably easy to inadvertently create a negative conditioned response, such as fear, anxiety, or discouragement. It may take a great deal of effort to overcome a few early experiences of failure. For example, many children develop a strong fear or distrust of anything connected with mathematics. Because they have experienced early failure, any testing situation will probably serve only to trigger more fear, and therefore bring about still more failure. A teacher confronted with fearful students strongly conditioned to fail should try to create "failure-proof" situations that permit the student to regain some level of comfort before testing is resumed.

Jeff was an eighth-grader who was so frightened of anything connected with mathematics that he became extremely disruptive during math class. He seemed especially frightened of being called on. One day his teacher took him aside and asked why he wouldn't answer any questions in math class. He told the teacher that last year, every time he made a mistake, the teacher would call him stupid and the other students would laugh. His eighth-grade teacher said that for the next few weeks she would not call on him unless she was sure he had the answer; if he did, he should wink at her and she would try to call on him. She kept a record of the number of times per math period that Jeff asked to be called on. It looked something like the graph in Figure 13–2.

By day 9 Jeff's teacher could see him becoming more comfortable with answering questions. At that point she asked to speak with

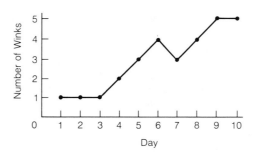

Figure 13–2. Jeff's Record

Jeff alone again and explained that even if he did not know the correct answer, she would most certainly not call him stupid. Jeff agreed to let her call on him even if he didn't wink. What his teacher discovered, to her delight, was that he had already become comfortable enough to raise his hand and answer without fear. She had succeeded in extinguishing a fear response through the 26 successive correct responses he had given.

Ms. Krantz teaches an eleventh-grade, 10-week unit in literature. When her students come in the first day, they see an unusual sight. She has her desk pushed to the side of the room. Where the desk would normally be, there is a speaker's lectern and a large three-legged stool behind it. As soon as the first bell rings, she stands behind the lectern and says: "Good morning. For the next 10 weeks, I will be your English teacher. I expect you to read at least two books a week. I want you to know them inside out. There will be at least two quizzes a week. Be on your toes. You will work harder for me than you've ever worked before."

There follow in Ms. Krantz's class many periods of lectures and assignments, punctuated by tests, followed by disappointed comments by Ms. Krantz about how poorly her students read. Toward the end of the unit, she announces that now that the hard work is done, she would like to spend the remaining two weeks really talking about literature with the students. However, she ends up spending much of that time angrily chiding her students for having no interest in mature literary conversation. Ms. Krantz has unintentionally created such an unpleasant learning environment that she, the classroom, and for many students, even the books themselves have become very distasteful conditioned stimuli.

Some of the ways teachers create negative emotional conditioning are by:

"Nailing" students—trapping them when it's obvious they don't know the right answer or haven't been paying attention.

Never smiling.

Being irrationally strict.

Rushing students on tests.

Being sarcastic, making jokes at a student's expense, or ridiculing.

Withholding praise, not recognizing effort or improvement.

Physically punishing students.

Punishing the whole class for the misbehavior of a few.

Can you add some other examples?

Hopefully, you don't want to create such an environment, so being aware of how easily negative emotional reactions are learned will help you to avoid teaching them. We have presented Pavlovian

A strong fear response can so inhibit people that they become immobilized, unable to do anything, totally confused, or unable to organize their thoughts.

Some examples of this type of negative emotional response are listed below. Have you ever experienced any of them? Can you think of others?

Freezing so that you couldn't remember anything on an important essay test.

Forgetting your lines in a play.

Getting totally confused in a speech.

Finding yourself tongue-tied (or totally confused) when being interviewed for an important job.

Pavlov's work (and Wolpe's too) lends itself to eliminating negative emotional responses. In the earlier sections of this book, we have focused on ways of creating positive feelings. You probably have many ideas of your own on how to create a positive emotional climate in your classroom. Why not list below what you feel are the three most important things a teacher should do to enhance positive feelings?

1.

2.

3.

Lawful behavior *refers to what science attempts to discover as the underlying order inherent in what seem at first to be isolated facts.*

If you have never seen how a Skinner Box works, you might visit the psychology laboratory at your college and ask to see one.

conditioning in some depth for two reasons. First, Pavlov was the first person to present a systematic theory of conditioning, and all psychologists after him have been affected by his discoveries and the language he used to describe them. Second, an understanding of a few simple principles may give you greater control over the emotional environment when you become a teacher.

Reinforcing Desired Behavior

B. F. Skinner (1953) is concerned not with feelings but with bits of behavior he calls *operants*. He is not especially interested in how operants come into being. He is interested in how we can increase desirable behavior and reduce undesirable behavior.

Just as Pavlov's work was rooted in a particular method of experimentation, so is Skinner's. It may be helpful to begin by describing Skinner's basic procedure, so that it can be compared to Pavlov's. Although Skinner had not studied psychology as an undergraduate, he eventually studied for his Ph.D. degree in experimental psychology at Harvard. He was very interested in the work of the famous American behaviorist John Watson, whose thinking had been influenced by his Russian contemporary, Pavlov. Skinner was fascinated with Pavlov's method of looking for lawful behavior, but found it difficult to move from Pavlov's study of salivation to important everyday human problems. He wanted to know what living organisms did as they moved around within an environment, not what they did when tied down in a laboratory harness.

Skinner devised a number of physical settings in which animals could roam fairly freely. The early ones were kind of "Rube Goldberg" contraptions, but finally he hit on a remarkably simple device that is still used in every beginning experimental psychology course as well as in highly sophisticated research. Usually called the *Skinner Box,* it has three solid sides, one transparent side, and a metal grid floor. In the box are a lever (called a bar press), a food pellet dispenser, a liquid dispenser, a source of light, and a rat. The lever is attached to a recording device consisting of graph paper wound around a drum and a stylus pen. The drum rotates at a set speed. The stylus is attached to the lever, so each time the rat presses the lever the press is recorded on the drum, yielding a *cumulative curve,* which describes the rate of bar pressing over time. A typical curve is illustrated in Figure 13–3.

To the experimenter this curve says: the rat made no bar presses in the first 5 minutes, had made 10 by the 10th minute, 20 by the 15th minute, none between the 15th and 20th minutes, and 40 responses by the 30th minute.

Only gradually did the full impact of his method of exploration become clear even to Skinner himself. As he succeeded in distinguishing his work from Pavlov's, several clear differences emerged. In the Pavlovian scheme there could be no response without a stimulus. For example, salivation was caused either by meat powder on the

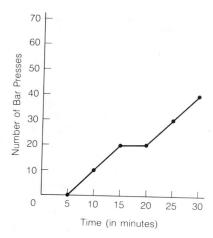

Figure 13–3. Typical Skinner Box Response Rate Curve

tongue or by a sound stimulus associated at first with the meat powder. Skinner called Pavlovian responses (those elicited by a stimulus) *respondents,* that is, responses to stimuli. The unit of behavior Skinner himself studied was of another sort. Unlike respondents, these behaviors are not elicited or "caused" by any known or obvious stimulus. They occur spontaneously; they are emitted, for whatever reason, by the organism. According to Skinner their cause is unimportant. He called these behaviors *operants.*

In simpler terms we might say that for Pavlov the stimulus (sight of food) precedes the behavior (salivation). For Skinner first the organism behaves (rat exploring the Skinner Box bumps the bar press) and then some environmental change (appearance of a food pellet, which the rat eats) may strengthen or reinforce the behavior. Pavlovian responses are basically emotional responses, often involving the increase or decrease of fear or pleasure. Because these responses seem to be elicited by external stimuli, they were once thought to be involuntary. Now there is increasing evidence that these responses may be brought under voluntary control. Techniques like yoga and Transcendental Meditation probably involve a self-conditioning of internal responses like respiration rate and even heartbeat. By contrast, Skinnerian responses are usually considered to be muscular, that is, involving voluntary behaviors. (Recently, however, the application of Skinner's principles to teaching machines has demonstrated that cognition, or thinking, can also be conditioned.) Furthermore, while Pavlovian conditioning is based on the principle of associations or pairing of two stimuli (the CS and UCS), Skinnerian conditioning focuses on the principle of reinforcement.

Skinner is not interested in the cause of behavior. His basic question is "What environmental conditions will weaken or strengthen a given behavior?" Returning to the example of the rat in the Skinner

The type of learning that Pavlov described is called either classical conditioning, *because Pavlov's was the classic (or first) explanation of conditioning, or* respondent conditioning *to emphasize the fact that a reaction (UCR) to a stimulus (UCS) is originally an automatic response.*

The kind of learning Skinner studied is called operant conditioning *because a behavior—an operant—is strengthened by being reinforced. Sometimes psychologists use the term* instrumental conditioning *rather than operant conditioning since a particular behavior (e.g., a rat's pushing the bar in the Skinner Box) is instrumental in bringing about reinforcement (e.g., the food pellet).*

Box, if the rat happens to press the bar, a pellet of food is delivered. If the rat associates the delivery of the food with increased bar pressing, we would then say that the food *reinforces* (strengthens) the bar-pressing response. Food is considered to be a *primary reinforcer* — if an organism is sufficiently food-deprived, it will "work" for a food reward.

Primary reinforcers are stimuli, such as food and water, that are automatically or naturally reinforcing. An animal or person does not have to learn to seek them; they are necessary to survival.

It is obvious that both animals and humans will change their behavior for rewards other than food. For example, a dog often will learn merely because his master says "good dog" and gives him a pat. Skinner says that stimuli like the pat and the words "good dog" are not naturally reinforcing, but that the animals learn that they have a reward value by originally receiving a food reward when they first heard the words "good dog." Such reinforcers are called *secondary reinforcers* or *learned reinforcers* because they have acquired reinforcing properties as a result of being paired with primary reinforcers. People respond mainly to secondary reinforcers. For example, we will work hard to do things to receive praise or recognition from someone we like or admire or put in extra effort at a job if we know it might lead to a promotion or pay raise.

With animals primary reinforcers are most effective in promoting learning. That's why circus animal trainers use food as reinforcement for the "tricks" that their animals do. In the learning laboratory, psychologists use either food or water as the reinforcer in their experiments with rats, pigeons, rabbits, etc.

A clear understanding of the nature of what Skinner calls *positive reinforcement* is helpful to the teacher. Positive reinforcement means any stimulus that, added to a situation, increases the probability of a response. Often the very actions a teacher performs to try to suppress a behavior may actually strengthen the behavior. For example, Johnny gets out of his seat, and his teacher shouts "Sit down!" The more his teacher yells at him, the more Johnny continues to get out of his seat. An observer would point out that shouting "sit down" may be rewarding to Johnny. It's possible that he is seeking recognition, and each time he is yelled at he gains the attention of this teacher (and his peers). What the teacher is doing to suppress his behavior may, in fact, be functioning as a reward and may be strengthening it. It is very important that teachers examine their own behavior to see whether they are rewarding undesirable behavior rather than desirable behavior.

On the other hand, for human beings, with their more advanced brains, all sorts of secondary reinforcers acquire reward power. In general, secondary reinforcers are used to reinforce learning both at home and in school. Some of the more common secondary reinforcers are praise, good grades, promotions, money, and peer approval. Only under special circumstances, usually with the severely retarded or disturbed, are primary reinforcers used to promote learning.

Like Pavlov, Skinner provided a useful language for discussing certain learning phenomena. In the following pages, we will explore some of the concepts of operant conditioning developed by Skinner and others.

Positive Reinforcement.   A stimulus which, when added to a situation, strengthens the probability of a response's recurring. For example, in the use of the Skinner Box, the presentation of food is considered positive reinforcement. Remember that the only way we know that something is reinforcing is if we can observe a change in behavior. As teachers, we assume that praise, good grades, kind looks, and other similar actions are reinforcing. Some students may be more responsive to these than others.

Try to list below two examples from your own school experience in which teachers reinforced undesirable behavior without realizing it.

1.

2.

Karen was a 10-year-old who often became disruptive in class, continually running and bothering other children. Her teacher, at wit's end, spoke to the principal, who suggested that any time Karen was getting out of hand, the teacher could send her down to speak with

Many children enjoy the positive reinforcement that comes from some sort of tangible recognition of their progress.

him. The principal was a kind man and spent a great deal of time talking with Karen each time she was sent out of class. Karen liked the principal very much. As time went on, her classroom behavior seemed to worsen rather than improve, until the school psychologist was consulted. As the teacher, the principal, and the psychologist talked, they realized that Karen was being rewarded for her poor behavior by trips to see the principal. They then decided to explain to Karen that she could have a scheduled meeting time with the principal twice a week but that the appointment could be kept only if she had behaved in class on the days prior to the appointment. Karen's behavior improved a great deal after this new arrangement was worked out.

The critical problem for the classroom teacher is to find out what is reinforcing to her students. Then she can use those things to encourage desirable behavior. Students differ in what is reinforcing for them. A good teacher learns that Jack needs a chance to be recognized by his peers, Andrea likes physical expression such as a hug, and David responds well to verbal praise. The better a teacher knows her students, the more ways she can develop to reinforce their behavior.

Extinction. The removal of reinforcement. If the rat continues to press the bar, but the feeding mechanism is disconnected, the rat will stop after a certain number of presses. We say that the behavior has been extinguished. When a teacher notices that a teaching behavior is unintentionally reinforcing, the best procedure is to remove the reinforcement and look for some acceptable behavior to reinforce. For example, it might be better to ignore a child who never pays attention in class rather than call on him when he isn't paying attention. When

Behavior modification *promotes learning by systematically using principles of operant conditioning. A useful guide on the application of behavior modification in the classroom is Krumboltz and Krumboltz,* Changing Children's Behavior *(1972).*

he is paying attention, the teacher should provide some positive reinforcement, such as letting him answer a question, smiling at him, or commenting to him individually at the end of the class.

Punishment.   Any act that suppresses a previous response. Scolding and hitting may be examples of punishing stimuli if, in fact, they suppress a given response. The major value of punishment is that it may provide an opportunity to reinforce a more appropriate behavior while the unwanted action is suppressed. The danger of punishment is that it may have positive reinforcement value for some people or that it may raise so much emotion that it disorganizes learning (e.g., hitting a child who is having a tantrum). Punishment often generates hostility and unpleasant feelings directed at the teacher, which can generalize to the subject as well—it is only a short step from hating the math teacher to hating the subject of math itself.

Nonetheless, there are times when it is necessary to punish. Punishment may be required when a student behaves in a way that endangers himself or others—for example, running away during a fire drill, disrupting an assembly, or threatening another student with bodily harm. Such actions must be stopped immediately. If you must punish, Good and Brophy (1977, p. 64) provide excellent guidelines:

> In general, effective punishment is mild rather than severe, immediate rather than delayed, informative rather than merely punitive, and tailored to the specific misbehavior involved in ways that are likely to help the student to see why the misbehavior is inappropriate and to resolve to avoid it in the future. Punishment is never a solution in itself, although it may be a necessary part of a solution in situations where students have not responded to more positive appeals. In any case, it is most effective when combined with explanations, discussions, and other socialization methods designed to change not only the overt behavior but also the student's underlying attitudes and beliefs. Sometimes this may have to be delayed until the student can be seen individually, but it should not be forgotten.

If a teacher threatens punishment, it is urgent that he carry it out. Teachers who threaten but do not consistently follow through soon lose all authority because they unwittingly encourage students to test them. If you must sometimes punish, it is best to predict the consequences first.

A final word about punishment. A recent U.S. Supreme Court decision (1977) has upheld the right of teachers to punish students physically. While the law of the land now permits such punishment (although some state laws ban it), the laws of learning strongly suggest that physical punishment is an ineffective means of controlling behavior, and one that frequently backfires. As modeling behavior it teaches students that might makes right. To punish students physically is to encourage them to handle problems through physical punishment. Usually when a teacher feels like physically punishing, it is because of his own rage, frustration, and feelings of failure at his craft. Learn to recognize these feelings and try to find some other outlet for

What are your feelings about the value of punishment in school situations?

Think back to your own experiences with punishment. How effective was punishment in eliminating your "undesirable behavior"? Are there some approaches that you feel are more effective than others?

Research shows that children who were physically abused by their parents are much more likely to become child abusers than other children. It seems that the model their parents provided had a profound effect on them even though they undoubtedly hated the abuse they received as children.

your anger. Later, when you have gained control of yourself, you can try to think of ways of avoiding the problem in the future.

Premack's Principle. Sometimes a behavior occurs, but not as frequently as the teacher may wish. David Premack (1965), a Skinnerian psychologist, has suggested one way to increase behaviors that do not occur often. He points out that behavior the child already favors, which therefore occurs frequently, can be used as a reward to encourage desired behavior that occurs infrequently. For example, a teacher may inform a child who enjoys playing out of doors during recess that she will have a shorter recess if she does not complete her work. This often motivates the student to work harder to earn the desired rewards.

Shaping. Often the desired operant is not present. In such cases it is necessary to start by reinforcing some small aspect of the desired behavior, and only when that bit is reliably established, to move a step closer to the final desired behavior. For example, if a student has difficulty sitting still for a full class period, it might seem wise to wait until, for some reason, he does sit still for a whole period and then reward him. In fact, this may mean the total withholding of reward, because you may wait forever for the accomplishment. The teacher could shape the desired behavior by rewarding the student for sitting still for two minutes. Probably the child is already capable of this behavior although he does it infrequently. After a sufficient number of reinforcements, he is likely to sit still for two minutes more often. Then the teacher can aim for five-minute periods. This procedure would be repeated until the child can sit still for the desired time. Patience and consistency are crucial for successful shaping.

Shaping is also the underlying principle in programmed learning, in which a complex set of concepts or principles are broken down into little "bits," each of which is reinforced before the student encounters the next "bit." Complex concepts in biology, for example, would be presented in small steps, with positive reinforcement provided as the student mastered each new "bit" of learning in the workbook.

A good place to find more about programmed learning is Skinner, The Technology of Teaching (1968).

Modeling Desired Behavior

We have seen that teachers have some degree of influence on students through their effects on emotional (Pavlovian) behavior and on overt (Skinnerian) behavior. We often think teachers promote learning by specific actions toward students. Often teachers do not clearly understand these actions, and so they have unpredictable effects on students.

Bandura (1969) and other researchers have studied still another method of inspiring behavior. In this mode of learning, the learner sees the behavior modeled by another person and may imitate it, either immediately or at some future time. Modeling differs from both Pavlovian and Skinnerian conditioning in that a person can learn a new behavior simply by observing it in someone else. For example, although you may have never taught, if you were asked to teach a lesson tomorrow, you would probably "model" your approach after teachers you have observed in your years as a student. Imitative learning, according to Bandura, is more likely to occur if the model is seen as attractive (possessing power, status, competence, etc.) and worth imitating. Modeling seems to promote learning in two ways. First, an individual may learn new responses by noting the behavior of

Example: Liebert and Baron (1972) have done research on the effects of television on aggression in children. Their findings suggest that television gives children "ideas" for solving problems through violence, such as fighting, stealing, or killing. As the child sees his hero (whether it is Superman, John Wayne, Batman, etc.) engage in aggressive behavior and receive rewards and recognition, the child's own inhibitions against aggression as a way of solving problems are lowered.

Probably you have heard the statement, "Teachers teach as they were taught." In other words, teachers tend to do what was done to them rather than what their education professors told them to do. This statement implies that if future teachers are to learn new approaches to teaching, they must experience them not simply be told about them.

To what extent are the teachers in your education courses practicing what they preach by using new teaching approaches?

Try to recall one of your teachers who practiced what he or she preached and one who didn't.

What were the consequences of the behavior modeled by each of these teachers for you and the other members of your class?

someone else. Second, the individual's inhibitions to act may be strengthened or weakened by observing the consequences of the model's behavior.

Modeling is a powerful influence on learning in all areas of a child's experience. Parents are probably the most important models in a child's life, but brothers and sisters, teachers, and peers are also quite important. Parents often show an intuitive understanding of modeling's power when they say "Do as I say, not as I do." The reality, however, is that children are more likely to do what their parents do than what their parents say. For example, parents who tell their children not to smoke but who smoke themselves are more likely to have children who grow up to be smokers than are parents who don't smoke.

In the classroom modeling is a valuable tool for promoting learning. Modeling may spark a new behavior and give the teacher opportunity to reinforce the behavior once it becomes part of the student's repertoire. For example, if your goal was to get your students to speak a foreign language, you would model the language best by speaking to students in that language rather than in English. Then you would reinforce students who imitated you. However, modeling also may have negative consequences. A teacher who becomes angry frequently and attempts to control the class by shouting is, through modeling, teaching students to shout.

Another potent effect of modeling is what Bandura calls *vicarious reinforcement*. When a teacher reinforces one student's behavior, other students are affected also. If a child is praised for a particular behavior—let's say helping a less able student—other children may try the same behavior in order to receive the same praise. On the other hand, if a teacher embarrasses a student in front of the whole class for not knowing an answer, many of the other children probably will be afraid to try to answer questions.

Modeling can be very useful in creating a teaching–learning environment in which cooperation and I–thou relationships exist. As a teacher models coping behavior rather than defending behavior, students are more likely to engage in coping behavior themselves. The more a teacher treats students with the respect, concern, and dignity that he expects from them, the more likely students are to return the consideration. In sum, a teacher must continually examine the type of behavior he is modeling in his classroom in order to make certain that his method—his approach to teaching—is supporting his message—his own philosophy and goals as a teacher.

Promoting Cognitive Clarification

For many years the field of psychology seemed divided between those who thought of people as thinking beings, and those who saw them as creatures of habit. In Chapter 4 we spoke of taking a strong theoretical position and going "all the way" with it. We pointed out that it is important for theory builders to be committed to their theories so they can plumb their depths. But there are dangers in deep theoretical commitments. Perhaps one of the greatest dangers is the loss of communication among people with different theoretical allegiances and the questioning that could result from such interchange. For example, Freud held a deep commitment to his particular theory of the unconscious. He believed that apparently illogical behavior was motivated by feelings locked deep within the mind. He held that as people came to understand their feelings through *psychoanalysis,* their insight would lead to behavioral change.

At roughly the same time as Freud, the American psychologist John B. Watson was a strong spokesman for the opposite point of view, which he called *behaviorism*. He believed that feelings or ideas had little to do with behavior and that insight into them was a dead end. He held that if parents would observe a set of simple laws for training children, their children would grow into well-behaved adults.

At their most extreme positions, insight-oriented psychologists (like Freud and many others we'll mention later) remain convinced that once we understand why we do something we consciously don't want to do, we will stop doing it. Equally convinced behaviorists (e.g., Skinner) believe that if the correct set of reinforcement and extinction procedures could be defined, we would stop doing what we didn't want to do in the first place. Each position has merit. When we understand why we do things, we may be strongly motivated to change. On the other hand, we may get so much reinforcement for repeating a habit that all the insight in the world would be insufficient to make change.

It might be helpful to look back at our model of learning facilitation presented in Figure 13–1. We have discussed three elements of the model: (1) enhancing positive feelings, (2) reinforcing desirable behavior, and (3) modeling desirable behavior. Now we will focus on the fourth element of the model, *promoting cognitive clarification*—the discussion and analysis of thoughts, feelings, and behavior. This area of learning facilitation draws heavily on the insight-oriented psychologies of Freud and cognitive psychology. We will focus here on *cognitive psychology* and its implications for facilitating learning.

Whenever psychology turns itself inward toward the process of perception or thought, its concern is cognitive. The strict behaviorist position has sometimes been described as a "black box" theory. We are asked to imagine what behaviorists call *the organism* (which could be a person, an earthworm, or any animal) as if it were a black box. We are to assume that we cannot know what goes on inside the black box, but if we stimulate it, it will emit responses. Behaviorists study the relationship between stimuli and responses, seeking laws that govern that relationship.

While behaviorists concentrate on what is outside the box, cognitive psychologists are concerned with the black box itself (see Fig. 13–4). They believe that the mind is where stimuli are coded and stored, and that the mind dictates our behaviors. In other words, what people think and feel is critical in determining how they act. Cognitive psychologists argue, moreover, that there are ways of coming to know the thoughts and feelings that cause people to behave in a particular way.

Psychoanalysis is the name Freud gave to his approach to helping people with emotional problems. Through many sessions over months or years, feelings that may have been affecting the patient's behavior are brought to a conscious level, where they can be understood and discussed with the analyst. For further discussion of Freud's theories, see Chapter 6.

Some emerging theories provide a more eclectic view of learning. Cognitive learning theories explore the relationship between cognition —our thoughts —and learning.

Behaviorists point out that there is no way we can know what goes on inside a person's brain. We can't study thoughts and feelings since there is no way to observe them objectively. We can, however, observe what people do and what events come to increase or decrease the likelihood of a particular response.

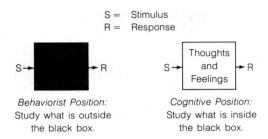

Figure 13-4. Behaviorist vs. Cognitive Theories

Throughout this book we have emphasized the importance of thoughts and feelings in influencing both the way we perceive the world and the way we respond to it. Learning involves not just a change in behavior but the internalization (or incorporation into our minds) of experiences, thoughts, and feelings.

Cognition has been a major concern throughout this book. For example, in Chapter 2 we explored the development of self-concept, the picture or "map" of the self we carry around in our heads. Bruner's concept of discovery (Chapters 4 and 5) is rooted in the idea that we are driven to make sense of our environment and organize it into a context within our brains. Ausubel (Chapter 4) is concerned with the meaningful presentation of instructional material. Piaget's developmental scheme (Chapter 5) and Guilford's concept (Chapter 8) of measuring intelligence as information processing are based on the belief that people learn actively; they are not merely passive receivers of information. Maslow's description of knowing and understanding as a need within a hierarchy (Chapter 9) is also consonant with a cognitive viewpoint.

Max Wertheimer (1880–1943) was a pioneer in the scientific study of cognition. He expressed the then revolutionary idea that the study of the elements of behavior in isolation would not lead to understanding human behavior itself. His point of view is best expressed by the German word *Gestalt,* which may be translated as an organized whole rather than a collection of parts. For example, a musical piece played by an orchestra is a collection of separate notes, each with a rhythmic value; but we hear the piece as a totality. It is the relationship among the tones and their rhythmic values, not the individual notes, that make the piece memorable for us. In the same way, we perceive a series of dots in a long row as a line rather than simply as a series of dots. Such observations interested the Gestalt psychologists because they indicate that the senses bring bits of information to the brain, but the brain must collect, organize, and make sense of the information it receives. Gestalt psychology is the study of how the brain processes information into meanings.

Among the areas explored by Wertheimer and his followers, three stand out as especially relevant to the study of educational psychology.

Prägnanz.   When people perceive fragmentary, incomplete, or assymetrical terms, they tend to see them as more complete or more perfect than they are. This is not necessarily the result of effort; it seems to occur spontaneously. Furthermore, once a Gestalt, or whole perception, is registered in the mind, it becomes strongly entrenched. Take, for example, the well-known goblet illusion shown in Figure 13–5.

Figure 13-5. The Goblet Illusion

Many people see the figure above as a goblet, and only with great effort (such as blocking out half the picture, squinting, tilting) can they see two human profiles facing one another. Some people perceive the profiles immediately and must work to find the goblet. One is really no more "correct" or objectively true than the other, but the mind finds it hard to hold both perceptions at the same moment. Such perceptions were originally investigated in terms of the senses, particularly vision (as in the goblet illusion), but they extend into our whole internal organization of the world. Sometimes the apparently innate predisposition to organize perception can cause us a great deal of trouble. We may latch on to a particular perception and become its victim. This tendency to focus on a single organization to the exclusion of others is called *fixation*.

Once you knew that there were two ways of seeing Figure 13-5, did you find it hard to hold both pictures in your mind at the same time? Did you find yourself shifting back and forth between the two pictures?

A few years ago a riddle that illustrates the problem of fixation gained wide popularity. A boy is badly injured in an accident. He is rushed to the hospital and prepared for surgery. The doctor is summoned, but refuses to perform the operation, saying only, "I cannot operate on this boy, he is my own son." But the doctor is not the boy's father! Who is the doctor?

Because many people are predisposed to think of a physician, particularly a surgeon, as male, it is often difficult for them to realize that the doctor is the boy's mother. Discussion of such a riddle is an excellent way of helping people see how they are often blinded by their perceptions. People do not simply take information into their brains and respond "objectively" to it. Rather, their minds work actively on the experiences they take in through their senses. The Gestalt psychologists emphasize that human beings cannot help "distorting" and interpret their experiences to fit in with their own biases, values, feelings, etc.

As teachers it's helpful to continually remind ourselves that, as a result of our experiences and stage of development, we may perceive things very differently than our students do.

The more we can help students to analyze why they feel the way they do, the more we can help them toward self-understanding.

Purposiveness. Purposiveness refers to the idea that behavior is goal-oriented, i.e., directed toward some end or purpose. If, as the Gestalt psychologists believe, people are organized by their own perceptions, it then follows that people's behavior is influenced by how they think of themselves. In this sense students who believe themselves stupid and who see grades as a necessary goal may easily turn to cheating as a means of reaching the goal. To the cognitive

*Try to think of some reasons Tom
might hang back in his science class.
Then pick one of your reasons and try
to offer one suggestion to help Tom
change his introverted behavior.*

psychologist, people do things because those things have meaning
for them, and they do them in ways consistent with their own sense of
what the world is and where they fit into it. Consequently, self-concept
is a very important determinant of how people will behave.

For example, Tom is an extremely quiet student who always iso-
lates himself and stays off in a corner, never participating in his science class. Rather than simply viewing this as laziness or lack of
interest, a teacher who is thinking in a cognitive frame asks, "What
purpose might Tom have in hanging back like this?" Thinking of behavior as having meaning or purpose leads the teacher to develop
new strategies to help the student restructure his view of himself and,
therefore, his goals.

Insight.   Insight involves a sudden reorganization of the field of
experience, for example, having a new idea or discovering the solution to a problem. This phenomenon, sometimes depicted in cartoons
by a lightbulb shining over a character's head, has been called the
"aha!" or "eureka!" experience.

Psychologists have long debated the nature of problem-solving
behavior. Early behaviorists like E. L. Thorndike (1932) believed that
problems were solved through a process of trial and error. Thorndike
put cats in special cages and then observed the way they found their
way out to get to food. The means of getting out of the cage was
pulling a chain. Thorndike noted that the cats would perform random
acts, such as pushing the sides of the cage, until they happened to
pull the chain. When put back in the cage, the cats did not immediately go for the chain, but repeated the same random activities.
Only after many trials did they begin to pull the chain immediately.
From this experiment, Thorndike reasoned that the cats learned by
trial and error, and that it was only because the pulling of the chain
was rewarded and the other behavior unrewarded, that the cats
gradually learned to pull the chain to escape.

Köhler (1925), a German psychologist doing research with chimpanzees in the 1920s, thought otherwise. He presented caged chimpanzees with fruit that was suspended out of their reach. Boxes were
left lying in the cage. Köhler observed that the chimpanzees seemed
to stop, study the problem, and sooner or later bring the box over to
where they could stand on it to reach the fruit. Once they saw they
could do this, they did it whenever they wanted fruit. Köhler held that
this was a demonstration of insight. In order to solve the problem of
how to get the fruit, the chimps had to "perceive" a new use for the
box.

*If you would like to learn more about
the early history of cognitive views of
learning, you might consult Hill,*
Learning: A Survey of Psychological
Interpretations *(1971).*

From the cognitive viewpoint what is important in human behavior
is the internal process not physical actions. Insightful thinking requires
that the thinker be able to hold the problem in mind while he searches
through his mind for various possible solutions until a correct one
suddenly comes to mind. At one time the rift between the behaviorist
psychologists, who were loyal to the trial-and-error theory, and the
cognitive psychologists, who espoused insightful learning, was so
deep that it seemed unresolvable. At the present time, however, there
is a growing recognition that we can't explain behavior by one or the
other theory alone—we seem to need both.

In terms of learning, we might say that if the goal of behavioral psychology is to improve our habits, then the goal of cognitive psychology is to improve our thinking. A variety of educational techniques have as their goal, or include as an important subgoal, cognitive restructuring or, as we described it earlier, cognitive clarification. The goal of Freudian psychotherapy is insight into one's own motives and feelings as a means of changing behavior. Group therapy helps people understand how they perceive others and how others perceive them. The more aware they become of these perceptions, the more likely they are to change them and, possibly, their behavior. Consciousness-raising groups enable women to learn from one another how society has created certain roles and expectations for them. As they understand the effects of these roles and expectations, they can work on ways of altering their concepts of themselves. Modern Gestalt-oriented therapies try to get us in touch with our bodily feelings, such as aches, pains, and muscular tensions. Often understanding the source of these feelings helps us to reshape our understanding of ourselves and our world.

In the classroom we are continually making cognitive clarifications. The statement of a *behavioral objective* is a good example. It is clarifying for teachers because it requires that they put into words what they are trying to accomplish. It is useful for students because it helps them know where they are going in a particular unit of study. If the student or teacher gets off the track, a reexamination of the original goal may help in getting back on track. The goal statement helps to elicit the appropriate behavior. As she observes the behavior of her students, a teacher may see that a strategy is not working and say, "Maybe my goal is not well stated. Perhaps I have to go back and rethink what I really want to accomplish."

Generally speaking, when the teacher asks herself whether she has accomplished her goal, she is asking whether she has helped her students to develop or strengthen some concept. The thrust of much contemporary cognitive psychology is concerned with how we develop concepts.

A behavioral objective is a specific statement of what a student must do to accomplish an educational objective. For example, a teacher might specify for a reading lesson:

After reading a two-page story, the student will summarize the main idea of the story in three sentences.

Concept Learning

It is hard to believe, but there was a time in your life when you did not know that there were such things as tables. Probably your first contact with tables occurred when you abandoned the high chair. One day your mother or father said, "You are too big for the high chair now—come sit at the table." Being one or two years old, you thought that was what *table* was: "the place in my house where I sit now that I am too big for the high chair." Gradually, you met other tables—a work table in school, a three-legged table, a folding card table, and so on. Soon the idea grew that a table could take many shapes, have different numbers of legs, and serve different purposes. So, little by little, you developed the concept *table*.

Complications arose. What about four-legged objects you sit on? Were they also tables? No, you learned; they were *chairs*. They also came in different sizes and shapes. They, too, had differing numbers of legs. There followed other complications. You learned the concepts *desk, dresser, bed,* and so on. Soon a new and larger, more inclusive concept arose—*furniture.* All of these objects were *furniture.* But just as a chair is not a table, and a desk, although it is like a table, is not a table, so, too, not all objects are furniture. For example, a sink is not furniture, although a dry sink might be, especially if it isn't used to wash dishes.

You can see that there are two tasks involved in developing a concept. One is to generalize—to have a class large enough to include all the relevant examples of the concept. The other is to discriminate—to know when properly to exclude an example from the concept. We sometimes refer to that which we include as an *example,* and that which we discriminate out as a *nonexample..*

Concepts often include subconcepts. As your concept enlarges to include subconcepts, the lines of example and nonexample shift. The following figures are all examples of the concept *triangles:*

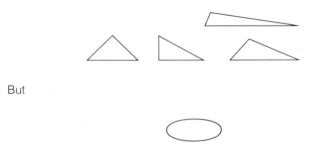

But

is a nonexample. If the larger concept of *geometric shapes* is being studied, all of the above figures are examples, as are the following:

Obviously, concepts are often more complex than the classification of objects such as shapes. Concepts are often powerful abstractions, which help us make sense of ever larger amounts of data. Gagné (1970, p. 203) calls higher order concepts *rules.* For example, to understand the rule *round things roll,* the learner must first have the concepts *round, things,* and *roll.* Gagné holds that there is a logical instructional sequence that connects these concepts:

Step 1: Inform the learner about the form of the performance to be expected when learning is completed.
Step 2: Question the learner in a way that requires the restatement (recall) of the previously learned concepts that make up the rule.
Step 3: Use verbal statements (cues) that will lead the learner to put the rule together, as a chain of concepts, in the proper order.
Step 4: By means of a question, ask the learner to "demonstrate" one or more concrete instances of the rule.

Gagné is concerned with strengthening understanding and ability to think. The more concepts we have to use in organizing our experience, the more effectively we will be able to solve problems.

Step 5: (Optional, but useful for later instruction) By a suitable question, require the learner to make a verbal statement of the rule.

Gagné believes that this sequence is the basis of orderly concept learning, "whether practiced by a teacher, film, or a textbook."

Concepts are valuable to the extent that they enhance our understanding. As teachers, we hope that concepts will have meaning for our students. Poor teaching often leads the teacher to believe that a concept has been mastered, when in fact students have merely learned it by rote.

If you ask a student to divide 26,480 by 20, he might be able to do it by the process of long division, and come up with the answer 1324. However, if you asked him to estimate how many 20s there are in 26,480, he might have no idea at all nor any way of thinking the problem through. Good teaching demands that we build toward concepts in such a way that they have meaning for the student.

It was customary in the nineteenth century to teach concepts by rote, or memorized rules. Students were judged by their ability to recall and identify rules. Grammatical ability, for instance, was defined by the knowledge of rules such as: "A sentence is a complete thought, including a subject and a predicate." Unfortunately, it is quite possible to know this definition by heart and still be unable to write a good sentence, let alone recognize one.

Klausmeier, Ghatala, and Frayer, Conceptual Learning and Development: A Cognitive View (1974) presents a good integration of current thinking on concept learning.

Facilitating Concept Learning

We have spoken earlier of the two major instructional theories, the discovery approach and the expository approach. Both agree that concept learning is of crucial importance because it organizes bits of information into units of increasing meaning. Bruner believes that concepts are best developed *inductively*. The student is encouraged to plunge into the unknown and to search out the organizing principles, or concepts, that make the unknown meaningful. Bruner wants students to think like scientists—to be curious, to ask questions, to seek relationships.

Ausubel believes that relatively few students will ever be scientists; most lack the imagination and creativity necessary for them to become such high-level thinkers. Only those students who reach the top, so to speak, will develop high levels of problem-solving ability. Consequently, Ausubel emphasizes the orderly exposition and presentation of knowledge.

There is as yet little convincing evidence that any one instructional method is best for all students. Some are reached by the kindling of curiosity and excitement that are at the heart of discovery teaching. For others discovery learning seems too much like a "sink or swim" method, and they may drown, or at least become so afraid of the water that they won't go in again. For the latter a more orderly, expository approach seems preferable. The teacher who understands the underlying principles of each approach and is aware that different students have different needs seeks ways of matching the degree of structure to the needs of the student.

In terms of results, the advocates of the discovery method believe that it leads to a great deal of transfer of learning. Not only is the student learning geometry, for example, she is also learning the process of knowledge-getting, and she will use that skill when studying science, algebra, and other areas with a high symbolic content. Expository method advocates are more concerned with the mastery of a particular subject and the building of a firm sequence so that more and more complex and abstract concepts can be presented and mastered.

Ausubel (1977, p. 165) uses the term *verbatim,* meaning *word-for-word,* to refer to information that is "swallowed whole" by the student. He points out that as long as the learner's intention is to "internalize . . . an arbitrary and verbatim series of words, both the learning process and the learning outcome must be rote or meaningless." Ausubel suggests three reasons students develop a rote-learning set. First, they may have learned that some teachers are only satisfied with a rote response. If you do not respond with the exact words they expect, you are the loser. Second, they have developed such a level of anxiety and are so discouraged by previous failure that they stick to the safest course of action, which is to try desperately to remember by heart. Finally, if students feel that it is safer to hide their uncertainty than to admit to not understanding something, they can create the impression of understanding by memorizing a few key phrases they can rattle off at appropriate times.

In the final section of this chapter we would like to help you see how cognitive clarification can be combined with reinforcing desirable behavior as a means of facilitating learning. In a classroom anecdote we will integrate practical suggestions drawn from behavioristic views of learning with those based on cognitive views.

A useful reminder: "Teachers frequently forget that pupils become very adept at using abstract terms with apparent appropriateness — when they have to —even though their understanding of the underlying concepts is virtually nonexistent" (Ausubel, 1977, p. 165).

What school subjects have you learned by rote rather than understanding? What factors led you to this type of learning?

From Behavior Modification to Self-Behavior Modification: An Eclectic Perspective on Facilitating Learning

Usually when we think of behavior modification, we imagine a teacher applying principles of reinforcement and learning in order to control student behavior. Recently, however, behavior modification has been reexamined (Goldfried and Merbaum, 1973; Thoresen and Mahoney, 1974), and it has become increasingly apparent that, in many instances, control can and should be in the hands of the learner not in the hands of the teacher. Behavior modification applies psychological principles of learning to changing behavior. Self–behavior modification (or self-modification) is a more eclectic approach, which draws on both habit-learning and cognitive theory, with its goal of clarification of thinking. Advocates of self-behavior modification believe that for a person to gain control over his own behavior, he must become aware of both the undesirable behaviors he wishes to eliminate and the desirable behaviors he hopes to learn. This process involves cognitive clarification. Then he can learn specific techniques for changing his behavior.

An interesting current use of self–behavior modification is biofeedback training. By this technique, a person might learn, for example, how to control her respiration rate and other bodily processes in order to relax and reduce feelings of anxiety. Although someone else could do the conditioning, imagine the pleasurable sense of self-control that comes with learning to reduce your own anxiety and relax by yourself. Another use of self-modification has been the application of Skinnerian principles to problems like cigarette smoking and overeating. Here, too, the individual identifies the habit she wishes to change and uses learning principles to change her behavior. Usually self-modification techniques allow for a great deal of discussion and analysis of one's thoughts and feelings before and during the attempts to alter behavior.

Self–behavior modification is very applicable to the classroom setting. What follows is an example of the shift from teacher control to student control of an unwanted behavior. JoAnn, a sixth grader, is unruly. She is constantly calling out answers, much to the annoyance of her fellow students and her teacher. The teacher might approach her alone in the following manner:

Teacher: JoAnn, you and I both know how angry the other kids are getting about your calling out.

JoAnn: Yes, I know, but I can't help it.

Teacher: Maybe together we can figure out a way of helping you stop.

JoAnn: It can't be done. Everyone is always shouting at me to shut up, but I keep doing it. I want to stop, but I can't.

Teacher: Let's try something. Can you figure out some of the things that make you call out?

JoAnn: Yes, whenever I have my hand up you don't call on me.

Teacher: Well, I can't every time your hand is up. But sometimes I do, like this morning in arithmetic.

JoAnn: But when I answered, you said it was wrong.

Teacher: It was wrong. But I guess it made you feel bad to have it pointed out.

JoAnn: But whenever you call on Jimmy, he's right.

Teacher: Do you think that your feelings about Jimmy might have something to do with your calling out?

JoAnn: Well, maybe I'm a little jealous of him and some of the other kids who always get the right answers.

Teacher: What does that have to do with your calling out?

JoAnn: Well, I think one reason I may do it is to prove that I'm not dumb. Sometimes I don't know the answers to three or four questions you ask in a row. Then when I do know an answer I'm

Biofeedback draws heavily on principles of classical (Pavlovian) conditioning.

Many self-help groups like "Weight Watchers," "Neurotics Anonymous," and stopping-smoking clinics use self-modification procedures.

Have you ever visited any of them? What do you think are the strengths of their approach?

Note the importance here of the teacher's helping JoAnn to clarify and think through why she is calling out.

afraid you won't call on me. So I call out to make sure you know that I know the answer and want to give it.

Teacher: Maybe you could do something to let me know when you know the right answer, even if I can't call on you right then.

JoAnn: Like what?

Teacher: Perhaps you could write the answer down as soon as you know it, and show it to me later. That way, I'd know you knew it, and you would be learning not to call out and get everyone angry.

JoAnn: But how would that help me?

Teacher: Well, as you write the answer down, you will be reminding yourself that you do know the work, and that you don't have to call out. As you stop calling out, the other students will think you're a better sport. You could even show any one who asks the answers you have written down to prove that you do know the work. Why don't you try this technique this afternoon and then come talk with me about how you feel it has worked after I dismiss the class?

JoAnn: Thanks. I don't know if it will work, but I guess I might as well try it.

By helping JoAnn to "see" what she knows, her teacher is providing reinforcement.

Here the teacher has enlisted JoAnn's cooperation in solving the problem. Such a cooperative approach demonstrates the teacher's genuine concern for helping JoAnn.

In this example, the teacher is helping JoAnn focus on the problem and encouraging her to begin taking some responsibility for changing her own behavior. By getting JoAnn to talk about and analyze what she feels might be causing her problem, the teacher is promoting cognitive clarification. The teacher believes that JoAnn still needs some external reinforcement, but delays it by having her write down some correct answers by herself. JoAnn must control herself, giving herself internal messages such as, "I *do* know some answers," and "I can keep from calling out." As she shows the teacher (or any of the students) what she has written down, she receives external reinforcement for the new behavior. The locus of control has shifted away from the teacher and is now shared by JoAnn and the teacher. As JoAnn makes progress, the teacher's ultimate aim will be to have her take complete control of her own behavior in this area. The teacher has used a very eclectic approach to facilitating JoAnn's learning.

Conclusions

An effective teacher is a learning facilitator—a person who makes learning easier by creating conditions that promote learning and eliminating conditions that interfere with it. This view of teaching has been heavily influenced by the thinking of Carl Rogers. However, we have gone far beyond Rogers by presenting in this chapter a model of learning facilitation that incorporates four major elements. Each of these elements offers suggestions for teaching that grow out of one of four theories of learning. Because we see teachers as either masters of the laws of learning or victims of them, we have gone into these laws in some depth.

The first element we presented in our model of learning facilitation is called *enhancing positive feelings*. If students are to learn, they must feel comfortable, secure, and open to new experiences. By understanding some basic principles of Pavlovian conditioning, teachers can improve the classroom atmosphere and minimize the fear, anxiety, and tension that many teachers unwittingly create.

Reinforcing desired behavior is a second area of our model. You have probably recognized its importance as you have thought about how different rewards further your own learning. The more teachers learn about their students, the more they discover what they can do to reward students for desired behavior and to avoid rewarding students for undesired behavior.

Modeling desired behavior is the third element of the model. All people are influenced by the behavior of others. This is especially true in the classroom, where students have many people to imitate, peers as well as the teacher. Teachers are powerful models. They can help students learn desirable behavior if they continually demonstrate it in their own actions.

The fourth element in our learning facilitation model is *promoting cognitive clarification*. This element is derived from the cognitive psychology view that in order to change their behavior and thus learn, people must think. By helping students clarify their own motives, perceptions, feelings, and thoughts, teachers prepare them for more effective learning.

Our purpose in this chapter has been to provide many approaches to promoting learning, drawn from a number of theoretical orientations. In some circumstances one approach will work; in other circumstances another approach may be more effective. As a teacher you must decide which approach to try. We have also emphasized the desirability of shifting control of behavior from the teacher to the student. The more teachers can make students aware of how learning occurs, the more they help students feel self-reliant and self-controlled. Generally this process progresses from teacher control, to control shared by both teacher and student, to student self-control.

Some Good Books

Bandura, Albert. *Principles of Behavior Modification.* New York: Holt, Rinehart and Winston, 1969. A comprehensive review of the application of reinforcement theory to behavioral change, with a good presentation of Bandura's special interest, modeling.

Bigge, Morris L. *Learning Theories for Teachers.* New York: Harper & Row, 1971. An excellent teacher-oriented guide to learning theories, with a balanced presentation of both the behaviorist and the cognitive positions.

Dacey, John S. *New Ways to Learn: The Psychology of Education.* Stamford, Conn.: Greylock, 1976. Dacey has provided here a good brief introduction to educational psychology. His chapter entitled "Encouraging Learning" explores the educational implications of Pavlov's classical conditioning, Skinner's operant conditioning, and Bandura's theory of modeling.

Gagné, Robert. *Essentials of Learning for Instruction.* Hinsdale, Ill.: Dryden, 1974. This paperback is a thought-provoking introduction to Gagné's information-processing model of learning.

Goldfried, M. R. and M. Merbaum, eds. *Behavior Change through Self-Control.* New York: Holt, Rinehart and Winston, 1973. A collection of papers exploring the relationship between cognitive control and behavioral change.

Joyce, Bruce and Marsha Weil. *Models of Teaching.* Englewood Cliffs, N.J.: Prentice-Hall, 1972. This book provides an excellent integration of major theories of teaching and their classroom applications.

Kovel, Joel. *A Complete Guide to Therapy: From Psychoanalysis to Behavior Modification.* New York: Pantheon, 1976. Kovel introduces the major psychotherapies, including psychoanalysis, Gestalt therapy, Rogerian therapy, and behavior therapy. The theories presented also have many implications for teaching.

Rogers, Carl. *Freedom to Learn.* Columbus, Ohio: Merrill, 1969. In this collection of articles, Rogers acquaints the reader with the psychological sources of his view of the teacher as learning facilitator.

Skinner, B. F. *About Behaviorism.* New York: Knopf, 1974. In his most recent book, B. F. Skinner answers the charges of many critics of behaviorism.

Thoresen, Carl E., ed. *Behavior Modification in Education. 72nd Yearbook, Part I, National Society for the Study of Education.* Chicago: University of Chicago Press, 1973. An excellent overview of research and issues on the use of behavior modification in educational settings.

Thoresen, Carl E. and M. J. Mahoney. *Behavioral Self-Control.* New York: Holt, Rinehart and Winston, 1974. This book explores the behaviorist approach and its implications for self-directed learning. Such an integration of behavioristic and humanistic concepts is often called humanistic behaviorism.

Wolpe, Joseph. *The Practice of Behavior Therapy.* New York: Oxford, 1969. The basic principles of behavior therapy presented in this book are useful in the elimination of phobias and anxieties.

Articles, Studies, and Other References

Bevans, William. "Perceptual Learning, An Overview." *Journal of General Psychology,* January 1961: 65–99. This article describes the relationship between Gestalt theory and cognitive learning, and compares them to the behaviorist position.

Bruner, Jerome. "The Growth of Mind." *American Psychologist* 20 (1965): 1007–1017. Based upon Bruner's research on intellectual development in children and the educational process, this article provides the reader with a good grasp of the cognitive position on learning.

Mahoney, Michael J. "Reflections on the Cognitive Learning Trend in Psychotherapy." *American Psychologist* 32 (1977): 5–12. A review paper setting forth the cognitive-learning concept in terms of psychotherapy, but very relevant to the field of education as well.

McKeachie, W. J. "The Decline and Fall of the Laws of Learning." *Educational Researcher* 3 (March 1974): 7–11. In this review of much behaviorist research on learning, McKeachie argues that many of the old Skinnerian laws inadequately explain learning because they don't take into account the full complexity and uniqueness of human beings.

Suggestions for Action-Oriented Learning

1. Make arrangements to observe the classes of four of your former teachers (preferably two of your "better" teachers and two that weren't so good). Use the model of learning facilitation to analyze how they go about (1) enhancing positive feelings, (2) reinforcing desired behavior, (3) modeling desired behavior, and (4) promoting cognitive clarification. Prepare a report summarizing your findings. (Be certain that you don't mention the names or schools of your teachers.)

2. Visit a class that uses a token economy or some other behaviorist approach to reward desirable behavior. How successful did you feel the approach was? Would you like to learn in such a setting? Why or why not?

3. Get involved in a volunteer tutoring program (or other type of educational program) in which you must teach a person or group once a week for a semester. Keep a log on your thoughts and feelings about teaching. At the end of the semester analyze and evaluate in a paper what you learned about yourself as a teacher and about facilitating learning.

4. If you had to name the most important element of the learning facilitation model, which would you choose—enhancing positive feelings, reinforcing desired behavior, modeling desired behavior, or promoting cognitive clarification? Justify your choice.

5. Pick an undesirable behavior you would like to change in yourself, such as smoking, overeating, procrastinating, watching too much television, biting your fingernails, etc. Try to develop an approach to eliminating it that involves self–behavior modification. Draw on principles discussed in this chapter to help you develop strategies for changing your behavior.

6. Develop an essay entitled "The Teacher I Hope to Be," in which you describe the type of behavior you hope to model as a teacher and why you feel that behavior is important.

14
Evaluating
Learning and Teaching

In this chapter we would like to explore with you the importance of evaluation in assessing student learning and in improving teaching. We hope to help you see the purposes of evaluation in a diagnostic–prescriptive model of teaching. At the same time we want to aid you in clarifying your own views about evaluation and in understanding a variety of evaluative approaches for use in the classroom. Before we discuss what we feel evaluation ought to be, we want you to think about what it all too often is—an adversary process in which teachers test, mark, grade, and judge students. The first two sections of this chapter, therefore, will encourage you to think about your own school experiences with evaluation and the pros and cons of grading.

We believe very strongly that evaluation is critical in any learning process. However, we question equating tests and grades with true evaluation. Tests and grades often interfere with evaluation rather than promote it.

Grading as Evaluation

There are few aspects of education that generate as much feeling and controversy as evaluation. In most U.S. schools evaluation has come to mean grading—a process usually disliked and often feared by students. Typically, grades such as As, Bs, Cs, Ds, and Fs indicate how students compare with their peers in the same subject or class. Any grading process involves two basic components: *evaluation* and *measurement*. *Evaluation* is a process which examines the outcomes of educational practices. The evaluator asks, has the program itself been satisfactory, or has the student achieved satisfactorily within the program? In either case, the word *satisfactory* implies that the evaluator is making a value judgment. *Measurement* is a useful tool in evaluation, although not the only one. Measurement is the process of determining or quantifying a student's achievement through some assessment device such as a test, questionnaire, inventory, or scale. Evaluation involves judgments about measurements. For example, SAT scores have declined over the last 10 years or so—that is a measurement. Exploring the implications of this decline would be accomplished through evaluation. On another level, when a teacher looks at a student's scores for the semester and decides that, taking everything into account, he will give an overall A instead of a B, he is making an evaluative judgment. The teacher can shift from measurement to evaluation in a split second, but such haste often hinders clear thinking. In any approach to grading, problems can arise with both the measuring devices used to assess learning (objective tests, essay exams, term papers, course projects, etc.) and the standards used for reporting how "well" a student has done.

Test scores, marks, and grades that compare students against each other have become so much a part of American education that many teachers and students accept them without question. These people often assume that (1) competition for grades evokes the best performance from students, (2) the desire for high grades motivates students to work hard, and (3) good grades provide positive reinforcement, which strengthens learning, while poor grades serve as negative reinforcement. Each of these assumptions is open to question. In preparation for a critical look at the role of grades and evaluation in the teaching–learning process, we would like you to complete Exploration 14–1.

How did you feel about grading when you were in high school? To what extent were your attitudes influenced by the grades you received?

Have your attitudes toward grading changed since you entered college? How? Why?

What are some factors that might influence the teacher in making such a decision? Can you name three?

1.

2.

3.

Exploration 14–1: Examining Your Own
Feelings about Different Evaluative Practices

It might be interesting to go through these anecdotes with another person. By learning of someone else's experiences and feelings, you will better understand your own attitudes about different approaches to evaluation.

Read the anecdotes that follow. Place a √ next to each one that triggers a memory of a similar experience you had as a student. Below each anecdote describe how you would feel if you were a student in that situation. If you actually experienced such a situation, try to record your feelings at that time.

___ Teacher: "OK, class, put away your books. We are going to have a surprise quiz now."

___ Student (to teacher): "This final grade isn't fair. I came to every class and I never worked so hard in a course in my life. I did my best and really showed improvement. But you didn't take my improvement into account; you just looked at the grade on my final paper."

Have you ever been labeled an underachiever?

___ Teacher (to student): "A comparison of your actual course work with your I.Q. scores shows clearly that you are not working up to your potential. You have the ability to be doing much better in this course."

___ Teacher: "Boys and girls, you should know by now that every time you don't do your homework I put a 0 in my grade book."

Do you think this type of advising occurs frequently?

___ Teacher (or counselor): "Bill, there is no point in your trying to become a lawyer (or teacher, doctor, etc.) because of your poor grades and low SAT scores."

___ Student: "I just know I won't get into a good college because I always do poorly on standardized tests like the College Board Exams even though I get good grades in my classes."

___ Teacher (to class): "The reason I give so many tests and papers is to keep you people on your toes and to make sure that I have lots of marks in my grade book so that your final grade will be fair."

—— Student (after multiple-choice test is returned): "Mr. Brown, you said you will only take answer *a* for 11, but *c* also makes sense. And I saw it in another book, too." Teacher: "I will only accept *a;* that's what it said in our book."

—— Student (to other students): "It's so unfair. We really talked a lot in class about what a beautiful book *Catcher in the Rye* was, and what it meant personally to each of us. Then on the test, Ms. Vinton asked a lot of silly questions like 'What season of the year was the story set in?'"

—— Teacher: "Duane, that is a horrible report card. You make sure that you bring it back to me signed by your mother or father. Also, I'll expect to hear from them so that I can set up an appointment to talk with them about your school work this last quarter."

How effective do you feel this approach will be in getting Duane to improve?

—— Teacher (to class): "If you don't really settle down and get to work, this class is going to get the lowest set of grades I've ever given."

—— Any additions?

The examples were selected to illustrate the fear, suspicion, distrust, self-doubts, and downright hostility students can feel as they confront rigid and punitive evaluation practices. Sometimes even good teachers who have generally cooperative relationships with their students find themselves in battle with students when testing day comes or when they must return course projects with grades. On the other hand, there are both teachers and students who argue that grades provide a very important means of evaluation and are essential in schools. The following paragraphs explore the debate about the value of grades. As you read the arguments pro and con, be thinking about your own experiences with grades. Consider to what extent you agree or disagree with each statement.

Have you ever talked with any teachers who disliked having to give grades?

Why did they feel that way?

How do you think you will feel about giving grades when you become a teacher?

Arguments in Support of Grading

1. Society needs grades. How else can we judge who should be permitted to become a doctor, teacher, or engineer, or hold

Do you feel grades in medical school are an important indication of how good a doctor someone will be? Why or why not?

How about prospective teachers? Do you feel that students who have high grades in college and graduate school will make better teachers? Why or why not?

Some advocates of grading don't emphasize competition. They measure students against a standard rather than against each other and give as many high grades as students earn.

What do you think would happen if all college courses were made pass/fail?

As you read the criticisms raised by Kirschenbaum, Simon, and Napier, think back to your own experiences in high school. You might try to answer some of the following questions.

Did you study primarily to get good grades rather than to learn? How often did you do extra work that you knew would not be on a test?

Was there cheating in your school? Why did it occur? How often did you cheat?

any responsible position? Grades give us a reasonable indication of how much a person knows. We certainly wouldn't want to hire a doctor who had failed certain medical school courses, or for that matter who had just gotten through with Cs.

2. Competition is good—it encourages people to try harder. Everyone likes to be recognized and do well. As people realize that only a small number of high grades will be given out, they will study more seriously. Competition brings out the best in people.

3. Grades are motivating. If students didn't know that they were going to be graded in some way, they probably wouldn't bother to do the work necessary to learn a particular subject. The fear of not doing well puts pressure on students to study.

4. Students need grades as feedback on how they are doing. Grades give students knowledge of their success or failure, so they serve as reinforcers.

5. Students who have worked extra hard want the satisfaction of public acknowledgment of their efforts. Letter grades give that sort of recognition. Pass/fail grades, on the other hand, lump everyone together and make no distinction between those who did really well and those who barely scraped by.

6. Parents need grades in order to know how their children are doing and how they compare with other children.

7. Schools need grades. Grades provide a simple, easy-to-use assessment of a student's achievement. Grades determine who gets promoted, which courses students should take, and which track they should be placed in. Colleges and graduate schools use grades as admissions criteria.

Arguments against Grading

Kirschenbaum, Simon, and Napier (1971) have written a thoughtful critique of current school evaluation practices. They have titled it after a question we are sure you have asked or been asked many times in your schooling—especially when report cards have just been given out—"Wad-ja-get?" Drawing upon their experience in many schools, the authors have described the reaction of the students in a hypothetical school, Mapleton High, to grading practices. Here is a summary of the major student criticisms of grading at Mapleton High:

1. Grades have become more important to students than learning. We don't study because we are interested in learning but in order to achieve good grades on our tests.

2. Grades encourage cheating. Because grades are made so important, we try to get them by any means possible. A better educational system with better evaluative procedures would lessen cheating, or maybe do away with it.

3. Grades divide teachers and students into warring camps. Teachers and students should work and grow together, but students lose respect for teachers when they "con" or "brownnose" them. Students and teachers often lose valuable classroom time arguing about grades instead of thinking about ideas.

4. Grades discourage students from developing their own goals. We spend so much of our time doing what teachers want us to do that we have little chance to really explore what interests us.

5. Grading stifles creativity. Once you figure out what a teacher wants, you stand a chance of getting a good grade. But if you choose to be original or creative, you risk offending the teacher or the possibility that the teacher won't understand what you're trying to do.

6. Grades are not applied fairly. Some teachers are, in general, harder markers than others. Some play favorites within a class. The way you dress, talk, act, or the "side of the tracks" you come from may influence a teacher a great deal.

7. Grades create an unhealthy atmosphere in the school. We are forced to compete for grades. This makes for jealousy and an unwillingness to help a classmate out because it might hurt our grades. School becomes a rat race instead of an enjoyable place.

8. Grades lead to other problems in school. The power to grade becomes a weapon that enables teachers to not respond to what might be constructive criticism. When the teacher holds all the power, students are often afraid to stand up and say what they think is wrong for fear that they will be penalized.

If you were a teacher what would you do to eliminate cheating? How would you respond to students caught cheating?

Have you found that grades stifled your creativity?

Are there things that teachers can do to encourage creativity even when they must give grades?

Was grading used as a weapon by teachers in your high school? How about in college?

In an essay entitled "The Student as Nigger" (1972), Jerry Farber described college as a place where students were forced to "bow down" and give up their identities in the classroom to teachers who acted the way white slave owners had with their black slaves.

In order to raise what we feel are important issues regarding evaluation in school settings, we have emphasized the extremes— viewpoints that support current grading practices and those that seriously question current practices. Many views fall somewhere between these extremes. Clearly, we do not support the grading practices current in most schools. All too often students see grades as ends (or goals) rather than as means toward learning. Grades often interfere with real learning and create adversary relationships between teachers and students and among students themselves. However, grades appear to be with us for some time. And, as we pointed out, there are important arguments that support their use. Our purpose so far in this chapter has been to encourage you to question rather than blindly accept existing evaluative practices.

Tests and grades may not be necessary in promoting learning, but evaluation is essential. All learning requires some feedback that tells us how we are doing, provides reinforcement, and helps us see where to make modifications. For example, when we learn to drive a car, some feedback comes to us directly as we feel the wheels of the

Why is it that grades are seen as so essential in school learning? People learn to walk, talk, sing, play baseball, play chess, figure out their income tax, carry out their jobs, etc., all without grades.

car on the road or find ourselves stopping more smoothly. But some comes from the comments, encouragement, and suggestions of the person who is teaching us to drive. All of this feedback is evaluation, yet it is not given in the form of grades. Even the road test requires only that we score above some acceptable level.

In the remaining sections of this chapter, we will introduce a model that views evaluation as much more than a process of testing and grading. After discussing this model of evaluation, we will provide some specific suggestions for evaluating both learning and teaching.

A Model of Evaluation

Not all approaches to evaluation have the adversary quality seen in Exploration 14–1. An interesting case in point is the Greek philosopher Socrates, who has stood for centuries as a model of great teaching. Plato depicts his ideal teacher, Socrates, whose method was to elicit and order the student's knowledge through dialogue with the student.

This form of education is characterized by a great deal of intimacy and exchange between teacher and learner. Because of the way he taught, Socrates was supplied with a continuing flow of information from his students. Sometimes this was in the form of questions, when the students were unclear, or as disagreement with a point that Socrates was making. A great deal of trust existed between Socrates and his students. They were there with him because they wanted to be, and he, in return, loved and honored them.

One of the problems of mass education and compulsory schooling is that not all students are in school because they want to be.

It is hard to imagine Socrates devising a mid-term or final examination in order to test either his effectiveness as a teacher or his students' success in learning what he had taught. But this does not suggest that there was no evaluation going on; in fact, there was continual evaluation. Socrates checked to see that his students were "with" him. He also gave them the opportunity to challenge him. He was monitoring their progress from minute to minute. The reader senses that, at the conclusion of a dialogue, Socrates would know what his student had learned, and whether the student would be capable of intelligent discussion of the subject with other people.

The key to Socrates' approach was his commitment to dialogue as a means of promoting learning. He established I–thou relationships with his students and saw his role as probing, questioning, and encouraging.

In the United States schooling generally does not take place in as intimate and trusting an environment as the one that Socrates created. Some college courses handle many hundreds of students in one lecture. The average high school teacher may face as many as 150 students a day. And even elementary teachers must often work with 25 to 30 or more students at the same time. As we move away from the intimate Socratic model and toward educational settings with more students, the problems of evaluation become increasingly complex. However, evaluation that emphasizes continuous feedback and a cooperative (rather than adversary) relationship with students is still possible no matter what the size of a class.

Probably you can recall teachers who had cooperative relationships with their students even though the classes were large.

Undoubtedly you can also recall some small classes (or even one-to-one relationships) in which there was a battle rather than cooperation between teacher and students.

In attempting to unravel some of the complexities of evaluation, it may be helpful to think first of two simple organizing concepts. We might call them the *what* and the *how* of evaluation. Any evaluator first must define, as clearly as possible, what is to be evaluated, and then how the evaluation can be best accomplished. Michael Scriven (1967) has divided the *what* of evaluation into two categories—*product* and *process*—and the *how* into two categories—*formative evaluation* and *summative evaluation.* Scriven has organized the four important aspects of evaluation into a model (shown in Figure 14–1). Before we explore that model, we will define briefly and give examples of each of Scriven's four major areas.

Product Evaluation.   In product evaluation, probably the most common type of evaluation, a teacher is concerned with what students have learned. The focus here is on achievement—how much and how well students have learned the particular subject matter, whether it be history, mathematics, biology, English, etc. Examples of product are the learning of facts, theories, principles, attitudes, values, etc. Product evaluation is often done through tests made up by teachers.

Process Evaluation.   Process evaluation is concerned with the evaluation of an individual's (or group's) procedures or ability to solve problems. A science teacher who emphasizes process learning would be more concerned with a student's ability to use the scientific method than with the information (or content) he could remember. This type of evaluation is concerned more with what people do than with what they know. For example, a psychology teacher might say to a group of students, "For your paper, I would like you to pick one of the following theories—behaviorism, psychoanalysis, humanism, or cognitivism—and then analyze Bill's behavior from that theoretical perspective." The teacher's interest is in seeing how well students can think in a particular theoretical perspective rather than that they can recall all four perspectives.

Process evaluation can also take account of the behavior of teacher and students and the interaction between them in a classroom. A teacher concerned with this type of evaluation will look at such things as how interested the students appear to be in the class sessions, how hard they work, how well they get along with each other, what types of questions they ask, and the general classroom atmosphere.

Formative Evaluation.   Through formative evaluation a teacher can assess progress during a learning experience rather than at its end. She might try to check on what her students are learning during an individual class, within a topic area, or as part of a unit. Such an evaluation procedure gives the teacher feedback on the progress students are making so that she can make modifications if she finds they aren't learning what she wants.

Summative Evaluation.   While formative evaluation takes place in the middle of a learning experience, summative evaluation takes place at the end of a topic area, a unit, or semester's work. Semester grades in a course are summative in that they provide feedback on what students have accomplished at the completion of a total experience.

In this science course the teacher might ask each student to carry out his own scientific experiment. Such a technique would be primarily a process evaluation since the teacher's major goal would not be learning how much the students had achieved but assessing their ability to use the scientific method.

Teachers usually gather this data primarily by observing the class, through course evaluations completed by students, and through the comments of supervisors who observe lessons.

A new source of this type of data is videotaping. A videotaped lesson can provide teachers with a "picture" of their teaching behavior and the atmosphere they have created.

A good teacher can discover whether her students understand what is being studied by observing them in discussion and as they do classwork, by looking over their homework, or by asking such questions as "How did you like today's lesson?" or "What should we do tomorrow?"

Now that you have a basic understanding of Scriven's four elements of evaluation, let's put them together in the model shown in Figure 14–1.

HOW

	Formative	Summative
Product	A	B
Process	C	D

WHAT

Figure 14–1. Scriven's Model of Evaluation

Try to think of one or two other examples for each of the four types of evaluation. Write them in the spaces below.

Formative Evaluation of Product

   1.

   2.

Summative Evaluation of Product

   1.

   2.

Formative Evaluation of Process

   1.

   2.

Summative Evaluation of Process

   1.

   2.

Were you ever labeled by a grade you received in school? How did you feel in that situation?

How did that labeling affect your subsequent performance?

As you look at the model, it should be clear that there are two ways of evaluating product (cells *A* and *B*) and two ways of evaluating process (cells *C* and *D*). We will explain each of these types of evaluation through an example.

Formative Evaluation of Product—Cell *A*.   This type of evaluation involves getting interim feedback on achievement. For example, a teacher might use a reading test to find out how the members of a class are progressing. Such feedback would help the teacher make modifications in her reading instruction.

Summative Evaluation of Product—Cell *B*.   The old standard final exam, which tests a student's achievement in a course, is one example of this type of evaluation.

Formative Evaluation of Process—Cell *C*.   One example would be a teacher's asking students to turn in rough drafts of their proposals for a chemistry research experiment. The proposals would indicate what the students were learning of the scientific method, and could be returned to them with suggestions for improvements.

Another example is a teacher's asking students to complete an anonymous course evaluation in the middle of a semester. Such a process evaluation would help the teacher learn how the students were receiving the course at a time when modifications were possible.

Summative Evaluation of Process—Cell *D*.   The final report of each chemistry student's research experiment is an example of summative evaluation of process. Another example is a course evaluation that all the members of a class complete at the end of a semester.

Our purpose in exposing you to the model presented in Figure 14–1 has been to help you see that there is much more to evaluation than testing. We believe that the major value of evaluation is to provide continuous feedback to both teacher and students on what is taking place in the classroom. We feel very strongly that evaluation should be used to improve the teaching–learning process rather than to label or judge students, as happens in so many classrooms. In the remaining two sections of this chapter we will discuss some specific suggestions for evaluating learning and teaching.

Approaches to Evaluating Student Learning

Throughout this book we have argued for a diagnostic–prescriptive approach to teaching, which demands almost continuous evaluation to determine which learning experiences students are benefiting from and which aren't working. Just as a physician must try to find out what is wrong with a patient before prescribing any medicine or program of treatment, so a good teacher diagnoses what a student needs to learn before giving the student any learning activities. As a physician says to a patient, "Call and let me know how you're doing," a good teacher uses techniques (e.g., tests, quizzes, homework assignments, projects, observation, etc.) to find out how the student is doing.

Effective teachers carry out diagnosis, prescription, and evaluation almost intuitively. Consider the following illustration. Ms. Warren is a third-grade teacher with fourteen years of elementary teaching experience. On the first day of school in September, she begins her process of diagnosis, prescription, and evaluation. She might play some games with the children as a way of finding out who they are and some of the things they are interested in. Probably she also does things to help them feel comfortable. She may informally test how well the children read, do arithmetic, and write. Whatever introductory activities she carries out, she is noting both the strengths and the weaknesses of her individual students. In short, she is diagnosing what they need to learn.

How frequently did you encounter teachers who, like Ms. Warren, spent a lot of time diagnosing what students needed?

The more data Ms. Warren gathers, the more she begins to try different prescriptions. For example, José may be able to read at fourth-grade level, but needs help with comprehension. So Ms. Warren gets José started on reading at an easier level and assigns him questions that test his comprehension. She might have noticed that most of the children are below their grade level in arithmetic skills, so she does a few lessons to review concepts that they should have learned in second grade. Throughout the year this process of finding out what students need (diagnosis), involving them in different learning activities (prescription), and checking how they are progressing (evaluation) continues. Evaluation is critical in the process because it tells Ms. Warren how effectively her prescriptions are working. As she receives feedback on the children's learning, she is able to rediagnose and modify the learning activities to fit the new diagnosis.

The diagnostic–prescriptive– evaluative process we are describing here includes a great deal of formative evaluation—evaluation that will help the teacher continually modify and improve her approach as she goes along.

We would now like to provide you with some guidelines for carrying out effective evaluation in the classroom.

Educational Objectives

In planning any type of instruction, goals—what the teacher is trying to accomplish—are very important. Goals develop out of a teacher's own philosophy of education and take into account both the subject and the students. In recent years a great deal of research and writing has supported the concept of teachers' specifying accurately what it is they want students to learn. There has been a shift away from teachers' thinking simply in terms of their own goals to the state-

If you would like to learn more about the use of behavioral objectives to improve instruction, you might look for either R. W. Burns, New Approaches to Behavioral Objectives *(1972); or R. F. Mager,* Preparing Instructional Objectives *(1962).*

The critical element in behavioral objectives is that they be stated in terms of observable behavior. Then, when a learning experience is complete, the teacher can evaluate by asking students to "demonstrate" their learning.

ment of specific objectives students are expected to achieve as a result of specific learning experiences. Such statements are often referred to as *behavioral objectives.* A behavioral objective is a clear, specific statement of what a student should be able to do, in terms of observable behavior, as an outcome of some learning activity. The following are two examples of behavioral objectives:

General Science—The student will define *osmosis* in his own words.

Civics—The student will write three ways in which the governments of England and the United States are alike and three ways in which they are different.

The more clearly a teacher states the objectives she wishes her students to accomplish, the easier it is to evaluate whether the students have accomplished those objectives. When objectives are stated in terms of observable behavior, an objective (rather than subjective) evaluative procedure is built in. The behavioral objectives theory has received both praise and criticism. Some praise the fact that it links evaluation to goals and makes the whole evaluative process less subjective. However, critics argue that behavioral objectives foster compartmentalized learning of bits and pieces of knowledge rather than the learning of concepts, principles, and relationships. Another criticism is that the easiest things to evaluate behaviorally may be the least important. For example, it is easier to state goals that emphasize memory or rote learning in behavioral terms than it is to state goals that emphasize thinking. In any case, evaluation is meaningless unless it is done in response to goals and objectives.

Bloom (1956) has developed a useful way of organizing cognitive objectives into a hierarchy of six different categories involving increasingly complex thinking:

1. *Knowledge—Acquiring information.*

2. *Comprehension—Understanding.*

3. *Application—Using knowledge in concrete situations.*

4. *Analysis—Being able to break down material into its elements.*

5. *Synthesis—Putting together elements; integrating.*

6. *Evaluation—Making judgments about the value of some knowledge.*

We should point out that there are different types of educational objectives. Here we would like to identify three major types of objectives, which we have discussed throughout this book without labeling them. They are *cognitive objectives, affective objectives,* and *psychomotor objectives. Cognitive objectives* are concerned with a person's thinking and problem-solving abilities. *Affective objectives* emphasize a person's learning of attitudes, values, interests, and feelings. *Psychomotor objectives* center around a person's movement and motor skills.

In our continuing concern for the total person in this book, we have always been supportive of a school's helping children with all three types of learning—cognitive, affective, and psychomotor. However, we recognize that in most schools attention has centered on the child's cognitive learning with little time left over for affective and psychomotor learning. The reasons for this emphasis on the cognitive are quite complex but three come quickly to mind. First, in Western culture thinking and reasoning have been emphasized as the most important ways of solving problems. Second, people can generally agree on the cognitive content to be taught, while they differ widely on the subjective issues of affective learning such as attitudes and values and what types of psychomotor learning to emphasize. Third, cognitive learning appears easier to evaluate objectively than affective learning.

Methods of Evaluating Student Learning

There are many methods of evaluating learning open to teachers. Unfortunately, in too many classrooms the only method employed is testing. And as it is frequently carried out, testing is adversary, with the teacher trying to "trick" students or "catch" them on something they didn't study. When students (especially as they get older) feel they are being tricked or pressured by tests, they often join the battle against the teacher and cheat or try to outmaneuver the teacher. In this atmosphere everyone loses, teacher and students alike.

The question for teachers is not whether to evaluate, but how to evaluate and how to present the results of evaluation to students. There are many types of measurement devices a teacher can use. Let's begin with traditional testing.

Teacher-made tests can be divided into *objective tests* and *essay tests*. An objective test, which might include, for example, multiple-choice items, true–false items, or matching items, can cover wide subject matter and has a clear-cut scoring system. However, as most of us know, such tests may encourage us to try to remember trivial points and to fragment our knowledge. Essay tests, on the other hand, lead students to put together their own response to a rather broad question. The students must integrate their knowlege and be able to explain what they know, not just recall it. The scoring, however, is very subjective and laborious for the teacher. The more specific an essay question, the easier it is to score and the less subjective is the scoring process. But as essay questions are made more and more specific, they require less real thinking and often encourage students to memorize.

There is no reason that tests have to occur with closed books during a class period. Two variations on the testing theme are open-book tests and take-home tests. The potential value of open-book and take-home tests is that neither requires memorization; each emphasizes process learning (learning of concepts and principles) rather than content learning. With these types of tests, students usually must apply their knowledge in some problem-solving situation. The disadvantage of a take-home test is that the teacher cannot know if a student worked on the test alone.

Term papers or other types of written reports can be useful in evaluating learning in virtually any subject. Short critical reaction papers written in response to issues or topics being studied also can be useful. A strength of these approaches is that they push students to develop their own ideas and express them in their own ways. However, these approaches may be difficult for students who know the material but don't express themselves well in writing. Furthermore, because papers generally are narrow in focus, they don't provide feedback on the full breadth of a student's learning in a course.

If you think back to your own high school years, you can probably see the cognitive emphasis in the curriculum. Subjects with heavy cognitive orientation were the major subjects—English, math, social studies, languages, science. Subjects with emphasis on affective and/or psychomotor learning—art, music, drama, dance, physical education—were minor subjects you would fill in around your major subjects if you had time.

Try to think back to the classroom situations in which you cheated and those in which you didn't cheat. What were the differences between them?

On the basis of your school experiences, which do you prefer—objective tests or essay tests? Why?

How do you think your feelings about tests when you were a student might influence your approaches to testing as a teacher?

Another disadvantage of take-home tests is that they may discriminate against children who don't have reference books at home.

On the basis of your own experience, what do you feel are the merits of projects rather than tests as a means of evaluation? Why do you feel that way?

Journals also provide students with formative evaluation as they see their own growth with each new entry.

Discuss with other students your experiences with:

Journals

Individual projects

Group projects

Class presentations

Check lists, rating scales, and questionnaires are especially useful for getting feedback on affective learning, which will not be graded or judged, but which teachers need to assess their progress.

Standardized tests like College Board Exams, Graduate Record Exams, Law School Aptitude Tests, etc. are all norm-referenced.

A criticism of norm-referenced evaluation is that it fosters unhealthy competition and hurts the self-concepts of students who often score low.

How do you feel about this criticism?

Other evaluative devices that involve creating products are journals, individual projects, group projects, and class presentations. Journals (which are similar to diaries) are collections of critical written responses to readings, lectures, class discussions, etc. Journals provide students with a chance to personalize their learning as they decide what to record. Journals allow for evaluation of the thinking process and personal growth rather than of specific content.

Individual projects give students a chance to learn actively as they implement their own ideas. For example, a fifth grader might do a science project involving breeding white mice, a tenth grader might develop a film on a local political campaign, or an English student might write and put together a collection of poems. Students learn to work together in group projects and through class presentations in which they teach something they have learned to the class. All of these projects require a great deal of planning, and allow students to delve deeply into some area of their own interest. However, they generally sacrifice breadth of learning for depth in the chosen area.

Teachers can also evaluate student learning through observation. They may use check lists, questionnaires, and rating scales to observe and record students' performance in the classroom or laboratory. Teachers can note participation by individual class members and the kind of thinking students demonstrate in their questions. Teachers also might use many other types of evaluation devices, such as those accompanying learning kits for commercial reading and mathematics programs and texts and programmed learning materials. As teachers begin to see that evaluation provides them with important feedback rather than just grades for students, they will discover a variety of evaluative measures.

Providing Evaluative Feedback to Students

There are two basic approaches that can be used in providing evaluative feedback to students. They are *norm-referenced evaluation* and *criterion-referenced evaluation.*

Norm-Referenced Evaluation. This method of evaluation compares a student's learning with the learning of other students. The actual "amount" of learning is not important. Teachers who use curve grading are using norm-referenced evaluation, since the student with the highest score receives the highest grade even if he got only 40 percent of the test items correct.

Criterion-Referenced Evaluation. This approach measures the performance of each student against an objective criterion. There is no predetermined number of passes or failures. Everyone passes who achieves whatever has been determined as the criterion. This means of evaluation has been influenced by the behavioral objectives approach. If educational objectives are stated in behavioral terms, then it should be easy to assess whether students have achieved those objectives. If they have, then we say they "pass."

A teacher's purposes will determine whether norm-referenced or criterion-referenced evaluation is more useful. If the teacher wants to discriminate qualitatively between students, she might employ norm-referenced evaluation. If she is concerned with helping students get to a minimum level of performance no matter how long it takes, then criterion-referenced evaluation may be appropriate. When students with different abilities work at their own rates in individualized instruction, then criterion-referenced evaluation is called for.

Whatever approach is used, evaluation must be carried out in the context of a cooperative relationship between teacher and student. The evaluative process should give the student feedback on his own learning that will show both his strengths and weaknesses. If the feedback is all negative, the student may give up or become defensive; if it is all positive, the student won't see where he can improve. A good teacher uses a student's strengths to work on his weaknesses.

Another important issue is the student's role in the evaluation process. Most teachers believe that they are educating students toward autonomy, but they may forget this as they carry out their evaluative procedures. In the traditional model the teacher evaluates the student. A more participatory model engages the student in the process of her own evaluation through a variety of means, including cooperative goal-setting and *contract learning,* self-testing, and teacher–student evaluation conferences. A teacher who believes in autonomy should attempt to move the student toward the ability to think honestly and self-critically, i.e., to evaluate her own learning.

Different students in the same class may be at different stages in their movement toward self-evaluation. If we can vary teaching methods to accommodate individual learning styles, we should be able to adjust evaluation procedures similarly. There is no logical reason for every student to be evaluated in the same way.

A particular type of criterion-referenced evaluation is a mastery test. *If people reach a minimum specified level of achievement on this type of test, they are considered to have "mastered" the material. Driving tests, state bar exams for lawyers, or state licensing exams for psychologists are all mastery tests.*

In contract learning *the teacher and the student make an agreement regarding what the student will learn and how evaluation will take place.*

Evaluating Teaching and Programs

Current procedures for the evaluation of teaching and educational programs face problems in many ways identical to those for the evaluation of student learning. Teachers often feel as put upon by administrators as students feel put upon by teachers.

Traditional supervision procedures can have a negative effect on teachers. Some traditional administrators deal with teachers very much as they expect their teachers to deal with students. Just as they believe that teachers should create compliant students, they reward compliant teachers. In short, the relationship between administrator and teacher is all too often adversary rather than cooperative.

Even relatively open administrators and supervisors often have difficulty in creating growth situations for teachers. For example, Flanders' system for observing and recording teacher–student interaction has great potential for helping teachers look more honestly at their own behavior. However, in many schools it and other similar methods have been used in attempts to force teachers to alter their teaching approaches. When it is so employed, it has an impact opposite to that Flanders intended. Just as classroom teachers must think about how

*If you need to refresh your under-
standing of Flanders' Interaction
Analysis, return to Chapter 1, where
we explored it in some depth.*

to most effectively provide evaluative feedback to students, supervisors must think through their evaluation procedures and how to present the results. Teachers who feel that a supervisor is their enemy
probably will not grow from the experience of supervision.

The concept of autonomy is as important in helping teachers
grow as in helping students grow. We hope that, like student evaluation, teacher evaluation will move toward self-evaluation. So far, few
schools can boast that they have achieved this objective. But imagine
a school that truly helped teachers as well as students to grow!

Conclusions

Our goal in this chapter has been to help you realize the importance of evaluation to both learners and teachers. As students learn,
some type of feedback is necessary to let them know how they are
progressing. Teachers, too, require feedback so that they can assess
how well their students are doing and decide what modifications to
make in their teaching. Therefore, good evaluation always involves
much more than grading students. In fact, evaluation can be carried
out without grades. Yet in many schools evaluation and grading have
become synonymous.

*As we saw in our model of evaluation,
teachers are in the best possible position to evaluate their own teaching.
Good teachers constantly observe
their students' behavior and monitor
their own behavior. They evaluate
their students' process and product
learning formatively and summatively
and always consider the implications for improving their own teaching.*

We have presented both the pros and cons of grading and have
tried to stimulate your thinking about evaluation designed to eliminate
the anxiety, fear, and distrust associated with so many current approaches. Evaluation does not have to foster adversary relationships
between teacher and students.

The model presented in Figure 14–1 calls attention to four different types of evaluation and their interactions. *Formative evaluation* is
ongoing evaluation throughout a learning experience, while *summative evaluation* sums up at the end of the experience. *Product evaluation* is concerned with the amount of new knowledge the student has
gained. *Process evaluation,* on the other hand, is concerned with a
person's growth or with the communications process taking place.
Each of these four types of evaluation can be helpful to both student
and teacher in the process of diagnosis, prescription, and evaluation.

In the final sections of this chapter we pointed out that good
evaluation and the clear statement of educational objectives go hand
in hand. We introduced many methods of evaluation in addition to
traditional testing, such as term papers, reaction papers, journals, individual projects, group projects, and class presentations. We also
discussed the advantages and disadvantages of evaluative procedures that compare students with each other—*norm-referenced
evaluation*—and procedures that are concerned with mastery—
criterion-referenced evaluation. Our concluding section dealt with the
role of evaluation in fostering the continuing growth of teachers.

Some Good Books

Bloom, Benjamin S., ed. *Taxonomy of Educational Objectives. Handbook I: Cognitive Domain*. New York: McKay, 1956. A pioneer work,

which sets forth a full scheme for the statement and evaluation of cognitive educational objectives.

Bloom, Benjamin S., J. Thomas Hastings, and George Madaus, eds. *Handbook on Formative and Summative Evaluation of Student Learning.* New York: McGraw-Hill, 1971. This book can be quite helpful to teachers interested in using both formative and summative evaluation in the classroom.

Cronbach, L. J. *Essentials of Psychological Testing.* 3rd ed. New York: Harper & Row, 1970. A well-organized guide to the basic principles of test construction and use.

Ebel, Robert L. *Essentials of Educational Measurement.* Englewood Cliffs, N.J.: Prentice-Hall, 1972. A good basic text on principles of educational measurement and evaluation and their application to the classroom.

Glasser, William. *Schools Without Failure.* New York: Harper & Row, 1969. This book is very relevant to the debate about the effects of grading. Glasser states that with the overemphasis on memorization and grades, many children begin to view themselves as failures early in their school careers.

Hoffman, B. and J. Barzun. *The Tyranny of Testing.* New York: Collier, 1962. A free-wheeling critique of mass testing. Hoffman believes testing inflicts punishment upon creative thinkers.

Kirschenbaum, Howard, Sidney B. Simon, and Rodney W. Napier. *Wad-Ja-Get: The Grading Game in American Education.* New York: Hart, 1971. A thorough examination of grading in American education, as seen through the eyes of teachers, students, administrators, and parents. It concludes with the pros and cons of some alternatives to traditional grading practices.

Krathwohl, D. R., B. S. Bloom, and B. B. Masia. *Taxonomy of Educational Objectives. Handbook II: Affective Domain.* New York: McKay, 1964. This volume provides a framework for thinking about and writing affective educational objectives, i.e., objectives concerned with attitudes and values.

Mager, Robert F. *Preparing Instructional Objectives.* Palo Alto, Calif.: Fearon, 1962. This paperback has become a classic for helping teachers write behavioral objectives.

Ten Brink, T. D. *Evaluation: A Practical Guide for Teachers.* New York: McGraw-Hill, 1974. A good general reference on classroom evaluation.

Articles, Studies, and Other References

Block, J. H. "Criterion-Referenced Measurements: Potential." *School Review* 79 (1971): 289–298. This article argues for evaluation according to some standard of performance rather than by comparing one student with another.

Ebel, Robert L. "Should We Get Rid of Grades?" *Measurement in Education* 5 (1974): 1–5. Ebel analyzed 22 common criticisms of grades and concluded that the only valid criticisms implied the need to improve our grading systems not abolish them.

Van Hoven, J. B. "Reporting Pupil Progress: A Broad Rationale for New Practices." *Phi Delta Kappan* 53 (1972): 365–366. Van Hoven argues for a much broader approach to reporting on pupil progress than through grades alone.

Suggestions for Action-Oriented Learning

1. Observe a number (at least five) of high school classes in different subject areas. Ask each teacher to tell you what his three major goals are and how he goes about evaluating each goal. Discuss with each teacher his feelings about grading. Did the teachers' views have elements in common? What did you learn about the evaluative process from your visits?

2. Visit an alternative school, open classroom, or some other nontraditional learning environment. How does this type of educational program handle evaluation? Do you think the program you visited is any more successful at evaluating than traditional schools? Why or why not?

3. Develop a survey to give to members of your class on the extent of cheating in their experiences at the elementary, junior high, high school, and college levels. Ask questions designed to get at (1) how frequently students cheated, (2) how common cheating was among their peers, (3) how they justified their own cheating, and (4) what situations students were likely to cheat in. Be sure to make the questionnaire anonymous and to clear it with your teacher before distributing it.

4. Try to review all the grades you have received throughout your school experiences. (Maybe you still have your old report cards!) Develop an autobiographical paper that expresses how your grades affected your self-concept as you went through school.

15
Epilogue: Toward Humanizing and Individualizing Teaching and Learning

A teacher is a very important person. You may recall that we opened Chapter 1 with this simple observation. Now, as you complete this book, we hope you understand why we began that way. Few professionals spend as much time with as many different individuals as teachers do. In the course of a 40-year teaching career, an elementary school teacher might work with over 1000 children. A typical junior high or high school teacher in the same time might easily teach 5000 different students.

Other than his parents and, in some cases, his close relatives, there are probably few adults who have a greater influence on an individual's development than his teachers. And that influence can extend far beyond the immediate contact between teacher and student in school. As a good teacher helps people grow, those people in turn may raise their own children differently, work differently, or relate to others differently—extending the influence of the teacher. As you have reflected on the positive impacts of your best teachers and the negative effects of your worst teachers, you have undoubtedly seen just how powerful a teacher's influence can be.

In beginning to imagine yourself as a teacher, you have probably thought about some of the changes you would like to make in the teaching–learning process. Maybe you can recall saying, "When I'm a teacher . . . I'll treat each student as a unique individual." Or "I would never humiliate a student as Mr. X did." Or "I won't forget what it was like when I was a student." Yet your own educational experiences have by now made it all too likely that you will do "what was done to you"; in other words, you will teach as you were taught, not as you were taught to teach. The models you have encountered in your years as a student have, by no means, been all good. It will take a great deal of effort for you to continually check out your implicit theories of teaching in order to avoid falling into the behaviors you have experienced rather than those you genuinely believe in.

Even if you obtain a position in the most progressive school, there will be pressure on you to compromise your own educational values. You will have to face realities such as large classes, inadequate instructional materials, "discipline problems," inflexible scheduling arrangements, wide differences in student ability, and at times overwhelming paper work. The expectations of other teachers, administrators, parents, and even your own students, can keep you from being creative and can perpetuate the status quo. Many teachers before you have lost their ideals and somehow forgotten what it was like to be a student—even though most of them were students for at least 16 years. If you are to resist this indoctrination process and not end up as another frustrated teacher whose lessons are boring, whose students are turned off, and for whom teaching is just a job not a profession, you will have to work hard. Becoming a good teacher and learning how to be effective as a change agent aren't easy. You must grow in your knowledge of your subject and in your understanding of yourself, your students, the teaching–learning process, and the social environment in which you work.

The enjoyment and personal satisfaction that can come to a person through teaching are hard to match.

As a helping person, your greatest resource, as Combs pointed out, is yourself. Developing a philosophy of education you can articulate is necessary in guiding your thinking about teaching. Being able to draw upon your experiences as a student and your knowledge of learning and development can help you empathize with students and understand their needs.

Throughout this book we have encouraged you to view any learner as a whole person rather than as an English or mathematics student, someone who is bright or slow, or an extrovert or introvert. In Chapter 4 we presented four major theories of teaching, each of which centers on a different aspect of a student's nature—behavior, feelings, thinking, or interactions with others. While each perspective by itself is limited, together they give us a picture of the student as a total person. In the next several paragraphs we will suggest future directions you may want to pursue in developing effective ways to respond to the needs of students.

According to the behavioristic perspective presented in Chapters 4 and 13, teachers must concern themselves with what students *do*. Whether this doing takes the form of Billy's continually getting the wrong answer on his math homework or of Ann's disrupting the class, a teacher ought to be aware of these behaviors and possibly seek to change them. In a group discussion a teacher must notice how the communication is taking place and, if necessary, intervene so that the students will change what they are doing. Through reinforcing desirable behaviors the teacher can help young people to change and learn.

Two important educational applications of behavioristic techniques involve behavior modification and programmed learning. *Be-*

havior modification is simply the systematic use of reinforcement theory through praise, smiles, pats on the back, grades, tokens, or other extrinsic reinforcers to change behavior in the direction of instructional goals. *Programmed learning* systematically organizes learning materials into small, digestible units, which provide an opportunity for immediate reinforcement to students. Programmed learning lends itself to individualized instruction, in which students work alone at their own rates. As you think further about teaching, you may want to do some reading on both of these techniques.

Unfortunately, teachers haven't concerned themselves as directly with students' feelings as with their academic learning and classroom behavior. Yet as we have seen, how students feel about themselves and others very definitely affects how they learn and relate to others. Teachers who understand students' feelings and accept them probably will do a better job of prescribing meaningful educational experiences. We believe that not only should teachers help children grow emotionally, but academic learning should help students clarify their feelings, values, and attitudes. Within the field of humanistic education today, there are many movements designed to help teachers incorporate affective objectives (those concerned with the emotional aspects of learning) into the curriculum at all grade levels. If you are interested, you may want to read further in the important emerging areas of values clarification, confluent education, and moral education.

Serious teachers also must deal with students' thinking. As we have seen in Guilford's work on the structure of the intellect, the process of thinking is complex and the variety of our intellectual capabilities is great. Helping children learn to understand as well as recall, to question as well as answer, to think divergently as well as convergently is important if they are to become creative adults capable of independent thinking. The research of both Bruner and Piaget has helped us understand intellectual development and provides important implications for teachers. Discovery and inquiry approaches to teaching, such as those developed by Bruner, are designed to help students engage in meaningful cognitive learning.

Finally, we must not forget social learning. Any school is a social environment, in which students interact with many people of approximately their own age and with adults. Students usually learn a great deal incidentally from both their peers and their teachers. The concern with being accepted and receiving positive feedback from others, whether they are adults or fellow students, leads to modeling and imitation. As Dewey has argued, social learning—learning how to live with others—should be an explicit part of the mission of schools, and consequently of the curriculum, rather than a type of learning that occurs incidentally. Movements to improve human relations, break down prejudice, and foster open communication within school settings already exist. As you continue to broaden your awareness of the teaching process, you may want to learn more about cooperative class projects, role playing, group discussion strategies, and various other group dynamics techniques that can promote social learning.

A major thesis of this book has centered around the need for both students and teachers to understand themselves better and develop their unique potential to the fullest extent. Yet, "doing one's own thing" and struggling for self-actualization are not always possible; in some circumstances they may not even be desirable. All human beings live in social environments, in which one individual's needs, drives, interests, and behaviors must be modified in order not to conflict with those of others. If teaching and learning are to prepare people for life, they must be humanized. As Buber has pointed out, such humanizing begins with a teacher's establishing I–thou relationships in the classroom and in the larger school setting. Such I–thou relationships emphasize cooperation, sharing, and open communication, and lead to coping rather than defending behavior by both students and teachers.

Helping people learn is not easy. As important as a humane and comfortable atmosphere is for learning, it is not enough. As a teacher you will continually have to diagnose learning needs, prescribe appropriate experiences, evaluate your students' progress, and modify your approaches to teaching. In your attempt to minimize conditions that interfere with learning and create conditions that promote learning, the more resources you have to draw on the better. The principles of emotional learning, reinforcement, modeling, and cognitive psychology presented in Chapter 13 can be helpful as strategies for facilitating learning.

If this book has been effective, it has led you to reflect on yourself as a helping person. We have tried to help you take a few steps forward in understanding the psychology of teaching and learning. Being a teacher—whether in a formal educational setting such as a school or more informally as a parent, coach, youth leader, or counselor—involves you in a communication process concerned with helping others grow. Not many experiences will demand as much from you as teaching will. But few human relationships provide as great an opportunity for self-fulfillment and continuous growth as teaching does.

Bibliography

Adams, G. R. "Classroom Aggression: Determinants, Controlling Mechanisms, and Guidelines for the Implementation of a Behavior Modification Program." *Psychology in the Schools* 10 (1973): 155–168.

Allen, V., ed. *Children as Teachers*. New York: Academic Press, 1976.

Alschuler, A. S., Tabor, D., and McIntyre, J. *Teaching Achievement Motivation*. Middletown, Conn.: Education Ventures, 1971.

Anastasi, A. *Psychological Testing*. 1st ed., 4th ed. New York: Macmillan, 1954, 1976.

Anderson, R. C. "Learning in Discussions: A Resume of the Authoritarian-Democratic Studies." In W. W. Charters, Jr. and N. L. Gage (eds.), *Readings in the Social Psychology of Education*. Boston: Allyn and Bacon, 1963.

Anglin, J., ed. *Beyond the Information Given*. New York: Norton, 1973.

Anrep, G. V. "Pitch Discrimination in the Dog." *Journal of Physiology* 53: 367–385.

"A Plea for Openness in Discussing the Nature-Nurture Question." *American Psychologist* 27 (1972): 660.

Ashton-Warner, Sylvia. *Teacher*. New York: Simon and Shuster, 1963.

Ausubel, D. P. *Educational Psychology: A Cognitive View*. New York: Holt, Rinehart and Winston, 1968.

Ausubel, D. P. "The Facilitation of Meaningful Verbal Learning in the Classroom." *Educational Psychologist* 12 (1977): 162–178.

Ausubel, D. P. *The Psychology of Meaningful Verbal Learning*. New York: Grune and Stratton, 1963.

Ausubel, D. P. and Robinson, F. D. *School Learning*. New York: Holt, Rinehart and Winston, 1969.

Avila, D. L., Combs, A. W., and Purkey, W. W., eds. *The Helping Relationship Sourcebook*. Boston: Allyn and Bacon, 1971.

Axline, V. *Dibs: In Search of Self*. New York: Ballantine, 1964.

Bandura, A. *Principles of Behavior Modification*. New York: Holt, Rinehart and Winston, 1969.

Bany, M. A. and Johnson, L. V. *Educational Social Psychology*. New York: Macmillan, 1975.

Barth, R. *Open Education and the American School*. New York: Agathon, 1972.

Barzun, J. *Teacher in America*. Garden City, N.Y.: Doubleday, 1955.

Becker, H. "Social Class Variation in the Teacher–Pupil Relationship." In R. C. Sprinthall and N. A. Sprinthall (eds.), *Educational Psychology*. New York: Van Nostrand, 1969, pp. 300–308.

Berlyne, D. E., "Curiosity and Education." In J. D. Krumboltz (ed.), *Learning and the Educational Process*. Chicago: Rand McNally, 1965, pp. 67–89.

Berne, E. *Games People Play*. New York: Grove, 1964.

Bevans, W. "Perceptual Learning, An Overview." *Journal of General Psychology,* January 1961: 65–69.

Bigge, M. L. *Learning Theories for Teachers*. New York: Harper & Row, 1971.

Binet, A. *Les Ideés Modernes sur Les Enfants*. Paris: Flamarion, 1909, pp. 54–55.

Block, J. B., ed. *Mastery Learning: Theory and Practice*. New York: Holt, Rinehart and Winston, 1971.

Block, J. H. "Criterion-Referenced Measurements: Potential." *School Review* 79 (1971): 289–298.

Block, N. J. and Dworkin, G., eds. *The I.Q. Controversy*. New York: Pantheon, 1976.

Bloom, B. S. *Stability and Change in Human Characteristics*. New York: Wiley, 1964.

Bloom, B. S., ed. *Taxonomy of Educational Objectives. Handbook I: Cognitive Domain*. New York: McKay, 1956.

Bloom, B.S., Hastings, J. T., and Madaus, G., eds. *Handbook on Formative and Summative Evaluation of Student Learning*. New York: McGraw-Hill, 1971.

Bogdan, R. and Taylor, S. "The Judged Not the Judges: An Insider's View of Mental Retardation." *American Psychologist* 31 (1976): 47–52.

Boyer, W. *Alternative Futures: Designing Social Change.* Dubuque, Iowa: Kendall Hunt, 1975.

Bradley, R. W. "Birth Order and School Related Behavior: A Heuristic Review." *Psychological Bulletin* 70 (1968): 45–51.

Brameld, T. *The Teacher as World Citizen—A Scenario of the 21st Century.* Palm Springs, Calif.: ETC Publications, 1976.

Brameld, T. *Toward a Reconstructed Philosophy of Education.* New York: Holt, Rinehart and Winston, 1956.

Brammer, L. M. *The Helping Relationship: Process and Skills.* Englewood Cliffs, N.J.: Prentice-Hall, 1973.

Braun, C. "Teacher Expectation: Sociopsychological Dynamics." *Review of Educational Research* 46 (1976): 185–213.

Bronfenbrenner, U. *Two Worlds of Childhood: U.S. and U.S.S.R.* New York: Simon and Schuster, 1970.

Brookover, W., Erikson, E. L., and Joiner, L. M. "Self-Concept of Ability and School Achievement, III." *Final Report of Cooperative Research Project #2831, U.S. Office of Education.* East Lansing, Mich.: Human Learning Research Institute, Michigan State University, 1967, pp. 142–143.

Brophy, J. and Evertson, C. *Learning from Teaching: A Developmental Perspective.* Boston: Allyn and Bacon, 1976.

Brophy, J. and Good, T. *Teacher-Student Relationships: Causes and Consequences.* New York: Holt, Rinehart and Winston, 1974.

Broudy, H. S. "How Can We Define Good Teaching?" *The Record* 70 (1969): 5.

Brown, G. *Human Teaching for Human Learning.* New York: Viking, 1971.

Brown, G. *The Live Classroom: Innovations through Confluent Education and Gestalt.* New York: Viking, 1975.

Bruner, J. S. "The Growth of Mind." *American Psychologist* 20 (1965): 1007–1017.

Bruner, J. S. *The Process of Education.* New York: Vintage, 1960.

Bruner, J.S. *Toward a Theory of Instruction.* New York: Norton, 1966.

Bruner, J.S., ed. *Play—Its Role in Development and Evolution.* New York: Basic Books, 1976.

Buber, M. *I and Thou.* 2nd ed. New York: Scribner's, 1958.

Burns, R. W. *New Approaches to Behavioral Objectives.* Dubuque, Iowa: William C. Brown, 1972.

Canfield, J. and Wells, H. C. *100 Ways to Enhance Self-Concept in the Classroom.* Englewood Cliffs, N.J.: Prentice-Hall, 1976.

Carnoy, M. and Levin, H. M. *The Limits of Educational Reform.* New York: McKay, 1976.

Charters, W. W., Jr. "The Social Background of Teaching." In N. L. Gage (ed.), *Handbook of Research on Teaching.* Chicago: Rand McNally, 1963, pp. 715–813.

Clarizio, H. F. "Natural vs. Accelerated Readiness." In H. F. Clarizio, R. C. Craig, and W. A. Mehrens (eds.), *Contemporary Issues in Educational Psychology.* 2nd ed. Boston: Allyn and Bacon, 1974, pp. 107–118.

Clifford, G. J. "A History of the Impact of Research on Teaching." In R. M. W. Travers (ed.), *Second Handbook of Research on Teaching.* Chicago: Rand McNally, 1973, 1–46.

Coladarci, A. P. "The Relevance of Educational Psychology." *Educational Leadership* 13 (1956): 489–492.

Coleman, J. S. *The Adolescent Society.* New York: Free Press, 1961.

Coleman, J. S. *Equality of Educational Opportunity.* Washington, D.C.: U.S. Government Printing Office, 1966.

Coleman, J. S. *Youth: Transition to Adulthood.* Chicago: University of Chicago Press, 1974.

Combs, A. W. *Florida Studies in the Helping Professions.* Gainesville, Fla.: University of Florida Press, 1969.

Combs, A. W. "The Personal Approach to Good Teaching." *Educational Leadership* 21 (1964): 369–377.

Combs, A. W., Avila, D. L., and Purkey, W. W. *Helping Relationships: Basic Concepts for the Helping Professions.* Boston: Allyn and Bacon, 1971.

Combs, A. W., Blume, R. A., Newman, A. J., and Wass, H. L. *The Professional Education of Teachers.* 2nd ed. Boston: Allyn and Bacon, 1974.

Combs, A. W., Richards, A. C., and Richards, F. *Perceptual Psychology: A Humanistic Approach to the Study of Persons.* New York: Harper & Row, 1976.

Combs, A. W. and Snygg, D. *Individual Behavior: A Perceptual Approach to Behavior.* New York: Harper & Row, 1959.

Conrad, D. *Education for Transformation.* Palm Springs, Calif.: ETC Publications, 1976.

Counts, G. S. *Dare the Schools Build a New Social Order?* New York: John Day, 1932.

Covington, M. V. and Beery, R. G. *Self-Worth and School Learning.* New York: Holt, Rinehart and Winston, 1976.

Cronbach, L. J. *Essentials of Psychological Testing.* 3rd ed. New York: Harper & Row, 1970.

Cronbach, L. J. "How Can Instruction Be Adapted to Individual Differences?" In R. Gagné, (ed.), *Learning and Individual Differences.* Columbus, Ohio: Merrill, 1967.

Cronbach, L. J. and Snow, R. E. *Aptitudes and Instructional Methods: A Handbook for Research on Interactions.* New York: Irvington Publishers/Naiburg Publishing Corporation, 1975.

Curwin, R. L. and Fuhrmann, B. S. *Discovering Your Teaching Self.* Englewood Cliffs, N.J.: Prentice-Hall, 1975.

Dacey, J. S. *New Ways to Learn: The Psychology of Education.* Stamford, Conn.: Greylock, 1976.

DeCecco, J. P. *The Psychology of Learning and Instruction.* Englewood Cliffs, N.J.: Prentice-Hall, 1968.

Deci, E. L. *Intrinsic Motivation.* New York: Plenum, 1975.

Dennis, W. and Najarian, P. "Infant Development Under Environmental Handicaps." *Psychological Monographs,* 1957, 7–1, No. 7.

Dewey, J. *The Child and the Curriculum: The School and Society.* Chicago: University of Chicago Press, 1956.

Dewey, J. *Experience and Education.* New York: Collier, 1938.

Dewey, J. *How We Think.* Boston: Heath, 1910.

Divoky, D. "Affective Education: Are We Going Too Far?" *Learning,* October 1975: 20–27.

Dreikurs, R., Grunwald, B., and Pepper, F. *Maintaining Sanity in the Classroom.* New York: Harper & Row, 1971.

Dubin, R. and Taveggia, T. *The Teaching-Learning Paradox: A Comparative Analysis of College Teaching Methods.* Eugene, Ore.: University of Oregon Press, 1968.

Dunkin, M. J. and Biddle, B. J. *The Study of Teaching.* New York: Holt, Rinehart and Winston, 1974.

Ebel, R. L. *Essentials of Educational Measurement.* Englewood Cliffs, N.J.: Prentice-Hall, 1972.

Ebel, R. L. "Shall We Get Rid of Grades?" *Measurement in Education* 5 (1974): 1–5.

Elashoff, J. D. and Snow, R. E. *Pygmalion Reconsidered.* Worthington, Ohio: Charles A. Jones, 1971.

Elkind, D. "Erik Erikson's Eight Ages of Man." In R. F. Biehler, *Psychology Applied to Teaching: Selected Readings.* Boston: Houghton Mifflin, 1972, pp. 120–137.

Elkind, D. *A Sympathetic Understanding of the Child from Six to Sixteen.* Boston: Allyn and Bacon, 1971.

English, F. "T. A.'s Disney World." *Psychology Today,* April 1973.

Epstein, S. "The Self-Concept Revisited or A Theory of a Theory." *American Psychologist* 28 (1973): 404–416.

Erikson, E. *Childhood and Society.* 2nd ed. New York: Norton, 1963.

Erikson, E. *Identity: Youth and Crisis.* New York: Norton, 1968.

Erikson, E. *Life History and the Historical Moment.* New York: Norton, 1975.

Evans, R. I. *Dialogue with Erik Erikson.* New York: Harper & Row, 1967.

Eysenck, H. J. *The I.Q. Argument.* New York: Library Press, 1971.

Fantini, M. *Alternative Education: A Sourcebook for Parents, Teachers, Students, and Administrators.* Garden City, N.Y.: Doubleday, 1976.

Farber, J. *The University of Tomorrowland.* New York: Pocket Books, 1972.

Farnham-Diggory, S. *Cognitive Processes in Education.* New York: Harper & Row, 1972.

Fiske, E. B. "Special Education Is Now a Matter of Civil Rights." The *New York Times Spring Survey of Education,* April 25, 1976.

Flanders, N. A. *Analyzing Teacher Behavior.* Reading, Mass.: Addison-Wesley, 1970.

Freire, P. *Pedagogy of the Oppressed.* New York: Seabury, 1970.

French, J. R. and Raven, B. "The Bases of Social Power." In D. Cartwright (ed.), *Studies in Social Power.* Ann Arbor, Mich.: Institute for Social Research, 1959, pp. 150–167.

Freud, S. *A General Introduction to Psychoanalysis.* New York: Washington Square Press, 1960.

Freud, S. *An Outline of Psychoanalysis.* New York: Norton, 1949.

Friedenberg, E. *The Vanishing Adolescent.* New York: Dell, 1959.

Friedlander, B. Z. "Some Remarks on Open Education." *American Educational Research Journal* 12 (1975): 465–468.

Fuller, F. F. "Concerns of Teachers: A Developmental Conceptualization." *American Educational Research Journal* 6 (1969): 207–226.

Furth, H. G. and Wachs, H. *Thinking Goes to School: Piaget's Theory in Practice.* New York: Oxford University Press, 1975.

Gage, N. L., ed. *Handbook of Research on Teaching.* Chicago: Rand McNally, 1963.

Gage, N. L. and Berliner, D. C. *Educational Psychology.* Chicago: Rand McNally, 1975.

Gagné, R. M. *The Conditions of Learning.* 2nd ed. New York: Holt, Rinehart and Winston, 1970.

Gagné, R. M. *Essentials of Learning for Instruction.* Hinsdale, Ill.: Dryden, 1974.

Gardner, H. "Book Review of J. Piaget's *The Grasp of Consciousness: Action and Concept in the Young Child.*" In The *New York Times Book Review,* August 1, 1976, p. 1.

Gartner, A., Kohler, M., and Riessman, F. *Children Teach Children: Learning by Teaching.* New York: Harper & Row, 1971.

Gaudrey, E. and Spielberger, C., eds. *Anxiety and Educational Achievement.* New York: Wiley, 1971.

Gazda, G. M. et al. *Human Relations Development—A Manual for Educators.* 2nd ed. Boston: Allyn and Bacon, 1977.

Ginott, H. G. *Between Parent and Child.* New York: Macmillan, 1965.

Ginott, H. G. *Between Parent and Teenager.* New York: Macmillan, 1969.

Ginott, H. *Teacher and Child.* New York: Macmillan, 1972.

Glasser, W. *Schools without Failure.* New York: Harper & Row, 1969.

Goble, F. G. *The Third Force: The Psychology of Abraham Maslow.* New York: Grossman, 1970.

Goldfried, M. R. and Merbaum, M., eds. *Behavior Change through Self-Control.* New York: Holt, Rinehart and Winston, 1973.

Good, T. and Brophy, J. *Educational Psychology: A Realistic Approach.* New York: Holt, Rinehart and Winston, 1977.

Gordon, I. J. "Affect and Cognition—A Reciprocal Relationship." *Educational Leadership,* April 1970.

Gordon, T. *P. E. T.: Parent Effectiveness Training.* New York: Peter H. Wyden, 1970.

Gordon, T. *T. E. T.: Teacher Effectiveness Training.* New York: McKay, 1974.

Gorman, A. H. *Teachers and Learners: The Interactive Process of Education.* 2nd ed. Boston: Allyn and Bacon, 1973.

Goslin, D. A., ed. *Handbook of Socialization Theory and Research.* Chicago: Rand McNally, 1969.

Gould, R. "Adult Life Stages: Growth toward Self-Tolerance." *Psychology Today,* February 1975.

Greenberg, H. *Teaching with Feeling.* New York: Pegasus, 1969.

Greene, D. and Lepper, M. R. "How to Turn Play into Work." *Psychology Today,* September 1974: 49–54.

Greenwood, G. E., Good, T. L., and Siegel, B. L. *Problem Situations in Teaching.* New York: Harper & Row, 1971.

Guilford, J. P. *The Nature of Human Intelligence.* New York: McGraw-Hill, 1967.

Guilford, J. P. "Three Faces of Intellect." *American Psychologist* 14 (1959): 469–479.

Hamachek, D. E. *Behavior Dynamics in Teaching, Learning, and Growth.* Boston: Allyn and Bacon, 1975.

Hamachek, D. E. *Encounters with the Self.* New York: Holt, Rinehart and Winston, 1971.

Hapgood, M., ed. *Supporting the Learning Teacher: A Sourcebook for Teacher Centers.* New York: Agathon, 1975.

Harris, T. A. *I'm OK, You're OK.* New York: Harper & Row, 1967.

Havelock, R. G. *The Change Agent's Guide to Innovation in Education.* Englewood Cliffs, N.J.: Educational Technology Publications, 1973.

Havighurst, R. L. *Developmental Tasks and Education.* New York: McKay, 1972.

Hawkins, D. "What It Means to Teach." *Teacher's College Record,* September 1973.

Henry, J. "In Suburban Classrooms." In R. Gross and B. Gross (eds.), *Radical School Reform.* New York: Simon and Schuster, 1969, pp. 77–92.

Herndon, J. *The Way It Spozed to Be.* New York: Simon and Schuster, 1968.

Herrnstein, R. "I.Q." *Atlantic* 228 (1971): 43–64.

Hill, W. F. *Learning: A Survey of Psychological Interpretations.* San Francisco: Chandler, 1971.

Hitt, W. D. "Two Models of Man." *American Psychologist* 24 (1969): 651–658.

Hoffman, B. and Barzun, J. *The Tyranny of Testing.* New York: Collier, 1962.

Holland, J. L. *The Psychology of Vocational Choice.* Waltham, Mass.: Blaisdell, 1966.

Holt, J. *How Children Fail.* New York: Pitman, 1964.

Holt, J. *How Children Learn.* New York: Pitman, 1967.

Holt, J. *Instead of Education.* New York: Dutton, 1976.

Howe, L. W. and Howe, M. M. *Personalizing Education: Values Clarification and Beyond.* New York: Hart, 1975.

Hughes, E. C., Becker, H.S., and Geer, B. "Student Culture and Academic Effort." In N. Sanford (ed.), *The American College.* New York: Wiley, 1962, pp. 515–530.

Hull, R. E. "Selecting an Approach to Individual Education." *Phi Delta Kappan* 55 (1973): 169–173.

Hunt, D. "Learning Styles and Teaching Strategies." *Behavioral and Social Science* 2 (1974): 22–34.

Hunt, D. E. and Sullivan, E. V. *Between Psychology and Education.* Hinsdale, Ill.: Dryden, 1974.

Hunt, J. McV. "Heredity, Environment, and Class or Ethnic Differences." In *Proceedings of the 1972 Invitational Conference on Testing Problems: Assessment in a Pluralistic Society.* Princeton, N.J.: Educational Testing Service, 1973, pp. 3–36.

Hunt, J. McV. *Intelligence and Experience.* New York: Ronald Press, 1961.

Hutchins, R. *The Conflict in Education.* New York: Harper and Bros., 1953.

Illich, I. *Deschooling Society.* New York: Harper & Row, 1971.

Inhelder, B. and Piaget, J. *The Growth of Logical Thinking from Childhood to Adolescence.* New York: Basic Books, 1958.

Jackson, P. *Life in Classrooms.* New York: Holt, Rinehart and Winston, 1968.

Jencks, C. *Inequality: A Reassessment of the Effect of Family and Schooling in America.* New York: Basic Books, 1972.

Jencks, C. and Bane, M. J. "Five Myths about Your I.Q." *Harper's,* February 1973.

Jensen, A. "How Much Can We Boost I.Q. and Scholastic Achievement?" *Harvard Educational Review* 39 (1969): 1–123.

Johnson, D. and Myklebust, H. *Learning Disabilities.* New York: Grune and Stratton, 1967.

Johnson, D. W. and Johnson, R. T. *Learning Together and Alone.* Englewood Cliffs, N.J.: Prentice-Hall, 1975.

Johnston, J. M. "Punishment of Human Behavior." *American Psychologist* 27 (1972): 1033–1054.

Jourard, S. "Healthy Personality and Self-Disclosure." *Mental Hygiene* 43 (1959): 499–507.

Joyce, B. and Weil, M. *Models of Teaching.* Englewood Cliffs, N.J.: Prentice-Hall, 1972.

Kaplan, A. *The Conduct of Inquiry.* San Francisco: Chandler, 1964.

Kaufman, Bel. *Up the Down Staircase.* New York: Avon, 1964.

Keniston, K. *Young Radicals: Notes on Committed Youth.* New York: Harcourt Brace Jovanovich, 1968.

Kimmel, D. C. *Adulthood and Aging: An Interdisciplinary, Developmental View.* New York: Wiley, 1974.

Kirman, W. J. *Modern Psychoanalysis in the Schools.* Dubuque, Iowa: Kendall Hunt, 1977.

Kirschenbaum, H., Simon, S. B., and Napier, R. W. *Wad-Ja-Get: The Grading Game in American Education.* New York: Hart, 1971.

Klausmeier, H. J. *Learning and Human Abilities: Educational Psychology.* 4th ed. New York: Harper & Row, 1975.

Klausmeier, H. J., Ghatala, E. S., and Frayer, D. A. *Conceptual Learning and Development: A Cognitive View.* New York: Academic Press, 1974.

Kohl, H. *On Teaching.* New York: Schocken, 1976.

Kohl, H. *The Open Classroom.* New York: Vintage, 1969.

Kohl, H. *36 Children.* New York: New American Library, 1967.

Kohlberg, L. "The Cognitive–Developmental Approach to Moral Education." *Phi Delta Kappan* 56 (1975): 670–677.

Kohlberg, L. *Collected Papers.* Cambridge, Mass.: Harvard Graduate School of Education, 1974.

Kohlberg, L. and Turiel, E. "Moral Development and Moral Education." In G. Lesser (ed.), *Psychology and Educational Practice.* Glenview, Ill.: Scott, Foresman, 1971.

Köhler, W. *The Mentality of Apes.* New York: Harcourt, Brace and World, 1925.

Kovel, J. *A Complete Guide to Therapy: From Psychoanalysis to Behavior Modification.* New York: Pantheon, 1976.

Kozol, J. *Death at an Early Age.* Boston: Houghton Miffiin, 1967.

Kozol, J. *Free Schools.* Boston: Houghton Mifflin, 1972.

Kozol, J. *The Night Is Dark and I Am Far from Home.* Boston: Houghton Mifflin, 1975.

Krasner, L. "The Classroom as a Planned Environment." *Educational Researcher* 5 (1976): 9–14.

Krathwohl, D. R., Bloom, B. S., and Masia, B. B. *Taxonomy of Educational Objectives. Handbook II: Affective Domain.* New York: McKay, 1964.

Krumboltz, J. D. and Krumboltz, H. B. *Changing Children's Behavior.* Englewood Cliffs, N.J.: Prentice-Hall, 1972.

Kübler-Ross, E. *Death: The Final Stage of Growth.* Englewood Cliffs, N.J.: Prentice-Hall, 1975.

Leacock, E. B. *Teaching and Learning in City Schools.* New York: Basic Books, 1969.

LeFrancois, G. R. *Psychology for Teaching.* 2nd ed. Belmont, Calif.: Wadsworth, 1975.

Leonard, G. *Education and Ecstasy.* New York: Dell, 1969.

Lerner, J. *Children with Learning Disabilities.* 2nd ed. Boston: Houghton Mifflin, 1975.

Lewin, K. "Group Dynamics and Social Change." In G. E. Swanson, T. M. Newcomb, and E. L. Hartley (eds.), *Readings in Social Psychology.* 3rd ed. New York: Holt, Rinehart and Winston, 1952.

Lewin, K. *Principles of Topological Psychology.* New York: McGraw-Hill, 1936.

Lewin, K., Lippitt, R., and White, R. "Patterns of Aggressive Behavior in Experimentally Created 'Social Climates.'" *Journal of Social Psychology* 10 (1939): 271–299.

Lieberman, M. *Education as a Profession.* Englewood Cliffs, N.J.: Prentice-Hall, 1956.

Liebert, R. M. and Baron, R. A. "Some Immediate Effects of Televised Violence on Children's Behavior." *Developmental Psychology* 6 (1972): 469–475.

Liebert, R. M., Neale, J. M., and Davidson, E. S. *The Early Window: Effects of Television on Children and Youth.* New York: Pergamon, 1973.

Lindgren, H. C. *Educational Psychology in the Classroom.* 5th ed. New York: Wiley, 1976.

Lowenthal, M. F., Thurnher, M., and Chiriboga, D. *Four Stages of Life: A Comparative Study of Women and Men Facing Transitions.* San Francisco: Jossey-Bass, 1975.

Lyon, H. *Learning to Feel—Feeling to Learn.* Columbus, Ohio: Merrill, 1971.

Madsen, C. H., Jr. and Madsen, C. K. *Teaching/Discipline.* 2nd ed. Boston: Allyn and Bacon, 1974.

Madsen, C. K. and Madsen, C. H., Jr. "What Is Behavior Modification? *Instructor,* October 1971: 47–56.

Mager, R. F. *Preparing Instructional Objectives.* Palo Alto, Calif.: Fearon, 1962.

Mahoney, M. J. "Reflections on the Cognitive Learning Trend in Psychotherapy." *American Psychologist* 32 (1977): 5–12.

Maier, H. W. *Three Theories of Child Development.* Rev. ed. New York: Harper & Row, 1969.

Man, A Course of Study. Washington, D.C.: Curriculum Development Associates, 1970.

Maslow, A. H. *The Farther Reaches of Human Nature.* New York: Viking, 1971.

Maslow, A. H. *Motivation and Personality.* New York: Harper & Row, 1954.

Maslow, A. H. *Toward a Psychology of Being.* 2nd ed. Princeton, N.J.: Van Nostrand, 1968.

Mattox, B. A. *Getting It Together: Dilemmas for the Classroom Based on Kohlberg's Approach.* San Diego: Pennant, 1975.

Maynard, Joyce. *Looking Back: Growing Up Old in the Sixties.* New York: Avon, 1972.

McClelland, D. C. "Toward a Theory of Motive Acquisition." *American Psychologist* 20 (1965): 321–333.

McGregor, D. *Leadership and Motivation.* Cambridge, Mass.: M.I.T. Press, 1966.

McKeachie, W. "The Decline and Fall of the Laws of Learning." *Educational Researcher,* March 1974: 7–11.

McKeachie, W. and Kulik, K. "Effective College Teaching." In F. Kerlinger (ed.), *Review of Research in Education.* Itaska, Ill.: Peacock, 1975.

Mead, M. *Culture and Commitment: A Study of the Generation Gap.* New York: Natural History Press/Doubleday, 1970.

Meeker, M. N. *The Structure of Intellect: Its Interpretation and Uses.* Columbus, Ohio: Merrill, 1969.

Miller, L. K. and Schneider, R. "The Use of a Token System in Project Head Start." *Journal of Applied Behavior Analysis* 3 (1970): 213–220.

Morris, F. L. "The Jensen Hypothesis: Was It White Perspective or White Racism?" In H. F. Clarizio, R. C. Craig, and W. A. Mehrens (eds.), *Contemporary Issues in Educational Psychology.* 2nd ed. Boston: Allyn and Bacon, 1974, pp. 627–637.

Morrison, D. W. *Personal Problem Solving in the Classroom.* New York: Wiley, 1977.

Napier, R. and Gershenfeld, M. K. *Groups: Theory and Experience.* Boston: Houghton Mifflin, 1973.

Napier, R., Hayman, J., and Moskowitz, G. *Classroom Dynamics: Viewing the Classroom as a Social System.* Monterey, Calif.: Brooks/Cole, 1976.

Nardine, F. E. "The Development of Competence." In G. S. Lesser (ed.), *Psychology and Educational Practice.* Glenview, Ill.: Scott, Foresman, 1971.

Neill, A. S. *Summerhill: A Radical Approach to Child Rearing.* New York: Hart, 1960.

Newman, R. G. *Groups in Schools.* New York: Simon and Schuster, 1974.

Orem, R. C., ed. *Montessori Today.* New York: Putnam, 1971.

Patterson, C. H. *Humanistic Education.* Englewood Cliffs, N.J.: Prentice-Hall, 1973.

Pavlov, I. P. *Conditioned Reflexes.* London: Oxford University Press, 1927.

Piaget, J. *The Construction of Reality in the Child.* Trans. M. Cook. New York: Basic Books, 1954.

Piaget, J. *The Moral Judgment of the Child.* London: Routledge and Kegan Paul, 1932.

Piaget, J. *The Origins of Intelligence in Children.* Trans. M. Cook. New York: International Universities Press, 1952.

Piaget, J. *Science of Education and the Psychology of the Child.* New York: Viking, 1970.

Pines, M. "Head Head Start." The *New York Times Magazine,* October 26, 1975, pp. 14ff.

Postman, N. and Weingartner, C. *The Soft Revolution.* New York: Delacorte, 1971.

Postman, N. and Weingartner, C. *Teaching as a Subversive Activity.* New York: Delacorte, 1969.

Premack, D. "Reinforcement Theory." In D. Levine (ed.), *Nebraska Symposium on Motivation.* Lincoln, Neb.: University of Nebraska Press, 1965, pp. 123–180.

Raths, L., Harmin, M., and Simon, S. *Values and Teaching.* Columbus, Ohio: Merrill, 1966.

Reinhold, R. "The Early Years Are Crucial." The *New York Times,* October 21, 1973.

Rest, J. "Developmental Psychology as a Guide to Value Education: A Review of Kohlbergian Programs." *Review of Educational Research* 44 (1974): 241–259.

Roe, A. "Early Determinants of Vocational Choice." *Journal of Counseling Psychology* 4 (1957): 212–217.

Rogers, C. "The Characteristics of a Helping Relationship." *Personnel and Guidance Journal* 37 (1958): 6–16.

Rogers, C. *Client-Centered Therapy.* Boston: Houghton Mifflin, 1951.

Rogers, C. "Forget You Are a Teacher." *Instructor,* August/September 1971.

Rogers, C. *Freedom to Learn.* Columbus, Ohio: Merrill, 1969.

Rogers, C. "The Interpersonal Relationship in the Facilitation of Learning." In R. W. Leeper (ed.), *Humanizing Education: The Person in the Process.* Washington, D.C.: Association for Supervision and Curriculum Development, 1967, pp. 1–18.

Rogers, C. *On Becoming a Person.* Boston: Houghton Mifflin, 1961.

Rogers, C. *On Personal Power: Inner Strength and Its Revolutionary Impact.* New York: Delacorte, 1977.

Rosenshine, B. and Furst, N. "The Use of Direct Observation to Study Teaching." In R. M. W. Travers (ed.), *Second Handbook of Research on Teaching.* Chicago: Rand McNally, 1973.

Rosenthal, R. and Jacobson, L. *Pygmalion in the Classroom.* New York: Holt, Rinehart and Winston, 1968.

Ryan, K., ed. *Don't Smile until Christmas: Accounts of the First Year of Teaching.* Chicago: University of Chicago Press, 1970.

Ryan, K. and Cooper, J. M. *Those Who Can Teach.* 2nd ed. Boston: Houghton Mifflin, 1975.

Ryans, D. G. *Characteristics of Teachers.* Washington, D. C.: American Council on Education, 1960.

Sarason, S. *The Creation of Settings and the Future Societies.* San Francisco: Jossey-Bass, 1972.

Satir, V. *Peoplemaking.* Palo Alto, Calif.: Science and Behavior Books, 1972.

Schmuck, R. A. and Schmuck, P. A. *Group Processes in the Classroom.* 2nd ed. Dubuque, Iowa: William C. Brown, 1975.

Scriven, M. "The Methodology of Evaluation." In R. W. Tyler et al. (eds.), *Perspectives of Curriculum Evaluation.* Chicago: Rand McNally, 1967.

Shaw, M. *Group Dynamics: The Psychology of Small Group Behavior.* 2nd ed. New York: McGraw-Hill, 1976.

Sheehy, G. *Passages: Predictable Crises of Adult Life.* New York: Dutton, 1976.

Shimahara, N., ed. *Educational Reconstruction: Promise and Challenge.* Columbus, Ohio: Merrill, 1973.

Shockley, W. "Negro I. Q. Deficit: Failure of 'Malicious Coincidence' Model Warrants New Research Proposals." *Review of Educational Research* 41 (1971): 227–248.

Silberman, C. *Crisis in the Classroom.* New York: Random House, 1970.

Silberman, C., ed. *The Open Classroom Reader.* New York: Vintage, 1973.

Simon, S., Howe, L., and Kirschenbaum, H. *Values Clarification: A Handbook of Practical Strategies for Teachers and Students.* New York: Hart, 1972.

Skinner, B. F. *About Behaviorism.* New York: Knopf, 1974.

Skinner, B. F. *Beyond Freedom and Dignity.* New York: Knopf, 1971.

Skinner, B. F. *Science and Human Behavior.* New York: Macmillan, 1953.

Skinner, B. F. *The Technology of Teaching*. New York: Appleton-Century-Crofts, 1968.

Skinner, B. F. *Walden Two*. New York: Macmillan, 1948.

Smith, B. O. *Teachers for the Real World*. Washington, D. C.: American Association of Colleges for Teacher Education, 1969.

Sommer, R. "Classroom Ecology." *Journal of Applied Behavioral Science* 3 (1967): 489–503.

Sprinthall, R. C. and Sprinthall, N. A. *Educational Psychology: A Developmental Approach*. 2nd ed. Reading, Mass.: Addison-Wesley, 1977.

Stephens, J. M. *The Process of Schooling: A Psychological Examination*. New York: Holt, Rinehart and Winston, 1967.

Stephens, J. M. and Evans, E. D. *Development and Classroom Learning*. New York: Holt, Rinehart and Winston, 1973.

Strike, K. "The Logic of Learning by Discovery." *Review of Educational Research,* Summer 1975: 461.

Sullivan, P. "Suicide by Mistake." *Psychology Today,* October 1976: 90ff.

Summerhill: For and Against. New York: Hart, 1970.

Super, D. E. *The Psychology of Careers*. New York: Harper and Bros., 1957.

Ten Brink, T. D. *Evaluation: A Practical Guide for Teachers*. New York: McGraw-Hill, 1974.

Terkel, S. *Working*. New York: Avon, 1975.

Thelen, H. "Tutoring by Students." *School Review* 77 (1969): 229–244.

Thoresen, C. E., ed. *Behavior Modification in Education. 72nd Yearbook, Part I, National Society for the Study of Education*. Chicago: University of Chicago Press, 1973.

Thoresen, C. E. and Mahoney, M. J. *Behavioral Self-Control*. New York: Holt, Rinehart and Winston, 1974.

Thorndike, E. L. *The Fundamentals of Learning*. New York: Teacher's College Press, 1932.

Thurstone, L. L. "Primary Mental Abilities." *Psychometric Monographs*. No. 1. Chicago: University of Chicago Press, 1938.

Tikunoff, W., Berliner, D., and Rist, R. *An Ethnographic Study of the Forty Classrooms of the Beginning Teacher Evaluation Study*. Technical Report No. 75–10–5. San Francisco: Far West Laboratory, 1975.

Toffler, A. *Future Shock*. New York: Bantam, 1971.

Toffler, A., ed. *Learning for Tomorrow: The Role of the Future in Education*. New York: Random House, 1974.

Toman, W. *Family Constellation: Its Effect on Personality and Social Behavior*. 3rd ed. New York: Springer, 1976.

Torrance, E. P. "The Risk of Being a Great Teacher." In E. P. Torrance and W. F. White, *Issues and Advances in Educational Psychology*. 2nd ed. Itaska, Ill.: Peacock, 1975.

Travers, R. M. W., ed. *Second Handbook of Research on Teaching*. Chicago: Rand McNally, 1973.

Turiel, E. "Stage Transitions in Moral Development." In R. M. W. Travers (ed.), *Second Handbook of Research on Teaching*. Chicago: Rand McNally, 1973, pp. 732–758.

Tyler, R. W. "Some Persistent Questions on the Defining of Objectives." In C. M. Lindvall (ed.), *Defining Educational Objectives*. Pittsburgh: University of Pittsburgh Press, 1964

Van Hoven, J. B. "Reporting Pupil Progress: A Broad Rationale for New Practices." *Phi Delta Kappan* 53 (1972): 365–366.

Van Til, W. *Education: A Beginning*. 2nd ed. Boston: Houghton Mifflin, 1974.

Wadsworth, B. J. *Piaget's Theory of Cognitive Development*. New York: McKay, 1971.

Watson, G. "What Psychology Can We Feel Sure About?" *Teacher's College Record* 1960: 253–257

White, B. L. *The First Three Years*. Englewood Cliffs; N.J.: Prentice-Hall, 1975.

White, B. L. and Watts, J. C. *Experience and Environment: Major Influences on the Development of the Young Child*. Vol. 1. Englewood Cliffs, N.J.: Prentice-Hall, 1973.

White, R. W. "Motivation Reconsidered: The Concept of Competence." *Psychological Review* 66 (1959): 297–233.

Wilson, G. T. and Davison, G. C. "Behavior Therapy: A Road to Self-Control." *Psychology Today* 5 (October 1975): 54–60.

Wilson, J. A. R. and Stier, L. D. "Instability of Subscores on Forms of SRA Primary Mental Ability Tests: Significance for Guidance." *Personnel and Guidance Journal* 40 (1962): 708–711.

Winn, M. *The Plug-In Drug*. New York: Viking, 1977.

Wolpe, J. *The Practice of Behavior Therapy*. New York: Oxford University Press, 1969.

Zajonc, R. B. "Family Configuration and Intelligence." *Science* 192 (1976): 227–236.

Zigmond, N. and Cecci, R. *Auditory Learning*. San Rafael, Calif.: Dimensions, 1968.

Name Index

Page numbers followed by *m* indicate material in margin notes. *Table* and *fig.* indicate material in tables and figures.

Subject Index

Page numbers followed by *m* indicate material in margin notes. *Table* and *fig.* indicate material in tables and figures.

Abstract thinking, 94, 95, 97
Achievement
  individual differences, 130–31
  vs. intelligence, 138*m*, 147, 159
  and motivation in learning, 178*m*
Adolescence
  Erikson on, 109–10
  and moral development, 119, 120
  Piaget on, 94, 95
  symbolic learning in, 88*m*
Adult education, 116*m*
Advance organizers, 68, 69
Affective theory of teaching, 60–61,
    66–67, 73, 74 *table*
Affirmative action, 16
Alternative schools, 238–40
Anxiety, 175, 254*m*, 271
Aptitude Treatment Interaction (ATI),
    132
Attendance officer, 133
Autocratic leadership style, 219–20

Back-to-Basics Movement, 184–85
Behavioral objectives, 59–60, 65,
    267
  in evaluation, 285–87, 290
  movement, 65*m*
Behaviorism, 65, 251–61, 263,
    266–67
  critiqued by Bruner, 176–77
  critiqued by Maslow, 179
  and extrinsic motivation, 174–75.
    See also Behavioristic theory of
    teaching
Behavioristic theory of teaching,
    9–12, 59–60, 64–66, 73, 74
    table, 295–96
  objectives in, 59–60, 65
  on punishment, 48
  reward and praise in, 60, 66

Behavior modification, 74 *table,*
    174–75, 259*m*, 270–72,
    295–96. *See also* Self-behavior
    modification
Bender-Gestalt test, 135 *table,*
    138–39, 140
Biofeedback training, 271
Birth order, 26*m*–27*m*, 131
Blacks
  home-to-school transition, 30
  and intelligence tests, 158–59
  as teachers, 16
Body language, 9*m*, 221–22

California Test of Mental Maturity,
    153
Change agent, teacher as, 14*m*,
    15*m*, 294
  in classroom, 229–32
  in community, 236–40
  in school, 233–36
Cheating, 280, 280*m*–81*m*
Classical conditioning, 251–56
Class, origin of teacher, 15–16, 17
Classroom
  communication in, 9–12, 220–23
  defending and coping behavior in,
    224–25
  discipline problems in, 89–90
  groups in, 209–10, 212–18
  leadership in, 218–20
  open, 231–32
  seating arrangements in, 38–40,
    43–44, 222–23
  social–emotional functions in, 218
  as social environment, 209–12
  as social system, 69–70
  student-centered, 221
  teacher as change agent in,
    229–32

teacher behavior in, 7–12
teacher-centered, 221.
  See also Groups in classroom;
    Teacher-class relationship
Class-teacher relationship. *See*
    Teacher-class relationship
Coercive power, 219
Cognitive clarification, 247, 249 *fig.,*
    262–70, 273
  and concept learning, 267–70
Cognitive growth
  Bruner on, 85–90, 97–98
  concrete operations stage in,
    93–94, 95, 96
  formal operations stage in, 94, 95,
    96
  and moral development, 119
  Piaget on, 91–96, 97
  predisposition in, 86–87, 96,
    176–77
  preoperational development in,
    93, 94–95, 96
  and reinforcement, 89–90, 97
  sensorimotor stage in, 92–93, 94,
    96, 97
  sequence in, 86, 88–89, 97
  structure in, 86, 87–88, 96
  and structure of intelligence,
    160–66.
  See also Learning
Cognitive psychology, 264–67
  vs. behaviorism, 263–64
  and concept learning, 267–70
  on insight, 266–67.
  See also Gestalt psychology;
    Phenomenological psychology
Cognitive theory of teaching, 62–63,
    67–69, 73–74, 74 *table,* 296
  critical thought in, 62–63, 69
  and structure of subject matter, 68

309